Distributed Computing

**WILEY SERIES ON PARALLEL
AND DISTRIBUTED COMPUTING**

Editor: Albert Y. Zomaya

A complete list of titles in this series appears at the end of this volume.

Distributed Computing

Fundamentals, Simulations and Advanced Topics

Second Edition

Hagit Attiya
Jennifer Welch

A JOHN WILEY & SONS, INC., PUBLICATION

Library of Congress Cataloging-in-Publication Data is available.

ISBN 0-471-45324-2

Printed in the United States of America.

10 9 8 7 6 5 4 3 2

Preface

The explosive growth of distributed computing systems makes understanding them imperative. Yet achieving such understanding is notoriously difficult, because of the uncertainties introduced by asynchrony, limited local knowledge, and partial failures. The field of distributed computing provides the theoretical underpinning for the design and analysis of many distributed systems: from wide-area communication networks, through local-area clusters of workstations to shared-memory multiprocessors.

This book aims to provide a coherent view of the theory of distributed computing, highlighting common themes and basic techniques. It introduces the reader to the fundamental issues underlying the design of distributed systems—communication, coordination, synchronization, and uncertainty—and to the fundamental algorithmic ideas and lower bound techniques. Mastering these techniques will help the reader design correct distributed applications.

This book covers the main elements of the theory of distributed computing, in a unifying approach that emphasizes the similarities between different models and explains inherent discrepancies between them. The book presents up-to-date results in a precise, and detailed, yet accessible manner. The emphasis is on fundamental ideas, not optimizations. More difficult results are typically presented as a series of increasingly complex solutions. The exposition highlights techniques and results that are applicable in several places throughout the text. This approach exposes the inherent similarities in solutions to seemingly diverse problems.

The text contains many accompanying figures and examples. A set of exercises, ranging in difficulty, accompany each chapter. The notes at the end of each chapter provide a bibliographic history of the ideas and discuss their practical applications in existing systems.

Distributed Computing is intended as a textbook for graduate students and advanced undergraduates and as a reference for researchers and professionals. It should be useful to anyone interested in learning fundamental principles concerning how to make distributed systems work, and why they sometimes fail to work. The expected prerequisite knowledge is equivalent to an undergraduate course in analysis of (sequential) algorithms. Knowledge of distributed systems is helpful for appreciating the applications of the results, but it is not necessary.

This book presents the major models of distributed computing, varying by the mode of communication (message passing and shared memory), by the synchrony assumptions (synchronous, asynchronous, and clocked), and by the failure type (crash and Byzantine). The relationships between the various models are demonstrated by simulations showing that algorithms designed for one model can be run in another model. The book covers a variety of problem domains within the models, including leader election, mutual exclusion, consensus, and clock synchronization. It presents several recent developments, including fast mutual exclusion algorithms, queue locks, distributed shared memory, the wait-free hierarchy, and failure detectors.

Part I of the book introduces the major issues—message passing and shared memory communication, synchronous and asynchronous timing models, failures, proofs of correctness, and lower bounds—in the context of three canonical problems: leader election, mutual exclusion, and consensus. It also presents the key notions of causality of events and clock synchronization.

Part II addresses the central theme of simulation between models of distributed computing. It consists of a series of such simulations and their applications, including more powerful interprocess communication from less powerful interprocess communication, shared memory from message passing, more synchrony from less synchrony, and more benign kinds of faults from less benign kinds of faults.

Part III samples advanced topics that have been the focus of recent research, including randomization, the wait-free hierarchy, asynchronous solvability, and failure detectors.

An introductory course based in this book could cover Chapters 2 through 10, omitting Section 10.3. A more theoretical course could cover Chapters 2, 3, 4, 5, Section 14.3, and Chapters 10, 15, 11 and 17. Other courses based on this book are possible; consider the chapter dependencies on the next page. The book could also be used as a supplemental text in a more practically oriented course, to flesh out the treatment of logical and vector clocks (Chapter 6), clock synchronization (Chapters 6 and 13), fault tolerance (Chapters 5 and 8), distributed shared memory (Chapter 9), and failure detectors (Chapter 17).

Changes in the second edition: We have made the following changes:

- We added a new chapter (Chapter 17) on failure detectors and their application to solving consensus in asynchronous systems and deleted two chapters, those on bounded timestamps (formerly Chapter 16) and sparse network covers (formerly Chapter 18).

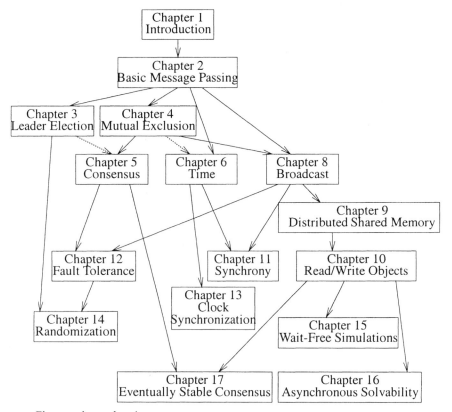

Chapter dependencies.

- We added new material to the existing chapters on fast mutual exclusion and queue locks (Chapter 4), practical clock synchronization (Chapters 6 and 13), and the processor lower bound for simulating shared memory with message passing (Chapter 10).

- We corrected errors and improved the presentation throughout. Improvements include a simpler proof of the round lower bound for consensus (Chapter 5) and a simpler randomized consensus algorithm in Chapter 14.

Acknowledgments for the first edition: Many people contributed to our view of distributed computing in general, and to this book in particular. Danny Dolev and Nancy Lynch introduced us to this subject area. Fred Schneider provided moral support in continuing the book and ideas for organization. Oded Goldreich and Marc Snir inspired a general scientific attitude.

Our graduate students helped in the development of the book. At the Technion, Ophir Rachman contributed to the lecture notes written in 1993–94, which were the origin of this book. Jennifer Walter read many versions of the book very carefully at TAMU, as did Leonid Fouren, who was the teaching assistant for the class at the Technion.

The students in our classes suffered through confusing versions of the material and provided a lot of feedback; in particular, we thank Eyal Dagan, Eli Stein (Technion, Spring 1993), Saad Biaz, Utkarsh Dhond, Ravishankar Iyer, Peter Nuernberg, Jingyu Zhang (TAMU, Fall 1996), Alla Gorbach, Noam Rinetskey, Asaf Shatil, and Ronit Teplixke (Technion, Fall 1997).

Technical discussions with Yehuda Afek, Brian Coan, Eli Gafni, and Maurice Herlihy helped us a lot. Several people contributed to specific chapters (in alphabetic order): Jim Anderson (Chapter 4), Rida Bazzi (Chapter 12), Ran Cannetti (Chapter 14), Soma Chaudhuri (Chapter 3), Shlomi Dolev (Chapters 2 and 3), Roy Friedman (Chapters 8 and 9), Sibsankar Haldar (Chapters 10), Martha Kosa (Chapter 9), Eyal Kushilevitz (Chapter 14), Dahlia Malkhi (Chapter 8), Mark Moir (Chapter 4), Gil Neiger (Chapter 5), Boaz Patt-Shamir (Chapters 6, 7 and 11), Sergio Rajsbaum (Chapter 6), and Krishnamurthy Vidyasankar (Chapters 10).

Acknowledgments for the second edition: We appreciate the time that many people spent using the first edition and giving us feedback. We benefited from many of Eli Gafni's ideas. Panagiota Fatourou provided us with a thoughtful review. Evelyn Pierce carefully read Chapter 10. We received error reports and suggestions from Uri Abraham, James Aspnes, Soma Chaudhuri, Jian Chen, Lucia Dale, Faith Fich, Roy Friedman, Mark Handy, Maurice Herlihy, Ted Herman, Lisa Higham, Iyad Kanj, Idit Keidar, Neeraj Koul, Ajay Kshemkalyani, Marios Mavronicolas, Erich Mikk, Krzysztof Parzyszej, Antonio Romano, Eric Ruppert, Cheng Shao, T.N. Srikanta, Jennifer Walter, and Jian Xu.

Several people affiliated with John Wiley & Sons deserve our thanks. We are grateful to Albert Zomaya, the editor-in-chief of the Wiley Series on Parallel and Distributed Computing for his support. Our editor Val Moliere and program coordinator Kirsten Rohstedt answered our questions and helped keep us on track.

Writing this book was a long project, and we could not have lasted without the love and support of our families. Hagit thanks Osnat, Rotem and Eyal, and her parents. Jennifer thanks George, Glenn, Sam, and her parents.

The following web site contains supplementary material relating to this book, including pointers to courses using the book and information on exercise solutions and lecture notes for a sample course:

http://www.cs.technion.ac.il/~hagit/DC/

Dedicated to our parents:
Malka and David Attiya
Judith and Ernest Lundelius

Contents

1

Introduction

This chapter describes the subject area of the book, explains the approach taken, and provides an overview of the contents.

1.1 DISTRIBUTED SYSTEMS

A *distributed system* is a collection of individual computing devices that can communicate with each other. This very general definition encompasses a wide range of modern-day computer systems, ranging from a VLSI chip, to a tightly-coupled shared memory multiprocessor, to a local-area cluster of workstations, to the Internet. This book focuses on systems at the more loosely coupled end of this spectrum. In broad terms, the goal of parallel processing is to employ all processors to perform one large task. In contrast, each processor in a distributed system generally has its own semiindependent agenda, but for various reasons, including sharing of resources, availability, and fault tolerance, processors need to coordinate their actions.

Distributed systems are ubiquitous today throughout business, academia, government, and the home. Typically they provide means to share resources, for instance, special purpose equipment such as color printers or scanners, and to share data, crucial for our information-based economy. Peer-to-peer computing is a paradigm for distributed systems that is becoming increasingly popular for providing computing resources and services. More ambitious distributed systems attempt to provide improved performance by attacking subproblems in parallel, and to provide improved availability in case of failures of some components.

Although distributed computer systems are highly desirable, putting together a properly functioning system is notoriously difficult. Some of the difficulties are pragmatic, for instance, the presence of heterogeneous hardware and software and the lack of adherence to standards. More fundamental difficulties are introduced by three factors: asynchrony, limited local knowledge, and failures. The term *asynchrony* means that the absolute and even relative times at which events take place cannot always be known precisely. Because each computing entity can only be aware of information that it acquires, it has only a local view of the global situation. Computing entities can fail independently, leaving some components operational while others are not.

The explosive growth of distributed systems makes it imperative to understand how to overcome these difficulties. As we discuss next, the field of distributed computing provides the theoretical underpinning for the design and analysis of many distributed systems.

1.2   THEORY OF DISTRIBUTED COMPUTING

The study of algorithms for sequential computers has been a highly successful endeavor. It has generated a common framework for specifying algorithms and comparing their performance, better algorithms for problems of practical importance, and an understanding of inherent limitations (for instance, lower bounds on the running time of any algorithm for a problem, and the notion of NP-completeness).

The goal of distributed computing is to accomplish the same for distributed systems. In more detail, we would like to identify fundamental problems that are abstractions of those that arise in a variety of distributed situations, state them precisely, design and analyze efficient algorithms to solve them, and prove optimality of the algorithms.

But there are some important differences from the sequential case. First, there is not a single, universally accepted model of computation, and there probably never will be, because distributed systems tend to vary much more than sequential computers do. There are major differences between systems, depending on how computing entities communicate, whether through messages or shared variables; what kind of timing information and behavior are available; and what kind of failures, if any, are to be tolerated.

In distributed systems, different complexity measures are of interest. We are still interested in time and (local) space, but now we must consider communication costs (number of messages, size and number of shared variables) and the number of faulty vs. nonfaulty components.

Because of the complications faced by distributed systems, there is increased scope for "negative" results, lower bounds, and impossibility results. It is (all too) often possible to prove that a particular problem cannot be solved in a particular kind of distributed system, or cannot be solved without a certain amount of some resource. These results play a useful role for a system designer, analogous to learning that some problem is NP-complete: they indicate where one should not put effort in trying to solve the problem. But there is often more room to maneuver in a distributed system: If it turns out that your favorite problem cannot be solved under a particular set of assumptions, then you can change the rules! Perhaps a slightly weaker problem statement can suffice for your needs. An alternative is to build stronger guarantees into your system.

Since the late 1970s, there has been intensive research in applying this theoretical paradigm to distributed systems. In this book, we have attempted to distill what we believe is the essence of this research. To focus on the underlying concepts, we generally care more about computability issues (i.e., whether or not some problem can be solved) than about complexity issues (i.e., how expensive it is to solve a problem). Section 1.3 gives a more detailed overview of the material of the book and the rationale for the choices we made.

1.3 OVERVIEW

The book is divided into three parts, reflecting three goals. First, we introduce the core theory, then we show relationships between the models, and finally we describe some current issues.

Part I, *Fundamentals*, presents the basic communication models, shared memory and message passing; the basic timing models, synchronous, asynchronous, and clocked; and the major themes, role of uncertainty, limitations of local knowledge, and fault tolerance, in the context of several canonical problems. The presentation highlights our emphasis on rigorous proofs of algorithm correctness and the importance of lower bounds and impossibility results.

Chapter 2 defines our basic message-passing model and builds the reader's familiarity with the model and proofs of correctness using some simple distributed graph algorithms for broadcasting and collecting information and building spanning trees. In Chapter 3, we consider the problem of electing a leader in a ring network. The algorithms and lower bounds here demonstrate a separation of models in terms of complexity. Chapter 4 introduces our basic shared memory model and uses it in a study of the mutual exclusion problem. The technical tools developed here, both for algorithm design and for the lower bound proofs, are used throughout the rest of the book. Fault tolerance is first addressed in Chapter 5, where the consensus problem (the fundamental problem of agreeing on an input value in the presence of failures) is studied. The results presented indicate a separation of models in terms of computability. Chapter 6 concludes Part I by introducing the notion of causality between events in a distributed system and describing the mechanism of clocks.

Part II, *Simulations*, shows how simulation is a powerful tool for making distributed systems easier to design and reason about. The chapters in this part show how to provide powerful abstractions that aid in the development of correct distributed algorithms, by providing the illusion of a better-behaved system. These abstractions are message broadcasts, shared objects with strong semantics, synchrony, less destructive faults, and fault-tolerant clocks.

To place the simulation results on a rigorous basis, we need a more sophisticated formal model than we had in Part I; Chapter 7 presents the essential features of this model. In Chapter 8, we study how to provide a variety of broadcast mechanisms using a point-to-point message-passing system. The simulation of shared objects by message-passing systems and using weaker kinds of shared objects is covered in Chapters 9 and 10. In Chapter 11, we describe several ways to simulate a more synchronous system with a less synchronous system. Chapter 12 shows how to simulate less destructive failures in the presence of more destructive failures. Finally, in Chapter 13 we discuss the problem of synchronizing clocks in the presence of failures.

Part III, *Advanced Topics*, consists of a collection of topics of recent research interest. In these chapters, we explore some issues raised earlier in more detail, present some results that use more difficult mathematical analyses, and give a flavor of other areas in the field.

Chapter 14 indicates the benefits that can be gained from using randomization (and weakening the problem specification appropriately) in terms of "beating" a lower bound or impossibility result. In Chapter 15, we explore the relationship between the ability of a shared object type to solve consensus and its ability to provide fault-tolerant implementations of other object types. In Chapter 16 three problems that can be solved in asynchronous systems subject to failures are investigated; these problems stand in contrast to the consensus problem, which cannot be solved in this situation. The notion of a failure detector as a way to abstract desired system behavior is presented in Chapter 17, along with ways to use this abstraction to solve consensus in environments where it is otherwise unsolvable.

1.4 RELATIONSHIP OF THEORY TO PRACTICE

Distributed computing comes in many flavors. In this section, we discuss the main kinds and their relationships to the formal models employed in distributed computing theory.

Perhaps the simplest, and certainly the oldest, example of a distributed system is an operating system for a conventional sequential computer. In this case processes on the same hardware communicate with the same software, either by exchanging messages or through a common address space. To time-share a single CPU among multiple processes, as is done in most contemporary operating systems, issues relating to the (virtual) concurrency of the processes must be addressed. Many of the problems faced by an operating system also arise in other distributed systems, such as mutual exclusion and deadlock detection and prevention.

Multiple-instruction multiple-data (MIMD) machines with shared memory are *tightly coupled* and are sometimes called *multiprocessors*. These consist of separate hardware running common software. Multiprocessors may be connected with a bus or, less frequently, by a switching network. Alternatively, MIMD machines can be *loosely coupled* and not have shared memory. They can be either a collection of workstations on a local area network or a collection of processors on a switching network.

Even more loosely coupled distributed systems are exemplified by autonomous hosts connected by a network, either wide area such as the Internet or local area such as Ethernet. In this case, we have separate hardware running separate software, although the entities interact through well-defined interfaces, such as the TCP/IP stack, CORBA, or some other groupware or middleware.

Distributed computing is notorious for its surplus of models; moreover, the models do not translate exactly to real-life architectures. For this reason, we chose not to organize the book around models, but rather around fundamental *problems* (in Part I), indicating where the choice of model is crucial to the solvability or complexity of a problem, and around *simulations* (in Part II), showing commonalities between the models.

In this book, we consider three main models based on communication medium and degree of synchrony. Here we describe which models match with which architectures. The *asynchronous shared memory* model applies to tightly-coupled machines, in the common situation where processors do not get their clock signal from a single source. The *asynchronous message-passing* model applies to loosely-coupled machines and to wide-area networks. The *synchronous message-passing* model is an idealization of message-passing systems in which some timing information is known, such as upper bounds on message delay. More realistic systems can simulate the synchronous message-passing model, for instance, by synchronizing the clocks. Thus the synchronous message-passing model is a convenient model in which to design algorithms; the algorithms can then be automatically translated to more realistic models.

In addition to communication medium and degree of synchrony, the other main feature of a model is the kind of faults that are assumed to occur. Much of this book is concerned with crash failures. A processor experiences a crash failure if it ceases to operate at some point without any warning. In practice, this is often the way components fail. We also study the Byzantine failure model. The behavior of Byzantine processors is completely unconstrained. This assumption is a very conservative, worst-case assumption for the behavior of defective hardware and software. It also covers the possibility of intelligent, that is, human, intrusion.

Chapter Notes

Representative books on distributed systems from a systems perspective include those by Coulouris, Dollimore, and Kindberg [85], Nutt [202], and Tanenbaum [249, 250]. The book edited by Mullender [195] contains a mixture of practical and theoretical material, as does the book by Chow and Johnson [82]. Other textbooks that cover distributed computing theory are those by Barbosa [45], Lynch [175], Peleg [208], Raynal [226], and Tel [252].

Part I

Fundamentals

2

Basic Algorithms in Message-Passing Systems

In this chapter we present our first model of distributed computation, for message-passing systems with no failures. We consider the two main timing models, synchronous and asynchronous. In addition to describing formalism for the systems, we also define the main complexity measures—number of messages and time—and present the conventions we will use for describing algorithms in pseudocode.

We then present a few simple algorithms for message-passing systems with arbitrary topology, both synchronous and asynchronous. These algorithms broadcast information, collect information, and construct spanning trees of the network. The primary purpose is to build facility with the formalisms and complexity measures and to introduce proofs of algorithm correctness. Some of the algorithms will be used later in the book as building blocks for other, more complex, algorithms.

2.1 FORMAL MODELS FOR MESSAGE PASSING SYSTEMS

This section first presents our formal models for synchronous and asynchronous message-passing systems with no failures. It then defines the basic complexity measures, and finally it describes our pseudocode conventions for describing message passing algorithms.

2.1.1 Systems

In a message-passing system, processors communicate by sending messages over communication channels, where each channel provides a bidirectional connection

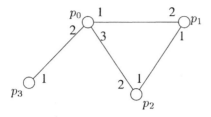

Fig. 2.1   A simple topology graph.

between two specific processors. The pattern of connections provided by the channels describes the *topology* of the system. The topology is represented by an undirected graph in which each node represents a processor and an edge is present between two nodes if and only if there is a channel between the corresponding processors. We will deal exclusively with connected topologies. The collection of channels is often referred to as the *network*. An algorithm for a message-passing system with a specific topology consists of a local program for each processor in the system. A processor's local program provides the ability for the processor to perform local computation and to send messages to and receive messages from each of its neighbors in the given topology.

More formally, a *system* or *algorithm* consists of n processors $p_0, \ldots, p_{n-1}$; i is the *index* of processor p_i. Each *processor* p_i is modeled as a (possibly infinite) state machine with state set Q_i. The processor is identified with a particular node in the topology graph. The edges incident on p_i in the topology graph are labeled arbitrarily with the integers 1 through r, where r is the degree of p_i (see Fig. 2.1 for an example). Each state of processor p_i contains $2r$ special components, $outbuf_i[\ell]$ and $inbuf_i[\ell]$, for every ℓ, $1 \le \ell \le r$. These special components are sets of messages: $outbuf_i[\ell]$ holds messages that p_i has sent to its neighbor over its ℓth incident channel but that have not yet been delivered to the neighbor, and $inbuf_i[\ell]$ holds messages that have been delivered to p_i on its ℓth incident channel but that p_i has not yet processed with an internal computation step. The state set Q_i contains a distinguished subset of *initial states*; in an initial state every $inbuf_i[\ell]$ must be empty, although the $outbuf_i[\ell]$ components need not be.

The processor's state, excluding the $outbuf_i[\ell]$ components, comprises the *accessible* state of p_i. Processor p_i's transition function takes as input a value for the accessible state of p_i. It produces as output a value for the accessible state of p_i in which each $inbuf_i[\ell]$ is empty. It also produces as output at most one message for each ℓ between 1 and r: This is the message to be sent to the neighbor at the other end of p_i's ℓth incident channel. Thus messages previously sent by p_i that are waiting to be delivered cannot influence p_i's current step; each step processes all the messages waiting to be delivered to p_i and results in a state change and at most one message to be sent to each neighbor.

A *configuration* is a vector $C = (q_0, \ldots, q_{n-1})$ where q_i is a state of p_i. The states of the *outbuf* variables in a configuration represent the messages that are in transit on the communication channels. An *initial configuration* is a vector $(q_0, \ldots, q_{n-1})$ such that each q_i is an initial state of p_i; in words, each processor is in an initial state.

Occurrences that can take place in a system are modeled as events. For message-passing systems, we consider two kinds of events. One kind is a *computation event*, denoted *comp(i)*, representing a computation step of processor p_i in which p_i's transition function is applied to its current accessible state. The other kind is a *delivery event*, denoted *del(i, j, m)*, representing the delivery of message m from processor p_i to processor p_j.

The behavior of a system over time is modeled as an execution, which is a sequence of configurations alternating with events. This sequence must satisfy a variety of conditions, depending on the specific type of system being modeled. We classify these conditions as either safety or liveness conditions. A *safety condition* is a condition that must hold in every finite prefix of the sequence; for instance, "every step by processor p_i immediately follows a step by processor p_0." Informally, a safety condition states that nothing bad has happened yet; for instance, the example just given can be restated to require that a step by p_1 never immediately follows a step by any processor other than p_0. A *liveness condition* is a condition that must hold a certain number of times, possibly an infinite number of times. For instance, the condition "eventually p_1 terminates" requires that p_1's termination happen once; the condition "p_1 takes an infinite number of steps" requires that the condition "p_1 just took a step" must happen infinitely often. Informally, a liveness condition states that eventually something good happens. Any sequence that satisfies all required safety conditions for a particular system type will be called an *execution*. If an execution also satisfies all required liveness conditions, it will be called *admissible*.

We now define the conditions required of executions and admissible executions for two types of message-passing systems, asynchronous and synchronous.

2.1.1.1 *Asynchronous Systems*

A system is said to be asynchronous if there is no fixed upper bound on how long it takes for a message to be delivered or how much time elapses between consecutive steps of a processor. An example of an asynchronous system is the Internet, where messages (for instance, E-mail) can take days to arrive, although often they only take seconds. There are usually upper bounds on message delays and processor step times, but sometimes these upper bounds are very large, are only infrequently reached, and can change over time. Instead of designing an algorithm that depends on these bounds, it is often desirable to design an algorithm that is independent of any particular timing parameters, namely, an asynchronous algorithm.

An *execution segment* α of a asynchronous message-passing system is a (finite or infinite) sequence of the following form:

$$C_0, \phi_1, C_1, \phi_2, C_2, \phi_3, \ldots$$

where each C_k is a configuration and each ϕ_k is an event. If α is finite then it must end in a configuration. Furthermore, the following conditions must be satisfied:

- If $\phi_k = del(i, j, m)$, then m must be an element of $outbuf_i[\ell]$ in C_{k-1}, where ℓ is p_i's label for channel $\{p_i, p_j\}$. The only changes in going from C_{k-1} to C_k

are that m is removed from *outbuf$_i$*$[\ell]$ in C_k and m is added to *inbuf$_j$*$[h]$ in C_k, where h is p_j's label for channel $\{p_i, p_j\}$. In words, a message is delivered only if it is in transit and the only change is to move the message from the sender's outgoing buffer to the recipient's incoming buffer. (In the example of Fig. 2.1, a message from p_3 to p_0 would be placed in *outbuf$_3$*$[1]$ and then delivered to *inbuf$_0$*$[2]$.)

- If $\phi_k = comp(i)$, then the only changes in going from C_{k-1} to C_k are that p_i changes state according to its transition function operating on p_i's accessible state in C_{k-1} and the set of messages specified by p_i's transition function are added to the *outbuf$_i$* variables in C_k. These messages are said to be *sent* at this event. In words, p_i changes state and sends out messages according to its transition function (local program) based on its current state, which includes all pending delivered messages (but not pending outgoing messages). Recall that the processor's transition function guarantees that the *inbuf* variables are emptied.

An *execution* is an execution segment $C_0, \phi_1, C_1, \phi_2, C_2, \phi_3, \ldots$, where C_0 is an initial configuration.

With each execution (or execution segment) we associate a *schedule* (or schedule segment) that is the sequence of events in the execution, that is, $\phi_1, \phi_2, \phi_3, \ldots$. Not every sequence of events is a schedule for every initial configuration; for instance, $del(1, 2, m)$ is not a schedule for an initial configuration with empty *outbuf*s, because there is no prior step by p_1 that could cause m to be sent. Note that if the local programs are deterministic, then the execution (or execution segment) is uniquely determined by the initial (or starting) configuration C_0 and the schedule (or schedule segment) σ and is denoted $exec(C_0, \sigma)$.

In the asynchronous model, an execution is *admissible* if each processor has an infinite number of computation events and every message sent is eventually delivered. The requirement for an infinite number of computation events models the fact that processors do not fail. It does not imply that the processor's local program must contain an infinite loop; the informal notion of termination of an algorithm can be accommodated by having the transition function not change the processor's state after a certain point, once the processor has completed its task. In other words, the processor takes "dummy steps" after that point. A schedule is *admissible* if it is the schedule of an admissible execution.

2.1.1.2 *Synchronous Systems*   In the synchronous model processors execute in lockstep: The execution is partitioned into rounds, and in each round, every processor can send a message to each neighbor, the messages are delivered, and every processor computes based on the messages just received. This model, although generally not achievable in practical distributed systems, is very convenient for designing algorithms, because an algorithm need not contend with much uncertainty. Once an algorithm has been designed for this ideal timing model, it can be automatically simulated to work in other, more realistic, timing models, as we shall see later.

Formally, the definition of an execution for the synchronous case is further constrained over the definition from the asynchronous case as follows. The sequence of alternating configurations and events can be partitioned into disjoint rounds. A *round* consists of a deliver event for every message in an *outbuf* variable, until all *outbuf* variables are empty, followed by one computation event for every processor. Thus a round consists of delivering all pending messages and then having every processor take an internal computation step to process all the delivered messages.

An execution is *admissible* for the synchronous model if it is infinite. Because of the round structure, this implies that every processor takes an infinite number of computation steps and every message sent is eventually delivered. As in the asynchronous case, assuming that admissible executions are infinite is a technical convenience; termination of an algorithm can be handled as in the asynchronous case.

Note that in a synchronous system with no failures, once the algorithm is fixed, the only relevant aspect of executions that can differ is the initial configuration. In an asynchronous system, there can be many different executions of the same algorithm, even with the same initial configuration and no failures, because the interleaving of processor steps and the message delays are not fixed.

2.1.2 Complexity Measures

We will be interested in two complexity measures, the number of messages and the amount of time, required by distributed algorithms. For now, we will concentrate on worst-case performance; later in the book we will sometimes be concerned with expected-case performance.

To define these measures, we need a notion of the algorithm terminating. We assume that each processor's state set includes a subset of *terminated* states and each processor's transition function maps terminated states only to terminated states. We say that the system (algorithm) has *terminated* when all processors are in terminated states and no messages are in transit. Note that an admissible execution must still be infinite, but once a processor has entered a terminated state, it stays in that state, taking "dummy" steps.

The *message complexity* of an algorithm for either a synchronous or an asynchronous message-passing system is the maximum, over all admissible executions of the algorithm, of the total number of messages sent.

The natural way to measure time in synchronous systems is simply to count the number of rounds until termination. Thus the *time complexity* of an algorithm for a synchronous message-passing system is the maximum number of rounds, in any admissible execution of the algorithm, until the algorithm has terminated.

Measuring time in an asynchronous system is less straightforward. A common approach, and the one we will adopt, is to assume that the maximum message delay in any execution is one unit of time and then calculate the running time until termination. To make this approach precise, we must introduce the notion of time into executions.

A *timed* execution is an execution that has a nonnegative real number associated with each event, the *time* at which that event occurs. The times must start at 0, must be nondecreasing, must be strictly increasing for each individual processor[1], and must increase without bound if the execution is infinite. Thus events in the execution are ordered according to the times at which they occur, several events can happen at the same time as long as they do not occur at the same processor, and only a finite number of events can occur before any finite time.

We define the *delay* of a message to be the time that elapses between the computation event that sends the message and the computation event that processes the message. In other words, it consists of the amount of time that the message waits in the sender's *outbuf* together with the amount of time that the message waits in the recipient's *inbuf*.

The *time complexity* of an asynchronous algorithm is the maximum time until termination among all timed admissible executions in which every message delay is at most one. This measure still allows arbitrary interleavings of events, because no lower bound is imposed on how closely events occur. It can be viewed as taking any execution of the algorithm and normalizing it so that the longest message delay becomes one unit of time.

2.1.3   Pseudocode Conventions

In the formal model just presented, an algorithm would be described in terms of state transitions. However, we will seldom do this, because state transitions tend to be more difficult for people to understand; in particular, flow of control must be coded in a rather contrived way in many cases.

Instead, we will describe algorithms at two different levels of detail. Simple algorithms will be described in prose. Algorithms that are more involved will also be presented in pseudocode. We now describe the pseudocode conventions we will use for synchronous and asynchronous message-passing algorithms.

Asynchronous algorithms will be described in an interrupt-driven fashion for each processor. In the formal model, each computation event processes all the messages waiting in the processor's *inbuf* variables at once. For clarity, however, we will generally describe the effect of each message individually. This is equivalent to the processor handling the pending messages one by one in some arbitrary order; if more than one message is generated for the same recipient during this process, they can be bundled together into one big message. It is also possible for the processor to take some action even if no message is received. Events that cause no message to be sent and no state change will not be listed.

The local computation done within a computation event will be described in a style consistent with typical pseudocode for sequential algorithms. We use the reserved word "terminate" to indicate that the processor enters a terminated state.

An asynchronous algorithm will also work in a synchronous system, because a synchronous system is a special case of an asynchronous system. However, we will often be considering algorithms that are specifically designed for synchronous

---

[1]*comp(i)* is considered to occur at p_i and *del(i, j, m)* at both p_i and p_j.

systems. These synchronous algorithms will be described on a round-by-round basis for each processor. For each round we will specify what messages are to be sent by the processor and what actions it is to take based on the messages just received. (Note that the messages to be sent in the first round are those that are initially in the *outbuf* variables.) The local computation done within a round will be described in a style consistent with typical pseudocode for sequential algorithms. Termination will be implicitly indicated when no more rounds are specified.

In the pseudocode, the local state variables of processor p_i will not be subscripted with i; in discussion and proof, subscripts will be added when necessary to avoid ambiguity.

Comments will begin with //.

In the next sections we will give several examples of describing algorithms in prose, in pseudocode, and as state transitions.

2.2 BROADCAST AND CONVERGECAST ON A SPANNING TREE

We now present several examples to help the reader gain a better understanding of the model, pseudocode, correctness arguments, and complexity measures for distributed algorithms. These algorithms solve basic tasks of collecting and dispersing information and computing spanning trees for the underlying communication network. They serve as important building blocks in many other algorithms.

Broadcast

We start with a simple algorithm for the *(single message) broadcast* problem, assuming a spanning tree of the network is given. A distinguished processor, p_r, has some information, namely, a message $\langle M \rangle$, it wishes to send to all other processors. Copies of the message are to be sent along a tree that is rooted at p_r and spans all the processors in the network. The spanning tree rooted at p_r is maintained in a distributed fashion: Each processor has a distinguished channel that leads to its *parent* in the tree as well as a set of channels that lead to its *children* in the tree.

Here is the prose description of the algorithm. Figure 2.2 shows a sample asynchronous execution of the algorithm; solid lines depict channels in the spanning tree, dashed lines depict channels not in the spanning tree, and shaded nodes indicate processors that have received $\langle M \rangle$ already. The root, p_r, sends the message $\langle M \rangle$ on all the channels leading to its children (see Fig. 2.2(a)). When a processor receives the message $\langle M \rangle$ on the channel from its parent, it sends $\langle M \rangle$ on all the channels leading to its children (see Fig. 2.2(b)).

The pseudocode for this algorithm is in Algorithm 1; there is no pseudocode for a computation step in which no messages are received and no state change is made.

Finally, we describe the algorithm at the level of state transitions: The state of each processor p_i contains:

- A variable *parent$_i$*, which holds either a processor index or nil

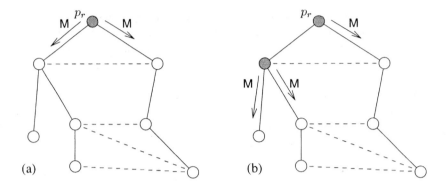

Fig. 2.2   Two steps in an execution of the broadcast algorithm.

- A variable *children_i*, which holds a set of processor indices

- A Boolean *terminated_i*, which indicates whether p_i is in a terminated state

Initially, the values of the *parent* and *children* variables are such that they form a spanning tree rooted at p_r of the topology graph. Initially, all *terminated* variables are false. Initially, $outbuf_r[j]$ holds $\langle M \rangle$ for each j in *children_r*;[2] all other *outbuf* variables are empty. The result of *comp(i)* is that, if $\langle M \rangle$ is in an $inbuf_i[k]$ for some k, then $\langle M \rangle$ is placed in $outbuf_i[j]$, for each j in *children_i*, and p_i enters a terminated state by setting *terminated_i* to true. If $i = r$ and *terminated_r* is false, then *terminated_r* is set to true. Otherwise, nothing is done.

Note that this algorithm is correct whether the system is synchronous or asynchronous. Furthermore, as we discuss now, the message and time complexities of the algorithm are the same in both models.

What is the message complexity of the algorithm? Clearly, the message $\langle M \rangle$ is sent exactly once on each channel that belongs to the spanning tree (from the parent to the child) in both the synchronous and asynchronous cases. That is, the total number of messages sent during the algorithm is exactly the number of edges in the spanning tree rooted at p_r. Recall that a spanning tree of n nodes has exactly $n - 1$ edges; therefore, exactly $n - 1$ messages are sent during the algorithm.

Let us now analyze the time complexity of the algorithm. It is easier to perform this analysis when communication is synchronous and time is measured in rounds.

The following lemma shows that by the end of round t, the message $\langle M \rangle$ reaches all processors at distance t (or less) from p_r in the spanning tree. This is a simple claim, with a simple proof, but we present it in detail to help the reader gain facility with the model and proofs about distributed algorithms. Later in the book we will leave such simple proofs to the reader.

---

[2]Here we are using the convention that *inbuf* and *outbuf* variables are indexed by the neighbors' indices instead of by channel labels.

Algorithm 1 Spanning tree broadcast algorithm.

Initially $\langle M \rangle$ is in transit from p_r to all its children in the spanning tree.

Code for p_r:
1: upon receiving no message: // first computation event by p_r
2:      terminate

Code for p_i, $0 \le i \le n - 1$, $i \ne r$:
3: upon receiving $\langle M \rangle$ from parent:
4:      send $\langle M \rangle$ to all children
5:      terminate

Lemma 2.1 *In every admissible execution of the broadcast algorithm in the synchronous model, every processor at distance t from p_r in the spanning tree receives the message $\langle M \rangle$ in round t.*

Proof.   The proof proceeds by induction on the distance t of a processor from p_r.

The basis is $t = 1$. From the description of the algorithm, each child of p_r receives $\langle M \rangle$ from p_r in the first round.

We now assume that every processor at distance $t - 1 \ge 1$ from p_r in the spanning tree receives the message $\langle M \rangle$ in round $t - 1$.

We must show that every processor p_i at distance t from p_r in the spanning tree receives $\langle M \rangle$ in round t. Let p_j be the parent of p_i in the spanning tree. Since p_j is at distance $t - 1$ from p_r, by the inductive hypothesis, p_j receives $\langle M \rangle$ in round $t - 1$. By the description of the algorithm, p_j then sends $\langle M \rangle$ to p_i in the next round. $\square$

By Lemma 2.1, the time complexity of the algorithm is d, where d is the depth of the spanning tree. Recall that d is at most $n - 1$, when the spanning tree is a chain.

Thus we have:

Theorem 2.2 *There is a synchronous broadcast algorithm with message complexity $n - 1$ and time complexity d, when a rooted spanning tree with depth d is known in advance.*

A similar analysis applies when communication is asynchronous. Once again, the key is to prove that by time t, the message $\langle M \rangle$ reaches all processors at distance t (or less) from p_r in the spanning tree. This implies that the time complexity of the algorithm is also d when communication is asynchronous. We now analyze this situation more carefully.

Lemma 2.3 *In every admissible execution of the broadcast algorithm in an asynchronous system, every processor at distance t from p_r in the spanning tree receives message $\langle M \rangle$ by time t.*

Proof.   The proof is by induction on the distance t of a processor from p_r.

The basis is $t = 1$. From the description of the algorithm, $\langle M \rangle$ is initially in transit to each processor p_i at distance 1 from p_r. By the definition of time complexity for the asynchronous model, p_i receives $\langle M \rangle$ by time 1.

We must show that every processor p_i at distance t from p_r in the spanning tree receives $\langle M \rangle$ in round t. Let p_j be the parent of p_i in the spanning tree. Since p_j is at distance $t - 1$ from p_r, by the inductive hypothesis, p_j receives $\langle M \rangle$ by time $t - 1$. By the description of the algorithm, p_j sends $\langle M \rangle$ to p_i when it receives $\langle M \rangle$, that is, by time $t - 1$. By the definition of time complexity for the asynchronous model, p_i receives $\langle M \rangle$ by time t. $\qquad\square$

Thus we have:

Theorem 2.4 *There is an asynchronous broadcast algorithm with message complexity $n - 1$ and time complexity d, when a rooted spanning tree with depth d is known in advance.*

Convergecast

The broadcast problem requires one-way communication, from the root, p_r, to all the nodes of the tree. Consider now the complementary problem, called *convergecast*, of collecting information from the nodes of the tree to the root. For simplicity, we consider a specific variant of the problem in which each processor p_i starts with a value x_i and we wish to forward the maximum value among these values to the root p_r. (Exercise 2.3 concerns a general convergecast algorithm that collects all the information in the network.)

Once again, we assume that a spanning tree is maintained in a distributed fashion, as in the broadcast problem. Whereas the broadcast algorithm is initiated by the root, the convergecast algorithm is initiated by the *leaves*. Note that a leaf of the spanning tree can be easily distinguished, because it has no children.

Conceptually, the algorithm is recursive and requires each processor to compute the maximum value in the subtree rooted at it. Starting at the leaves, each processor p_i computes the maximum value in the subtree rooted at it, which we denote by v_i, and sends v_i to its parent. The parent collects these values from all its children, computes the maximum value in its subtree, and sends the maximum value to its parent.

In more detail, the algorithm proceeds as follows. If a node p_i is a leaf, then it starts the algorithm by sending its value x_i to its parent (see Fig. 2.3(a)). A non-leaf node, p_j, with k children, waits to receive messages containing $v_{i_1}, \ldots, v_{i_k}$ from its children $p_{i_1}, \ldots, p_{i_k}$. Then it computes $v_j = \max\{x_j, v_{i_1}, \ldots, v_{i_k}\}$ and sends v_j to its parent. (See Figure 2.3(b).)

The analyses of the message and time complexities of the convergecast algorithm are very much like those of the broadcast algorithm. (Exercise 2.2 indicates how to analyze the time complexity of the convergecast algorithm.)

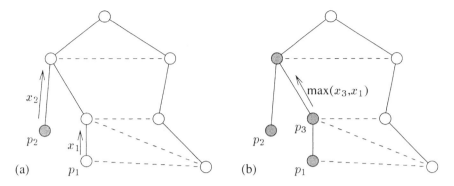

Fig. 2.3 Two steps in an execution of the convergecast algorithm.

Theorem 2.5 *There is an asynchronous convergecast algorithm with message complexity $n - 1$ and time complexity d, when a rooted spanning tree with depth d is known in advance.*

It is sometimes useful to combine the broadcast and convergecast algorithms. For instance, the root initiates a request for some information, which is distributed with the broadcast, and then the responses are funneled back to the root with the convergecast.

2.3 FLOODING AND BUILDING A SPANNING TREE

The broadcast and convergecast algorithms presented in Section 2.2 assumed the existence of a spanning tree for the communication network, rooted at a particular processor. Let us now consider the slightly more complicated problem of broadcast without a preexisting spanning tree, starting from a distinguished processor p_r. First we consider an asynchronous system.

The algorithm, called *flooding*, starts from p_r, which sends the message $\langle M \rangle$ to all its neighbors, that is, on all its communication channels. When processor p_i receives $\langle M \rangle$ for the first time, from some neighboring processor p_j, it sends $\langle M \rangle$ to all its neighbors except p_j (see Figure 2.4).

Clearly, a processor will not send $\langle M \rangle$ more than once on any communication channel. Thus $\langle M \rangle$ is sent at most twice on each communication channel (once by each processor using this channel); note that there are executions in which the message $\langle M \rangle$ is sent twice on all communication channels, except those on which $\langle M \rangle$ is received for the first time (see Exercise 2.6). Thus it is possible that $2m - (n - 1)$ messages are sent, where m is the number of communication channels in the system, which can be as high as $\frac{n(n-1)}{2}$.

We will discuss the time complexity of the flooding algorithm shortly.

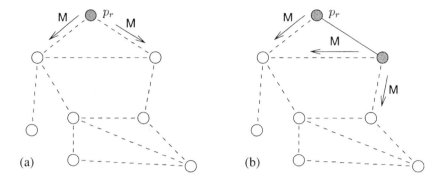

Fig. 2.4 Two steps in an execution of the flooding algorithm; solid lines indicate channels that are in the spanning tree at this point in the execution.

Effectively, the flooding algorithm induces a spanning tree, with the root at p_r, and the parent of a processor p_i being the processor from which p_i received $\langle M \rangle$ for the first time. It is possible that p_i received $\langle M \rangle$ concurrently from several processors, because a *comp* event processes all messages that have been delivered since the last *comp* event by that processor; in this case, p_i's parent is chosen arbitrarily among them.

The flooding algorithm can be modified to explicitly construct this spanning tree, as follows: First, p_r sends $\langle M \rangle$ to all its neighbors. As mentioned above, it is possible that a processor p_i receives $\langle M \rangle$ for the first time from several processors. When this happens, p_i picks one of the neighboring processors that sent $\langle M \rangle$ to it, say, p_j, denotes it as its parent and sends a $\langle parent \rangle$ message to it. To all other processors, and to any other processor from which $\langle M \rangle$ is received later on, p_i sends an $\langle already \rangle$ message, indicating that p_i is already in the tree. After sending $\langle M \rangle$ to all its other neighbors (from which $\langle M \rangle$ was not previously received), p_i waits for a response from each of them, either a $\langle parent \rangle$ message or an $\langle already \rangle$ message. Those who respond with $\langle parent \rangle$ messages are denoted as p_i's children. Once all recipients of p_i's $\langle M \rangle$ message have responded, either with $\langle parent \rangle$ or $\langle already \rangle$, p_i terminates (see Figure 2.5).

The pseudocode for the modified flooding algorithm is in Algorithm 2.

Lemma 2.6 *In every admissible execution in the asynchronous model, Algorithm 2 constructs a spanning tree of the network rooted at p_r.*

Proof. Inspecting the code reveals two important facts about the algorithm. First, once a processor sets its *parent* variable, it is never changed (and it has only one parent). Second, the set of children of a processor never decreases. Thus, eventually, the graph structure induced by *parent* and *children* variables is static, and the *parent* and *children* variables at different nodes are consistent, that is, if p_j is a child of p_i, then p_i is p_j's parent. We show that the resulting graph, call it G, is a directed spanning tree rooted at p_r.

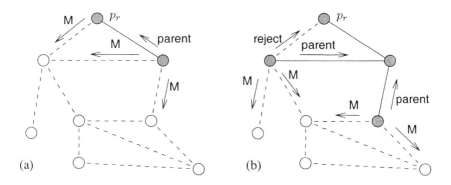

Fig. 2.5 Two steps in the construction of the spanning tree.

Why is every node reachable from the root? Suppose in contradiction some node is not reachable from p_r in G. Since the network is connected, there exist two processors, p_i and p_j, with a channel between them such that p_j is reachable from p_r in G but p_i is not. Exercise 2.4 asks you to verify that a processor is reachable from p_r in G if and only if it ever sets its *parent* variable. Thus p_i's *parent* variable remains nil throughout the execution, and p_j sets its *parent* variable at some point. Thus p_j sends $\langle M \rangle$ to p_i in Line 9. Since the execution is admissible, the message is eventually received by p_i, causing p_i to set its *parent* variable. This is a contradiction.

Why is there no cycle? Suppose in contradiction there is a cycle, say, $p_{i_1}, p_{i_2}, \ldots,$ p_{i_k}, p_{i_1}. Note that if p_i is a child of p_j, then p_i receives $\langle M \rangle$ for the first time after p_j does. Since each processor is the parent of the next processor in the cycle, that would mean that p_{i_1} receives $\langle M \rangle$ for the first time before p_{i_1} (itself) does, a contradiction.

☐

Clearly, the modification to construct a spanning tree increases the message complexity of the flooding algorithm only by a constant multiplicative factor.

In the asynchronous model of communication, it is simple to see that by time t, the message $\langle M \rangle$ reaches all processors that are at distance t (or less) from p_r. Therefore:

Theorem 2.7 *There is an asynchronous algorithm to find a spanning tree of a network with m edges and diameter D, given a distinguished node, with message complexity $O(m)$ and time complexity $O(D)$.*

The modified flooding algorithm works, unchanged, in the synchronous case. Its analysis is similar to that for the asynchronous case. However, in the synchronous case, unlike the asynchronous, the spanning tree constructed is guaranteed to be a *breadth-first search* (BFS) tree:

Lemma 2.8 *In every admissible execution in the synchronous model, Algorithm 2 constructs a* BFS *tree of the network rooted at p_r.*

Algorithm 2 Modified flooding algorithm to construct a spanning tree:
code for processor p_i, $0 \leq i \leq n - 1$.

Initially *parent* $= \bot$, *children* $= \emptyset$, and *other* $= \emptyset$.

1: upon receiving no message:
2:    if $p_i = p_r$ and *parent* $= \bot$ then   // root has not yet sent $\langle M \rangle$
3:      send $\langle M \rangle$ to all neighbors
4:      *parent* $:= p_i$

5: upon receiving $\langle M \rangle$ from neighbor p_j:
6:    if *parent* $= \bot$ then   // p_i has not received $\langle M \rangle$ before
7:      *parent* $:= p_j$
8:      send $\langle$parent$\rangle$ to p_j
9:      send $\langle M \rangle$ to all neighbors except p_j
10:   else send $\langle$already$\rangle$ to p_j

11: upon receiving $\langle$parent$\rangle$ from neighbor p_j:
12:   add p_j to *children*
13:   if *children* $\cup$ *other* contains all neighbors except *parent* then
14:     terminate

15: upon receiving $\langle$already$\rangle$ from neighbor p_j:
16:   add p_j to *other*
17:   if *children* $\cup$ *other* contains all neighbors except *parent* then
18:     terminate

Proof. We show by induction on t that at the beginning of round t, (1) the graph constructed so far according to the *parent* variables is a BFS tree consisting of all nodes at distance at most $t - 1$ from p_r, and (2) $\langle M \rangle$ messages are in transit only from nodes at distance exactly $t - 1$ from p_r.

The basis is $t = 1$. Initially, all *parent* variables are nil, and $\langle M \rangle$ messages are outgoing from p_r and no other node.

Suppose the claim is true for round $t - 1 \geq 1$. During round $t - 1$, the $\langle M \rangle$ messages in transit from nodes at distance $t - 2$ are received. Any node that receives $\langle M \rangle$ is at distance $t - 1$ or less from p_r. A recipient node with a non-nil *parent* variable, namely, a node at distance $t - 2$ or less from p_r, does not change its *parent* variable or send out an $\langle M \rangle$ message. Every node at distance $t - 1$ from p_r receives an $\langle M \rangle$ message in round $t - 1$ and, because its *parent* variable is nil, it sets it to an appropriate parent and sends out an $\langle M \rangle$ message. Nodes not at distance $t - 1$ do not receive an $\langle M \rangle$ message and thus do not send any.   □

Therefore:

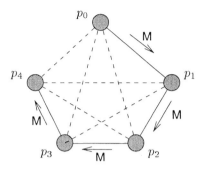

Fig. 2.6 A non-BFS tree.

Theorem 2.9 *There is a synchronous algorithm to find a* BFS *tree of a network with* m *edges and diameter* D, *given a distinguished node, with message complexity* $O(m)$ *and time complexity* $O(D)$.

In an asynchronous system, it is possible that the modified flooding algorithm does not construct a BFS tree. Consider a fully connected network with five nodes, p_0 through p_4, in which p_0 is the root (see Fig. 2.6). Suppose the $\langle M \rangle$ messages quickly propagate in the order p_0 to p_1, p_1 to p_2, p_2 to p_3, and p_3 to p_4, while the other $\langle M \rangle$ messages are very slow. The resulting spanning tree is the chain p_0 through p_4, which is not a BFS tree. Furthermore, the spanning tree has depth 4, although the diameter is only 1. Note that the running time of the algorithm is proportional to the diameter, not the number of nodes. Exercise 2.5 asks you to generalize these observations for graphs with n nodes.

The modified flooding algorithm can be combined with the convergecast algorithm described above, to request and collect information. The combined algorithm works in either synchronous or asynchronous systems. However, the time complexity of the combined algorithm is different in the two models; because we do not necessarily get a BFS tree in the asynchronous model, it is possible that the convergecast will be applied on a tree with depth $n - 1$. However, in the synchronous case, the convergecast will always be applied on a tree whose depth is at most the diameter of the network.

2.4 CONSTRUCTING A DEPTH-FIRST SEARCH SPANNING TREE FOR A SPECIFIED ROOT

Another basic algorithm constructs a *depth-first search* (DFS) tree of the communication network, rooted at a particular node. A DFS tree is constructed by adding one node at a time, more gradually than the spanning tree constructed by Algorithm 2, which attempts to add all the nodes at the same level of the tree concurrently.

The pseudocode for depth-first search is in Algorithm 3.

Algorithm 3 Depth-first search spanning tree algorithm for a specified root: code for processor p_i, $0 \leq i \leq n - 1$.

Initially *parent* $= \perp$, *children* $= \emptyset$, *unexplored* $=$ all neighbors of p_i

```
 1:  upon receiving no message:
 2:      if p_i = p_r and parent = ⊥ then                    // root wakes up
 3:          parent := p_i
 4:          explore()

 5:  upon receiving ⟨M⟩ from p_j:
 6:      if parent = ⊥ then                          // p_i has not received ⟨M⟩ before
 8:          parent := p_j
 9:          remove p_j from unexplored
10:          explore()
11:      else
12:          send ⟨already⟩ to p_j                          // already in tree
13:          remove p_j from unexplored
14:  upon receiving ⟨already⟩ from p_j:
15:      explore()

16:  upon receiving ⟨parent⟩ from p_j:
17:      add p_j to children
18:      explore()

19:  procedure explore():
20:      if unexplored ≠ ∅ then
21:          let p_k be a processor in unexplored
22:          remove p_k from unexplored
23:          send ⟨M⟩ to p_k
24:      else
25:          if parent ≠ p_i then send ⟨parent⟩ to parent
26:          terminate                  // DFS subtree rooted at p_i has been built
```

The correctness of Algorithm 3 essentially follows from the correctness of the sequential DFS algorithm, because there is no concurrency in the execution of this algorithm. A careful proof of the next lemma is left as an exercise.

Lemma 2.10 *In every admissible execution in the asynchronous model, Algorithm 3 constructs a DFS tree of the network rooted at p_r.*

To calculate the message complexity of the algorithm, note that each processor sends $\langle M \rangle$ at most once on each of its adjacent edges; also, each processor generates at most one message (either $\langle$already$\rangle$ or $\langle$parent$\rangle$) in response to receiving $\langle M \rangle$ on each of its adjacent edges. Therefore, at most $4m$ messages are sent by Algorithm 3.

Showing that the time complexity of the algorithm is $O(m)$ is left as an exercise for the reader. We summarize:

Theorem 2.11 *There is an asynchronous algorithm to find a depth-first search spanning tree of a network with m edges and n nodes, given a distinguished node, with message complexity $O(m)$ and time complexity $O(m)$.*

2.5   CONSTRUCTING A DEPTH-FIRST SEARCH SPANNING TREE WITHOUT A SPECIFIED ROOT

Algorithm 2 and Algorithm 3 build a spanning tree for the communication network, with reasonable message and time complexities. However, both of them require the existence of a distinguished node, from which the construction starts. In this section, we discuss how to build a spanning tree when there is no distinguished node. We assume, however, that the nodes have unique identifiers, which are natural numbers; as we shall see in Section 3.2, this assumption is necessary.

To build a spanning tree, each processor that wakes up spontaneously attempts to build a DFS tree with itself as the root, using a separate copy of Algorithm 3. If two DFS trees try to connect to the same node (not necessarily at the same time), the node will join the DFS tree whose root has the higher identifier.

The pseudocode appears in Algorithm 4. To implement the above idea, each node keeps the maximal identifier it has seen so far in a variable *leader*, which is initialized to a value smaller than any identifier.

When a node wakes up spontaneously, it sets its *leader* to its own identifier and sends a DFS message carrying its identifier. When a node receives a DFS message with identifier y, it compares y and *leader*. If $y > leader$, then this might be the DFS of the processor with maximal identifier; in this case, the node changes *leader* to be y, sets its *parent* variable to be the node from which this message was received, and continues the DFS with identifier y. If $y = leader$, then the node already belongs to this spanning tree. If $y < leader$, then this DFS belongs to a node whose identifier is smaller than the maximal identifier seen so far; in this case, no message is sent, which stalls the DFS tree construction with identifier y. Eventually, a DFS message carrying the identifier *leader* (or a larger identifier) will arrive at the node with identifier y, and connect it to its tree.

Only the root of the spanning tree constructed explicitly terminates; other nodes do not terminate and keep waiting for messages. It is possible to modify the algorithm so that the root sends a termination message using Algorithm 1.

Proving correctness of the algorithm is more involved than previous algorithms in this chapter; we only outline the arguments here. Consider the nodes that wake up spontaneously, and let p_m be the node with the maximal identifier among them; let m be p_m's identifier.

First observe that ⟨leader⟩ messages with leader id m are never dropped because of discovering a larger leader id, by definition of m.

Algorithm 4 Spanning tree construction: code for processor p_i, $0 \le i \le n - 1$.

Initially *parent* $= \perp$, *leader* $= -1$, *children* $= \emptyset$, *unexplored* $=$ all neighbors of p_i

1: upon receiving no message:
2:     if *parent* $= \perp$ then   // wake up spontaneously
3:         *leader* $:=$ *id*
4:         *parent* $:= p_i$
5:         explore()

6: upon receiving ⟨leader,*new-id*⟩ from p_j:
7:     if *leader* $<$ *new-id* then   // switch to new tree
8:         *leader* $:=$ *new-id*
9:         *parent* $:= p_j$
10:         *children* $:= \emptyset$
11:         *unexplored* $:=$ all neighbors of p_i except p_j
12:         explore()
13:     else if *leader* $=$ *new-id* then
14:         send ⟨already,*leader*⟩ to p_j // already in same tree
                    // otherwise, *leader* $>$ *new-id* and the DFS for *new-id* is stalled

15: upon receiving ⟨already,*new-id*⟩ from p_j:
16:     if *new-id* $=$ *leader* then explore()

17: upon receiving ⟨parent,*new-id*⟩ from p_j:
18:     if *new-id* $=$ *leader* then   // otherwise ignore message
19:         add p_j to *children*
20:         explore()

21: procedure explore():
22:     if *unexplored* $\ne \emptyset$ then
23:         let p_k be a processor in *unexplored*
24:         remove p_k from *unexplored*
25:         send ⟨leader,*leader*⟩ to p_k
26:     else
27:         if *parent* $\ne p_i$ then send ⟨parent,*leader*⟩ to *parent*
28:         else terminate as root of spanning tree

Second, ⟨already⟩ messages with leader id m are never dropped because they have the wrong leader id. Why? Suppose p_i receives an ⟨already⟩ message from p_j with leader id m. The reason p_j sent this message to p_i is that it received a ⟨leader⟩ message from p_i with leader id m. Once p_i sets its leader id to m, it never resets it, because m is the largest leader id in the system. Thus when p_i receives p_j's ⟨already⟩

message with leader id m, p_i still has its leader id as m, the message is accepted, and the exploration proceeds.

Third, ⟨parent⟩ messages with leader id m are never dropped because they have the wrong leader id. The argument is the same as for ⟨already⟩ messages.

Finally, messages with leader id m are never dropped because the recipient has terminated. Suppose in contradiction that some p_i has terminated before receiving a message with leader id m. Then p_i thinks it is the leader, but its id, say i, is less than m. The copy of Algorithm 3 with leader id i must have reached every node in the graph, including p_m. But p_m would not have responded to the leader message, so this copy of Algorithm 3 could not have completed, a contradiction.

Thus the copy of Algorithm 3 for leader id m completes, and correctness of Algorithm 3 implies correctness of Algorithm 4.

A simple analysis of the algorithm uses the fact that, in the worst case, each processor tries to construct a DFS tree. Therefore, the message complexity of Algorithm 4 is at most n times the message complexity of Algorithm 3, that is, $O(nm)$. The time complexity is similar to the time complexity of Algorithm 3, that is, $O(m)$.

Theorem 2.12 *Algorithm 4 finds a spanning tree of a network with m edges and n nodes, with message complexity $O(n \cdot m)$ and time complexity $O(m)$.*

Exercises

2.1 Code one of the simple algorithms in state transitions.

2.2 Analyze the time complexity of the convergecast algorithm of Section 2.2 when communication is synchronous and when communication is asynchronous.

Hint: For the synchronous case, prove that during round $t + 1$, a processor at height t sends a message to its parent. For the asynchronous case, prove that by time t, a processor at height t has sent a message to its parent.

2.3 Generalize the convergecast algorithm of Section 2.2 to collect all the information. That is, when the algorithm terminates, the root should have the input values of all the processors. Analyze the bit complexity, that is, the total number of bits that are sent over the communication channels.

2.4 Prove the claim used in the proof of Lemma 2.6 that a processor is reachable from p_r in G if and only if it ever sets its *parent* variable.

2.5 Describe an execution of the modified flooding algorithm (Algorithm 2) in an asynchronous system with n nodes that does not construct a BFS tree.

2.6 Describe an execution of Algorithm 2 in some asynchronous system, where the message is sent twice on communication channels that do not connect a parent and its children in the spanning tree.

2.7 Perform a precise analysis of the time complexity of the modified flooding algorithm (Algorithm 2), for the synchronous and the asynchronous models.

2.8 Explain how to eliminate the ⟨*already*⟩ messages from the modified flooding algorithm (Algorithm 2) in the synchronous case and still have a correct algorithm. What is the message complexity of the resulting algorithm?

2.9 Do the broadcast and convergecast algorithms rely on knowledge of the number of nodes in the system?

2.10 Modify Algorithm 3 so that it handles correctly the case where the distinguished node has no neighbors.

2.11 Modify Algorithm 3 so that all nodes terminate.

2.12 Prove that Algorithm 3 constructs a DFS tree of the network rooted at p_r.

2.13 Prove that the time complexity of Algorithm 3 is $O(m)$.

2.14 Modify Algorithm 3 so it constructs a DFS numbering of the nodes, indicating the order in which the message ⟨M⟩ arrives at the nodes.

2.15 Modify Algorithm 3 to obtain an algorithm that constructs a DFS tree with $O(n)$ time complexity.

Hint: When a node receives the message ⟨M⟩ for the first time, it notifies all its neighbors but passes the message only to one of them.

2.16 Prove Theorem 2.12.

2.17 Show that in Algorithm 4 if the *leader* variable is not included in the ⟨parent⟩ message and the test in Line 18 is not performed, then the algorithm is incorrect.

Chapter Notes

The first part of this chapter introduced our formal model of a distributed message-passing system; this model is closely based on that used by Attiya, Dwork, Lynch, and Stockmeyer [27], although many papers in the literature on distributed algorithms have used similar models.

Modeling each processor in a distributed algorithm as a state machine is an idea that goes back at least to Lynch and Fischer [176]. Two early papers that explicitly represent an execution of a distributed system as a sequence of state transitions are by Owicki and Lamport [204] and by Lynch and Fischer [176]. The same idea is, more implicitly, present in the paper by Owicki and Gries [203].

A number of researchers (e.g., Fischer, Lynch, and Paterson [110]) have used the term "admissible" to distinguish those executions that satisfy additional constraints from all executions: That is, the term "execution" refers to sequences that satisfy some relatively basic syntactic constraints, and "admissible" indicates that additional properties are satisfied. But the details vary from paper to paper. Emerson's chapter [103] contains an informative discussion of safety and liveness properties and many references.

The asynchronous time complexity measure was first proposed by Peterson and Fischer [214] for the shared memory case and is naturally extended to the message passing case, as in Awerbuch's paper [36].

The formal model introduced in this chapter, and used throughout Part I of this book does not address composition or interactions with users; Part II takes up these issues.

The second part of the chapter presented a few algorithms for message-passing systems, to demonstrate how to use the formalisms and complexity measures presented earlier. The algorithms solve the problems of broadcast, convergecast, DFS, BFS, and leader election; Gafni [115] includes these problems in a set of useful "building blocks" for constructing algorithms for message-passing systems.

The algorithms presented in the chapter appear to be folklore. The broadcast and convergecast algorithms of Section 2.2 are described by Segall [240], who also describes an asynchronous algorithm for finding a BFS tree rooted at a distinguished node. A BFS tree is useful for broadcasting information in a network within minimum time, as it allows information to be routed between processors along shortest paths. The algorithm for constructing a DFS tree from a specified root (Algorithm 3) first appeared in Cheung [78]. An algorithm to construct a DFS tree with linear time complexity (Exercise 2.15) was presented by Awerbuch [37].

Algorithm 4 for constructing a spanning tree works by *extinction* of the DFS trees of processors with low identifiers. This algorithm is folklore, and our presentation of it is inspired by the algorithm of Gallager [117]. The message complexity of Gallager's algorithm is $O(m + n \log n)$; it carefully balances the expansion of the trees constructed by different processors by guaranteeing that only small trees are extinguished and not much work is being lost.

Exercise 2.17 was suggested by Uri Abraham.

Algorithm 4 and Gallager's algorithm produce spanning trees of the networks without taking into account the cost of sending messages on different communication links. If weights are assigned to edges representing communication links according to their costs, then a *minimum-weight spanning tree* of the network minimizes the communication cost of broadcast and convergecast.

An algorithm for constructing a minimum-weight spanning tree was given by Gallager, Humblet, and Spira [118]; the message complexity of this algorithm is $O(m + n \log n)$. The next chapter includes lower bounds indicating that $\Omega(n \log n)$ messages are needed to elect a leader. The time complexity of the algorithm for finding a minimum-weight spanning tree is $O(n \log n)$; Awerbuch [39] presented an algorithm for finding a minimum-weight spanning tree with $O(n)$ time complexity and $O(n \log n)$ message complexity.

Because only one node terminates as the root in any spanning tree algorithm, it can be called a *leader*; leaders are very useful, and Chapter 3 is dedicated to the problem of electing them with as few messages as possible in a ring topology.

3

Leader Election in Rings

In this chapter, we consider systems in which the topology of the message passing system is a ring. Rings are a convenient structure for message-passing systems and correspond to physical communication systems, for example, token rings. We investigate the *leader election* problem, in which a group of processors must choose one among them to be the leader. The existence of a leader can simplify coordination among processors and is helpful in achieving fault tolerance and saving resources— recall how the existence of the special processor p_r made possible a simple solution to the broadcast problem in Chapter 2. Furthermore, the leader election problem represents a general class of symmetry-breaking problems. For example, when a deadlock is created, because of processors waiting in a cycle for each other, the deadlock can be broken by electing one of the processors as a leader and removing it from the cycle.

3.1 THE LEADER ELECTION PROBLEM

The leader election problem has several variants, and we define the most general one below. Informally, the problem is for each processor eventually to decide that either it is the leader or it is not the leader, subject to the constraint that exactly one processor decides that it is the leader. In terms of our formal model, an algorithm is said to solve the leader election problem if it satisfies the following conditions:

- The terminated states are partitioned into *elected* and *not-elected* states. Once a processor enters an elected (respectively, not-elected) state, its transition

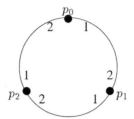

Fig. 3.1   A simple oriented ring.

function will only move it to another (or the same) elected (respectively, not-elected) state.

- In every admissible execution, exactly one processor (the *leader*) enters an elected state and all the remaining processors enter a not-elected state.

We restrict our attention to the situation in which the topology of the system is a ring. In particular, we assume that the edges in the topology graph go between p_i and p_{i+1}, for all i, $0 \le i < n$, where addition is mod n. Furthermore, we assume that processors have a consistent notion of left and right, resulting in an *oriented* ring. Formally, this assumption is modeled by requiring that, for every i, $0 \le i < n$, p_i's channel to p_{i+1} is labeled 1, also known as *left* or *clockwise*, and p_i's channel to p_{i-1} is labeled 2, also known as *right* or *counterclockwise* (as usual, addition and subtraction are mod n). Figure 3.1 contains a simple example of a three-node ring. (See the chapter notes for more on orientation.)

3.2   ANONYMOUS RINGS

A leader election algorithm for a ring system is *anonymous* if processors do not have unique identifiers that can be used by the algorithm. More formally, every processor in the system has the same state machine. In describing anonymous algorithms, recipients of messages can be specified only in terms of channel labels, for example, left and right neighbors.

A potentially useful piece of information for an algorithm is n, the number of processors. If n is not known to the algorithm, that is, n is not hardcoded in advance, the algorithm is said to be "uniform," because the algorithm looks the same for every value of n. Formally, in an anonymous *uniform* algorithm, there is only one state machine for all processors, no matter what the ring size. In an anonymous *nonuniform* algorithm, for each value of n, the ring size, there is a single state machine, but there can be different state machines for different ring sizes, that is, n can be explicitly present in the code.

We show that there is no anonymous leader election algorithm for ring systems.

For generality and simplicity, we prove the result for nonuniform algorithms and synchronous rings. Impossibility for synchronous rings immediately implies the same result for asynchronous rings (see Exercise 3.1). Similarly, impossibility for nonuniform algorithms, that is, algorithms in which n, the number of processors, is known, implies impossibility for algorithms when n is unknown (see Exercise 3.2).

Recall that in a synchronous system, an algorithm proceeds in rounds, where in each round all pending messages are delivered, following which every processor takes one computation step. The initial state of a processor includes in the *outbuf* variables any messages that are to be delivered to the processor's right and left neighbors in the first round.

The idea behind the impossibility result is that in an anonymous ring, the symmetry between the processors can always be maintained; that is, without some initial asymmetry, such as provided by unique identifiers, symmetry cannot be broken. Specifically, all processors in the anonymous ring algorithm start in the same state. Because they are identical and execute the same program (i.e., they have the same state machine), in every round each of them sends exactly the same messages; thus they all receive the same messages in each round and change state identically. Consequently, if one of the processors is elected, then so are all the processors. Hence, it is impossible to have an algorithm that elects a single leader in the ring.

To formalize this intuition, consider a ring R of size $n > 1$ and assume, by way of contradiction, that there exists an anonymous algorithm, A, for electing a leader in this ring. Because the ring is synchronous and there is only one initial configuration, there is a unique admissible execution of A on R.

Lemma 3.1 *For every round k of the admissible execution of A in R, the states of all the processors at the end of round k are the same.*

Proof. The proof is by induction on k. The base case, $k = 0$ (before the first round), is straightforward because the processors begin in the same initial state.

For the inductive step, assume the lemma holds for round $k - 1$. Because the processors are in the same state in round $k - 1$, they all send the same message m_r to the right and the same message m_ℓ to the left. In round k, every processor receives the message m_ℓ on its right edge and the message m_r on its left edge. Thus all processors receive exactly the same messages in round k; because they execute the same program, they are in the same state at the end of round k. □

The above lemma implies that if at the end of some round some processor announces itself as a leader, by entering an elected state, so do all other processors. This contradicts the assumption that A is a leader election algorithm and proves:

Theorem 3.2 *There is no nonuniform anonymous algorithm for leader election in synchronous rings.*

3.3   ASYNCHRONOUS RINGS

This section presents upper and lower bounds on the message complexity for the leader election problem in asynchronous rings. Because Theorem 3.2 just showed that there is no anonymous leader election algorithm for rings, we assume in the remainder of this chapter that processors have unique identifiers.

We assume that each processor in a ring has a unique identifier. Every natural number is a possible identifier. When a state machine (local program) is associated with each processor p_i, there is a distinguished state component id_i that is initialized to the value of that identifier.

We will specify a ring by listing the processors' identifiers in clockwise order, beginning with the smallest identifier. Thus each processor p_i, $0 \leq i < n$, is assigned an identifier id_i. Note that two identifier assignments, one of which is a cyclic shift of the other, result in the same ring by this definition, because the indices of the underlying processors (e.g., the 97 of processor p_{97}) are not available.

The notions of uniform and nonuniform algorithms are slightly different when unique identifiers are available.

A (non-anonymous) algorithm is said to be *uniform* if, for every identifier, there is a state machine and, regardless of the size of the ring, the algorithm is correct when processors are assigned the unique state machine for their identifier. That is, there is only one local program for a processor with a given identifier, no matter what size ring the processor is a part of.

A (non-anonymous) algorithm is said to be *nonuniform* if, for every n and every identifier, there is a state machine. For every n, given any ring of size n, the algorithm in which every processor has the state machine for its identifier *and for ring size n* must be correct.

We start with a very simple leader election algorithm for asynchronous rings that requires $O(n^2)$ messages. This algorithm motivates a more efficient algorithm that requires $O(n \log n)$ messages. We show that this algorithm has optimal message complexity by proving a lower bound of $\Omega(n \log n)$ on the number of messages required for electing a leader.

3.3.1   An $O(n^2)$ Algorithm

In this algorithm, each processor sends a message with its identifier to its left neighbor and then waits for messages from its right neighbor. When it receives such a message, it checks the identifier in this message. If the identifier is greater than its own identifier, it forwards the message to the left; otherwise, it "swallows" the message and does not forward it. If a processor receives a message with its own identifier, it declares itself a leader by sending a termination message to its left neighbor and terminating as a leader. A processor that receives a termination message forwards it to the left and terminates as a non-leader. Note that the algorithm does not depend on the size of the ring, that is, it is uniform.

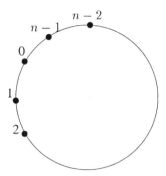

Fig. 3.2 Ring with $\Theta(n^2)$ messages.

Note that, in any admissible execution, only the message of the processor with the maximal identifier is never swallowed. Therefore, only the processor with the maximal identifier receives a message with its own identifier and will declare itself as a leader. All the other processors receive termination messages and are not chosen as leaders. This implies the correctness of the algorithm.

Clearly, the algorithm never sends more than $O(n^2)$ messages in any admissible execution. Moreover, there is an admissible execution in which the algorithm sends $\Theta(n^2)$ messages: Consider the ring where the identifiers of the processors are $0, \ldots, n - 1$ and they are ordered as in Figure 3.2. In this configuration, the message of processor with identifier i is sent exactly $i + 1$ times. Thus the total number of messages, including the n termination messages, is $n + \sum_{i=0}^{n-1} (i + 1) = \Theta(n^2)$.

3.3.2 An $O(n \log n)$ Algorithm

A more efficient algorithm is based on the same idea as the algorithm we have just seen. Again, a processor sends its identifier around the ring and the algorithm guarantees that only the message of the processor with the maximal identifier traverses the whole ring and returns. However, the algorithm employs a more clever method for forwarding identifiers, thus reducing the worst-case number of messages from $O(n^2)$ to $O(n \log n)$.

To describe the algorithm, we first define the *k-neighborhood* of a processor p_i in the ring to be the set of processors that are at distance at most k from p_i in the ring (either to the left or to the right). Note that the k-neighborhood of a processor includes exactly $2k + 1$ processors.

The algorithm operates in phases; it is convenient to start numbering the phases with 0. In the kth phase a processor tries to become a *winner* for that phase; to be a winner, it must have the largest id in its 2^k-neighborhood. Only processors that are winners in the kth phase continue to compete in the $(k + 1)$-st phase. Thus fewer processors proceed to higher phases, until at the end, only one processor is a winner and it is elected as the leader of the whole ring.

In more detail, in phase 0, each processor attempts to become a phase 0 winner and sends a ⟨probe⟩ message containing its identifier to its 1-neighborhood, that is, to each of its two neighbors. If the identifier of the neighbor receiving the probe is greater than the identifier in the probe, it swallows the probe; otherwise, it sends back a ⟨reply⟩ message. If a processor receives a reply from both its neighbors, then the processor becomes a phase 0 winner and continues to phase 1.

In general, in phase k, a processor p_i that is a phase $k-1$ winner sends ⟨probe⟩ messages with its identifier to its 2^k-neighborhood (one in each direction). Each such message traverses 2^k processors one by one. A probe is swallowed by a processor if it contains an identifier that is smaller than its own identifier. If the probe arrives at the last processor in the neighborhood without being swallowed, then that last processor sends back a ⟨reply⟩ message to p_i. If p_i receives replies from both directions, it becomes a phase k winner, and it continues to phase $k+1$. A processor that receives its own ⟨probe⟩ message terminates the algorithm as the leader and sends a termination message around the ring.

Note that in order to implement the algorithm, the last processor in a 2^k-neighborhood must return a reply rather than forward a ⟨probe⟩ message. Thus we have three fields in each ⟨probe⟩ message: the identifier, the phase number, and a hop counter. The hop counter is initialized to 0, and is incremented by 1 whenever a processor forwards the message. If a processor receives a phase k message with a hop counter 2^k, then it is the last processor in the 2^k-neighborhood.

The pseudocode appears in Algorithm 5. Phase k for a processor corresponds to the period between its sending of a ⟨probe⟩ message in line 4 or 15 with third parameter k and its sending of a ⟨probe⟩ message in line 4 or 15 with third parameter $k+1$. The details of sending the termination message around the ring have been left out in the code, and only the leader terminates.

The correctness of the algorithm follows in the same manner as in the simple algorithm, because they have the same swallowing rules. It is clear that the probes of the processor with the maximal identifier are never swallowed; therefore, this processor will terminate the algorithm as a leader. On the other hand, it is also clear that no other ⟨probe⟩ can traverse the whole ring without being swallowed. Therefore, the processor with the maximal identifier is the only leader elected by the algorithm.

To analyze the worst-case number of messages that is sent during any admissible execution of the algorithm, we first note that the probe distance in phase k is 2^k, and thus the number of messages sent on behalf of a particular competing processor in phase k is $4 \cdot 2^k$. How many processors compete in phase k, in the worst case? For $k = 0$, the number is n, because all processors could begin the algorithm. For $k \geq 1$, every processor that is a phase $k-1$ winner competes in phase k. The next lemma gives an upper bound on the number of winners in each phase.

Lemma 3.3 *For every $k \geq 1$, the number of processors that are phase k winners is at most $\frac{n}{2^k+1}$.*

Proof. If a processor p_i is a phase k winner, then every processor in p_i's 2^k-neighborhood must have an id smaller than p_i's id. The closest together that two

---

Algorithm 5 Asynchronous leader election: code for processor p_i, $0 \leq i < n$.

Initially, $asleep = $ true

```
1:   upon receiving no message:
2:       if asleep then
3:           asleep := false
4:           send ⟨probe,id,0,1⟩ to left and right

5:   upon receiving ⟨probe,j,k,d⟩ from left (resp., right):
6:       if j = id then terminate as the leader
7:       if j > id and d < 2^k then                    // forward the message
8:           send ⟨probe,j,k,d + 1⟩ to right (resp., left)   // increment hop counter
9:       if j > id and d ≥ 2^k then                    // reply to the message
10:          send ⟨reply,j,k⟩ to left (resp., right)
                                        // if j < id, message is swallowed

11:  upon receiving ⟨reply,j,k⟩ from left (resp., right):
12:      if j ≠ id then send ⟨reply,j,k⟩ to right (resp., left)   // forward the reply
13:      else                                          // reply is for own probe
14:          if already received ⟨reply,j,k⟩ from right (resp., left) then
15:              send ⟨probe,id,k + 1,1⟩                // phase k winner
```

---

phase k winners, p_i and p_j, can be is if the left side of p_i's 2^k-neighborhood is exactly the right side of p_j's 2^k-neighborhood. That is, there are 2^k processors in between p_i and p_j. The maximum number of phase k winners is achieved when this dense packing continues around the ring. The number of winners in this case is $\frac{n}{2^k+1}$. ☐

By the previous lemma, there is only one winner once the phase number is at least $\log(n-1)$. In the next phase, the winner elects itself as leader. The total number of messages then, including the $4n$ phase 0 messages and n termination messages, is at most:

$$5n + \sum_{k=1}^{\lceil \log(n-1) \rceil + 1} 4 \cdot 2^k \cdot \frac{n}{2^{k-1}+1} < 8n(\log n + 2) + 5n$$

To conclude, we have the following theorem:

Theorem 3.4 *There is an asynchronous leader election algorithm whose message complexity is $O(n \log n)$.*

Note that, in contrast to the simple algorithm of Section 3.3.1, this algorithm uses bidirectional communication on the ring. The message complexity of this algorithm is not optimal with regard to the constant factor, 8; the chapter notes discuss papers that achieve smaller constant factors.

3.3.3 An $\Omega(n \log n)$ Lower Bound

In this section, we show that the leader election algorithm of Section 3.3.2 is asymptotically optimal. That is, we show that any algorithm for electing a leader in an asynchronous ring sends at least $\Omega(n \log n)$ messages. The lower bound we prove is for uniform algorithms, namely, algorithms that do not know the size of the ring.

We prove the lower bound for a special variant of the leader election problem, where the elected leader must be the processor with the maximum identifier in the ring; in addition, all the processors must know the identifier of the elected leader. That is, before terminating each processor writes to a special variable the identity of the elected leader. The proof of the lower bound for the more general definition of the leader election problem follows by reduction and is left as Exercise 3.5.

Assume we are given a uniform algorithm A that solves the above variant of the leader election problem. We will show that there exists an admissible execution of A in which $\Omega(n \log n)$ messages are sent. Intuitively, this is done by building a "wasteful" execution of the algorithm for rings of size $n/2$, in which many messages are sent. Then we "paste together" two different rings of size $n/2$ to form a ring of size n, in such a way that we can combine the wasteful executions of the smaller rings and force $\Theta(n)$ additional messages to be received.

Although the preceding discussion referred to pasting together executions, we will actually work with schedules. The reason is that executions include configurations, which pin down the number of processors in the ring. We will want to apply the same sequence of events to different rings, with different numbers of processors. Before presenting the details of the lower bound proof, we first define schedules that can be "pasted together."

Definition 3.1 *A schedule σ of A for a particular ring is* open *if there exists an edge e of the ring such that in σ no message is delivered over the edge e in either direction; e is an* open *edge of σ.*

Note that an open schedule need not be admissible; in particular, it can be finite, and processors may not have terminated yet.

Intuitively, because the processors do not know the size of the ring, we can paste together two open schedules of two small rings to form an open schedule of a larger ring. Note that this argument relies on the fact that the algorithm is uniform and works in the same manner for every ring size.

We now give the details. For clarity of presentation, we assume that n is an integral power of 2 for the rest of the proof. (Exercise 3.6 asks you to prove the lower bound for other values of n.)

Theorem 3.5 *For every n and every set of n identifiers, there is a ring using those identifiers that has an open schedule of A in which at least $M(n)$ messages are received, where $M(2) = 1$ and $M(n) = 2M(\frac{n}{2}) + \frac{1}{2}(\frac{n}{2} - 1)$ for $n > 2$.*

Since $M(n) = \Theta(n \log n)$, this theorem implies the desired lower bound. The proof of the theorem is by induction. Lemma 3.6 is the base case ($n = 2^1$) and

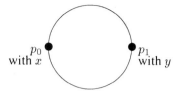

Fig. 3.3 Illustration for Lemma 3.6.

Lemma 3.7 is the inductive step ($n = 2^i, i > 1$). For the base case ring consisting of two processors, we assume that there are actually two distinct links connecting the processors.

Lemma 3.6 *For every set consisting of two identifiers, there is a ring R using those two identifiers that has an open schedule of A in which at least one message is received.*

Proof. Assume R contains processors p_0 and p_1 and the identifier of p_0 (say, x) is larger than the identifier of p_1 (say, y) (see Fig. 3.3).

Let α be an admissible execution of A on the ring. Since A is correct, eventually p_1 must write p_0's identifier x in α. Note that at least one message must be received in α; otherwise, if p_1 does not get a message from p_0 it cannot discover that the identifier of p_0 is x. Let σ be the shortest prefix of the schedule of α that includes the first event in which a message is received. Note that the edge other than the one over which the first message is received is open. Since exactly one message is received in σ and one edge is open, σ is clearly an open schedule that satisfies the requirements of the lemma. ☐

The next lemma provides the inductive step of the pasting procedure. As mentioned above, the general approach is to take two open schedules on smaller rings in which many messages are received and to paste them together at the open edges into an open schedule on the bigger ring in which the same messages plus extra messages are received. Intuitively, one can see that two open schedules can be pasted together and still behave the same (this will be proved formally below). The key step, however, is forcing the additional messages to be received. After the two smaller rings are pasted together, the processors in the half that does not contain the eventual leader must somehow learn the id of the eventual leader, and this can only occur through message exchanges. We unblock the messages delayed on the connecting open edges and continue the schedule, arguing that many messages must be received. Our main problem is how to do this in a way that will yield an open schedule on the bigger ring so that the lemma can be applied inductively. The difficulty is that if we pick in advance which of the two edges connecting the two parts to unblock, then the algorithm can choose to wait for information on the other edge. To avoid this problem, we first create a 'test' schedule, learning which of the two edges, when

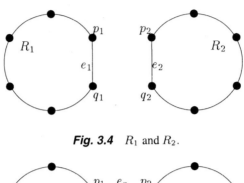

Fig. 3.4 R_1 and R_2.

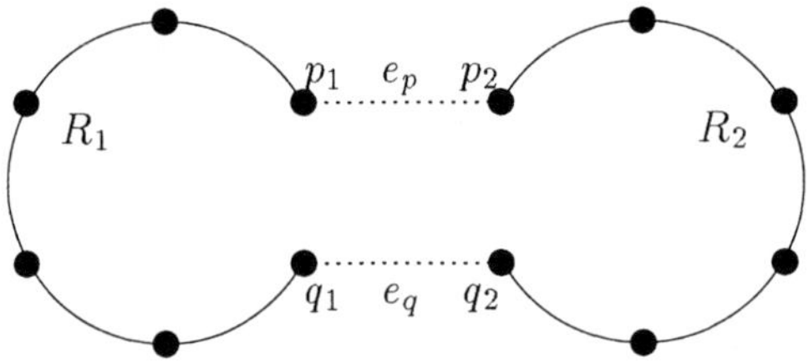

Fig. 3.5   Pasting together R_1 and R_2 into R.

unblocked, causes the larger number of messages to be received. We then go back to our original pasted schedule and only unblock that edge.

Lemma 3.7 *Choose $n > 2$. Assume that for every set of $\frac{n}{2}$ identifiers, there is a ring using those identifiers that has an open schedule of A in which at least $M\left(\frac{n}{2}\right)$ messages are received. Then for every set of n identifiers, there is a ring using those identifiers that has an open schedule of A in which at least $2M\left(\frac{n}{2}\right) + \frac{1}{2}\left(\frac{n}{2} - 1\right)$ messages are received.*

Proof.   Let S be a set of n identifiers. Partition S into two sets S_1 and S_2, each of size $\frac{n}{2}$. By assumption, there exists a ring R_1 using the identifiers in S_1 that has an open schedule σ_1 of A in which at least $M\left(\frac{n}{2}\right)$ messages are received. Similarly, there exists ring R_2 using the identifiers in S_2 that has an open schedule σ_2 of A in which at least $M\left(\frac{n}{2}\right)$ messages are received. Let e_1 and e_2 be the open edges of σ_1 and σ_2, respectively. Denote the processors adjacent to e_1 by p_1 and q_1 and the processors adjacent to e_2 by p_2 and q_2. Paste R_1 and R_2 together by deleting edges e_1 and e_2 and connecting p_1 to p_2 with edge e_p and q_1 to q_2 with edge e_q; denote the resulting ring by R. (This is illustrated in Figs. 3.4 and 3.5.)

We now show how to construct an open schedule σ of A on R in which $2M\left(\frac{n}{2}\right) + \frac{1}{2}\left(\frac{n}{2} - 1\right)$ messages are received. The idea is to first let each of the smaller rings execute its wasteful open schedule separately.

We now explain why σ_1 followed by σ_2 constitutes a schedule for A in the ring R. Consider the occurrence of the event sequence σ_1 starting in the initial configuration for ring R. Since the processors in R_1 cannot distinguish during these events whether R_1 is an independent ring or a sub-ring of R, they execute σ_1 exactly as though R_1

was independent. Consider the subsequent occurrence of the event sequence σ_2 in the ring R. Again, since no messages are delivered on the edges that connect R_1 and R_2, processors in R_2 cannot distinguish during these events whether R_2 is an independent ring or a sub-ring of R. Note the crucial dependence on the uniformity assumption.

Thus $\sigma_1\sigma_2$ is a schedule for R in which at least $2M\left(\frac{n}{2}\right)$ messages are received.

We now show how to force the algorithm into receiving $\frac{1}{2}\left(\frac{n}{2}-1\right)$ additional messages by unblocking either e_p or e_q, but not both.

Consider every finite schedule of the form $\sigma_1\sigma_2\sigma_3$ in which e_p and e_q both remain open. If there is a schedule in which at least $\frac{1}{2}\left(\frac{n}{2}-1\right)$ messages are received in σ_3, then the lemma is proved.

Suppose there is no such schedule. Then there exists some schedule $\sigma_1\sigma_2\sigma_3$ that results in a "quiescent" configuration in the corresponding execution. A processor state is said to be *quiescent* if there is no sequence of computation events from that state in which a message is sent. That is, the processor will not send another message until it receives a message. A configuration is said to be *quiescent* (with respect to e_p and e_q) if no messages are in transit except on the open edges e_p and e_q and every processor is in a quiescent state.

Assume now, without loss of generality, that the processor with the maximal identifier in R is in the sub-ring R_1. Since no message is delivered from R_1 to R_2, processors in R_2 do not know the identifier of the leader, and therefore no processor in R_2 can terminate at the end of $\sigma_1\sigma_2\sigma_3$ (as in the proof of Lemma 3.6).

We claim that in every admissible schedule extending $\sigma_1\sigma_2\sigma_3$, every processor in the sub-ring R_2 must receive at least one additional message before terminating. This holds because a processor in R_2 can learn the identifier of the leader only through messages that arrive from R_1. Since in $\sigma_1\sigma_2\sigma_3$ no message is delivered between R_1 and R_2, such a processor will have to receive another message before it can terminate. This argument depends on the assumption that all processors must learn the id of the leader.

The above argument clearly implies that an additional $\Omega\left(\frac{n}{2}\right)$ messages must be received on R. However, we cannot conclude our proof here because the above claim assumes that both e_p and e_q are unblocked (becasue the schedule must be admissible), and thus the resulting schedule is not open. We cannot a priori claim that many messages will be received if e_p alone is unblocked, because the algorithm might decide to wait for messages on e_q. However, we can prove that it suffices to unblock only one of e_p or e_q and still force the algorithm to receive $\Omega\left(\frac{n}{2}\right)$ messages. This is done in the next claim.

Claim 3.8 *There exists a finite schedule segment σ_4 in which $\frac{1}{2}\left(\frac{n}{2}-1\right)$ messages are received, such that $\sigma_1\sigma_2\sigma_3\sigma_4$ is an open schedule in which either e_p or e_q is open.*

Proof. Let σ_4'' be such that $\sigma_1\sigma_2\sigma_3\sigma_4''$ is an admissible schedule. Thus all messages are delivered on e_p and e_q and all processors terminate. As we argued above, since each of the processors in R_2 must receive a message before termination, at least $\frac{n}{2}$ messages are received in σ_4'' before A terminates. Let σ_4' be the shortest prefix of σ_4'' in which $\frac{n}{2}-1$ messages are received. Consider all the processors in R that received

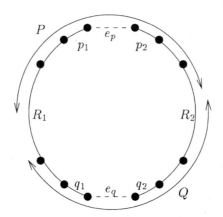

Fig. 3.6   Illustration for Claim 3.8.

messages in σ_4'. Since α_4' starts in a quiescent configuration in which messages are in transit only on e_p and e_q, these processors form two consecutive sets of processors P and Q. P contains the processors that are awakened because of the unblocking of e_p and thus contains at least one of p_1 and p_2. Similarly, Q contains the processors that are awakened because of the unblocking of e_q and thus contains at least one of q_1 and q_2 (see Fig. 3.6).

Since at most $\frac{n}{2} - 1$ processors are included in these sets and the sets are consecutive, it follows that the two sets are disjoint. Furthermore, the number of messages received by processors in one of the sets is at least $\frac{1}{2}(\frac{n}{2} - 1)$. Without loss of generality, assume this set is P, that is, the one containing p_1 or p_2. Let σ_4 be the subsequence of σ_4' that contains only the events on processors in P. Since in σ_4' there is no communication between processors in P and processors in Q, $\sigma_1\sigma_2\sigma_3\sigma_4$ is a schedule. By assumption, at least $\frac{1}{2}(\frac{n}{2} - 1)$ messages are received in σ_4. Furthermore, by construction, no message is delivered on e_q. Thus $\sigma_1\sigma_2\sigma_3\sigma_4$ is the desired open schedule.   □

To summarize, we started with two separate schedules on R_1 and R_2, in which $2M(\frac{n}{2})$ messages were received. We then forced the ring into a quiescent configuration. Finally, we forced $\frac{1}{2}(\frac{n}{2} - 1)$ additional messages to be received from the quiescent configuration, while keeping either e_p or e_q open. Thus we have constructed an open schedule in which at least $2M(\frac{n}{2}) + \frac{1}{2}(\frac{n}{2} - 1)$ messages are received.   □

3.4 SYNCHRONOUS RINGS

We now turn to the problem of electing a leader in a synchronous ring. Again, we present both upper and lower bounds. For the upper bound, two leader election algorithms that require $O(n)$ messages are presented. Obviously, the message complexity of these algorithms is optimal. However, the running time is not bounded by any function (solely) of the ring size, and the algorithms use processor identifiers in an unusual way. For the lower bound, we show that any algorithm that is restricted to use only comparisons of identifiers, or is restricted to be time bounded (that is, to terminate in a number of rounds that depends only on the ring size), requires at least $\Omega(n \log n)$ messages.

3.4.1 An $O(n)$ Upper Bound

The proof of the $\Omega(n \log n)$ lower bound for leader election in an asynchronous ring presented in Section 3.3.3, heavily relied on delaying messages for arbitrarily long periods. It is natural to wonder whether better results can be achieved in the synchronous model, where message delay is fixed. As we shall see, in the synchronous model information can be obtained not only by receiving a message but also by *not* receiving a message in a certain round.

In this section, two algorithms for electing a leader in a synchronous ring are presented. Both algorithms require $O(n)$ messages. The algorithms are presented for a unidirectional ring, where communication is in the clockwise direction. Of course, the same algorithms can be used for bidirectional rings. The first algorithm is nonuniform, and requires all processors in the ring to start at the same round, as is provided for in the synchronous model. The second algorithm is uniform, and processors may start in different rounds, that is, the algorithm works in a model that is slightly weaker than the standard synchronous model.

3.4.1.1 The Nonuniform Algorithm The nonuniform algorithm elects the processor with the minimal identifier to be the leader. It works in phases, each consisting of n rounds. In phase i $(i \geq 0)$, if there is a processor with identifier i, it is elected as the leader, and the algorithm terminates. Therefore, the processor with the minimal identifier is elected.

In more detail, phase i includes rounds $n \cdot i + 1, n \cdot i + 2, \ldots, n \cdot i + n$. At the beginning of phase i, if a processor's identifier is i, and it has not terminated yet, the processor sends a message around the ring and terminates as a leader. If the processor's identifier is not i and it receives a message in phase i, it forwards the message and terminates the algorithm as a non-leader.

Because identifiers are distinct, it is clear that the unique processor with the minimal identifier terminates as a leader. Moreover, exactly n messages are sent in the algorithm; these messages are sent in the phase in which the winner is found. The number of rounds, however, depends on the minimal identifier in the ring. More precisely, if m is the minimal identifier, then the algorithm takes $n \cdot (m + 1)$ rounds.

Note that the algorithm depends on the requirements mentioned—knowledge of n and synchronized start. The next algorithm overcomes these restrictions.

3.4.1.2 The Uniform Algorithm The next leader election algorithm does not require knowledge of the ring size. In addition, the algorithm works in a slightly weakened version of the standard synchronous model, in which the processors do not necessarily start the algorithm simultaneously. More precisely, a processor either wakes up spontaneously in an arbitrary round or wakes up upon receiving a message from another processor (see Exercise 3.7).

The uniform algorithm uses two new ideas. First, messages that originate at different processors are forwarded at different rates. More precisely, a message that originates at a processor with identifier i is delayed $2^i - 1$ rounds at each processor that receives it, before it is forwarded clockwise to the next processor. Second, to overcome the unsynchronized starts, a preliminary wake-up phase is added. In this phase, each processor that wakes up spontaneously sends a "wake-up" message around the ring; this message is forwarded without delay. A processor that receives a wake-up message before starting the algorithm does not participate in the algorithm and will only act as a *relay*, forwarding or swallowing messages. After the preliminary phase the leader is elected among the set of participating processors.

The wake-up message sent by a processor contains the processor's identifier. This message travels at a regular rate of one edge per round and eliminates all the processors that are not awake when they receive the message. When a message from a processor with identifier i reaches a participating processor, the message starts to travel at a rate of 2^i; to accomplish this slowdown, each processor that receives such a message delays it for $2^i - 1$ rounds before forwarding it. Note that after a message reaches an awake processor, all processors it will reach are awake. A message is in the *first phase* until it is received by a participating processor; after reaching a participating processor, a message is in the *second phase*, and it is forwarded at a rate of 2^i.

Throughout the algorithm, processors forward messages. However, as in previous leader election algorithms we have seen, processors sometimes swallow messages without forwarding them. In this algorithm, messages are swallowed according to the following rules:

1. A participating processor swallows a message if the identifier in the message is larger than the minimal identifier it has seen so far, including its own identifier.

2. A relay processor swallows a message if the identifier in the message is larger than the minimal identifier it has seen so far, not including its own id.

The pseudocode appears in Algorithm 6.

As we prove below, n rounds after the first processor wakes up, only second-phase messages are left, and the leader is elected among the participating processors. The swallowing rules guarantee that only the participating processor with the smallest identifier receives its message back and terminates as a leader. This is proved in Lemma 3.9.

For each i, $0 \le i < n$, let id_i be the identifier of processor p_i and $\langle id_i \rangle$ be the message originated by p_i.

Lemma 3.9 *Only the processor with the smallest identifier among the participating processors receives its own message back.*

Algorithm 6 Synchronous leader election: code for processor $p_i, 0 \leq i < n$.

Initially *waiting* is empty and *status* is asleep

```
1:  let R be the set of messages received in this computation event
2:  S := ∅                                        // the messages to be sent

3:  if status = asleep then
4:      if R is empty then                        // woke up spontaneously
5:          status := participating
6:          min := id
7:          add ⟨id,1⟩ to S                        // first phase message
8:      else
9:          status := relay
10:         min := ∞

9:  for each ⟨m,h⟩ in R do
10:     if m < min then
11:         become not elected
12:         min := m
13:         if (status = relay) and (h = 1) then    // m stays first phase
14:             add ⟨m,h⟩ to S
15:         else                                   // m is/becomes second phase
16:             add ⟨m,2⟩ to waiting tagged with current round number
17:     elseif m = id then become elected
                                                   // if m > min then message is swallowed

18: for each ⟨m,2⟩ in waiting do
19:     if ⟨m,2⟩ was received 2^m − 1 rounds ago then
20:         remove ⟨m⟩ from waiting and add to S

21: send S to left
```

Proof. Let p_i be the participating processor with the smallest identifier. (Note that at least one processor must participate in the algorithm.) Clearly, no processor, participating or not, can swallow $\langle id_i \rangle$.

Furthermore, since $\langle id_i \rangle$ is delayed at most 2^{id_i} rounds at each processor, p_i eventually receives its message back.

Assume, by way of contradiction, that some other processor p_j, $j \neq i$, also receives back its message $\langle id_j \rangle$. Thus, $\langle id_j \rangle$ must pass through all the processors in the ring, including p_i. But $id_i < id_j$, and since p_i is a participating processor, it does not forward $\langle id_j \rangle$, a contradiction. $\qquad\square$

The above lemma implies that exactly one processor receives its message back. Thus this processor will be the only one to declare itself a leader, implying the correctness of the algorithm. We now analyze the number of messages sent during an admissible execution of the algorithm.

To calculate the number of messages sent during an admissible execution of the algorithm we divide them into three categories:

1. First-phase messages

2. Second-phase messages sent before the message of the eventual leader enters its second phase

3. Second-phase messages sent after the message of the eventual leader enters its second phase

Lemma 3.10 *The total number of messages in the first category is at most n.*

Proof.   We show that at most one first-phase message is forwarded by each processor, which implies the lemma.

Assume, by way of contradiction, that some processor p_i forwards two messages in their first phase, $\langle id_j \rangle$ from p_j and $\langle id_k \rangle$ from p_k. Assume, without loss of generality, that p_j is closer to p_i than p_k is to p_i, in terms of clockwise distance. Thus, $\langle id_k \rangle$ must pass through p_j before it arrives at p_i. If $\langle id_k \rangle$ arrives at p_j after p_j woke up and sent $\langle id_j \rangle$, $\langle id_k \rangle$ continues as a second-phase message, at a rate of 2^{id_k}; otherwise, p_j does not participate and $\langle id_j \rangle$ is not sent. Thus either $\langle id_k \rangle$ arrives at p_i as a second phase message or $\langle id_j \rangle$ is not sent, a contradiction.   □

Let r be the first round in which some processor starts executing the algorithm, and let p_i be one of these processors. To bound the number of messages in the second category, we first show that n rounds after the first processor starts executing the algorithm, all messages are in their second phase.

Lemma 3.11 *If p_j is at (clockwise) distance k from p_i, then a first-phase message is received by p_j no later than round $r + k$.*

Proof.   The proof is by induction on k. The base case, $k = 1$, is obvious because p_i's neighbor receives p_i's message in round $r + 1$. For the inductive step, assume that the processor at (clockwise) distance $k - 1$ from p_i receives a first-phase message no later than round $r + k - 1$. If this processor is already awake when it receives the first-phase message, it has already sent a first-phase message to its neighbor p_j; otherwise, it forwards the first-phase message to p_j in round $r + k$.   □

Lemma 3.12 *The total number of messages in the second category is at most n.*

Proof.   As shown in the proof of Lemma 3.10, at most one first-phase message is sent on each edge. Since by round $r + n$ one first-phase message was sent on every edge, it follows that after round $r + n$ no first-phase messages are sent. By Lemma 3.11, the message of the eventual leader enters its second phase at most n rounds after the first message of the algorithm is sent. Thus messages from the second category are sent only in the n rounds following the round in which the first processor woke up.

Message $\langle i \rangle$ in its second phase is delayed $2^i - 1$ rounds before being forwarded. Thus $\langle i \rangle$ is sent at most $\frac{n}{2^i}$ times in this category. Since messages containing smaller identifiers are forwarded more often, the maximum number of messages is obtained when all the processors participate, and when the identifiers are as small as possible, that is, $0, 1, \ldots, n - 1$. Note that second-phase messages of the eventual leader (in our case, 0) are not counted in this category. Thus the number of messages in the second category is at most $\sum_{i=1}^{n-1} \frac{n}{2^i} \leq n$. □

Let p_i be the processor with the minimal identifier; no processor forwards a message after it forwards $\langle id_i \rangle$. Once $\langle id_i \rangle$ returns to p_i, all the processors in the ring have already forwarded it, and therefore we have the following lemma:

Lemma 3.13 *No message is forwarded after $\langle id_i \rangle$ returns to p_i.*

Lemma 3.14 *The total number of messages in the third category is at most $2n$.*

Proof. Let p_i be the eventual leader, and let p_j be some other participating processor. By Lemma 3.9, $id_i < id_j$. By Lemma 3.13, there are no messages in the ring after p_i receives its message back. Since $\langle id_i \rangle$ is delayed at most 2^{id_i} rounds at each processor, at most $n \cdot 2^{id_i}$ rounds are needed for $\langle id_i \rangle$ to return to p_i. Therefore, messages in the third category are sent only during $n \cdot 2^{id_i}$ rounds. During these rounds, $\langle id_j \rangle$ is forwarded at most

$$\frac{1}{2^{id_j}} \cdot n \cdot 2^{id_i} = n \cdot 2^{id_i - id_j}$$

times. Hence, the total number of messages transmitted in this category is at most

$$\sum_{j=0}^{n-1} \frac{n}{2^{id_j - id_i}}$$

By the same argument as in the proof of Lemma 3.12, this is less than or equal to

$$\sum_{k=0}^{n-1} \frac{n}{2^k} \leq 2n$$

□

Lemmas 3.10, 3.12, and 3.14 imply:

Theorem 3.15 *There is a synchronous leader election algorithm whose message complexity is at most $4n$.*

Now consider the time complexity of the algorithm. By Lemma 3.13, the computation ends when the elected leader receives its message back. This happens within $O(n2^i)$ rounds since the first processor starts executing the algorithm, where i is the identifier of the elected leader.

3.4.2 An $\Omega(n \log n)$ Lower Bound for Restricted Algorithms

In Section 3.4.1, we presented two algorithms for electing a leader in synchronous rings whose worst-case message complexity is $O(n)$. Both algorithms have two undesirable properties. First, they use the identifiers in a nonstandard manner (to decide how long a message should be delayed). Second, and more importantly, the number of rounds in each admissible execution depends on the identifiers of processors. The reason this is undesirable is that the identifiers of the processors can be huge relative to n.

In this section, we show that both of these properties are inherent for any message efficient algorithm. Specifically, we show that if an algorithm uses the identifiers only for comparisons it requires $\Omega(n \log n)$ messages. Then we show, by reduction, that if an algorithm is restricted to use a bounded number of rounds, independent of the identifiers, then it also requires $\Omega(n \log n)$ messages.

The synchronous lower bounds cannot be derived from the asynchronous lower bound (of Theorem 3.5), because the algorithms presented in Section 3.4.1 indicate that additional assumptions are necessary for the synchronous lower bound to hold. The synchronous lower bound holds even for nonuniform algorithms, whereas the asynchronous lower bound holds only for uniform algorithms. Interestingly, the converse derivation, of the asynchronous result from the synchronous, is correct and provides an asynchronous lower bound for nonuniform algorithms, as explored in Exercise 3.11.

3.4.2.1 Comparison-Based Algorithms
In this section, we formally define the concept of comparison-based algorithms.

For the purpose of the lower bound, we assume that all processors begin executing at the same round.

Recall that a ring is specified by listing the processors' identifiers in clockwise order, beginning with the smallest identifier. Note that in the synchronous model an admissible execution of the algorithm is completely defined by the initial configuration, because there is no choice of message delay or relative order of processor steps. The initial configuration of the system, in turn, is completely defined by the ring, that is, by the listing of processors' identifiers according to the above rule. When the choice of algorithm is clear from context, we will denote the admissible execution determined by ring R as $exec(R)$.

Two processors, p_i in ring R_1 and p_j in ring R_2, are *matching* if they both have the same position in the respective ring specification. Note that matching processors are at the same distance from the processor with the smallest identifier in the respective rings.

Intuitively, an algorithm is comparison based if it behaves the same on rings that have the same order pattern of the identifiers. Formally, two rings, $x_0, \ldots, x_{n-1}$ and $y_0, \ldots, y_{n-1}$, are *order equivalent* if for every i and j, $x_i < x_j$ if and only if $y_i < y_j$. Recall that the *k-neighborhood* of a processor p_i in a ring is the sequence of $2k + 1$ identifiers of processors $p_{i-k}, \ldots, p_{i-1}, p_i, p_{i+1}, \ldots, p_{i+k}$ (all indices are calculated modulo n). We extend the notion of order equivalence to k-neighborhoods in the obvious manner.

We now define what it means to "behave the same." Intuitively, we would like to claim that in the admissible executions on order equivalent rings R_1 and R_2, the same messages are sent and the same decisions are made. In general, however, messages sent by the algorithm contain identifiers of processors; thus messages sent on R_1 will be different from messages sent on R_2. For our purpose, however, we concentrate on the message pattern, that is, when and where messages are sent, rather than their content, and on the decisions. Specifically, consider two executions α_1 and α_2 and two processors p_i and p_j. We say that the behavior of p_i in α_1 is *similar* in round k to the behavior of p_j in α_2 if the following conditions are satisfied:

1. p_i sends a message to its left (right) neighbor in round k in α_1 if and only if p_j sends a message to its left (right) neighbor in round k in α_2

2. p_i terminates as a leader in round k of α_1 if and only if p_j terminates as a leader in round k of α_2

We say that that the behaviors of p_i in α_1 and p_j in α_2 are *similar* if they are similar in all rounds $k \geq 0$. We can now formally define comparison-based algorithms.

Definition 3.2 *An algorithm is* comparison based *if for every pair of order-equivalent rings R_1 and R_2, every pair of matching processors have similar behaviors in $exec(R_1)$ and $exec(R_2)$.*

3.4.2.2 Lower Bound for Comparison-Based Algorithms

Let A be a comparison-based leader election algorithm. The proof considers a ring that is highly symmetric in its order patterns, that is, a ring in which there are many order-equivalent neighborhoods. Intuitively, as long as two processors have order-equivalent neighborhoods they behave the same under A. We derive the lower bound by executing A on a highly symmetric ring and arguing that if a processor sends a message in a certain round, then all processors with order-equivalent neighborhoods also send a message in that round.

A crucial point in the proof is to distinguish rounds in which information is obtained by processors from rounds in which no information is obtained. Recall that in a synchronous ring it is possible for a processor to obtain information even without receiving a message. For example, in the nonuniform algorithm of Section 3.4.1, the fact that no message is received in rounds 1 through n implies that no processor in the ring has the identifier 0. The key to the proof that follows is the observation that the nonexistence of a message in a certain round r is useful to processor p_i only if a message could have been received in this round in a different, but order-equivalent, ring. For example, in the nonuniform algorithm, if some processor in the ring had the identifier 0, a message would have been received in rounds $1, \ldots, n$. Thus a round in which no message is sent in any order-equivalent ring is not useful. Such useful rounds are called active, as defined below:

Definition 3.3 *A round* r *is* active *in an execution on a ring* R *if some processor sends a message in round* r *of the execution. When* R *is understood from context, we denote by* r_k *the index of the* k*th active round.*[1]

Recall that, by definition, a comparison-based algorithm generates similar behaviors on order-equivalent rings. This implies that, for order equivalent rings R_1 and R_2, a round is active in $exec(R_1)$ if and only if it is active in $exec(R_2)$.

Because information in messages can travel only k processors around the ring in k rounds, the state of a processor after round k depends only on its k-neighborhood. We have, however, a stronger property that the state of a processor after the kth *active* round depends only on its k-neighborhood. This captures the above intuition that information is obtained only in active rounds and is formally proved in Lemma 3.16. Note that the lemma does not require that the processors be matching (otherwise the claim follows immediately from the definition) but does require that their neighborhoods be identical. This lemma requires the hypothesis that the two rings be order equivalent. The reason is to ensure that the two executions under consideration have the same set of active rounds; thus r_k is well-defined.

Lemma 3.16 *Let* R_1 *and* R_2 *be order-equivalent rings, and let* p_i *in* R_1 *and* p_j *in* R_2 *be two processors with identical* k*-neighborhoods. Then the sequence of transitions that* p_i *experiences in rounds 1 through* r_k *of* $exec(R_1)$ *is the same as the sequence of transitions that* p_j *experiences in rounds 1 through* r_k *of* $exec(R_2)$.

Proof.   Informally, the proof shows that after k active rounds, a processor may learn only about processors that are at most k away from itself.

The formal proof follows by induction on k. For the base case $k = 0$, note that two processors with identical 0-neighborhoods have the same identifiers, and thus they are in the same state.

For the inductive step, assume that every two processors with identical $(k - 1)$-neighborhoods are in the same state after the $(k - 1)$-st active round. Since p_i and p_j have identical k-neighborhoods, they also have identical $(k - 1)$-neighborhoods; therefore, by the inductive hypothesis, p_i and p_j are in the same state after the $(k - 1)$-st active round. Furthermore, their respective neighbors have identical $(k - 1)$-neighborhoods. Therefore, by the inductive hypothesis, their respective neighbors are in the same state after the $(k - 1)$-st active round.

In the rounds between the $(k-1)$-st active round and the kth active round (if there are any), no processor receives any message and thus p_i and p_j remain in the same state as each other, and so do their respective neighbors. (Note that p_i might change its state during the nonactive rounds, but since p_j has the same transition function, it makes the same state transition.) In the kth active round, if both p_i and p_j do not receive messages they are in the same states at the end of the round. If p_i receives a message from its right neighbor, p_j also receives an identical message from its

---

[1]Recall that once the ring is fixed, the whole admissible execution is determined because the system is synchronous.

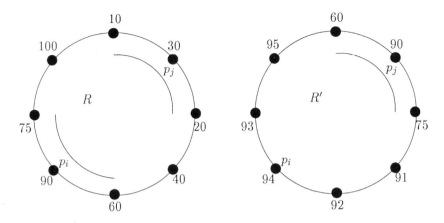

Fig. 3.7 Example for the proof of Lemma 3.17; $k = 1$ and $n = 8$.

right neighbor, because the neighbors are in the same state, and similarly for the left neighbor. Hence, p_i and p_j are in the same state at the end of the kth active round, as needed. □

Lemma 3.17 extends the above claim from processors with identical k-neighborhoods to processors with order-equivalent k-neighborhoods. It relies on the fact that A is comparison based. Furthermore, it requires the ring R to be spaced, which intuitively means that for every two identifiers in R, there are n unused identifiers between them, where n is the size of the ring. Formally, a ring of size n is *spaced* if for every identifier x in the ring, the identifiers $x - 1$ through $x - n$ are not in the ring.

Lemma 3.17 *Let R be a spaced ring and let p_i and p_j be two processors with order-equivalent k-neighborhoods in R. Then p_i and p_j have similar behaviors in rounds 1 through r_k of exec(R).*

Proof. We construct another ring R' that satisfies the following:

- p_j's k-neighborhood is the same as p_i's k-neighborhood from R

- the identifiers in R' are unique

- R' is order equivalent to R with p_j in R' matching p_j in R

R' can be constructed because R is spaced (see an example in Fig. 3.7).

By Lemma 3.16, the sequence of transitions that p_i experiences in rounds 1 through r_k of $exec(R)$ is the same as the sequence of transitions that p_j experiences in rounds 1 through r_k of $exec(R')$. Thus p_i's behavior in rounds 1 through r_k of $exec(R)$ is similar to p_j's behavior in rounds 1 through r_k of $exec(R')$. Since the algorithm is comparison based and p_j in R' is matching to p_j in R, p_j's behavior in rounds 1 through r_k of $exec(R')$ is similar to p_j's behavior in rounds 1 through r_k of $exec(R)$.

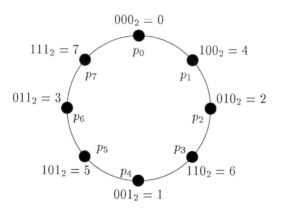

Fig. 3.8 The ring R_8^{rev}.

Thus p_i's behavior and p_j's behavior in rounds 1 through r_k of $exec(R)$ are similar.

□

We can now prove the main theorem:

Theorem 3.18 *For every $n \geq 8$ that is a power of 2, there exists a ring S_n of size n such that for every synchronous comparison-based leader election algorithm A, $\Omega(n \log n)$ messages are sent in the admissible execution of A on S_n.*

Proof. Fix any such algorithm A. The key to this proof is the construction of S_n, a highly symmetric ring, in which many processors have many order equivalent neighborhoods. S_n is constructed in two steps.

First, define the n-processor ring R_n^{rev} as follows. For each i, $0 \leq i < n$, let p_i's identifier be $\text{rev}(i)$, where $\text{rev}(i)$ is the integer whose binary representation using $\log n$ bits is the reverse of the binary representation of i. (See the special case $n = 8$ in Fig. 3.8.) Consider any partitioning of R_n^{rev} into consecutive segments of length j, where j is a power of 2. It can be shown that all these segments are order equivalent (see Exercise 3.9).

S_n is a spaced version of R_n^{rev}, obtained by multiplying each identifier in R_n^{rev} by $n + 1$ and then adding n to it. These changes do not alter the order equivalence of segments.

Lemma 3.19 quantifies how many order-equivalent neighborhoods of a given size there are in S_n. This result is then used to show, in Lemma 3.20, a lower bound on the number of active rounds of the algorithms and to show, in Lemma 3.21, a lower bound on the number of messages sent in each active round. The desired bound of $\Omega(n \log n)$ is obtained by combining the latter two bounds.

Lemma 3.19 *For all $k < n/8$, and for all k-neighborhoods N of S_n, there are more than $\frac{n}{2(2k+1)}$ k-neighborhoods of S_n that are order equivalent to N (including N itself).*

Proof. N consists of a sequence of $2k + 1$ identifiers. Let j be the smallest power of 2 that is bigger than $2k + 1$. Partition S_n into $\frac{n}{j}$ consecutive segments such that one segment totally encompasses N. By the construction of S_n, all of these segments are order equivalent. Thus there are at least $\frac{n}{j}$ neighborhoods that are order equivalent to N. Since $j < 2(2k + 1)$, the number of neighborhoods order equivalent to N is more than $\frac{n}{2(2k+1)}$. $\qquad\square$

Lemma 3.20 *The number of active rounds in* $exec(S_n)$ *is at least* $n/8$.

Proof. Let T be the number of active rounds. Suppose in contradiction $T < n/8$. Let p_i be the processor that is elected the leader in $exec(S_n)$. By Lemma 3.19, there are more than $\frac{n}{2(2T+1)}$ T-neighborhoods that are order equivalent to p_i's T-neighborhood. By assumption on T,

$$\frac{n}{2(2T + 1)} > \frac{n}{2(2n/8 + 1)} = \frac{2n}{n + 4}$$

and, since $n \geq 8$, $\frac{2n}{n+4} > 1$. Thus there exists some processor p_j other than p_i whose T-neighborhood is order equivalent to p_i's T-neighborhood. By Lemma 3.17, p_j is also elected, contradicting the assumed correctness of A. $\qquad\square$

Lemma 3.21 *At least* $\frac{n}{2(2k+1)}$ *messages are sent in the kth active round of* $exec(S_n)$, *for each* k, $1 \leq k \leq n/8$.

Proof. Consider the kth active round. Since it is active, at least one processor sends a message, say p_i. By Lemma 3.19, there are more than $\frac{n}{2(2k+1)}$ processors whose k-neighborhoods are order equivalent to p_i's k-neighborhood. By Lemma 3.17, each of them also sends a message in the kth active round. $\qquad\square$

We now finish the proof of the main theorem. By Lemma 3.20 and Lemma 3.21, the total number of messages sent in $exec(S_n)$ is at least

$$\sum_{k=1}^{n/8} \frac{n}{2(2k + 1)} \geq \frac{n}{6} \sum_{k=1}^{n/8} \frac{1}{k} > \frac{n}{6} \ln \frac{n}{8}$$

which is $\Omega(n \log n)$. $\qquad\square$

Note that in order for this theorem to hold, the algorithm need not be comparison based for *every* set of identifiers drawn from the natural numbers, but only for identifiers drawn from the set $\{0, 1, \ldots, n^2 + 2n - 1\}$. The reason is that the largest identifier in S_n is $n^2 + n - 1 = (n + 1) \cdot rev(n - 1) + n$ (recall that n is a power of 2 and thus the binary representation of $n - 1$ is a sequence of 1s). We require the algorithm to be comparison based on *all* identifiers between 0 and $n^2 + 2n - 1$, and not just on identifiers that occur in S_n, because the proof of Lemma 3.17 uses the fact that the algorithm is comparison based on all identifiers that range from n less than the smallest in S_n to n greater than the largest in S_n.

3.4.2.3 Lower Bound for Time-Bounded Algorithms The next definition disallows the running time of an algorithm from depending on the identifiers: It requires the running time for each ring size to be bounded, even though the possible identifiers are not bounded, because they come from the set of natural numbers.

Definition 3.4 *A synchronous algorithm A is* time-bounded *if, for each n, the worst-case running time of A over all rings of size n, with identifiers drawn from the natural numbers, is bounded.*

We now prove the lower bound for time-bounded algorithms, by reduction to comparison-based algorithms. We first show how to map from time-bounded algorithms to comparison-based algorithms. Then we use the lower bound of $\Omega(n \log n)$ messages for comparison-based algorithms to obtain a lower bound on the number of messages sent by time-bounded algorithms. Because the comparison-based lower bound as stated is only for values of n that are powers of 2, the same is true here, although the lower bound holds for all values of n (see chapter notes).

To map from time-bounded to comparison-based algorithms, we require definitions describing the behavior of an algorithm during a bounded amount of time.

Definition 3.5 *A synchronous algorithm A is t-*comparison based over identifier set *S for ring size n if, for every two order equivalent rings, R_1 and R_2, of size n, every pair of matching processors have similar behaviors in rounds 1 through t of exec(R_1) and exec(R_2).*

Intuitively, an r-comparison based algorithm over S is an algorithm that behaves as a comparison-based algorithm in the first r rounds, as long as identifiers are chosen from S. If the algorithm terminates within r rounds, then this is the same as being comparison based over S for all rounds.

The first step is to show that every time-bounded algorithm behaves as a comparison-based algorithm over a subset of its inputs, provided that the input set is sufficiently large. To do this we use the finite version of Ramsey's theorem. Informally, the theorem states that if we take a large set of elements and we color each subset of size k with one of t colors, then we can find some subset of size ℓ such that all its subsets of size k have the same color. If we think of the coloring as partitioning into equivalence classes (two subsets of size k belong to the same equivalence class if they have the same color), the theorem says that there is a set of size ℓ such that all its subsets of size k are in the same equivalence class. Later, we shall color rings with the same color if the behavior of matching processors is similar in them.

For completeness, we repeat Ramsey's theorem:

Ramsey's Theorem (finite version) *For all integers k, ℓ, and t, there exists an integer $f(k, \ell, t)$ such that for every set S of size at least $f(k, \ell, t)$, and every t-coloring of the k-subsets of S, some ℓ-subset of S has all its k-subsets with the same color.*

In Lemma 3.22, we use Ramsey's theorem to map any time-bounded algorithm to a comparison-based algorithm.

Lemma 3.22 *Let* A *be a synchronous time-bounded algorithm with running time* $r(n)$. *Then, for every* n, *there exists a set* C_n *of* $n^2 + 2n$ *identifiers such that* A *is* $r(n)$-*comparison based over* C_n *for ring size* n.

Proof. Fix n. Let Y and Z be any two n-subsets of N (the natural numbers). We say that Y and Z are *equivalent subsets* if, for every pair of order equivalent rings, R_1 with identifiers from Y and R_2 with identifiers from Z, matching processors have similar behaviors in rounds 1 through $t(n)$ of $exec(R_1)$ and $exec(R_2)$. This definition partitions the n-subsets of N into finitely many equivalence classes, since the term 'similar behavior' only refers to the presence or absence of messages and terminated states. We color the n-subsets of N such that two n-subsets have the same color if and only if they are in the same equivalence class.

By Ramsey's theorem, if we take t to be the number of equivalence classes (colors), ℓ to be $n^2 + 2n$, and k to be n, then, since N is infinite, there exists a subset C_n of N of cardinality $n^2 + 2n$ such that all n-subsets of C_n belong to the same equivalence class.

We claim that A is an $r(n)$-comparison based algorithm over C_n for ring size n. Consider two order-equivalent rings, R_1 and R_2, of size n with identifiers from C_n. Let Y be the set of identifiers in R_1 and Z be the set of identifiers in R_2. Y and Z are n-subsets of C_n; therefore, they belong to the same equivalence class. Thus matching processors have similar behaviors in rounds 1 through $r(n)$ of $exec(R_1)$ and $exec(R_2)$. Therefore, A is an $r(n)$-comparison based over C_n for ring size n. $\qquad\square$

Theorem 3.18 implies that every comparison-based algorithm has worst-case message complexity $\Omega(n \log n)$. We cannot immediately apply this theorem now, because we have only shown that a time-bounded algorithm A is comparison based on a specific set of ids, not on all ids. However, we will use A to design another algorithm A', with the same message complexity as A, that is comparison based on rings of size n with ids from the set $\{0, 1, \ldots, n^2 + 2n - 1\}$. As was discussed just after the proof of Theorem 3.18, this will be sufficient to show that the message complexity of A' is $\Omega(n \log n)$. Thus the message complexity of A is $\Omega(n \log n)$.

Theorem 3.23 *For every synchronous time-bounded leader election algorithm* A *and every* $n \geq 8$ *that is a power of 2, there exists a ring* R *of size* n *such that* $\Omega(n \log n)$ *messages are sent in the admissible execution of* A *on* R.

Proof. Fix an algorithm A satisfying the hypotheses of the theorem with running time $r(n)$. Fix n; let C_n be the set of identifiers guaranteed by Lemma 3.22, and let $c_0, c_1, \ldots, c_{n^2+2n-1}$ be the elements of C_n in increasing order.

We define an algorithm A' that is comparison based on rings of size n with identifiers from the set $\{0, 1, \ldots, n^2+2n-1\}$ and that has the same time and message complexity as A. In algorithm A', a processor with identifier i executes algorithm A as if though had the identifier c_i. Since A is $r(n)$-comparison based over C_n for ring size n and since A terminates within $r(n)$ rounds, it follows that A' is comparison based on rings of size n with identifiers from the set $\{0, 1, \ldots, n^2 + 2n - 1\}$.

By Theorem 3.18, there is a ring of size n with identifiers from $\{0, 1, \ldots, n^2 + 2n - 1\}$ in which A' sends $\Omega(n \log n)$ messages. By the way A' was constructed, there is an execution of A in a ring of size n with identifiers from C_n in which the same messages are sent, which proves the theorem.   □

Exercises

3.1 Prove that there is no anonymous leader election algorithm for asynchronous ring systems.

3.2 Prove that there is no anonymous leader election algorithm for synchronous ring systems that is uniform.

3.3 Is leader election possible in a synchronous ring in which all but one processor have the same identifier? Either give an algorithm or prove an impossibility result.

3.4 Consider the following algorithm for leader election in an asynchronous ring: Each processor sends its identifier to its right neighbor; every processor forwards a message (to its right neighbor) only if it includes an identifier larger than its own.

Prove that the average number of messages sent by this algorithm is $O(n \log n)$, assuming that identifiers are uniformly distributed integers.

3.5 In Section 3.3.3, we have seen a lower bound of $\Omega(n \log n)$ on the number of messages required for electing a leader in an asynchronous ring. The proof of the lower bound relies on two additional properties: (a) the processor with the maximal identifier is elected, and (b) all processors must know the identifier of the elected leader.

Prove that the lower bound holds also when these two requirements are omitted.

3.6 Extend Theorem 3.5 to the case in which n is not an integral power of 2.

Hint: Consider the largest $n' < n$ that is an integral power of 2, and prove the theorem for n'.

3.7 Modify the formal model of synchronous message passing systems to describe the non-synchronized start model of Section 3.4.1. That is, state the conditions that executions and admissible executions must satisfy.

3.8 Prove that the order-equivalent ring R' in proof of Lemma 3.17 can always be constructed.

3.9 Recall the ring R_n^{rev} from the proof of Theorem 3.18. For every partition of R_n^{rev} into $\frac{n}{j}$ consecutive segments, where j is a power of 2, prove that all of these segments are order equivalent.

3.10 Consider an anonymous ring where processors start with binary inputs.

1. Prove there is no uniform synchronous algorithm for computing the AND of the input bits.

   Hint: Assume by way of contradiction that such an algorithm exists, and consider the execution of the algorithm on the all-ones ring; then embed this ring in a much larger ring with a single 0.

2. Present an asynchronous (nonuniform) algorithm for computing the AND; the algorithm should send $O(n^2)$ messages in the worst case.

3. Prove that $\Omega(n^2)$ is a lower bound on the message complexity of any asynchronous algorithm that computes the AND.

4. Present a synchronous algorithm for computing the AND; the algorithm should send $O(n)$ messages in the worst case.

3.11 Derive an $\Omega(n \log n)$ lower bound on the number of messages required for leader election in the asynchronous model of communication from the lower bound for the synchronous model. In the asynchronous model, the proof should not rely on the algorithm being comparison based or time-bounded.

Chapter Notes

This chapter consists of an in-depth study of the leader election problem in message-passing systems with a ring topology. Ring networks have attracted so much study because their behavior is easy to describe and because lower bounds derived for them apply to algorithms designed for networks with arbitrary topology. Moreover, rings correspond to token ring networks [18].

We first showed that it is impossible to choose a leader in an anonymous ring (Theorem 3.2); this result was proved by Angluin [17]. In Chapter 14, we describe how to use randomization to overcome this impossibility result.

We then presented algorithms for leader election in asynchronous rings. The $O(n^2)$ algorithm for leader election in asynchronous rings (presented in Section 3.3.1) is based on an algorithm of LeLann [165], who was the first to study the leader election problem, with optimizations of Chang and Roberts [70]. It can be viewed as a special case of Algorithm 4. Chang and Roberts also prove that, averaged over all possible inputs, the message complexity of this algorithm is $O(n \log n)$ (Exercise 3.4).

An $O(n \log n)$ algorithm for leader election in asynchronous rings was first suggested by Hirschberg and Sinclair [139]; this is the algorithm presented in Section 3.3.2. Subsequently, leader election in rings was studied in numerous papers, and we shall not list all of them here. The best algorithm currently known is due to Higham and Przytycka [137] and has message complexity $1.271n \log n + O(n)$.

The Hirschberg and Sinclair algorithm assumes that the ring is bidirectional; $O(n \log n)$ algorithms for the unidirectional case were presented by Dolev, Klawe, and Rodeh [95] and by Peterson [212].

The issue of orientation is discussed at length by Attiya, Snir, and Warmuth [33]; their paper contains the answer to Exercise 3.10.

A major part of this chapter was dedicated to lower bounds on the number of messages needed for electing a leader in a ring. The lower bound for the asynchronous case is due to Burns [61]. This lower bound applies only to *uniform* algorithms. A lower bound of $\Omega(n \log n)$ on the *average* message complexity of leader election in asynchronous rings was presented by Pachl, Korach, and Rotem [205]. In this lower bound, the average is taken over all possible rings of a particular size, and, therefore, the lower bound applies to nonuniform algorithms.

The linear algorithms as well as the lower bound for the synchronous case, presented in Section 3.4, are taken from the paper by Frederickson and Lynch [111]; our formal treatment of comparison-based algorithms is somewhat different from theirs. Constructions of symmetric rings of size n, where n is not an integral power of 2, appear in [33, 111]. Exercise 3.11 follows an observation of Eli Gafni.

4

Mutual Exclusion in Shared Memory

Having introduced the message-passing paradigm already, we now turn to the other major communication model for distributed systems, *shared memory*. In a shared memory system, processors communicate via a common memory area that contains a set of *shared variables*. We only consider *asynchronous* shared memory systems.[1]

Several types of variables can be employed. The *type* of a shared variable specifies the operations that can be performed on it and the values returned by the operations. The most common type is a *read/write* register, in which the operations are the familiar reads and writes such that each read returns the value of the latest preceding write. Other types of shared variables support more powerful operations, such as *read-modify-write*, *test&set*, or *compare&swap*. Registers can be further characterized according to their access patterns, that is, how many processors can access a specific variable with a specific operation. Not surprisingly, the type of shared variables used for communication determines the possibility and the complexity of solving a given problem.

In this chapter, we concentrate on the *mutual exclusion* problem. We present several algorithms and lower bounds. Our presentation highlights the connection between the type of shared memory accesses used and the cost of achieving mutual exclusion in terms of the amount of shared memory required.

We first give the formal definitions for shared memory systems. We then study the memory requirement for solving mutual exclusion when powerful variables are used. The main result here is that $\Theta(\log n)$ bits are necessary and sufficient for providing strong fairness properties for n processors. Finally, we consider systems

---

[1] Synchronous shared memory systems are studied in the PRAM model of parallel computation.

in which processors can only share read/write variables. We present two algorithms that provide mutual exclusion for n processors using $O(n)$ registers, one that relies on unbounded values and another that avoids them. We then show that any algorithm that provides mutual exclusion using only read/write registers must employ $\Omega(n)$ registers.

4.1 FORMAL MODEL FOR SHARED MEMORY SYSTEMS

Here we describe our formal model of shared memory systems. As in the case of message-passing systems, we model processors as state machines and model executions as alternating sequences of configurations and events. The difference is the nature of the configurations and events. In this section, we discuss in detail the new features of the model and only briefly mention those that are similar to the message-passing model. We also discuss the relevant complexity measures and pseudocode conventions for presenting shared memory algorithms. Later, in Chapters 9 and 10, we study alternative ways to model shared memory systems.

4.1.1 Systems

We assume the system contains n processors, $p_0, \ldots, p_{n-1}$, and m registers, $R_0, \ldots, R_{m-1}$.

As in the message-passing case, each processor is modeled as a state machine, but there are no special *inbuf* or *outbuf* state components.

Each register has a *type*, which specifies:

1. The values that can be taken on by the register

2. The operations that can be performed on the register

3. The value to be returned by each operation (if any)

4. The new value of the register resulting from each operation

An initial value can be specified for each register.

For instance, an integer-valued read/write register R can take on all integer values and has operations read(R, v) and write(R, v). The read(R, v) operation returns the value v, leaving R unchanged. The write(R, v) operation takes an integer input parameter v, returns no value, and changes R's value to v.

A *configuration* in the shared memory model is a vector

$$C = (q_0, \ldots, q_{n-1}, r_0, \ldots, r_{m-1})$$

where q_i is a state of p_i and r_j is a value of register R_j. Denote by $mem(C)$ the state of the memory in C, namely $(r_0, \ldots, r_{m-1})$. In an *initial configuration*, all processors are in their initial states and all registers contain initial values.

The *events* in a shared memory system are computation steps by the processors and are denoted by the index of the processor. At each computation step by processor p_i, the following happen atomically:

1. p_i chooses a shared variable to access with a specific operation, based on p_i's current state

2. The specified operation is performed on the shared variable

3. p_i's state changes according to p_i's transition function, based on p_i's current state and the value returned by the shared memory operation performed

We define an *execution segment* of the algorithm to be a (finite or infinite) sequence with the following form:

$$C_0, \phi_1, C_1, \phi_2, C_2, \phi_3 \ldots$$

where each C_k is a configuration and each ϕ_k is an event. Furthermore, the application of ϕ_k to C_{k-1} results in C_k, as follows. Suppose $\phi_k = i$ and p_i's state in C_{k-1} indicates that shared variable R_j is to be accessed. Then C_k is the result of changing C_{k-1} in accordance with p_i's computation step acting on p_i's state in C_{k-1} and the value of the register R_j in C_{k-1}; thus the only changes are to p_i's state and the value of the register R_j.

As in the message-passing model, an *execution* is an execution segment that begins in an initial configuration. As for message-passing systems, we need to define the *admissible* executions. In asynchronous shared memory systems the only requirement is that in an infinite execution, each processor has an infinite number of computation steps.

A *schedule* in the shared memory model is simply a sequence of processor indices, indicating the sequence of events in an execution (segment).

A schedule is *P-only*, where P is a set of processors, if the schedule consists solely of indices for processors in P. If P contains only a single processor, say p_i, then we write p_i-only.

As in the message-passing case, we assume that each processor's state set has a set of *terminated* states and each processor's transition function maps terminated states only to terminated states. Furthermore, when a processor is in a terminated state, it makes no further changes to any shared variables. We say that the system (algorithm) has terminated when all processors are in terminated states.

A configuration C and a schedule $\sigma = i_1 i_2 \ldots$ uniquely determine an execution segment resulting from applying the events in σ one after the other, starting from C; the execution is denoted $exec(C, \sigma)$. This execution segment is well-defined because processors are deterministic. If σ is finite, then $\sigma(C)$ is the final configuration in the execution segment $exec(C, \sigma)$. We say that configuration C' is *reachable from configuration* C if there exists a finite schedule σ such that $C' = \sigma(C)$. A configuration is simply *reachable* if it is reachable from the initial configuration.

The following notion plays a crucial role in lower bounds in this chapter and in several other chapters.

Definition 4.1 *Configuration C is similar to configuration C' with respect to a set of processors P, denoted $C \overset{P}{\sim} C'$, if each processor in P has the same state in C as in C' and $mem(C) = mem(C')$.*

If C and C' are similar with respect to P, then the processors in P do not observe any difference between C and C'.

4.1.2   Complexity Measures

Obviously in shared memory systems there are no messages to measure. Instead, we focus on the *space complexity*, the amount of shared memory needed to solve problems. The amount is measured in two ways, the number of distinct shared variables required, and the amount of shared space (e.g., number of bits or, equivalently, how many distinct values) required.

Although one could extend the definition of time complexity for message-passing systems (cf. Exercise 4.4) it is not clear whether this definition correctly captures the total time for executing an algorithm in a shared memory system. For example, the delay of an access to a shared register may depend on the contention—the number of processors concurrently competing for this register. Meaningful and precise definitions of time complexity for shared memory algorithms are the subject of current research; the chapter notes indicate some pointers. Instead, we sometimes count the number of steps taken by processors to solve a problem in the worst case; generally, we are only interested in whether the number is infinite, finite, or bounded.

4.1.3   Pseudocode Conventions

Shared memory algorithms will be described, for each processor, in a pseudocode similar to that used generally for sequential algorithms. The pseudocode will involve accesses both to local variables, which are part of the processor's state, and to shared variables. The names of shared variables are capitalized (e.g., *Want*), whereas the names of local variables are in lower case (e.g., *last*). The operations on shared variables will be in sans-serif (e.g., read). In terms of the formal model, a transition of a processor starts with an operation on a shared variable and continues according to the flow of control until just before the next operation on a shared variable.

In the special case of read/write variables, we employ an even more familiar style of code. Instead of explicitly saying read and write in the pseudocode, we use the familiar imperative style: a reference to a shared variable on the left-hand side of an assignment statement means write, whereas a reference on the right-hand side means read. A single statement of pseudocode may represent several steps in the formal model. In this case, the reads of the shared variables on the right-hand side of the assignment statement are performed in left-to-right order, the return values are saved in local variables, the specified computation is performed on the local variables, and finally the result is written to the variable on the left-hand side of the assignment statement. For instance, if X, Y, and Z are shared variables, the pseudocode statement $X := Y + Z$ means first, read Y and save result in a local variable, second, read Z and save result in a local variable, and third, write the sum of those local variables to X.

We also use the construct "wait until P", where P is some predicate involving shared variables. In terms of the formal model, this is equivalent to a loop in which the relevant shared variable is repeatedly read until P is true.

4.2 THE MUTUAL EXCLUSION PROBLEM

The *mutual exclusion* problem concerns a group of processors that occasionally need access to some resource that cannot be used simultaneously by more than a single processor, for example, some output device. Each processor may need to execute a code segment called a *critical section*, such that, informally speaking, at any time, at most one processor is in the critical section (*mutual exclusion*), and if one or more processors try to enter the critical section, then one of them eventually succeeds as long as no processor stays in the critical section forever (*no deadlock*).

The above properties do not provide any guarantee on an individual basis because a processor may try to enter the critical section and yet fail because it is always bypassed by other processors. A stronger property, which implies no deadlock, is *no lockout*: If a processor wishes to enter the critical section, then it will eventually succeed as long as no processor stays in the critical section forever. (This property is sometimes called *no starvation*.) Later we will see an even stronger property that limits the number of times a processor might be bypassed while trying to enter the critical section.

Original solutions to the mutual exclusion problem relied on special synchronization support such as semaphores and monitors. Here, we focus on *distributed* software solutions, using ordinary shared variables.

Each processor executes some additional code before and after the critical section to ensure the above properties; we assume the program of a processor is partitioned into the following sections:

Entry (trying): the code executed in preparation for entering the critical section

Critical: the code to be protected from concurrent execution

Exit: the code executed on leaving the critical section

Remainder: the rest of the code

Each processor cycles through these sections in the order: remainder, entry, critical, and exit (see Fig. 4.1). If a processor wants to enter the critical section it first executes the entry section; after that, the processor enters the critical section; then, the processor releases the critical section by executing the exit section and returning to the remainder section.

A mutual exclusion algorithm consists of code for the entry and exit sections and should work no matter what goes in the critical and remainder sections. In particular, a processor may transition from the remainder section to the entry section any number

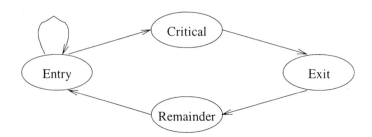

Fig. 4.1   Parts of the mutual exclusion code.

of times, either finite or infinite. We assume that the variables, both shared and local, accessed in the entry and exit sections are *not* accessed in the critical and remainder sections. We also assume that no processor stays in the critical section forever.

To capture these requirements, we make the following assumptions in the formal model. If a processor takes a step while in the remainder (resp., critical) section, it immediately enters the entry (resp., exit) section. The definition of admissible execution is changed to allow a processor to stop in the remainder section. Thus an execution is *admissible* if for every processor p_i, either p_i takes an infinite number of steps or p_i ends in the remainder section.

More formally, an algorithm for a shared memory system solves the mutual exclusion problem with no deadlock (or no lockout) if the following hold:

Mutual exclusion: In every configuration of every execution, at most one processor is in the critical section.

No deadlock: In every admissible execution, if some processor is in the entry section in a configuration, then there is a later configuration in which some processor is in the critical section.

No lockout: In every admissible execution, if some processor is in the entry section in a configuration, then there is a later configuration in which *that same* processor is in the critical section.

We also require that in an admissible execution, no processor is ever stuck in the exit section; this is called the *unobstructed exit* condition. In all the algorithms presented in this chapter, the exit sections are straight-line code (i.e., no loops), and thus the condition obviously holds.

Note that the mutual exclusion condition is required to hold in every execution, not just admissible ones. Exercise 4.1 explores the consequences of assuming that the condition need only hold for admissible executions.

Algorithm 7 Mutual exclusion using a test&set register: code for every processor.

Initially V equals 0

⟨Entry⟩:
1: wait until test&set(V) = 0
⟨Critical Section⟩
⟨Exit⟩:
2: reset(V)
⟨Remainder⟩

4.3 MUTUAL EXCLUSION USING POWERFUL PRIMITIVES

In this section, we study the memory requirements for solving mutual exclusion when powerful shared memory primitives are used. We show that one bit suffices for guaranteeing mutual exclusion with no deadlock. However, $\Theta(\log n)$ bits are necessary (and sufficient) for providing stronger fairness properties.

4.3.1 Binary Test&Set Registers

We start with a simple type of variable, called *test&set*. A test&set variable V is a binary variable that supports two atomic operations, test&set and reset, defined as follows:

test&set(V : memory address) returns binary value :
    temp := V
    V := 1
    return (*temp*)
reset(V : memory address):
    V := 0

The test&set operation atomically reads *and* updates the variable. (The variable is "tested" to see whether it equals 0, and if so it is "set" to 1.) The reset operation is merely a write.

There is a simple mutual exclusion algorithm with no deadlock that uses one test&set register. The pseudocode appears in Algorithm 7.

Assume the initial value of a test&set variable V is 0. In the entry section, processor p_i repeatedly tests V until it returns 0; the last test by p_i assigns 1 to V, causing any following test to return 1 and prohibiting any other processor from entering the critical section. In the exit section, p_i resets V to 0, so one of the processors waiting at the entry section can enter the critical section.

To see that the algorithm provides mutual exclusion, assume, by way of contradiction, that two processors, p_i and p_j, are in the critical section together at some point in an execution. Consider the earliest such point in the execution. Without loss of generality, assume that this point occurs when p_j enters the critical section, that is, p_i is already in the critical section. According to the code, when p_i enters the critical section most recently prior to this point, it tests V, sees that $V = 0$, and sets V to 1. Also according to the code, V remains equal to 1 until some processor leaves the critical section. By assumption that the point under consideration is the first violation of mutual exclusion, no processor other than p_i is in the critical section until p_j enters the critical section. Thus no processor leaves the critical section in the interval since p_i sets V to 1 just before entering the critical section and until p_j enters the critical section, implying that V remains 1. Finally, we see that when p_j enters the critical section, its test of V must return 1, and not 0, and thus p_j cannot enter the critical section after all, a contradiction.

To show that the algorithm provides no deadlock, assume in contradiction there is an admissible execution in which, after some point, at least one processor is in the entry section but no processor ever enters the critical section. Since no processor stays in the critical section forever in an admissible execution, there is a point after which at least one processor is in the entry section but no processor is in the critical section. The key is to note that $V = 0$ if and only if no processor is in the critical section. This fact can be shown by induction, because mutual exclusion holds. Thus any processor that executes Line 1 after the specified point discovers $V = 0$ and enters the critical section, a contradiction. Therefore, we have:

Theorem 4.1 *Algorithm 7 provides mutual exclusion and no deadlock with one test&set register.*

4.3.2 Read-Modify-Write Registers

In this section, we consider an even stronger type of register, one that supports read-modify-write operations.

A *read-modify-write* register V is a variable that allows the processor to read the current value of the variable, compute a new value as a function of the current value, and write the new value to the variable, all in one atomic operation. The operation returns the previous value of the variable. Formally, a read-modify-write (rmw) operation on register V is defined as follows:

rmw(V : memory address, f : function) returns value:
    temp := V
    $V := f(V)$
    return (*temp*)

The rmw operation takes as a parameter a function f that specifies how the new value is related to the old value. In this definition, the size and type of V are not constrained; in practice, of course, they typically are.

Clearly, the test&set operation is a special case of rmw, where $f(V) = 1$ for any value of V.

We now present a mutual exclusion algorithm that guarantees no lockout (and thus no deadlock), using only one read-modify-write register. The algorithm organizes processors into a FIFO queue, allowing the processor at the head of the queue to enter the critical section.

Algorithm 8 Mutual exclusion using a read-modify-write register:
code for every processor.

Initially $V = \langle 0, 0 \rangle$

$\langle$Entry$\rangle$:
1: $position :=$ rmw$(V, \langle V.first, V.last + 1 \rangle)$ // enqueueing at the tail
2: repeat
3:      $queue :=$ rmw(V, V) // read head of queue
4: until $(queue.first = position.last)$ // until becomes first
$\langle$Critical Section$\rangle$
$\langle$Exit$\rangle$:
5: rmw$(V, (V.first + 1, V.last))$ // dequeueing
$\langle$Remainder$\rangle$

The pseudocode appears in Algorithm 8. Each processor has two local variables, *position* and *queue*. The algorithm uses a read-modify-write register V consisting of two fields, *first* and *last*, containing "tickets" of the first and the last processors in the queue, respectively. When a new processor arrives at the entry section, it enqueues by reading V to a local variable and incrementing $V.last$, in one atomic operation. The current value of $V.last$ serves as the processor's ticket. A processor waits until it becomes first, that is, until $V.first$ is equal to its ticket. At this point, the processor enters the critical section. After leaving the critical section, the processor dequeues by incrementing $V.first$, thereby allowing the next processor on the queue to enter the critical section (see Fig. 4.2).

Only the processor at the head of the queue can enter the critical section, and it remains at the head until it leaves the critical section, thereby preventing other processors from entering the critical section. Therefore, the algorithm provides mutual exclusion. In addition, the FIFO order of enqueueing, together with the assumption that no processor stays in the critical section forever, provides the no lockout property of the algorithm, which implies no deadlock.

Note that no more than n processors can be on the queue at the same time. Thus all calculations can be done modulo n, and the maximum value of $V.first$ and $V.last$ is $n - 1$. Thus V requires at most $2\lceil \log_2 n \rceil$ bits (see Fig. 4.3).

We get:

Fig. 4.2 Data structures for Algorithm 8.

Fig. 4.3   Bounding the memory requirements of Algorithm 8.

Theorem 4.2 *There exists a mutual exclusion algorithm that provides no lockout, and thus no deadlock, using one read-modify-write register consisting of* $2\lceil \log_2 n \rceil$ *bits.*

One drawback of Algorithm 8 is that processors waiting for the critical section repeatedly read the same variable V, waiting for it to take on a specific value. This behavior is called *spinning*. In certain shared memory architectures, spinning can increase the time to access the shared memory (see chapter notes). Algorithm 9 implements the queue of waiting processors so that every waiting processor checks a different variable. The algorithm must use n shared variables, to allow n processors to wait simultaneously.

The algorithm uses an array *Flags* of binary variables, each of which can take on one of two values: *has-lock* or *must-wait*. A processor gets the index of the array element on which it should wait by using a read-modify-write operation on a variable *Last* (see Fig. 4.4). The processor waits until its array element contains the value *has-lock*; before going into the critical section, the processor sets its array element to *must-wait*; after leaving the critical section, the processor sets the next element in the array *Flags* to *has-lock*.

The next lemma states the invariant properties of Algorithm 9; its proof is left as an exercise (see Exercise 4.3(a)):

Lemma 4.3 *Algorithm 9 maintains the following invariants concerning the array Flags:*

1. *At most one element is set to has-lock.*

2. *If no element is set to has-lock then some processor is inside the critical section.*

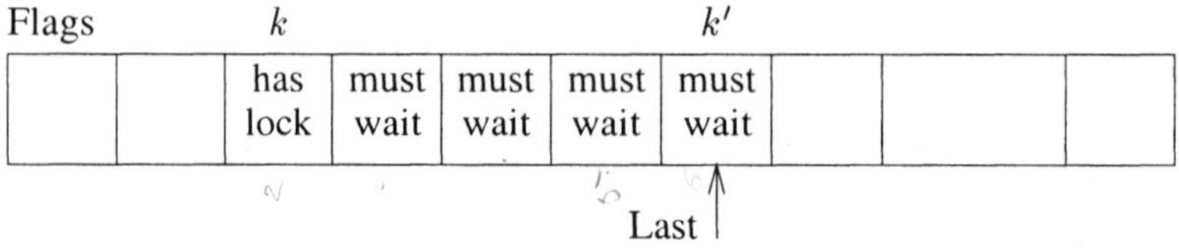

Flags		k				k'			
		has lock	must wait	must wait	must wait	must wait			

Last ↑

Fig. 4.4   Processor p_i threads itself on the queue and spins on *Flags*[k'].

Algorithm 9 Mutual exclusion using local spinning: code for every processor.

Initially $Last = 0$; $Flags[0] = has\text{-}lock$; $Flags[i] = must\text{-}wait$, $0 < i < n$.

⟨Entry⟩:
1:    $my\text{-}place :=$ rmw($Last$, $Last + 1$ mod n)   // thread yourself on queue
2:    wait until ($Flags[my\text{-}place] = has\text{-}lock$)   // spin
3:    $Flags[my\text{-}place] := must\text{-}wait$ // clean
⟨Critical Section⟩
⟨Exit⟩:
4:    $Flags[my\text{-}place+1$ mod $n] := has\text{-}lock$ // tap next in line
⟨Remainder⟩

---

   3. If Flags[k] is set to has-lock then exactly $(k - Last - 1)$ mod n *processors are in the entry section, each of them spinning on a different entry of Flags.*

These invariants imply that the algorithm provides mutual exclusion and no lock-out (in fact, FIFO entry); the proof is similar to the proof of Algorithm 8 (see Exercise 4.3(b)).

4.3.3   Lower Bound on the Number of Memory States

Previously, we have seen that one binary test&set register suffices to provide deadlock-free solutions to the mutual exclusion problem. However, in this algorithm, a processor can be indefinitely starved in the entry section. Then we have seen a mutual exclusion algorithm that provides no lockout by using one read-modify-write register of $2\lceil \log_2 n \rceil$ bits. In fact, to avoid lockout at least $\sqrt{n}$ distinct memory states are required. In the rest of this section we show a weaker result, that if the algorithm does not allow a processor to be overtaken an unbounded number of times then it requires at least n distinct memory states.

Definition 4.2 *A mutual exclusion algorithm provides k-bounded waiting if, in every execution, no processor enters the critical section more than k times while another processor is waiting in the entry section.*

   Note that the k-bounded waiting property, together with the no deadlock property, implies the no lockout property. The main result of this section is:

Theorem 4.4 *If an algorithm solves mutual exclusion with no deadlock and k-bounded waiting (for some k), then the algorithm uses at least n distinct shared memory states.*

Proof. The proof uses the following definition:

Definition 4.3 *A configuration of a mutual exclusion algorithm is* quiescent *if all processors are in the remainder section.*

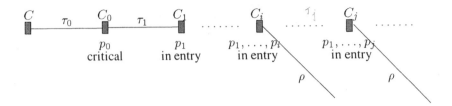

Fig. 4.5 Proof of Theorem 4.4.

Let C be the initial configuration of the algorithm. Note that it is quiescent. Let τ_0' be an infinite p_0-only schedule. Since $exec(C, \tau_0')$ is admissible (p_0 takes an infinite number of steps and the rest of the processors stay in the remainder section), the no deadlock property implies that there exists a finite prefix τ_0 of τ_0' such that p_0 is in the critical section in $C_0 = \tau_0(C)$. Inductively, construct for every $i, 1 \le i \le n - 1$, a p_i-only schedule τ_i such that p_i is in the entry section in $C_i = \tau_i(C_{i-1})$ (p_i takes a step to go from the remainder section to the entry section). Thus, p_0 is in the critical section and $p_1, \ldots, p_{n-1}$ are in the entry section at $C_{n-1} = \tau_0 \tau_1 \ldots \tau_{n-1}(C)$.

Assume, by way of contradiction, that there are strictly less than n distinct shared memory states. This implies that there are two configurations, C_i and C_j, $0 \le i < j \le n - 1$, with identical shared memory states, that is, $mem(C_i) = mem(C_j)$. Note that $p_0, \ldots, p_i$ do not take any steps in $\tau_{i+1} \ldots \tau_j$ and therefore, $C_i \overset{p_0,\ldots,p_i}{\sim} C_j$. Furthermore, in C_i and thus in C_j, p_0 is in the critical section, and $p_1, \ldots, p_i$ are in the entry section (see Fig. 4.5).

Apply an infinite schedule ρ' to C_i in which processors p_0 through p_i take an infinite number of steps and the rest take no steps. Since $exec(C, \tau_0 \tau_1 \ldots \tau_i \rho')$ is admissible (p_0 through p_i take an infinite number of steps, and the remaining processors stay in their remainder section), the no deadlock property implies that some processor $p_\ell, 0 \le \ell \le i$, enters the critical section an infinite number of times in $exec(C_i, \rho')$.

Let ρ be some finite prefix of ρ' in which p_ℓ enters the critical section $k + 1$ times. Since $C_i \overset{p_0,\ldots,p_i}{\sim} C_j$ and ρ is $\{p_0, \ldots, p_i\}$-only, it follows that p_ℓ enters the critical section $k + 1$ times in $exec(C_j, \rho)$. Note that p_j is in the entry section at C_j. Thus while p_j is in the entry section, p_ℓ enters the critical section $k+1$ times in $exec(C_j, \rho)$. Let σ be an infinite schedule in which p_0 through p_j take an infinite number of steps and the rest take no steps. The execution $exec(C, \tau_0 \tau_1 \ldots \tau_j \rho \sigma)$ is admissible, since p_0 through p_j take an infinite number of steps and the remaining processors stay in their remainder section. However, in the segment of this execution corresponding to ρ, p_j is bypassed more than k times by p_ℓ, violating the k-bounded waiting property. $\square$

It is worth understanding why this proof does not work if the algorithm only needs to satisfy no lockout instead of bounded waiting. We cannot prove that the admissible execution constructed at the end of the last paragraph fails to satisfy no-lockout; for instance, after p_j is bypassed $k+1$ times by p_ℓ, p_j might enter the critical section. This problem cannot be fixed by replacing $\rho\sigma$ with ρ', because the resulting execution is not admissible: p_{i+1} through p_j are stuck in their trying section because they take no steps in ρ', and non-admissible executions are not required to satisfy no lockout.

4.4 MUTUAL EXCLUSION USING READ/WRITE REGISTERS

In this section, we concentrate on systems in which processors access the shared registers only by read and write operations. We present two algorithms that provide mutual exclusion and no lockout for n processors, one that uses unbounded values and another that avoids them. Both algorithms use $O(n)$ separate registers. We then show that any algorithm that provides mutual exclusion, even with the weak property of no deadlock, must use n separate read/write registers, regardless of the size of each register. These results contrast with the situation where stronger primitives are used, in which a single register is sufficient.

4.4.1 The Bakery Algorithm

In this section, we describe the *bakery* algorithm for mutual exclusion among n processors; the algorithm provides mutual exclusion and no lockout.

The main idea is to consider processors wishing to enter the critical section as customers in a bakery.[2] Each customer arriving at the bakery gets a number, and the one with the smallest number is the next to be served. The number of a customer who is not standing in line is 0 (which does not count as the smallest ticket).

To make the bakery metaphor more concrete, we employ the following shared data structures: *Number* is an array of n integers, which holds in its ith entry the number of p_i; *Choosing* is an array of n Boolean values such that *Choosing*[i] is true while p_i is in the process of obtaining its number.

Each processor p_i wishing to enter the critical section tries to choose a number that is greater than all the numbers of the other processors and writes it to *Number*[i]. This is done by reading *Number*[0], ..., *Number*[$n-1$] and taking the maximum among them plus one. However, because several processors can read *Number* concurrently it is possible for several processors to obtain the same number. To break symmetry, we define p_i's ticket to be the pair (*Number*[i], i). Clearly, the tickets held by processors wishing to enter the critical section are unique. We use the lexicographic order on pairs to define an ordering between tickets.

After choosing its number, p_i waits until its ticket is minimal: For each other processor p_j, p_i waits until p_j is not in the middle of choosing its number and then compares their tickets. If p_j's ticket is smaller, p_i waits until p_j executes the critical section and leaves it. The pseudocode appears in Algorithm 10.

---

[2]Actually, in Israel, there are no numbers in the bakeries and the metaphor of a health care clinic is more appropriate.

Algorithm 10 The bakery algorithm: code for processor p_i, $0 \leq i \leq n - 1$.

Initially *Number*$[i] = 0$ and
Choosing$[i] =$ false, for i, $0 \leq i \leq n - 1$

$\langle$Entry$\rangle$:
1:   *Choosing*$[i] :=$ true
2:   *Number*$[i] := \max(\textit{Number}[0], \ldots, \textit{Number}[n - 1]) + 1$
3:   *Choosing*$[i] :=$ false
4:   for $j := 0$ to $n - 1(\neq i)$ do
5:          wait until *Choosing*$[j] =$ false
6:          wait until *Number*$[j] = 0$ or $(\textit{Number}[j], j) > (\textit{Number}[i], i)$
$\langle$Critical Section$\rangle$
$\langle$Exit$\rangle$:
7:   *Number*$[i] := 0$
$\langle$Remainder$\rangle$

We now prove the correctness of the bakery algorithm. That is, we prove that the algorithm provides the three properties discussed above, mutual exclusion, no deadlock and no lockout.

Fix an execution α of the algorithm. To show mutual exclusion, we first prove a property concerning the relation between tickets of processors.

Lemma 4.5 *In every configuration C of α, if processor p_i is in the critical section, and for some $k \neq i$, Number$[k] \neq 0$, then (Number$[k], k) > $ (Number$[i], i)$.*

Proof.   Since p_i is in the critical section in configuration C, it finished the for loop, in particular, the second wait statement (Line 6), for $j = k$. There are two cases, according to the two conditions in Line 6:
Case 1: p_i read that *Number*$[k] = 0$. In this case, when p_i finished Line 6 (the second wait statement) with $j = k$, p_k either was in the remainder or was not finished choosing its number (since *Number*$[k] = 0$). But p_i already finished Line 5 (the first wait statement) with $j = k$ and observed *Choosing*$[k] =$ false. Thus p_k was not in the middle of choosing its number. Therefore, p_k started reading the *Number* array after p_i wrote to *Number*$[i]$. Thus, in configuration C, *Number*$[i] < \textit{Number}[k]$, which implies $(\textit{Number}[i], i) < (\textit{Number}[k], k)$.
Case 2: p_i read that $(\textit{Number}[k], k) > (\textit{Number}[i], i)$. In this case, the condition will clearly remain valid until p_i exits the critical section or as long as p_k does not choose another number. If p_k chooses a new number, the condition will still be satisfied since the new number will be greater than *Number*$[i]$ (as in Case 1). $\square$

The above lemma implies that a processor that is in the critical section has the smallest ticket among the processors trying to enter the critical section. To apply this lemma, we need to prove that whenever a processor is in the critical section its number is nonzero.

Lemma 4.6 *If p_i is in the critical section, then Number$[i] > 0$.*

Proof. First, note that for any processor p_i, *Number*$[i]$ is always nonnegative. This can be easily proved by induction on the number of assignments to *Number* in the execution. The base case is obvious by the initialization. For the inductive step, each number is assigned either 0 (when exiting the critical section) or a number greater than the maximum current value, which is nonnegative by assumption.

Each processor chooses a number before entering the critical section. This number is strictly greater than the maximum current number, which is nonnegative. Therefore, the value chosen is positive. □

To prove mutual exclusion, note that if two processors, p_i and p_j, are simultaneously in the critical section, then *Number*$[i] \neq 0$ and *Number*$[j] \neq 0$, by Lemma 4.6. Lemma 4.5 can then be applied (twice), to derive that $(Number[i], i) < (Number[j], j)$ and $(Number[i], i) > (Number[j], j)$, which is a contradiction. This implies:

Theorem 4.7 *Algorithm 10 provides mutual exclusion.*

Finally, we show that each processor wishing to enter the critical section eventually succeeds (no lockout). This also implies the no deadlock property.

Theorem 4.8 *Algorithm 10 provides no lockout.*

Proof. Consider any admissible execution. Thus no processor stays in the critical section forever. Assume, by way of contradiction, that there is a starved processor that wishes to enter the critical section but does not succeed. Clearly, all processors wishing to enter the critical section eventually finish choosing a number, because there is no way to be blocked while choosing a number. Let p_i be the processor with the smallest $(Number[i], i)$ that is starved.

All processors entering the entry section after p_i has chosen its number will choose greater numbers and therefore will not enter the critical section before p_i. All processors with smaller numbers will eventually enter the critical section (since by assumption they are not starved) and exit it (since no processor stays in the critical section forever). At this point, p_i will pass all the tests in the for loop and enter the critical section, a contradiction. □

The numbers can grow without bound, unless there is a situation in which all processors are in the remainder section. Therefore, there is a problem in implementing the algorithm on real systems, where variables have finite size. We next discuss how to avoid this behavior.

4.4.2 A Bounded Mutual Exclusion Algorithm for Two Processors

In this section, we develop a two-processor mutual exclusion algorithm that uses bounded variables, as a preliminary step toward an algorithm for n processors.

Algorithm 11 A bounded mutual exclusion algorithm for two processors: allows lockout.

Initially *Want*[0] and *Want*[1] are 0

code for p_0	code for p_1
⟨Entry⟩:	⟨Entry⟩:
	1: *Want*[1] := 0
	2: wait until (*Want*[0] = 0)
3: *Want*[0] := 1	3: *Want*[1] := 1
	5: if (*Want*[0] = 1) then
	goto Line 1
6: wait until (*Want*[1] = 0)	
⟨Critical Section⟩	⟨Critical Section⟩
⟨Exit⟩:	⟨Exit⟩:
8: *Want*[0] := 0	8: *Want*[1] := 0
⟨Remainder⟩	⟨Remainder⟩

We start with a very simple algorithm that provides mutual exclusion and no deadlock for two processors p_0 and p_1; however, the algorithm gives priority to one of the processors and the other processor can starve. We then convert this algorithm to one that provides no lockout as well.

In the first algorithm, each processor p_i has a Boolean shared variable *Want*[i] whose value is 1 if p_i is interested in entering the critical section and 0 otherwise. The algorithm is asymmetric: p_0 enters the critical section whenever it is empty, without considering p_1's attempts to do so; p_1 enters the critical section only if p_0 is not interested in it at all. The code appears in Algorithm 11; line numbers are nonconsecutive for compatibility with the next algorithm.

Lemma 4.9 follows immediately from the code.

Lemma 4.9 *In any configuration of any execution, if p_i is after Line 3 and before Line 8 (including the critical section) then Want[i] = 1.*

This algorithm uses a flag mechanism to coordinate between processors competing for the critical section: p_i raises a flag (by setting *Want*[i]) and then inspects the other processor's flag (by reading *Want*[1 − i]). As proved Theorem 4.10, at least one of the processors observes the other processor's flag as raised and avoids entering the critical section.

Theorem 4.10 *Algorithm 11 provides mutual exclusion.*

Proof. Consider any execution. Assume, by way of contradiction, that both processors are in the critical section at some point. By Lemma 4.9, it follows that *Want*[0] = *Want*[1] = 1 at this point. Assume, without loss of generality, that p_0's last write to *Want*[0] before entering the critical section follows p_1's last write to *Want*[1] before entering the critical section. Note that p_0 reads *Want*[1] = 0 before

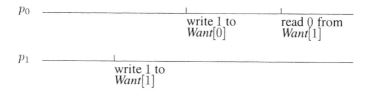

Fig. 4.6 Illustration for the proofs of Theorem 4.10 and Theorem 4.11.

entering the critical section (in Line 6), after its write to $Want[0]$, which by assumption, follows p_1's write to $Want[1]$. (see Fig. 4.6). But in this case, p_0's read of $Want[1]$ should return 1. A contradiction. □

We leave it to the reader to verify that this algorithm provides no deadlock (Exercise 4.7).

Note that if p_0 is continuously interested in entering the critical section, it is possible that p_1 will never enter the critical section because it gives up whenever p_0 is interested.

To achieve no lockout, we modify the algorithm so that instead of always giving priority to p_0, each processor gives priority to the other processor on leaving the critical section. A shared variable *Priority* contains the id of the processor that has priority at the moment, and is initialized to 0. This variable is read and written by both processors. The processor with the priority plays the role of p_0 in the previous algorithm, so it will enter the critical section. When exiting, it will give the priority to the other processor and will play the role of p_1 from the previous algorithm, and so on. We will show that this ensures no lockout.

The modified algorithm provides mutual exclusion in the same manner as Algorithm 11: A processor raises a flag and then inspects the other processor's flag; at least one of the processors observes the other processor's flag as raised and avoids entering the critical section.

The pseudocode for the algorithm appears in Algorithm 12; note that the algorithm is symmetric.

Lemma 4.9 is still valid for Algorithm 12, and can be used to prove:

Theorem 4.11 *Algorithm 12 provides mutual exclusion.*

Proof. Consider any execution. Assume, by way of contradiction, that both processors are in the critical section at some point. By Lemma 4.9, it follows that $Want[0] = Want[1] = 1$ at this point. Assume, without loss of generality, that p_0's last write to $Want[0]$ before entering the critical section follows p_1's last write to $Want[1]$ before entering the critical section. Note that p_0 can enter the critical section either through Line 5 or through Line 6; in both cases, p_0 reads $Want[1] = 0$. However, p_0's read of $Want[1]$ follows p_0's write to $Want[0]$, which by assumption, follows p_1's write to $Want[1]$ (see Fig. 4.6). But in this case, p_0's read of $Want[1]$ should return 1, a contradiction. □

Algorithm 12 A bounded mutual exclusion algorithm for two processors: with no lockout.

Initially *Want*[0] and *Want*[1] and *Priority* are all 0

code for p_0	code for p_1
⟨Entry⟩:	⟨Entry⟩:
1: *Want*[0] := 0	1: *Want*[1] := 0
2: wait until (*Want*[1] = 0	2: wait until *Want*[0] = 0
or *Priority* = 0)	or *Priority* = 1
3: *Want*[0] := 1	3: *Want*[1] := 1
4: if (*Priority* = 1) then	4: if (*Priority* = 0) then
5: if (*Want*[1] = 1) then	5: if (*Want*[0] = 1) then
goto Line 1	goto Line 1
6: else wait until (*Want*[1] = 0)	6: else wait until (*Want*[0] = 0)
⟨Critical Section⟩	⟨Critical Section⟩
⟨Exit⟩:	⟨Exit⟩:
7: *Priority* := 1	7: *Priority* := 0
8: *Want*[0] := 0	8: *Want*[1] := 0
⟨Remainder⟩	⟨Remainder⟩

We now show the no deadlock condition.

Theorem 4.12 *Algorithm 12 provides no deadlock.*

Proof. Consider any admissible execution. Suppose in contradiction there is a point after which at least one processor is forever in the entry section and no processor enters the critical section.

First consider the case when both processors are forever in the entry section. Since both processors are in the entry section, the value of *Priority* does not change. Assume, without loss of generality, that *Priority* = 0. Thus p_0 passes the test in Line 2 and loops forever in Line 6 with *Want*[0] = 1. Since *Priority* = 0, p_1 does not reach Line 6. Thus p_1 waits in Line 2, with *Want*[1] = 0. In this case, p_0 passes the test in Line 6 and enters the critical section, a contradiction.

Thus, it must be that only one processor is forever in the entry section, say p_0. Since p_1 does not stay in the critical section or exit section forever, after some point p_1 is forever in the remainder section. So after some point *Want*[1] equals 0 forever. Then p_0 does not loop forever in the entry section (see Lines 2, 5, and 6) and enters the critical section, a contradiction. □

Theorem 4.13 *Algorithm 12 provides no lockout.*

Proof. Consider any admissible execution. Assume, by way of contradiction, that some processor, say p_0, is starved. Thus from some point on, p_0 is forever in the entry section.

Case 1: Suppose p_1 executes Line 7 (setting *Priority* to 0) at some later point. Then *Priority* equals 0 forever after. Thus p_0 passes the test in Line 2 and skips Line 5. So p_0 must be stuck in Line 6, waiting for *Want*[1] to be 0, which never occurs. Thus p_1 is always executing between Lines 3 and 8. But since p_1 does not stay in the critical section forever, this would mean that p_1 is stuck in the entry section forever, violating no deadlock (Theorem 4.12).

Case 2: Suppose p_1 never executes Line 7 at some later point. Since there is no deadlock, it must be that p_1 is forever in the remainder section. Thus *Want*[1] equals 0 henceforth. Then p_0 can never be stuck at Line 2, 5, or 6 and it enters the critical section, a contradiction. $\qquad\square$

4.4.3   A Bounded Mutual Exclusion Algorithm for n Processors

To construct a solution for the general case of n processors we employ the algorithm for two processors. Processors compete pairwise, using the two-processor algorithm described in Section 4.4.2, in a *tournament tree* arrangement. The pairwise competitions are arranged in a complete binary tree. Each processor begins at a specific leaf of the tree. At each level, the winner gets to proceed to the next higher level, where it competes with the winner of the competition on the other side of the tree. The processor on the left side plays the role of p_0, and the processor on the right plays the role of p_1. The processor that wins at the root enters the critical section.

Let $k = \lceil \log n \rceil - 1$. Consider a complete binary tree with 2^k leaves (and a total of $2^{k+1} - 1$ nodes). The nodes of the tree are numbered inductively as follows. The root is numbered 1; the left child of a node numbered v is numbered $2v$ and the right child is numbered $2v + 1$. Note that the leaves of the tree are numbered $2^k, 2^k + 1, \ldots, 2^{k+1} - 1$ (see Fig. 4.7).

With each node we associate three binary shared variables whose roles are analogous to the variables used by the two-processor algorithm (Algorithm 12). Specifically, with node number v we associate shared variables $Want^v[0]$, $Want^v[1]$, and $Priority^v$, whose initial values are all 0.

The algorithm is recursive and instructs a processor what to do when reaching some node in the tree. The code for the algorithm consists of a procedure Node(v,*side*) that is executed when a processor accesses node number v while playing the role of processor *side*; the procedure appears in Algorithm 13. We associate a critical section with each node. A node's critical section (Lines 7 through 9) includes the entry code (Lines 1 through 6) executed at all the nodes on the path from that node's parent to the root, the original critical section, and the exit code (Lines 10 through 11) executed at all the nodes on the path from the root to that node's parent. To begin the competition for the (real) critical section, processor p_i executes Node($2^k + \lfloor i/2 \rfloor$, $i \bmod 2$); that is, this starts the recursion.

We now present the correctness proof of the algorithm.

We want to consider the "projection" of an execution of the tree algorithm onto node v, that is, we only consider steps that are taken while executing the code in Node($v, 0$) and Node($v, 1$). We will show that this is an execution of the 2-processor

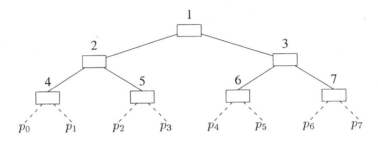

Fig. 4.7   The tournament tree for $n = 8$.

algorithm, if we view every processor that executes Node$(v, 0)$ as p_0 and every processor that executes Node$(v, 1)$ as p_1. Thus different processors play the roles of p_0 (for node v) throughout the execution, and the same for p_1. We now proceed more formally.

Fix any execution

$$\alpha = C_0\varphi_1 C_1\varphi_2 C_2 \dots$$

of the tournament tree algorithm. Let α_v be the sequence of alternating configurations and events

$$D_0\pi_1 D_1 \pi_2 D_2 \dots$$

defined inductively as follows. D_0 is the initial configuration of the 2-processor algorithm. Suppose α_v has been defined up to D_{i-1}. Let φ_j be the ith event of α that is a step in Node$(v, 0)$ or Node$(v, 1)$. Let $\varphi_j = k$, meaning p_k takes this step. Suppose without loss of generality that φ_j is a step in Node$(v, 0)$. Then let $\pi_i = 0$ (i.e., let p_0 take this step), and let D_i be the configuration in which the variables' states are those of the node v variables in C_j, the state of p_1 is the same as in D_{i-1}, and the state of p_0 is the same as the state of p_k in C_j except for the id being replaced with 0. (Note that all processors have the same code in the tournament tree algorithm except for their ids, and the id is only used in the start of the recursion to determine which leaf is the starting place.)

Lemma 4.14 *For every v, α_v is an execution of the 2-processor algorithm.*

Proof. Comparing the code of Node(v, i) with the 2-processor algorithm for p_i, $i = 0, 1$, shows that they are the same. The only thing we have to check is that only one processor performs instructions of Node(v, i) at a time. We show this by induction on the level of v, starting at the leaves.

Basis: v is a leaf. By construction only one processor ever performs the instructions of Node(v, i), $i = 0, 1$.

Induction: v is not a leaf. By the code, if a processor executes instructions of Node$(v, 0)$, then it is in the critical section for v's left child. By the inductive hypothesis and the fact that the 2-processor algorithm guarantees mutual exclusion (Theorem 4.11), only one processor at a time is in the critical section for v's left child.

Algorithm 13 The tournament tree algorithm:
A bounded mutual exclusion algorithm for n processors.

---

procedure Node(v: integer; *side*: 0..1)
1:   *Want^v*[*side*] := 0
2:   wait until (*Want^v*[1 − *side*] = 0 or *Priority^v* = *side*)
3:   *Want^v*[*side*] := 1
4:   if (*Priority^v* = 1 − *side*) then
5:      if (*Want^v*[1 − *side*] = 1) then goto Line 1
6:   else wait until (*Want^v*[1 − *side*] = 0)
7:   if ($v = 1$) then   // at the root
8:      ⟨Critical Section⟩
9:   else Node($\lfloor v/2 \rfloor$, v mod 2)
10: *Priority^v* := 1 − *side*
11: *Want^v*[*side*] := 0
end procedure

Thus only one processor at a time executes instructions of Node($v, 0$). Similarly, only one processor at a time executes instructions of Node($v, 1$). □

Lemma 4.15 *For all v, if α is admissible, then α_v is admissible.*

Proof. Pick a node v. The proof is by induction on the level of v, starting at the root.

Basis: Suppose v is the root. Since exit sections have no loops, it is sufficient to show that in α_v, no processor stays in the critical section forever. Since α is admissible, no processor stays in the real critical section forever. Since the critical section for α_v is the real critical section, the same is true of α_v.

Induction: Suppose v is not the root. Again, it is sufficient to show that in α_v, no processor stays in the critical section forever. Let u be v's parent. By the inductive hypothesis, α_u is admissible, and therefore, since there is no lockout in α_u (Theorem 4.13), the processor eventually enters the critical section for u. By the inductive hypothesis, the processor eventually exits the critical section for u, completes the exit section for u, and exits the critical section for v. □

Theorem 4.16 *Algorithm 13 provides mutual exclusion and no lockout.*

Proof. To show mutual exclusion, assume in contradiction there is an admissible execution in which two processors are in the critical section simultaneously. Lemma 4.14 implies that the restriction to the root of the tree is an admissible execution of the 2-processor algorithm. Since the 2-processor algorithm guarantees mutual exclusion by Theorem 4.11, two processors cannot be in the critical section simultaneously, a contradiction.

To show no lockout, assume in contradiction there is an admissible execution in which no processor stays in the critical section forever, and some processor, say p_i, is stuck in the entry section forever after some point. Let v be the leaf node associated with p_i in the tournament tree. Lemmas 4.14 and 4.15 imply that the restriction to v is an admissible execution of the 2-processor algorithm in which no processor stays in the critical section forever. Since the 2-processor algorithm has no lockout by Theorem 4.13, p_i cannot be locked out, a contradiction. $\qquad\square$

4.4.4 Lower Bound on the Number of Read/Write Registers

In this section, we show that any deadlock-free mutual exclusion algorithm using only shared read/write registers must use at least n shared variables, regardless of their size.

The proof allows the shared variables to be multi-writer, that is, every processor can write to every variable. Note that if variables are single-writer, then the lower bound is obvious, because every processor must write something (to a separate variable) before entering the critical section. Otherwise, a processor could enter the critical section without other processors knowing, and some other processor may enter concurrently, thereby violating mutual exclusion.

Fix a no deadlock mutual exclusion algorithm A. We will show that A uses at least n shared variables by showing that there is some reachable configuration of A in which each of the n processors is about to write to a distinct shared variable. The notion of being about to write to a variable is captured in the definition of a processor "covering" a variable:

Definition 4.4 *A processor* covers *a variable in a configuration if it is about to write it (according to its state in the configuration).*

We will use induction on the number of covered variables to show the existence of the desired configuration. For the induction to go through, we will need the configuration to satisfy an additional property, that of appearing to be quiescent to a certain set of processors. This notion is captured in the definition of P-quiescent:

Definition 4.5 *Configuration C is P-quiescent, where P is a set of processors, if there exists a reachable quiescent configuration D such that $C \overset{P}{\sim} D$.*

A useful fact about covered variables is that, under certain circumstances, a processor must write to at least one variable that is not covered before it can enter the critical section. The intuition is that the processor must inform the others that it is in the critical section, in order to avoid a violation of mutual exclusion, and this information must not be overwritten before it is observed by some other processor. The following lemma formalizes this fact.

Lemma 4.17 *Let C be a reachable configuration that is p_i-quiescent for some processor p_i. Then there exists a p_i-only schedule σ such that p_i is in the critical section in $\sigma(C)$, and during $exec(C, \sigma)$, p_i writes to some variable that is not covered by any other processor in C.*

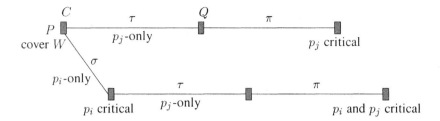

Fig. 4.8 Proof of Lemma 4.17.

Proof. First we show that σ exists. Since C is p_i-quiescent, there is a quiescent configuration D such that $C \overset{p_i}{\sim} D$. By the no deadlock condition, if p_i alone takes steps from D, it eventually enters the critical section. Thus if p_i alone takes steps from C, the same will happen.

Now we show that during $exec(C, \sigma)$, p_i writes to some variable that is not covered by any other processor in C. Suppose in contradiction during $exec(C, \sigma)$, p_i never writes to a variable that is not covered by any other processor in C. Let W be the set of variables that are covered in C by at least one processor other than p_i and let P be a set of processors, not including p_i, such that each variable in W is covered by exactly one processor in P (see Fig. 4.8).

Starting at C, let each processor in P take one step (in any order). The result is that all the variables that were covered in W have now been overwritten. Then invoke the no deadlock condition and the unobstructed exit condition successively to cause every processor that is not in the remainder section in C to go into the critical section (if necessary), complete the exit section, and enter the remainder section, where it stays. Let τ be this schedule and call the resulting configuration Q. Note that Q is quiescent.

Pick any processor p_j other than p_i. By the no deadlock condition, there is a p_j-only schedule from Q that causes p_j to enter the critical section. Call this schedule π. So at the end of $exec(C, \tau\pi)$, p_j is in the critical section.

Finally, observe that during τ and π, the other processors cannot tell whether p_i has performed the steps in σ or not, because the first part of τ overwrites anything that p_i may have written (since we are assuming p_i only writes to covered variables). Thus, at the end of $exec(C, \sigma\tau\pi)$, p_j is in the critical section, just as it was at the end of $exec(C, \tau\pi)$. But p_i is also in the critical section at the end of $exec(C, \sigma\tau\pi)$ since it took no steps during $\tau\pi$, violating mutual exclusion. □

The next lemma is the heart of the proof, showing inductively the existence of a number of covered variables.

Lemma 4.18 *For all k, $1 \le k \le n$, and for all reachable quiescent configurations C, there exists a configuration D reachable from C by a $\{p_0, \ldots, p_{k-1}\}$-only schedule such that $p_0, \ldots, p_{k-1}$ cover k distinct variables in D and D is $\{p_k, \ldots, p_{n-1}\}$-quiescent.*

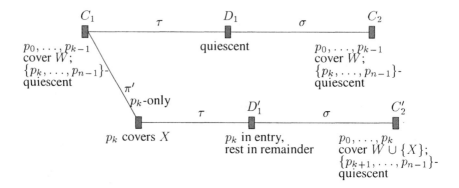

Fig. 4.9 Simple case in proof of Lemma 4.18.

Proof. By induction on k.

Basis: $k = 1$. For the basis, note that before entering the critical section, a processor must write to some shared variable. The desired configuration is obtained by considering the execution in which only p_0 takes steps and truncating it just before the first write by p_0.

In more detail: Fix a reachable quiescent configuration C. By Lemma 4.17, there exists a p_0-only schedule σ such that p_0 performs at least one write during $exec(C, \sigma)$.

Let σ' be the prefix of σ ending just before p_0 performs its first write, say to variable x. Let $D = \sigma'(C)$. Clearly, p_0 covers x in D. Since $mem(D) = mem(C)$ and only p_0 takes steps in σ', D is $\{p_1, \dots, p_{n-1}\}$-quiescent.

Induction: Assume the lemma is true for $k \geq 1$ and show it for $k + 1$.

For purposes of explanation, assume for now that every application of the inductive hypothesis causes the same set W of k variables to be covered by p_0 through p_{k-1}. Refer to Figure 4.9 for this simpler situation.

By the inductive hypothesis, we can get to a configuration C_1 that appears quiescent to p_k through p_{n-1} in which p_0 through p_{k-1} cover W. We must show how to cover one more variable, for a total of $k + 1$ covered variables.

Lemma 4.17 implies that we can get p_k to cover an additional variable, say X, by starting at C_1 and just having p_k take steps. Call this schedule π'. However, the resulting configuration does not necessarily appear quiescent to p_{k+1} through p_{n-1}, because p_k may have written to some (covered) variables.

From $\pi'(C_1)$, we can get to a $\{p_{k+1}, \dots, p_{n-1}\}$-quiescent configuration while still keeping X covered by p_k as follows. First, we overwrite all traces of p_k by having p_0 through p_{k-1} each take a step. Second, we successively invoke the no deadlock condition and the unobstructed exit condition to cause p_0 through p_{k-1} (in some order) to cycle through the critical section and into the remainder section. Call this schedule τ and let $D_1' = \tau(\pi'(C_1))$.

Finally, we would like to invoke the inductive hypothesis on D_1' to get to another configuration in which W is covered again and which appears quiescent to p_{k+1}

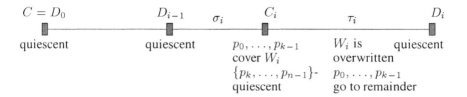

Fig. 4.10 General structure of the execution constructed in Lemma 4.18.

through p_{n-1}. This would be the desired configuration, because X is still covered, giving a total of $k+1$ covered variables.

But the inductive hypothesis requires that we start with a (totally) quiescent configuration, and D_1' is not quiescent because p_k is in the entry section. However, this problem can be solved by noting that applying τ to C_1 produces a configuration D_1 that is quiescent. Thus by the inductive hypothesis, there is a $\{p_0, \ldots, p_{k-1}\}$-only schedule σ such that $C_2 = \sigma(D_1)$ is $\{p_k, \ldots, p_{n-1}\}$-quiescent and W is covered by p_0 through p_{k-1}.

Since D_1 looks like D_1' to p_0 through p_{k-1}, p_0 through p_{k-1} do the same thing in $exec(D_1', \sigma)$ as in $exec(D_1, \sigma)$. Thus in $C_2' = \sigma(D_1')$, $k+1$ variables are covered (W plus X) and C_2' appears quiescent to p_{k+1} through p_{n-1}.

However, it may *not* be the case that every application of the inductive hypothesis causes the same set of k variables to be covered. But because only a finite number of shared variables is used by the algorithm, there is only a finite number of different possibilities for which k variables are covered. Thus we repeatedly apply the inductive hypothesis, cycling between quiescent configurations $(D_1, D_2, \ldots)$ and $\{p_k, \ldots, p_{n-1}\}$-quiescent configurations in which k variables are covered $(C_1, C_2, \ldots)$. Eventually we will find two configurations C_i and C_j in which the same set of k variables are covered. We can then use essentially the same argument as we did above with C_1 and C_2.

We now proceed with the details. Let C be a reachable quiescent configuration. We now inductively define an infinite execution fragment starting with $C = D_0$ and passing through configurations $C_1, D_1, \ldots, C_i, D_i, \ldots$ (see Fig. 4.10).

Given quiescent configuration D_{i-1}, $i > 0$, define configuration C_i as follows. By the inductive hypothesis, there exists a schedule σ_i such that $C_i = \sigma_i(D_{i-1})$ is $\{p_k, \ldots, p_{n-1}\}$-quiescent and in C_i, p_0 through p_{k-1} cover a set W_i of k distinct variables.

Given configuration C_i, $i > 0$, define D_i as follows. First, apply the schedule $0, \ldots, k-1$ to C_i. This schedule causes every variable in W_i to be written. Now successively invoke the no deadlock condition and the unobstructed exit condition k times in order to cause each of p_0 through p_{k-1}, in some order, to enter the critical section, exit the critical section, go to the remainder section, and stay there. Call this schedule τ_i. Let D_i be the resulting configuration, $\tau_i(C_i)$. Clearly D_i is quiescent.

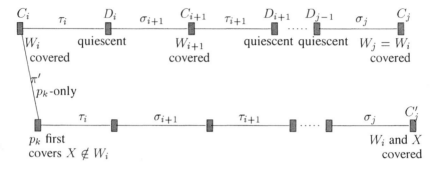

Fig. 4.11   Perturbation of the execution constructed in Lemma 4.18.

Since the set of variables is finite, there exist i and j, $1 \le i < j$, such that $W_i = W_j$.

Recall that C_i is $\{p_k, \ldots, p_{n-1}\}$-quiescent. By Lemma 4.17, there is a p_k-only schedule π such that p_k is in the critical section in $\pi(C_i)$, and during $exec(C_i, \pi)$, p_k writes to some variable not in W_i.

Let π' be the schedule of the prefix of $exec(C_i, \pi)$ just before p_k's first write to some variable, say X, not in W_i. Apply to C_i the schedule $\pi'\beta_i \ldots \beta_{j-1}$, where $\beta_\ell = \tau_\ell\sigma_{\ell+1}$, $i \le \ell < j - 1$. Let C'_j be the resulting configuration (see Figure 4.11).

We finish by showing that C'_j is the desired configuration D. Since π' is p_k-only, the beginning of τ_i writes to all variables in W_i, and $\beta_i \ldots \beta_{j-1}$ involves only p_0 through p_{k-1}, it follows that $C'_j \overset{P}{\sim} C_j$, where P is the set of all processors except p_k. Thus C'_j is $\{p_{k+1}, \ldots, p_{n-1}\}$-quiescent and, in C'_j, p_0 through p_{k-1} cover W_j and p_k covers X. Since X is not in W_i and $W_i = W_j$, it follows that X is not in W_j, and thus $k + 1$ distinct variables are covered in C'_j.   □

This lemma, instantiated with $k = n$ and C equal to the initial configuration, implies the existence of at least n distinct variables, namely the covered variables. Thus we have proved:

Theorem 4.19 *Any no deadlock mutual exclusion algorithm using only read/write registers must use at least n shared variables.*

4.4.5   Fast Mutual Exclusion

Previously, we have seen two general mutual exclusion algorithms, the bakery algorithm (Algorithm 10) and the tournament tree algorithm (Algorithm 13). In both algorithms, the number of steps a processor executes when trying to enter the critical section depends on n, even in the absence of *contention*, that is, when it is the only processor in the entry section. In most systems, it is expected that the typical contention is significantly smaller than n, that is, only a small number of processors are concurrently trying to enter the critical section.

Algorithm 14 Contention detector.

Initially, *door* := open, *race* := -1
1: *race* := *id*   // write identifier
2: if *door* = *closed* then return lose   // doorway closed
3: else   // doorway open
4:      *door* := *closed*   // close doorway
5:      if *race* = *id* then return win
6:      else return lose

A mutual exclusion algorithm is *fast* if a processor enters the critical section within a constant number of steps when it is the only processor trying to enter the critical section.

A fast algorithm clearly requires the use of multi-writer shared variables; if each variable is written only by a single processor, then a processor wishing to enter the critical section has to check at least n variables for possible competition.

The key for the algorithm is the correct combination of two mechanisms, one for providing fast entry when only a single processor wants the critical section, and the other for providing deadlock freedom when there is contention. We first describe a *contention detector* that allows a processor to detect whether there is contention for the critical section or not, by using only read and write operations.

The contention detector combines two mechanisms. First, a *doorway* mechanism catches a nonempty set of concurrent processors accessing the detector. A two-valued *door* flag is used: When it is *open*, the contention detector is free (and not yet accessed); *door* is set to *closed* after the first processor enters the contention detector.

Because *door* is not accessed atomically, two or more processors might be able to pass through the doorway concurrently. A simple race is used to pick one winner among this set of processors. This is done by having each processor write its identifier to a shared variable *race*, and then reading it to see whether some processor has written to *race* after it. A processor returns "win", and is said to *win* the contention detector, if it passes through the doorway and does not observe another processor in *race*;, otherwise, it returns "lose". The pseudocode is presented in Algorithm 14.

Theorem 4.20 *In every admissible execution of Algorithm 14:*
(1) At most one processor wins the contention detector.
(2) If processor p_i executes the contention detector alone, that is, no other processor starts the procedure before p_i completes it, then p_i wins the contention detector.

Proof. Let C be the set of processors that read *open* from *door*; note that this set is not empty, because the value of *door* is initially *open*. Processors in C are candidates for winning the contention detector, while other processors lose in Line 2.

Let p_j be the processor whose write to *race* is the last before *door* is set to *closed* for the first time. All processors that write to *race* after the write of processor p_j to *race* are not in C because they read *closed* from *door*. Every processor in C checks *race* after *door* is set to *closed*; thus it reads id_j or an identifier written afterwards.

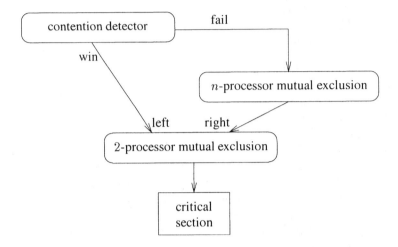

Fig. 4.12   Design of fast mutual exclusion algorithm.

Thus only if $p_j \in C$ and there is no later write to *race* does p_j win the contention detector. This implies (1).

Property (2) is simple to verify.   □

A processor may win the contention detector even if there is contention, but it is guaranteed that in this case, all other processors lose.

With the contention detector, it is simple to devise a fast mutual exclusion algorithm. Processors enter the contention detector and processors that lose in the contention detector use an ordinary mutual exclusion algorithm, for example, the bakery algorithm (Algorithm 10), so that a single processor is selected to enter the critical section. The winner of the n-processor mutual exclusion and the (possible) winner of the contention detector are arbitrated with a 2-processor mutual exclusion algorithm (Algorithm 12) to select the next processor to enter the critical section (see Fig. 4.12).

Figure 4.12 does not show the exit section of the fast mutual exclusion algorithm. In principle, the processor performs the exit sections of the modules it accessed on the entry to the critical section: first for the 2-processor mutual exclusion algorithm and then either for the contention detector or for the n-processor mutual exclusion algorithm.

However, the contention detector should be reset even if a processor reached the critical section along the so-called *slow path* (after losing the contention detector), so it can detect later intervals without contention. To do that in a correct manner, the contention detector is reset immediately after the processor leaves the critical section, while it is still in exclusion. The details of how this is done are rather sophisticated; see the chapter notes.

Note that when there is contention, however small, a processor may have to enter the critical section along the slow path, after reading n variables. The chapter notes discuss other algorithms that guarantee fast access to the critical section even when there is small contention.

Exercises

4.1 Suppose an algorithm satisfies the condition that in every *admissible* execution, at most one processor is in the critical section in any configuration. Show that this algorithm also satisfies the mutual exclusion condition.

4.2 An algorithm solves the *2-mutual exclusion* problem if at any time at most *two* processors are in the critical section. Present an algorithm for solving the 2-mutual exclusion problem by using read-modify-write registers.

4.3 (a) Prove, by induction on the length of the execution, the invariant properties of Algorithm 9, as stated in Lemma 4.3.

(b) Based on the invariants, prove that Algorithm 9 provides mutual exclusion and FIFO entry to the critical section.

4.4 Propose a method for measuring worst-case time complexity in the asynchronous shared memory model analogous to that in the asynchronous message-passing model.

4.5 Calculate the waiting time for the algorithm presented in Section 4.4.3 using the method from Exercise 4.4. That is, calculate how long a processor waits, in the worst case, since entering the entry section until entering the critical section. Assume that each execution of the critical section takes at most one time unit.

Hint: Use recursion inequalities.

4.6 Present an algorithm that solves the 2-mutual exclusion problem (defined in Exercise 4.2) and efficiently exploits the resources, that is, a processor does not wait when only one processor is in the critical section. The algorithm should use only read/write registers, but they can be unbounded.

4.7 Prove that Algorithm 11 provides no deadlock.

4.8 Modify the tournament tree mutual exclusion algorithm for n processors so that it can use an arbitrary two-processor mutual exclusion algorithm as "subroutines" at the nodes of the tree. Prove that your algorithm is correct. Try to minimize any assumptions you need to make about the two-processor algorithm.

4.9 Show why the variable *Choosing*[i] is needed in the bakery algorithm (Algorithm 10). Specifically, consider a version of Algorithm 10 in which this variable is omitted, and construct an execution in which mutual exclusion is violated.

4.10 Formalize the discussion at the beginning of Section 4.4.4 showing that n variables are required for no deadlock mutual exclusion if they are single-writer.

4.11 Show a simplified version of the lower bound presented in Section 4.4.4 for the case $n = 2$. That is, prove that any mutual exclusion algorithm for two processors requires at least two shared variables.

4.12 Write the pseudocode for the algorithm described in Figure 4.12, and prove that it satisfies the mutual exclusion and the no deadlock properties.

Which properties should the embedded components satisfy in order to provide the no lockout property?

4.13 Construct an execution of the algorithm from Exercise 4.12 in which there are two processors in the entry section and both read at least $\Omega(n)$ variables before entering the critical section.

4.14 Design a fast mutual exclusion algorithm using test&set operations.

Chapter Notes

We started this chapter by adapting the model of Chapter 2 to shared memory systems. This book considers only *asynchronous* shared memory systems; several books address the PRAM model of synchronous shared memory systems, for example, [142, 164].

Guaranteeing mutual exclusion is a fundamental problem in distributed computing, and many algorithms have been designed to solve it. We have only touched on a few of them in this chapter. Good coverage of this topic appears in the book by Raynal [225].

We first showed simple algorithms for achieving mutual exclusion using strong hardware primitives; these algorithms, presented in Section 4.3, are folklore. The lower bound of n on shared space for bounded waiting (Section 4.3.3) was proved by Burns, Jackson, Lynch, Fischer, and Peterson [62]. In the same paper they showed a lower bound of $\Omega(\sqrt{(n)})$ on the number of states of the shared memory for no lockout and a lower bound of $n/2$ if processors cannot remember anything about previous invocations of the mutual exclusion protocol. Chapter 14 discusses how to use randomization to guarantee no lockout with small shared variables, despite the lower bound.

In shared memory multiprocessors, copies of shared locations are *cached* locally at the processors; this means that if a processor is spinning on a particular location, then waiting will be done on the cached copy. Algorithm 9 is based on the *queue lock* algorithm of Anderson [16], who also discusses its architectural justification. The algorithm actually uses fetch&inc, a special instance of rmw that allows a processor to read a shared location and increment it by 1, in a single atomic operation. Graunke and Thakkar [125] present a variant using fetch&store (swapping a value between a local register and a shared memory location).

In Algorithm 9, different processors spin on the same location (an entry in the *Flags* array) at different times. This is quite harmful in distributed shared memory systems (described in Chapter 9), where it causes migration of shared memory between processors. An algorithm by Mellor-Crummey and Scott [184] avoids this problem by not assigning memory locations to different processors at different points during the execution.

The first mutual exclusion algorithm using only read/write operations was given by Dijkstra [90], who extended a two-processor algorithm of Dekker to an arbitrary number of processors.

This chapter presents three other algorithms for mutual exclusion using only read/write operations: The bakery algorithm (Algorithm 10) is due to Lamport [153]; the bounded algorithm for two processors (Algorithm 12) is due to Peterson [211]. The use of a tournament tree for generalizing to n processors (Algorithm 13) is adapted from a paper by Peterson and Fischer [214]. This paper, however, uses a different algorithm as the embedded two-processor algorithm. Their algorithms are more sophisticated and use only single-writer registers, whereas our algorithms use multi-writer registers. This presentation was chosen for simplicity and clarity.

Section 4.4.4 presents a lower bound on the number of read/write registers needed for achieving mutual exclusion without deadlock. This lower bound was proved by Burns and Lynch [63]; our proof organizes their ideas in a slightly different form.

Finally, we discussed the notion of fast mutual exclusion algorithms, guaranteeing that a processor enters the critical section within a constant number of steps when there is no contention. This notion was suggested by Lamport [160]. Our presentation follows Moir and Anderson [188] in abstracting the contention detector; the implementation of the contention detector is extracted from Lamport's original fast mutual exclusion algorithm. Rather than using the bakery algorithm when there is contention, Lamport uses a simpler n-processor algorithm that guarantees only no deadlock. Furthermore, "smashing" the 2-processor mutual exclusion procedure onto the other modules leads to a very compact algorithm, in which a processor performs only seven steps in order to enter the critical section in the absence of contention.

As Exercise 4.13 demonstrates, being fast provides no guarantee about the behavior of the algorithm in the presence of any contention, even a very low level. In an *adaptive* mutual exclusion algorithm, the number of steps a processor executes when trying to enter the critical section depends on k, a bound on the number of processors concurrently competing for the critical section, that is, the maximum contention. A recent survey of this topic is given by Anderson, Kim and Herman [15].

5

Fault-Tolerant Consensus

Coordination problems require processors to agree on a common course of action. Such problems are typically very easy to solve in reliable systems of the kind we have considered so far. In real systems, however, the various components do not operate correctly all the time. In this chapter, we start our investigation of the problems arising when a distributed system is unreliable. Specifically, we consider systems in which processors' functionality is incorrect.

In Section 5.1, we consider benign types of failures in synchronous message passing systems. In this case, a faulty processor crashes, that is, stops operating, but does not perform wrong operations (e.g., deliver messages that were not sent). We study the *consensus* problem, a fundamental coordination problem that requires processors to agree on a common output, based on their (possibly conflicting) inputs. Matching upper and lower bounds on the number of rounds required for solving consensus are shown.

In Section 5.2, we consider more severe types of (mis)behavior of the faulty processors, still in synchronous message-passing systems. We assume failures are *Byzantine*, that is, a failed processor may behave arbitrarily. We show that if we want to solve consensus, less than a third of the processors can be faulty. Under this assumption, we present two algorithms for reaching consensus in the presence of Byzantine failures. One algorithm uses the optimal number of rounds but has exponential message complexity; the second algorithm has polynomial message complexity, but it doubles the number of rounds.

Finally, we turn to asynchronous systems. We show that consensus cannot be achieved by a deterministic algorithm in asynchronous systems, even if only one processor fails in a benign manner by simply crashing. This result holds whether communication is via messages or through shared read/write variables. Chapter 15 considers the ability of other types of shared variables to solve consensus. Chapter 16 studies weaker coordination problems that can be solved in such asynchronous systems.

In this chapter, we study both synchronous and asynchronous message-passing systems and asynchronous shared memory systems. In each section, we discuss how to modify the model of the respective reliable system to include the specific type of faulty behavior.

5.1 SYNCHRONOUS SYSTEMS WITH CRASH FAILURES

In this section, we discuss a simple scenario for fault-tolerant distributed computing: a synchronous system in which processors fail by simply ceasing to operate. For all message-passing systems in this section, we assume that the communication graph is complete, that is, processors are located at the nodes of a clique. We further assume that the communication links are completely reliable and all messages sent are delivered.

5.1.1 Formal Model

We need to modify the formal definitions from Chapter 2 for a synchronous message-passing system to handle processor crashes.

A vital parameter of the system definition is f, the maximum number of processors that can fail. We call the system f-*resilient*.

Recall that in the reliable case, an execution of the synchronous system consists of a series of rounds. Each round consists of the delivery of all messages pending in *outbuf* variables, followed by one computation event for every processor.

For an f-resilient system, the definition of an execution is modified as follows. There exists a subset F of at most f processors, the *faulty* processors; the set of faulty processors can be different in different executions, so that it is not known in advance which processors are faulty. Each round contains exactly one computation event for every processor not in F and *at most* one computation event for every processor in F. Furthermore, if a processor in F does not have a computation event in some round, then it has no computation event in any subsequent round. Finally, in the last round in which a faulty processor has a computation event, an arbitrary subset of its outgoing messages are delivered.

This last property is quite important and causes the difficulties associated with this failure model. If every crash is a *clean* crash, in which either all or none of the crashed processor's outgoing messages from its last step are delivered, consensus can be solved very efficiently (see Exercise 5.2). But the uncertainty in the effect of the crash means that processors must do more work (e.g., exchange more messages) in order to solve consensus.

Algorithm 15 Consensus algorithm in the presence of crash failures:
code for processor p_i, $0 \leq i \leq n - 1$.

Initially $V = \{x\}$ // V contains p_i's input

1: round k, $1 \leq k \leq f + 1$:
2:      send $\{v \in V : p_i$ has not already sent $v\}$ to all processors
3:      receive S_j from p_j, $0 \leq j \leq n - 1$, $j \neq i$
4:      $V := V \cup \bigcup_{j=0}^{n-1} S_j$
5:      if $k = f + 1$ then $y := \min(V)$ // decide

5.1.2 The Consensus Problem

Consider a system in which each processor p_i has special state components x_i, the *input*, and y_i, the *output*, also called the *decision*. Initially, x_i holds a value from some well-ordered set of possible inputs and y_i is undefined. Any assignment to y_i is irreversible. A solution to the *consensus* problem must guarantee the following:

Termination: In every admissible execution, y_i is eventually assigned a value, for every nonfaulty processor p_i.

Agreement: In every execution, if y_i and y_j are assigned, then $y_i = y_j$, for all nonfaulty processors p_i and p_j. That is, nonfaulty processors do not decide on conflicting values.

Validity: In every execution, if, for some value v, $x_i = v$ for all processors p_i, and if y_i is assigned for some nonfaulty processor p_i, then $y_i = v$. That is, if all the processors have the same input, then any value decided upon must be that common input.

For two-element input sets, this validity condition is equivalent to requiring that every nonfaulty decision value be the input of some processor, as Exercise 5.1 asks you to show. Once a processor crashes, it is of no interest to the algorithm, and no requirements are placed on its decision.

Below we show matching upper and lower bounds of $f + 1$ on the number of rounds required for reaching consensus in an f-resilient system.

5.1.3 A Simple Algorithm

The pseudocode appears in Algorithm 15. In the algorithm, each processor maintains a set of the values it knows to exist in the system; initially, this set contains only its own input. In later rounds, a processor updates its set by joining it with the sets received from other processors and broadcasts any new additions to the set to all processors. This continues for $f + 1$ rounds. At this point, the processor decides on the smallest value in its set.

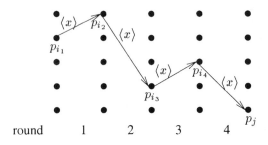

Fig. 5.1   Illustration for the proof of Lemma 5.1, $f = 3$.

Clearly, the algorithm requires exactly $f + 1$ rounds, which implies termination. Furthermore, it is obvious that the validity condition is maintained, because the decision value is an input of some processor. The next lemma is the key to proving that the agreement condition is satisfied.

Lemma 5.1 *In every execution, at the end of round $f + 1$, $V_i = V_j$, for every two nonfaulty processors p_i and p_j.*

Proof.   It suffices to show that if $x \in V_i$ at the end of round $f + 1$, then $x \in V_j$ at the end of round $f + 1$, for all nonfaulty processors p_i and p_j.

Let r be the first round in which x is added to V_i (in Line 4), for any nonfaulty processor p_i. If x is initially in V_i, let r be 0. If $r \leq f$ then, in round $r + 1 \leq f + 1$, p_i sends x to each p_j, which causes p_j to add x to V_j, if it is not already present.

Otherwise, suppose $r = f + 1$ and let p_j be a nonfaulty processor that receives x for the first time in round $f + 1$. Then there must be a chain of $f + 1$ processors $p_{i_1}, \ldots, p_{i_{f+1}}$ that transfers the value x to p_j. That is, p_{i_1} sends x to p_{i_2} in round 1, p_{i_2} sends x to p_{i_3} in round 2, etc., and finally p_{i_f} sends x to $p_{i_{f+1}}$ in round f, and $p_{i_{f+1}}$ sends x to p_j in round $f + 1$. (Fig. 5.1 illustrates this situation for $f = 3$.) Since each processor sends a particular value only once, the processors $p_{i_1}, \ldots, p_{i_{f+1}}$ form a set of $f + 1$ distinct processors. Thus there must be at least one nonfaulty processor among $p_{i_1}, \ldots, p_{i_{f+1}}$. However, this processor adds x to its set at a round $\leq f < r$, contradicting the assumption that r is minimal.   □

Therefore, nonfaulty processors have the same set in Line 5 and decide on the same value. This implies that the agreement condition is satisfied. Thus we have:

Theorem 5.2 *Algorithm 15 solves the consensus problem in the presence of f crash failures within $f + 1$ rounds.*

5.1.4   Lower Bound on the Number of Rounds

We now present a lower bound of $f + 1$ on the number of rounds required for reaching consensus in the presence of crash failures. This implies that the algorithm presented in Section 5.1.3 is optimal. We assume that $f \leq n - 2$.[1]

The intuition behind the lower bound is that if processors decide too early, they cannot distinguish between admissible executions in which they should make different decisions. The notion of indistinguishability is crucial to this proof and is central in our understanding of distributed systems. To capture this notion formally, we introduce the following definition of a processor's view of the execution.

Definition 5.1 *Let α be an execution and let p_i be a processor. The view of p_i in α, denoted by $\alpha | p_i$, is the subsequence of computation and message delivery events that occur in α at p_i together with the state of p_i in the initial configuration of α.*

Chapter 4 included a definition of two (shared memory) configurations being similar for a processor (Definition 4.1). Using the notion of view that was just defined, we can extend the definition of similarity to entire (message passing) executions. However, here we are only concerned if a *nonfaulty* processor cannot distinguish between the executions.

Definition 5.2 *Let α_1 and α_2 be two executions and let p_i be a processor that is nonfaulty in α_1 and α_2. Execution α_1 is similar to execution α_2 with respect to p_i, denoted $\alpha_1 \overset{p_i}{\sim} \alpha_2$, if $\alpha_1 | p_i = \alpha_2 | p_i$.*

Some technical details in the lower bound proof are made easier if we restrict attention to consensus algorithms in which every processor is supposed to send a message to every other processor at each round. This does not impair the generality of the result, because any consensus algorithm can be modified trivially to conform to this rule by adding dummy messages where necessary. We also assume that every processor keeps a history of all the messages it has received in all the previous rounds, so that a configuration contains the information concerning which processors have failed and how many rounds (or parts of rounds) have elapsed.

An execution is said to be *failure sparse* if there is at most one crash per round. Such executions are very useful in proving the lower bound — even a single failure can cause some information to be lost, and stretching out the failures over more rounds increases the amount of time in which there is uncertainty about the decision. In the remainder of this section, we only consider executions that are prefixes of admissible failure-sparse executions and configurations appearing in such executions. In particular, all definitions in this section are with respect to failure-sparse executions, and we will only explicitly mention "failure sparse" when the argument crucially depends on this property.

---

[1] If $f = n - 1$ then consensus can be achieved within f rounds, by a small modification to Algorithm 15; see Exercise 5.3.

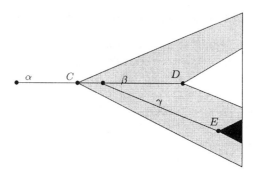

Fig. 5.2 Schematic of the set S of all admissible failure-sparse executions that include configuration C. Solid lines (α, β, γ) represent single executions. Shaded triangle with endpoint C, D or E represents all executions in S that include that configuration. If all decisions in the white triangle are 1, then D is 1-valent; if all decisions in the black triangle are 0, then E is 0-valent; in this case C is bivalent.

A key notion in this proof (and in others) is the set of decisions that can be reached from a particular configuration. The next few definitions formalize this notion.

The *valence* of configuration C is the set of all values that are decided upon by a nonfaulty processor in some configuration that is reachable from C in an (admissible failure sparse) execution that includes C. By the termination condition, the set cannot be empty. C is *univalent* if this set contains one value; it is *0-valent* if this value is 0, and *1-valent* if this value is 1. If the set contains two values then C is *bivalent*. Figure 5.2 shows an example of 0-valent, 1-valent, and bivalent configurations.

If some processor has decided in a configuration, the agreement condition implies that the configuration is univalent.

Theorem 5.3 *Any consensus algorithm for n processors that is resilient to f crash failures requires at least $f + 1$ rounds in some admissible execution, for all $n \geq f + 2$.*

Proof. Consider any consensus algorithm A for n processors and f crash failures, with $n \geq f + 2$.

The proof strategy is, first, to show that there exists an $(f - 1)$-round execution of A in which the configuration at the end is undecided. The next step is to show that with just one more round it is not possible for the processors to decide explicitly. Thus at least $f + 1$ rounds are required for decision.

The $(f - 1)$-round execution in the first stage is constructed by induction. Lemma 5.4 shows that there is an "undecided" initial configuration. Lemma 5.5 shows how to construct an undecided k-round execution out of an undecided $(k - 1)$-round execution, up to the limit of $f - 1$. The executions manipulated by the proof are failure-sparse ones, and thus "undecided" here means bivalent with respect to failure-sparse executions.

Lemma 5.4 *Algorithm A has a bivalent initial configuration.*

Proof. Suppose in contradiction that all initial configurations are univalent. Since the initial configuration in which all inputs are 0 is 0-valent and the initial configuration in which all inputs are 1 is 1-valent, there must exist two configurations that differ in the input of only one processor yet have different valences.

In particular, let I_0 be a 0-valent initial configuration and I_1 be a 1-valent initial configuration such that I_0 and I_1 differ only in the input of processor p_i.

Consider the schedule σ in which p_i fails initially and no other processors fail. Assume that σ is long enough to ensure that all the nonfaulty processors decide when starting from I_0. Note that the resulting execution is failure sparse. Since I_0 is 0-valent, applying σ to I_0 results in a decision of 0.

What happens if σ is applied to I_1? The processors other than p_i are nonfaulty and cannot tell the difference between these two executions (formally, the executions are similar with respect to every processor other than p_i). Thus the nonfaulty processors decide 0 in I_1, contradicting the 1-valence of I_1.

Thus there is at least one bivalent initial configuration. $\qquad\square$

Lemma 5.5 *For each k, $0 \leq k \leq f - 1$, there is a k-round execution of A that ends in a bivalent configuration.*

Proof. The proof is by induction on k. The base case, $k = 0$, follows from Lemma 5.4.

Assume that the lemma is true for $k - 1 \geq 0$ and show it is true for $k \leq f - 1$. Let α_{k-1} be the $(k - 1)$-round execution ending in a bivalent configuration whose existence is guaranteed by the inductive hypothesis.

Assume in contradiction that all one-round extensions of α_{k-1} with at most one additional crash end in a univalent configuration.

Without loss of generality, assume that the one-round failure-free extension of α_{k-1}, denoted β_k, leads to a 1-valent configuration. Since α_{k-1} ends in a bivalent configuration, there is another one-round extension of α_{k-1} that ends in a 0-valent configuration. Call this execution γ_k. Since we are working exclusively with failure-sparse execution, exactly one failure occurs in round k of γ_k. In the execution γ_k, let p_i be the processor that crashes and $q_1, \ldots, q_m$ be the processors to whom p_i fails to send (see Fig. 5.3); m is some value between 1 and n inclusive.

For each j, $0 \leq j \leq m$, define execution α_k^j to be the one-round extension of α_{k-1} in which p_i fails to send to $q_1, \ldots, q_j$. Note that $\alpha_k^0 = \beta_k$ and is 1-valent, whereas $\alpha_k^m = \gamma_k$ and is 0-valent.

What are the valences of the intermediate α_k^j executions? Somewhere in the sequence $\alpha_k^0, \alpha_k^1, \ldots, \alpha_k^{m-1}, \alpha_k^m$ there is a switch from 1-valent to 0-valent. Let j be such that α_k^j is 1-valent and α_k^{j+1} is 0-valent. Note that the only difference between α_k^j and α_k^{j+1} is that p_i sends to q_{j+1} in α_k^j but not in α_k^{j+1}.

The number of faulty processors in α_k^j (and also in α_k^{j+1}) is less than f, since at most $k - 1 < f - 1$ processors crash in α_{k-1} and p_i crashes in round k. Thus there is still one more processor that can crash without violating the bound f on the number of failures. Consider the admissible extensions δ_k^j and δ_k^{j+1} of α_k^j and α_k^{j+1}, respectively, in which q_{j+1} crashes at the beginning of round $k + 1$, without ever

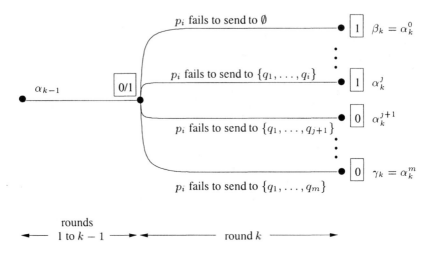

Fig. 5.3   Illustration for the proof that there is a k-round execution ending in a bivalent configuration (Lemma 5.5). Valences of configurations are indicated by values in boxes. Edge labels indicate to whom p_i fails to send.

getting a chance to reveal whether or not it received a message from p_i in round $k+1$, and no further processors crash. The two executions δ_k^j and δ_k^{j+1} are similar with respect to every nonfaulty processor, since the only difference between them is that p_i sends to q_{j+1} in δ_k^j but not in δ_k^{j+1}, yet q_{j+1} crashes before revealing this information. Thus α_k^j and α_k^{j+1} must have the same valence, which is a contradiction.

Thus there must exist a one-round extension of α_{k-1} with at most one additional crash that ends in a bivalent configuration.   □

From the previous lemma, we have an $(f-1)$-round execution that ends in a bivalent configuration. The next lemma concerns round f — this round may not preserve bivalence, but we show that nonfaulty processors cannot determine yet what decision to make, and thus an additional round is necessary.

Lemma 5.6 *If α_{f-1} is an $(f-1)$-round execution of A that ends in a bivalent configuration, then there exists a one-round extension of α_{f-1} in which some nonfaulty processor has not decided.*

Proof.   Let β_f be the one-round extension of α_{f-1} in which no failure occurs in round f. If β_f ends in a bivalent configuration, we are done. Suppose β_f ends in a univalent configuration, say 1-valent. Since the configuration at the end of α_{f-1} is bivalent, some other one-round extension of α results in a configuration that is either bivalent (in which case we are done) or 0-valent; call this execution γ_f. It must be that exactly one processor fails in round f of γ_f, that is, some processor p_i is faulty and fails to send a message to some nonfaulty processor p_j. The reason why p_j exists is that p_j cannot fail in round f, since p_i is the processor that fails in this round, and

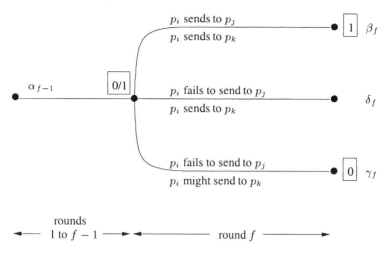

Fig. 5.4 Illustration for the proof that some processor is still undecided in round f (Lemma 5.6). Valences of configurations are indicated by values in boxes. Edge labels indicate to whom p_i fails or does not fail to send.

p_j cannot already have failed since otherwise there would be no observable difference between the executions. Consider a third one-round extension δ_f of α_{f-1} that is the same as γ_f except that p_i succeeds in sending to some nonfaulty processor p_k other than p_j; p_k must exist since $n \geq f + 2$. (It is possible for δ_f to be the same as γ_f.) See Fig. 5.4.

The executions β_f and δ_f are similar with respect to p_k. Thus at the end of round f in δ_f, p_k is either undecided or has decided 1, since β_f is 1-valent. Similarly, the executions γ_f and δ_f are similar with respect to p_j. Thus at the end of round f in δ_f, p_j is either undecided or has decided 0, since γ_f is 0-valent. Since the algorithm satisfies the agreement property, it cannot be the case in δ_f that both p_j and p_k have decided. $\qquad\qquad\square$

We now conclude the proof of Theorem 5.3. Lemmas 5.5 and 5.6 together imply the existence of an f-round execution in which some nonfaulty processor has not decided. In every admissible extension of this execution (for instance, the extension in which there are no further crashes), at least $f + 1$ rounds are required for termination. $\qquad\qquad\square$

5.2 SYNCHRONOUS SYSTEMS WITH BYZANTINE FAILURES

We now turn to study more severe, malicious failures, still in the context of synchronous systems. This model is often called the *Byzantine model*, because of the following metaphoric description of the consensus problem:

Several divisions of the Byzantine army are camped outside an enemy city. Each division is commanded by a general. The generals can communicate with each other only by reliable messengers. The generals should decide on a common plan of action, that is, they should decide whether to attack the city or not (cf. agreement), and if the generals are unanimous in their initial opinion, then that opinion should be the decision (cf. validity). The new wrinkle is that some of the generals may be traitors (that is why they are in the Byzantine army) and may try to prevent the loyal generals from agreeing. To do so, the traitors send conflicting messages to different generals, falsely report on what they heard from other generals, and even conspire and form a coalition.

5.2.1 Formal Model

We need to modify the definition of execution from Chapter 2 (for reliable synchronous message passing) to handle Byzantine processor failures. In an execution of an f-resilient Byzantine system, there exists a subset of at most f processors, the *faulty* processors.[2] In a computation step of a faulty processor, the new state of the processor and the contents of the messages sent are completely unconstrained. As in the reliable case, every processor takes a computation step in every round and every message sent is delivered in that round.

Thus a faulty processor can behave arbitrarily and even maliciously, for example, it can send different messages to different processors (or not send messages at all) when it is supposed to send the same message. The faulty processors can appear to coordinate with each other. In some situations, the recipient of a message from a faulty processor can detect that the sender is faulty, for instance, if the message is improperly formatted. Difficulties arise when the message received is plausible to the recipient, yet not correct. A faulty processor can also mimic the behavior of a crashed processor by failing to send any messages from some point onward.

5.2.2 The Consensus Problem Revisited

The definition of the consensus problem in the presence of Byzantine failures is the same as for crash failures and is repeated here. Each processor p_i has input and output state components, x_i and y_i; initially, x_i holds a value from some well-ordered set and y_i is undefined. Any assignment to y_i is irreversible. A solution to the consensus problem must guarantee the following:

Termination: In every admissible execution, y_i is eventually assigned a value, for every nonfaulty processor p_i.

Agreement: In every execution, if y_i and y_j are assigned, then $y_i = y_j$, for all nonfaulty processors p_i and p_j. That is, nonfaulty processors do not decide on conflicting values.

---

[2]In some of the literature, the upper bound on the number of Byzantine processors is denoted t, for *traitors*.

Validity: In every execution, if, for some value v, $x_i = v$ for all processors p_i, and if y_i is assigned for some nonfaulty processor p_i, then $y_i = v$. That is, if all the processors have the same input, then any value decided upon by a nonfaulty processor must be that common input.

For input sets whose size is larger than two, this validity condition is not equivalent to requiring that every nonfaulty decision value be the input of some processor, as Exercise 5.7 asks you to show. As in the crash case, no requirements are placed on the decisions of faulty processors.

We first show a lower bound on the ratio between faulty and nonfaulty processors. We then present two algorithms for reaching consensus in the presence of Byzantine failures. The first is relatively simple but uses exponential-size messages. The round complexity of this algorithm is $f + 1$ and matches the lower bound proved in Section 5.1.4. Recall that the $f + 1$ round lower bound was shown assuming crash failures. The same lower bound also holds in any system that is worse-behaved, including one with Byzantine failures; a Byzantine-faulty processor can act like a crash-faulty processor. The second algorithm is more complicated and doubles the number of rounds; however, it uses constant-size messages.

5.2.3 Lower Bound on the Ratio of Faulty Processors

In this section, we prove that if a third or more of the processors can be Byzantine, then consensus cannot be reached. We first show this result for the special case of a system with three processors, one of which might be Byzantine; the general result is derived by reduction to this special case.

Theorem 5.7 *In a system with three processors and one Byzantine processor, there is no algorithm that solves the consensus problem.*

Proof. Assume, by way of contradiction, that there is an algorithm for reaching consensus in a system with three processors, p_0, p_1, and p_2, connected by a complete communication graph. Let A be the local algorithm (state machine) for p_0, B the local algorithm for p_1, and C the local algorithm for p_2.

Consider a synchronous ring system with six processors in which p_0 and p_3 have A for their local algorithm, p_1 and p_4 have B for their local algorithm, and p_2 and p_5 have C for their local algorithm, as depicted in Figure 5.5(a). We cannot assume that such a system solves consensus, since the combination of A, B, and C only has to work correctly in a triangle. However, this system does have some particular, well-defined behavior, when each processor begins with an input value and there are no faulty processors.

The particular execution of the ring of interest is when the input values are 1 for p_0, p_1, and p_2 and 0 for p_3, p_4, and p_5 (see Fig. 5.5(a)). Call this execution β. This execution will be used to specify the behavior of faulty processors in some triangles.

Consider an execution α_1 of the algorithm in a triangle in which all processors start with input 1 and processor p_2 is faulty (see Fig. 5.5(b)). Furthermore, assume that processor p_2 is sending to p_0 the messages sent in β by p_5 (bottom left) to p_0

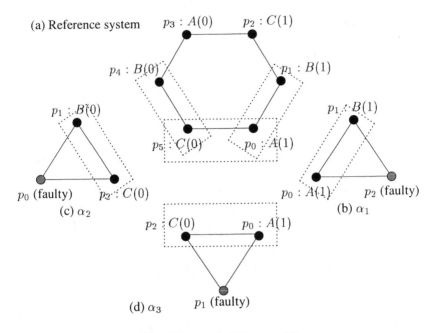

Fig. 5.5   Proof of Theorem 5.7.

and to p_1 the messages sent in β by p_2 (upper right) to p_1. By the validity condition, both p_0 and p_1 must decide 1 in α_1.

Now consider an execution α_2 of the algorithm in a triangle in which all processors start with input 0, and processor p_0 is faulty (Fig. 5.5(c)). Furthermore, assume that processor p_0 is sending to p_1 the messages sent in β by p_3 (top left) to p_4 and to p_2 the messages sent in β by p_0 (bottom right) to p_5. By the validity condition, both p_1 and p_2 must decide 0 in α_2.

Finally, consider an execution α_3 of the algorithm in a triangle where processor p_0 starts with input 1, processor p_2 starts with input 0, and processor p_1 is faulty (Fig. 5.5(d)). Furthermore, assume that processor p_1 is sending to p_2 the messages sent in β by p_4 (middle left) to p_5 and to p_0 the messages sent in β by p_1 (middle right) to p_0.

We now argue that $\alpha_1 \overset{p_0}{\sim} \alpha_3$. Since the messages sent by faulty processor p_2 are defined with reference to β, a simple induction on the round number verifies that p_0 has the same view in α_1 as it does in β and that p_1 has the same view in α_1 as it does in β. Similarly, induction on the round number verifies that p_0 has the same view in β as it does in α_3 and p_5 has the same view in β as p_2 does in α_3. Thus $\alpha_1 \overset{p_0}{\sim} \alpha_3$, and consequently, p_0 decides 1 in α_3.

But since $\alpha_2 \overset{p_2}{\sim} \alpha_3$ (cf. Exercise 5.10), p_2 decides 0 in α_3, violating the agreement condition, a contradiction. $\qquad\square$

We prove the general case by reduction to the previous theorem.

Theorem 5.8 *In a system with n processors and f Byzantine processors, there is no algorithm that solves the consensus problem if $n \leq 3f$.*

Proof. Assume, by way of contradiction, that there exists an algorithm that reaches consensus in a system with n processors, f of which might be Byzantine. Partition the processors into three sets, P_0, P_1, and P_2, each containing at most $n/3$ processors. Consider now a system with three processors, p_0, p_1, and p_2. We now describe a consensus algorithm for this system, which can tolerate one Byzantine failure.

In the algorithm, p_0 simulates all the processors in P_0, p_1 simulates all the processors in P_1, and p_2 simulates all the processors in P_2. We leave the details of the simulation to the reader. If one processor is faulty in the three-processor system, then since $n/3 \leq f$, at most f processors are faulty in the simulated system with n processors. Therefore, the simulated algorithm must preserve the validity and agreement conditions in the simulated system, and hence also in the three-processor system.

Thus we have a consensus algorithm for a system with three processors that tolerates the failure of one processor. This contradicts Theorem 5.7. $\qquad\square$

5.2.4 An Exponential Algorithm

In this section, we describe an algorithm for reaching consensus in the presence of Byzantine failures. The algorithm takes exactly $f + 1$ rounds, where f is the upper bound on the number of failures, and requires that $n \geq 3f + 1$. Thus the algorithm meets two of the lower bounds for consensus in the presence of Byzantine failure, on the number of rounds and resilience. However, it uses messages of exponential size.

The algorithm contains two stages. In the first stage, information is gathered by communication among the processors. In the second stage, each processor locally computes its decision value using the information collected in the previous stage.

It is convenient to describe the information maintained by each processor during the algorithm as a tree in which each path from the root to a leaf contains $f + 2$ nodes; thus the height of the tree is $f + 1$. We label nodes with sequences of processors' names in the following manner. The root is labeled with the empty sequence. Let v be an internal node in the tree labeled with the sequence $i_1, i_2, \ldots, i_r$; for every i between 0 and $n - 1$ that is not in this sequence, v has one child labeled $i_1, i_2, \ldots, i_r, i$. (Fig. 5.6 contains an example for a system with $n = 4$ and $f = 1$; the shadings in the nodes at level 2 will be used in Fig. 5.7.) Note that no processor appears twice in the label of a node. A node labeled with the sequence π *corresponds* to processor p_i if π ends with i.

In the first stage of the algorithm, information is gathered and stored in the nodes of the tree. In the first round of the information gathering stage, each processor sends its initial value to all processors, including itself.[3] When a nonfaulty processor p_i

---

[3] Although processors do not actually have channels to themselves, they can "pretend" that they do.

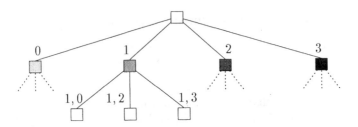

Fig. 5.6 The exponential information gathering tree; $n = 4, f = 1$.

receives a value x from processor p_j, it stores the received value at the node labeled j in its tree; a default value, $v_\perp$, is stored if x is not a legitimate value or if no value was received. In general, each processor broadcasts the rth level of its tree at the beginning of round r. When a processor receives a message from p_j with the value of the node labeled $i_1, \ldots, i_r$, it stores the value in the node labeled $i_1, \ldots, i_r, j$ in its tree. Figure 5.7 shows how the information received from p_2 in round 2, corresponding to the shaded nodes at level 2 in Figure 5.6, is stored at the nodes in level 3.

Intuitively, p_i stores in node $i_1, \ldots, i_r, j$ the value that "p_j says that p_{i_r} says that $\ldots$ that p_{i_1} said." Given a specific execution, we refer to this value as $tree_i(i_1, \ldots, i_r, j)$, omitting the subscript i when no confusion will arise.

Information gathering as described above continues for $f + 1$ rounds, until the entire tree has been filled in. At this point, the second stage of computing the decision value locally starts. Processor p_i computes the decision value by applying to each subtree a recursive data reduction function resolve. The value of the reduction function on p_i's subtree rooted at a node labeled with π is denoted $resolve_i(\pi)$, omitting the subscript i when no confusion will arise. The decision value is $resolve_i()$, that is, the result of applying the function to the root of the tree.

The function resolve is essentially a recursive majority vote and is defined for a node π as follows. If π is a leaf, then $resolve(\pi) = tree(\pi)$; otherwise, $resolve(\pi)$ is the majority value of $resolve(\pi')$, where π' ranges over all children of π ($v_\perp$ if no majority exists).

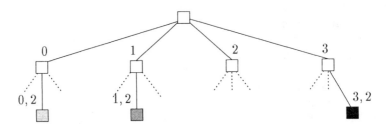

Fig. 5.7 How level 2 of p_2 is stored at level 3 of another processor.

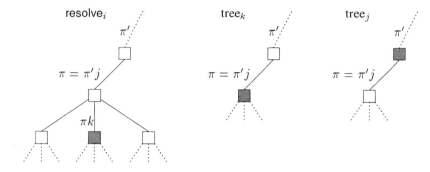

Fig. 5.8 Illustration for the proof of Lemma 5.9.

In summary, processor p_i gathers information for $f + 1$ rounds, computes the reduced value using resolve$_i$ and decides on resolve$_i()$.

We now prove that the algorithm is correct. Fix an admissible execution of the algorithm. We first prove Lemma 5.9, which is useful in establishing the validity condition. It states that nonfaulty processor p_i's resolved value for what another nonfaulty process p_j reports for node π' equals the value that p_j has stored in its tree in node π'.

A key aspect of the proof is that, if a node π in p_i's tree corresponds to p_j, then the value stored in $tree_i(\pi)$ was received by p_i in a message from p_j.

Lemma 5.9 *For every tree node label π of the form $\pi'j$, where p_j is nonfaulty,* resolve$_i(\pi) = tree_j(\pi')$, *for every nonfaulty processor p_i.*

Proof. The proof is by induction on the height of the node π in the tree, starting from the leaves.

The basis of the induction is when π is a leaf. By definition, resolve$_i(\pi)$ equals $tree_i(\pi)$. Note that $tree_i(\pi)$ stores the value for π' that p_j sent to p_i in the last round. Since p_j is nonfaulty, this value is $tree_j(\pi')$.

For the inductive step, let π be an internal node. Note that π has depth at most f. Since the tree has $f + 2$ levels, the root has degree n, and in every level of the tree the degree of nodes decreases by one, it follows that the degree of π is at least $n - f$. Since $n \geq 3f + 1$, the degree of π is at least $2f + 1$. Thus the majority of the children of π correspond to nonfaulty processors.

Let πk be some child of π that corresponds to a nonfaulty processor p_k (see Fig. 5.8). By the inductive hypothesis, resolve$_i(\pi k)$ equals $tree_k(\pi)$. Since p_j is nonfaulty, $tree_k(\pi)$ equals $tree_j(\pi')$, that is, p_j correctly reports to p_k the value that p_j has stored for π'.

Thus p_i resolves each child of π corresponding to a nonfaulty processor to $tree_j(\pi')$, and thus resolve$_i(\pi)$ equals the majority value, $tree_j(\pi')$. □

We can now show the validity condition. Suppose all nonfaulty processors start with the same input value, v. The decision of each nonfaulty processor p_i is resolve$_i()$, which is the majority of the resolved values for all children of the root. For each child j of the root where p_j is nonfaulty, Lemma 5.9 implies that resolve$_i(j)$ equals $tree_j()$, which is p_j's input v. Since a majority of the children of the root correspond to nonfaulty processors, p_i decides v.

The next lemma is used to show the agreement condition. A node π is *common* in an execution if all nonfaulty processors compute the same reduced value for π, that is, resolve$_i(\pi) =$ resolve$_j(\pi)$, for every pair of nonfaulty processors p_i and p_j. A subtree has a *common frontier* if there is a common node on every path from the root of the subtree to its leaves.

Lemma 5.10 *Let π be a node. If there is a common frontier in the subtree rooted at π, then π is common.*

Proof. The lemma is proved by induction on the height of π. The base case is when π is a leaf and it follows immediately.

For the inductive step, assume that π is the root of a subtree with height $k + 1$ and that the lemma holds for every node with height k. Assume in contradiction that π is not common. Since by hypothesis the subtree rooted at π has a common frontier, every subtree rooted at a child of π must have a common frontier. Since the children of π have height k, the inductive hypothesis implies that they are all common. Therefore, all processors resolve the same value for all the children of π and the lemma follows since the resolved value for π is the majority of the resolved values of its children. □

Note that the nodes on each path from a child of the root of the tree to a leaf correspond to different processors. Because the nodes on each such path correspond to $f + 1$ different processors, at least one of them corresponds to a nonfaulty processor and hence is common, by Lemma 5.9. Therefore, the whole tree has a common frontier, which implies, by Lemma 5.10, that the root is common. The agreement condition now follows. Thus we have:

Theorem 5.11 *There exists an algorithm for n processors that solves the consensus problem in the presence of f Byzantine failures within $f + 1$ rounds using exponential size messages, if $n > 3f$.*

In each round, every processor sends a message to every processor. Therefore, the total message complexity of the algorithm is $n^2(f + 1)$. Unfortunately, in each round, every processor broadcasts a whole level of its tree (the one that was filled in most recently) and thus the longest message contains $n(n - 1)(n - 2) \cdots (n - (f + 1)) = \Theta(n^{f+2})$ values.

5.2.5 A Polynomial Algorithm

The following simple algorithm uses messages of constant size, takes $2(f + 1)$ rounds, and assumes that $n > 4f$. It shows that it is possible to solve the consensus problem

---

Algorithm 16 A polynomial consensus algorithm in the presence of
Byzantine failures: code for p_i, $0 \le i \le n - 1$.

Initially $pref[i] = x$ // initial preference for self is for own input
and $pref[j] = v_\perp$, for any $j \ne i$ // default for others

1:    round $2k - 1$, $1 \le k \le f + 1$:   // first round of phase k
2:       send $\langle pref[i] \rangle$ to all processors
3:       receive $\langle v_j \rangle$ from p_j and assign to $pref[j]$, for all $0 \le j \le n - 1$, $j \ne i$
4:       let maj be the majority value of $pref[0], \ldots, pref[n - 1]$ ($v_\perp$ if none)
5:       let $mult$ be the multiplicity of maj

6:    round $2k$, $1 \le k \le f + 1$:   // second round of phase k
7:       if $i = k$ then send $\langle maj \rangle$ to all processors   // king of this phase
8:       receive $\langle king\text{-}maj \rangle$ from p_k ($v_\perp$ if none)
9:       if $mult > \frac{n}{2} + f$
10:        then $pref[i] := maj$
11:        else $pref[i] := king\text{-}maj$
12:       if $k = f + 1$ then $y := pref[i]$ // decide

---

with constant-size messages, although with an increase in the number of rounds and a decrease in the resilience.

The algorithm contains $f + 1$ phases, each taking two rounds. Each processor has a preferred decision (in short, *preference*) for each phase, initially its input value. At the first round of each phase, all processors send their preferences to each other. Let v_i^k be the majority value in the set of values received by processor p_i at the end of the first round of phase k. If there is no majority, then a default value, $v_\perp$, is used. In the second round of the phase, processor p_k, called the *king* of the phase, sends its majority value v_k^k to all processors. If p_i receives more than $n/2 + f$ copies of v_i^k (in the first round of the phase) then it sets its preference for the next phase to be v_i^k; otherwise, it sets its preference to be the phase king's preference, v_k^k, received in the second round of the phase. After $f + 1$ phases, the processor decides on its preference.

Each processor maintains a local array *pref* with n entries. The pseudocode appears in Algorithm 16.

The following lemmas are with respect to an arbitrary admissible execution of the algorithm. The first property to note is *persistence of agreement*:

Lemma 5.12 *If all nonfaulty processors prefer v at the beginning of phase k, then they all prefer v at the end of phase k, for all k, $1 \le k \le f + 1$.*

Proof. Since all nonfaulty processors prefer v at the beginning of phase k, each processor receives at least $n - f$ copies of v (including its own) in the first round of phase k. Since $n > 4f$, $n - f > n/2 + f$, which implies that all nonfaulty processors will prefer v at the end of phase k.   □

This immediately implies the validity property: If all nonfaulty processors start with the same input v, they continue to prefer v throughout the phases (because the preference at the end of one phase is the preference at the beginning of the next); finally, they decide on v at the end of phase $f + 1$.

Agreement is achieved by the king breaking ties. Because each phase has a different king and there are $f + 1$ phases, then at least one phase has a nonfaulty king.

Lemma 5.13 *Let g be a phase whose king p_g is nonfaulty. Then all nonfaulty processors finish phase g with the same preference.*

Proof. Suppose that all nonfaulty processors use the majority value received from the king for their preference (Line 11). Since the king is nonfaulty, it sends the same message and thus all the nonfaulty preferences are the same.

Suppose that some nonfaulty processor, say p_i, uses its own majority value, say v, for its preference (Line 10). Thus p_i receives more than $n/2 + f$ messages for v in the first round of phase g. Consequently every processor, including the king p_g, receives more than $n/2$ messages for v in the first round of phase g and sets its majority value to be v. Thus, no matter whether it executes Line 10 or Line 11 to set its preference, every nonfaulty processor has v for its preference. $\square$

Therefore, at phase $g + 1$ all processors have the same preference, and the persistence of agreement (Lemma 5.12) implies that they will decide on the same value at the end of the algorithm. This implies that the algorithm has the agreement property and solves the consensus problem.

Clearly, the algorithm requires $2(f + 1)$ rounds and messages contain one bit. Thus we have:

Theorem 5.14 *There exists an algorithm for n processors that solves the consensus problem in the presence of f Byzantine failures within $2(f+1)$ rounds using constant size messages, if $n > 4f$.*

5.3 IMPOSSIBILITY IN ASYNCHRONOUS SYSTEMS

We have seen that the consensus problem can be solved in synchronous systems in the presence of failures, both benign (crash) and severe (Byzantine). We now turn to asynchronous systems. We assume that the communication system is completely reliable and the only possible failures are caused by unreliable processors. We show that if the system is completely asynchronous, then there is no consensus algorithm even in the presence of a single processor failure. The result holds even if processors fail only by crashing. The asynchronous nature of the system is crucial for this impossibility proof.

This impossibility result holds both for shared memory systems, if only read/write registers are used, and for message-passing systems. We first present the proof for shared memory systems in the simpler case of an $(n - 1)$-resilient algorithm (also called a *wait-free* algorithm), where all but one of the n processors might fail. Then we use a simulation to deduce the same impossibility result for the harder case of shared memory systems with n processors only one of which might crash. Another simulation, of shared memory in message-passing systems, allows us to obtain the impossibility result for message-passing systems as well.

The only change to the formal model needed is to allow the possibility of processors crashing, in both shared memory and message-passing asynchronous systems. This is done for shared memory simply by changing the definition of admissible executions to require that all but f of the processors must take an infinite number of steps, where f is the resiliency of the system (number of failures to be tolerated). In addition, for message passing, the definition of admissible execution requires that all messages sent must be eventually delivered, except for messages sent by a faulty processor in its last step, which may or may not be delivered.

The precise problem statement is the same as for the synchronous model in Section 5.1.2; we emphasize that x_i and y_i are private state components of processor p_i, not shared variables. We concentrate on the case of trying to decide when the input set is simply $\{0, 1\}$.

5.3.1 Shared Memory—The Wait-Free Case

We first consider the relatively simple situation of $n > 1$ processors all but one of which might crash. That is, we show that there is no wait-free algorithm for consensus in the asynchronous case. We assume that the shared registers are single-writer but multi-reader. (Chapter 10 shows that multi-writer registers can be simulated with single-writer registers, and thus this impossibility result also holds for multi-writer registers.)

The proof proceeds by contradiction. We assume there is a wait-free algorithm and then create an admissible execution in which no processor decides. This proof relies on the notion of bivalence, which was first introduced in Section 5.1.4 for a specific class of executions (failure-sparse ones) in the synchronous model. We adapt the definition to the asynchronous model and generalize it for all admissible executions, as follows.

Throughout this section, we consider only configurations that are reachable from an initial configuration by a prefix of an admissible execution. The *valence* of configuration C is the set of all values that are decided upon, by any processor, in some configuration reachable from C. Here, the term "reachable" is with respect to any execution, and not just failure-sparse executions as it was in Section 5.1.4. In an asynchronous system, a faulty processor cannot be distinguished from a nonfaulty processor in a finite execution, and therefore, the definition of valence refers to the decision of any processor, not just the nonfaulty processors. Bivalence, univalence, 1-valence, and 0-valence are defined analogously to the definitions in Section 5.1.4, but again with regard to any execution, not just failure-sparse ones, and any processor, not just nonfaulty ones.

The proof constructs an infinite execution in which every configuration is bivalent and thus no processor can decide.

In this section, we are concerned with the similarity of *configurations* in a shared memory model, as opposed to the message-passing synchronous lower bound in Section 5.1.4, where we worked with similar *executions*. Here we review Definition 4.1, originally used to study mutual exclusion algorithms: Two configurations C_1 and C_2 are *similar* to processor p_i, denoted $C_1 \overset{p_i}{\sim} C_2$, if the values of all the shared variables and the state of p_i are the same in C_1 and C_2. Lemma 5.15 shows that if two univalent configurations are similar for a single processor, then they cannot have different valences.

Lemma 5.15 *Let C_1 and C_2 be two univalent configurations. If $C_1 \overset{p_i}{\sim} C_2$, for some processor p_i, then C_1 is v-valent if and only if C_2 is v-valent, for $v = 0, 1$.*

Proof. Suppose C_1 is v-valent. Consider an infinite execution from C_1 in which only p_i takes steps. Since the algorithm is supposed to be wait-free, this execution is admissible and eventually p_i must decide. Since C_1 is v-valent, p_i must eventually decide v. Apply the same schedule to C_2. Since $C_1 \overset{p_i}{\sim} C_2$ and only p_i takes steps, it follows that p_i decides v also in the execution from C_2. Thus C_2 is also v-valent. $\square$

Lemma 5.16 states that some initial configuration is bivalent. Exercise 5.15 asks you to prove this fact, which is just a simpler version of Lemma 5.4.

Lemma 5.16 *There exists a bivalent initial configuration.*

Note that given a configuration C, there are n possible configurations that can immediately follow C: one for every possible processor to take the next step. If C is bivalent and the configuration resulting by letting p_i take a step from C is univalent, then p_i is said to be *critical* in C. We next prove that not all the processors can be critical in a bivalent configuration:

Lemma 5.17 *If C is a bivalent configuration, then at least one processor is not critical in C.*

Proof. Assume, by way of contradiction, that all processors are critical in C. Since C is bivalent, it follows that there exist two processors, p_i and p_j, such that $i(C)$ is 0-valent and $j(C)$ is 1-valent. The rest of the proof depends on the type of accesses performed by the processors in these steps.

If p_i and p_j access different registers or if both read the same register, then $i(j(C))$ is the same as $j(i(C))$, which implies that $i(C)$ and $j(C)$ cannot have different valences.

Since registers are single-writer, the only remaining case is when one processor writes to a shared register and the other processor reads from the same register. Without loss of generality, assume that p_i writes to R and p_j reads from R. Consider the configurations $i(C)$ and $i(j(C))$, that is, the configurations resulting when p_i takes a step from C and when p_j and then p_i take a step from C (see Fig. 5.9). Note that $i(j(C))$ is 1-valent and $i(C)$ is 0-valent. However, $i(j(C)) \overset{p_i}{\sim} i(C)$, which contradicts Lemma 5.15. $\square$

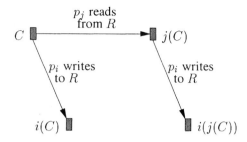

Fig. 5.9 Illustration for the proof of Lemma 5.17.

We now inductively create an admissible execution $C_0 i_1 C_1 i_2 \dots$ in which the configurations remain bivalent forever. Let C_0 be the initial bivalent configuration provided by Lemma 5.16. Suppose the execution has been created up to bivalent configuration C_k. By Lemma 5.17, some processor is not critical in C_k; denote this processor by p_{i_k}. Then p_{i_k} can take a step without resulting in a univalent configuration. We apply the event i_k to C_k to obtain C_{k+1}, which is bivalent, and repeat the process again.

The execution constructed in this manner is admissible for the wait-free case, because at least one processor takes an infinite number of steps. It is possible that after some point, all the p_{i_k}'s are the same, meaning that $n - 1$ processors have failed. The strong assumption of wait freedom made our life easier in constructing this counterexample execution (cf. the complications in modifying this proof for the 1-resilient case in Exercise 5.18).

To summarize, we have constructed an admissible execution in which all the configurations are bivalent. Therefore, no processor ever decides, contradicting the termination property of the algorithm and implying:

Theorem 5.18 *There is no wait-free algorithm for solving the consensus problem in an asynchronous shared memory system with n processors.*

5.3.2 Shared Memory—The General Case

The impossibility proof of Section 5.3.1 assumed that the consensus algorithm is wait-free, that is, each processor must be able to decide even when all other processors fail. However, a stronger claim holds: There is no consensus algorithm even if only one processor may fail. This section proves this impossibility result. There exists a direct proof of this claim (see the chapter notes and Exercise 5.18); here we prove the more general result by reduction to the impossibility result of Section 5.3.1. Specifically, we assume, by way of contradiction, that there is a consensus algorithm for a system of $n > 2$ processors that tolerates the failure of one processor and show that there is a wait-free consensus algorithm for a system of two processors, that is, an algorithm that tolerates the failure of one processor. (Note that in the case of two processors, an algorithm that tolerates the failure of one processor is wait-free, and vice versa.) As we just proved that there can be no wait-free algorithm for any value of n, including $n = 2$, the assumed 1-resilient algorithm cannot exist.

5.3.2.1 *Overview of Simulation*

The reduction works by having two processors *simulate* the code of the local algorithms (state machines) of the n processors. To explain the idea in more detail, let us denote the n *simulated* processors by $q_0, \ldots, q_{n-1}$ and, as usual, denote the two *simulating* processors by p_0 and p_1.

A simple approach to the simulation would be to let p_0 simulate half of the processors and let p_1 simulate the other half of the processors. Under this approach, however, a failure of a *single* simulating processor may lead to the failure of a *majority* of the simulated processors. Thus we would only be able to derive the impossibility of solving consensus when a majority of the processors may fail, and not when just a single processor may fail.

Instead, each of p_0 and p_1 goes through the codes of $q_0, \ldots, q_{n-1}$, in round-robin order, and tries to simulate their computation, one step at a time. Each simulating processor uses its input as the input for each simulated code. Once a decision is made by some simulated code, this decision is taken as the output by the simulating processor, which then stops the simulation.

It is possible that both p_0 and p_1 may try to simulate the same step, say, the kth, of the same simulated processor, q_j. To guarantee the consistency of the simulation, we require that p_0 and p_1 agree on each step of each simulated processor. Roughly and glossing over some details, this is done as follows: When a simulating processor simulates the kth step of q_j, it writes its suggestion for this step, then it checks to see whether the other processor has written a suggestion for the kth step of q_j. If the other processor has not yet written a suggestion, the first processor declares itself as the winner (by setting a flag to be 1), and its suggestion is used henceforth as the kth step for the simulated processor q_j. Otherwise, if the other processor has already written a suggestion, the first processor sets its flag to be 0. If both processors set their flags to 0, processors subsequently break the tie by using the suggestion of p_0 as the kth simulated step. (This is very similar to the asymmetric code for two-processor mutual exclusion, Algorithm 11.)

There are situations when it is not clear which processor wins, for example, if the flag of p_0 is 0 and the flag of p_1 is not yet set for the last simulated step of some processor q_j. In this case, we cannot know the result of this step until p_1 sets its flag. Thus the simulation of the code of q_j might be blocked if p_1 fails before writing its flag. Superficially, this seems to imply that the simulation algorithm is not wait-free. Yet, note that the reason we are blocked is that some simulating processor (in the above example, p_1) is in the middle of simulating a step of q_j. Clearly, this means it is not in the middle of simulating any step of any other simulated processor $q_{j'}$. As we shall show below, this means that the other processor (in the above example, p_0) can continue to simulate the other processors' codes on its own until it is able to decide. Thus the simulation of at most one processor can be stuck.

We now discuss the main details that were glossed over in the above description, namely, what a step is and what the suggestions made by simulating processors are. We make the following assumptions about the algorithm being simulated:

1. Each processor q_j can write to a single shared register, whose initial value is arbitrary

2. The code of each processor q_j consists of strictly alternating read steps and write steps, beginning with a read step

3. Each write step of each processor q_j writes q_j's current state into q_j's shared register

There is no loss of generality in making these assumptions, because any algorithm in which processors communicate by reading and writing single-writer multi-reader registers can be expressed in this form. (See Exercise 5.23.)

Thus q_j's computation is a sequence of *pairs* of read steps and write steps. Each pair can be viewed as a kind of "super-step" in which q_j reads the state of some other processor $q_{j'}$, changes its local state, based on its previous state and the value read, and writes its new state. Of course, the read and write are not done atomically—other steps of other processors can be interposed between them. The suggestions made by the simulating processors can be different and must be reconciled in the simulation. The state of the simulated processor can be read only after the suggestions are reconciled. Thus the suggestions are for the states of simulated processors (which equal the values of shared registers) at the end of the pairs, that is, after the write steps.

5.3.2.2 *The Simulation*
The algorithm employs the following shared data structures. For each simulating processor p_i, $i = 0, 1$, for each simulated processor q_j, $j = 0, \ldots, n - 1$, and for each integer $k \geq 0$, there are two registers, both written by p_i and read by p_{1-i}:

Suggest$[j, k, i]$: The state of simulated processor q_j at the end of the kth pair, as suggested by simulating processor p_i. The initial value is $\perp$.

Flag$[j, k, i]$: The competition flag of simulating processor p_i, for the kth pair of simulated processor q_j. The initial value is $\perp$.

In addition, each simulating processor maintains some local variables for bookkeeping during the simulation. The main local variable is an array *lastpair*, where *lastpair*$[j]$ is the number of pairs of steps by q_j that it has simulated. The meanings of the other local variables should be obvious from their usage in the code.

The pseudocode for the simulation appears in Algorithm 17. The function transition, given a simulated processor, the current state, and the value read, produces the next state of the simulated processor, according to its code.

5.3.2.3 *Correctness Proof*
All the lemmas are with respect to an arbitrary admissible execution of the simulation algorithm. We start with some basic properties of the synchronization structure of the algorithm. The following simple lemma holds because, for each pair, a simulating processor first sets its own suggestion and then

---

Algorithm 17 Simulating n processors and one failure:
code for p_i, $i = 0, 1$.

Initially $lastpair[j] = 0, 0 \leq j \leq n - 1$

```
 1:  j := 0                                              // start with q₀
 2:  while true do
 3:      if computed(j,lastpair[j]) then        // previous pair for qⱼ is computed
 4:          k, lastpair[j] := lastpair[j] + 1
 5:          if Flag[j, k, 1 − i] ≠ 1 then            // other processor has not won
 6:              s := get-state(j, k − 1)
 7:              if s is a decision state of qⱼ then
 8:                  decide same and terminate
 9:              r := simulated processor whose variable is
                        to be read next according to s
10:              v := get-read(r)
11:              Suggest[j, k, i] := transition(j, s, v)         // new state for qⱼ
12:              if Suggest[j, k, 1 − i] = ⊥ then              // pᵢ has won
13:                  Flag[j, k, i] := 1
14:              else Flag[j, k, i] := 0
15:      j := (j + 1) mod n                        // go to next simulated processor

16: function computed(j, k)                  // has kth pair of qⱼ been computed?
17:     if k = 0 then return true
18:     if Flag[j, k, 0] = 1 or Flag[j, k, 1] = 1 then return true
19:     if Flag[j, k, 0] = 0 and Flag[j, k, 1] = 0 then return true  // need not reread
20:     return false

21: function get-state(j, ℓ)                      // return state of qⱼ after ℓth pair
22:     if ℓ = 0 then return initial state of qⱼ with input equal to pᵢ's input
23:     w := winner(j, ℓ)                   // who won competition on ℓth pair of qⱼ?
24:     return Suggest[j, ℓ, w]

25: function get-read(r)                     // return current value of qᵣ's variable
26:     m := 1
27:     while computed(r, m) do m := m + 1
                // m − 1 is largest numbered pair that is computed for qᵣ
28:     if m − 1 = 0 then return initial value of qᵣ's variable
29:     return get-state(r, m − 1)

30: function winner(j, k)                   // who won competition on kth pair of qⱼ?
31:     if Flag[j, k, 1] = 1 then return 1 else return 0
```

---

checks the other processor's suggestion. Therefore, at least one of them sees the other processor's suggestion and sets its flag to be 0.

Lemma 5.19 *For every simulated processor q_j and every $k \geq 1$, at most one of $Flag[j, k, 0]$ and $Flag[j, k, 1]$ equals 1 in every configuration.*

This implies that if one processor's flag is set to 1, then the other processor's flag will be set to 0, if it is set at all. Note, however, that it is possible that both processors will set their flags to 0, if they write their suggestions "together" and then read each other's. We say that k is a *computed pair* of q_j either if $Flag[j, k, 0]$ and $Flag[j, k, 1]$ are both set or one of them is not set and the other one equals 1. We define the *winner* of the kth computed pair of q_j to be the simulating processor p_i, $i = 0, 1$, that sets $Flag[j,k,i]$ to 1, if there is such a processor, and to be p_0 otherwise. By Lemma 5.19, the winner is well-defined. Note that the function winner is only called for computed pairs and it returns the id of the winner, according to this definition. Furthermore, the procedures get-state and get-read return the winner's suggestion.

There is a slight asymmetry between get-state and get-read for pair 0: get-state returns the initial state of the processor, which includes the input value, whereas get-read returns the initial value of the register, which does not include the input value.

Each processor p_i executes Lines 4 through 14 of the main code with particular values of j and k at most once; we will refer to the execution of these lines as p_i's simulation of q_j's kth pair.

Lemma 5.20 states that if one processor simulates a pair on its own (in the sense made precise by the lemma), then its flag will be set to 1. As a result, its suggestion for this pair will be taken subsequently.

Lemma 5.20 *For every simulated processor q_j, and every $k \geq 1$, if simulating processor p_i executes Line 12 of its simulation of q_j's kth pair before p_{1-i} executes Line 11 of its simulation of q_j's kth pair, then p_i sets $Flag[j, k, i]$ to 1.*

Thus, if one processor simulates on its own, it is able to decide on the simulated pair without waiting for the other simulating processor. We can already argue progress:

Lemma 5.21 *Suppose simulating processor p_i never fails or decides. Then the values of its lastpair$[j]$ variable grow without bound, for all j, $0 \leq j \leq n - 1$, except possibly one.*

Proof. Suppose there exists a simulated processor q_{j_0} such that simulating processor p_i's *lastpair*$[j_0]$ variable does not grow without bound. Since the variable never decreases, it reaches some value k_0 and never changes. Since p_i is stuck on pair k_0 for q_{j_0}, p_i writes 0 to $Flag[j_0, k_0, i]$ and never finds $Flag[j_0, k_0, 1 - i]$ set. This behavior is caused by the other simulating processor, p_{1-i}, crashing after writing $Suggest[j_0, k_0, 1 - i]$ in Line 11 and before writing $Flag[j_0, k_0, 1 - i]$ in Line 13 or 14.

Suppose, in contradiction, that p_i also fails to make progress on q_{j_1} for some $j_1 \neq j_0$. Let k_1 be the highest value reached by p_i's *lastpair*$[j_1]$ variable. It is not hard to see that k_1 is at least 1.

By the assumption that p_i is stuck on the k_1-th pair for q_{j_1}, computed(j_1, k_1) is never true. Thus neither $Flag[j_1, k_1, i]$ nor $Flag[j_1, k_1, 1 - i]$ is ever set to 1. As a result, p_i executes Lines 6 through 14 of its simulation of q_{j_1}'s k_1-th pair. By Lemma 5.20, it must be that p_i executes Line 12 of its simulation of q_{j_1}'s k_1-th pair after p_{1-i} executes Line 11 of its simulation of q_{j_1}'s k_1-th pair, or else p_i would set its flag to 1. Thus p_i finds the other processor's suggestion already set and sets its flag to 0. Since computed(j_1, k_1) is never true, it must be that p_{1-i} never sets its flag, that is, it fails after Line 11 but before Line 13 or 14 of its simulation of q_{j_1}'s k_1-th pair. But this contradicts the fact that p_{1-i} fails during the simulation of q_{j_0}, not q_{j_1}.

$\square$

The above lemma guarantees that if one simulating processor does not halt, then it makes progress through the simulated codes of at least $n - 1$ processors. Yet this does not necessarily mean that the processor will eventually decide correctly, or even decide at all. This will follow only if we show that the codes are simulated correctly. To prove this, we explicitly construct, for each admissible execution α of the simulation, a corresponding admissible execution β of $q_0, \ldots, q_{n-1}$, in which the same state transitions are made and at most one (simulated) processor fails. Because the algorithm of $q_0, \ldots, q_{n-1}$ is assumed to solve the consensus problem in the presence of one fault, it follows that the nonfaulty simulated processors eventually decide correctly in β and, therefore, the nonfaulty simulating processors eventually decide correctly in α.

For every simulated processor q_j, and every $k \leq 1$, we first identify two points in α: one for the read done in the kth pair from the register of some other processor and another for the write to q_j's register in the kth pair. Note that because the simulated algorithm is for the read/write model, these points can be separate. The *read point* is when the winner of the kth pair of q_j returns from the last call to computed in Line 27 of get-read. This is the call that returns false, based on the values of the two flags that are read. The *write point* is when the winner of the kth pair of q_j sets its flag to 1, or, if neither flag is ever set to 1, when the second simulating processor writes 0 to its flag.

Strictly speaking, the read point specified above is not well-defined, because the execution of computed does two reads and thus does not correspond to a single event in α. Note, however, that one of these flags is the winner's own flag and, therefore, this read need not be from the shared memory, but can instead be done from a copy in the local memory. Therefore, the execution of computed translates into a single shared memory operation, and the read point is well-defined.[4]

The next lemma shows that the values returned by get-read in α are consistent with the read and write points defined.

Lemma 5.22 *Let v be the value suggested by the winner of q_j's kth pair, that is, v is the value written to $Suggest[j, k, i]$, where $i = $ winner(j, k). Then, in α, any read*

---

[4]Another solution is to use atomic snapshots, which will be defined in Chapter 10.

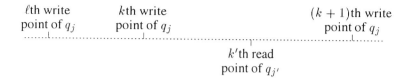

Fig. 5.10 Illustration for the proof of Lemma 5.22, $\ell \leq k$.

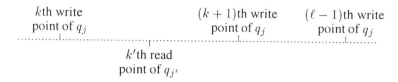

Fig. 5.11 Illustration for the proof of Lemma 5.22, $\ell > k + 1$.

from the register of q_j whose read point is between the kth write point of q_j and the $(k+1)$st write point of q_j (if it exists) returns v.

Proof. Consider some pair, say the k'-th, of $q_{j'}$ that reads from the register of q_j, such that its read point is between the kth write point of q_j and the next write point of q_j. Without loss of generality, assume p_0 is the winner for this pair of $q_{j'}$ and let ℓ be the value of m when p_0 finishes Line 27 of procedure get-read. We argue that $\ell = k + 1$, which proves the lemma.

If $\ell \leq k$ then, since the write point of the kth pair of q_j is before the read point of the k'th pair of $q_{j'}$, the write point of the ℓth pair of q_j is also before the read point of the k'th pair of $q_{j'}$ (see Fig. 5.10). Therefore, either the winner of the ℓth pair of q_j has set its flag to 1 or both simulating processors wrote 0 to their flags, before the read point of the k'th pair of $q_{j'}$. Thus when p_0 checks computed(j, ℓ) in the while loop of get-read, it continues the loop beyond ℓ, a contradiction.

On the other hand, if $\ell > k + 1$, then the write point for the $(\ell - 1)$th pair of q_j is after the read point of the k'th pair of $q_{j'}$ (see Fig. 5.11). Therefore, at the read point of the k'th pair of $q_{j'}$, the winner of the ℓth pair of q_j has not written 1 to its flag, and one of the processors has not written at all to its flag. Therefore, in Line 27 of get-read, p_0 finds computed$(j, k + 1)$ false and exits the while loop at $k + 1$, which is less than ℓ, a contradiction. $\qquad\square$

We now construct an execution β of $q_0, \ldots, q_{n-1}$ based on execution α; we will show a precise correspondence between the two executions that will allow us to deduce the desired impossibility.

Consider the sequence of read and write points, for all simulated processors, in α. (The occurrence of the points forms a sequence because each point is an atomic occurrence in α.) Let σ be the sequence of simulated processor indices corresponding to the read and write points. Define an initial configuration C_0, in which the input value of each q_i is the input value of the simulating processor that is the winner for the first pair of q_i. If there is no winner for the first pair of q_i, then use p_0's input as the input value of q_i in C_0. Let β be the execution of $q_0, \ldots, q_{n-1}$ obtained by starting with C_0 and applying computation events in the order specified by σ. In other words, we let the simulated processors take steps in the order of their read and write points in α.

Lemma 5.23 shows that the values suggested by the winners for the pairs in α are consistent with the states and register values in β.

Lemma 5.23 *Let q_j be any processor and k be such that q_j executes at least $k > 0$ pairs in β. Then in α,*
(a) eventually computed(j, k) is true, and, after that point,
(b) the value of Suggest$[j, k, w]$, where w is winner(j, k), is equal to the value of q_j's state (and shared register) after its kth pair in β.

Proof.   (a) By the construction of β from α, if q_j executes at least k pairs in β, it must be that computed(j, k) is set to true.

(b) We will prove this by induction on the prefixes of α.

For the basis, we consider the initial configuration of α. Since every processor has completed 0 pairs at this point, the lemma is vacuously true.

Suppose the lemma is true for prefix α' of α. Let π be the next event in α following α'. If π does not cause any additional pair to be computed, then the lemma remains true.

Suppose π causes computed(j, k) to become true. Let i be winner(j, k).

First, we show that p_i's execution of get-state$(j, k - 1)$ returns the correct value. If $k = 1$ (this is the first pair by q_j), then get-state$(j, k - 1)$ returns the initial state of q_j, with input equal to p_i's input. If $k > 1$, then get-state$(j, k - 1)$ returns Suggest$[j, k - 1, w]$, where w is winner$(j, k - 1)$. By the inductive hypothesis, Suggest$[j, k - 1, w]$ equals the value of q_j's state (and shared register) after its $(k - 1)$-st pair in β. Let s be the value returned by get-state$(j, k - 1)$.

Suppose the read step of q_j's kth pair involves reading the register of q_r and at the time of this read, q_r has performed h pairs (and thus h writes).

We now show that p_i's execution of get-read(r) returns the correct value. If $h = 0$, then get-read(r) returns the initial value of q_r's variable. If $h > 0$, then get-read(r) returns Suggest$[r, h, w']$, where w' is winner(r, h). By the inductive hypothesis, Suggest$[r, h, w']$, equals the value of q_r's state (and shared register) after its hth pair in β. By construction of β, the read point of this execution of get-read is between the hth and $(h + 1)$st write points of q_r. By Lemma 5.22, the value read is correct. Let v be the value returned by get-read(r).

Thus the winning suggestion for q_j's kth pair is transition(j, s, v), which is the value of q_j's state after its kth pair in β. $\square$

Exercise 5.24 asks you to put together the pieces shown by Lemma 5.21 and Lemma 5.23 in order to prove that Algorithm 17 correctly simulates an n-processor consensus algorithm with two processors. Consequently, if there is a 1-resilient consensus algorithm for n processors, then there is a 1-resilient consensus algorithm for two processors. But a 1-resilient consensus algorithm for two processors is wait-free, and Theorem 5.18 states that no such algorithm can exist. Thus we have proved:

Theorem 5.24 *There is no consensus algorithm for a read/write asynchronous shared memory system that can tolerate even a single crash failure.*

5.3.3 Message Passing

Finally, we extend the result of Section 5.3.2 to message-passing systems. Again, this is done by simulation; that is, we show how to simulate a message-passing algorithm by a shared memory algorithm. Therefore, if there is a message-passing algorithm for consensus there would be a shared memory algorithm for consensus, which is impossible (Theorem 5.24).

The simulation is simple: For each ordered pair of processors we have a separate single-writer single-reader register. The "sender" writes every new message it wishes to send in this register by appending the new message to the prior contents, and the "receiver" polls this register at every step to see whether the sender has sent anything new. This can be very easily done, if we assume that registers can hold an infinite number of values.

Because the receiver needs to check whether a message was sent by a number of senders, it has to poll a number of registers (one for each sender). However, in each computation step, the receiver can read only one register. Therefore, the reader should read the registers in a round-robin manner, checking each register only once every number of steps. This scheme introduces some delay, because a message is not necessarily read by the reader immediately after it is written by the sender. However, this delay causes no problems, because the message-passing algorithm is asynchronous and can withstand arbitrary message delays. As a result:

Theorem 5.25 *There is no algorithm for solving the consensus problem in an asynchronous message-passing system with n processors, one of which may fail by crashing.*

Exercises

5.1 Show that for two-element input sets, the validity condition given in Section 5.1.2 is equivalent to requiring that every nonfaulty decision be the input of some processor.

5.2 Consider a synchronous system in which processors fail by *clean* crashes, that is, in a round, a processor either sends all its messages or none. Design an algorithm that solves the consensus problem in one round.

5.3 (a) Modify Algorithm 15 to achieve consensus within f rounds, in the case $f = n - 1$.

Algorithm 18 k-set consensus algorithm in the presence of crash failures: code for processor p_i, $0 \leq i \leq n - 1$.

Initially $V = \{x\}$

1:    round r, $1 \leq r \leq \frac{f}{k} + 1$:   // assume that k divides f
2:       send V to all processors
3:       receive S_j from p_j, $0 \leq j \leq n - 1$, $j \neq i$
4:       $V := V \cup \bigcup_{j=0}^{n-1} S_j$
5:       if $r = f/k + 1$ then $y := \min(V)$ // decide

(b) Show that f is a lower bound on the number of rounds required in this case.

5.4 Design a consensus algorithm for crash failures with the following *early stopping* property: If f' processors fail in an execution, then the algorithm terminates within $O(f')$ rounds.

Hint: Processors need not decide in the same round.

5.5 Define the *k-set consensus* problem as follows. Each processor starts with some arbitrary integer value x_i and should output an integer value y_i such that:

Validity: $y_i \in \{x_0, \ldots, x_{n-1}\}$, and

k-Agreement: the number of different output values is at most k.

Show that Algorithm 18 solves the k-set consensus problem in the presence of f crash failures, for any $f < n$. The algorithm is similar to Algorithm 15 (for consensus in the presence of crash failures) and is based on collecting information.

What is the message complexity of the algorithm?

5.6 Present a synchronous algorithm for solving the k-set consensus problem in the presence of $f = n - 1$ crash failures using an algorithm for consensus as a black box. Using Algorithm 15 as the black box, the round complexity of the algorithm should be $(\frac{n}{k} + 1)$, and its message complexity should be $O(\frac{n^2}{k}|V|)$, where $|V|$ is the number of possible input values. For simplicity assume that k divides n.

5.7 Show that, if the input set has more than two elements, the validity condition given in Section 5.2.2 is not equivalent to requiring that every nonfaulty decision be the input of some processor. In particular, design an algorithm that satisfies the validity condition of Section 5.2.2 but does not guarantee that every nonfaulty decision is the input of some processor.

Hint: Consider the exponential message and phase king algorithms when the size of the input set is larger than 2.

5.8 Consider the exponential message consensus algorithm described in Section 5.2.4. By the result of Section 5.2.3, the algorithm does not work correctly if $n = 6$ and $f = 2$. Construct an execution for this system in which the algorithm violates the conditions of the consensus problem.

5.9 Repeat Exercise 5.8 for the polynomial message algorithm of Section 5.2.5.

5.10 Prove that $\alpha_2 \overset{p_2}{\sim} \alpha_3$ in the proof of Theorem 5.7.

5.11 Modify the exponential information gathering algorithm in Section 5.2.4 to reduce the number of messages to be $O(f^3 + fn)$.

5.12 Show that to satisfy the stronger validity condition (every nonfaulty decision is some nonfaulty input) for Byzantine failures, n must be greater than $\max(3, m) \cdot f$, where m is the size of the input set.

5.13 Assuming n is sufficiently large, modify the exponential message algorithm of Section 5.2.4 to satisfy the stronger validity condition of Exercise 5.12.

5.14 Assuming n is sufficiently large, modify the polynomial message algorithm of Section 5.2.5 to satisfy the stronger validity condition of Exercise 5.12.

5.15 Prove Lemma 5.16. That is, assume there is a wait-free consensus algorithm for the asynchronous shared memory system and prove that it has a bivalent initial configuration.

5.16 Consider a variation of the consensus problem in which the validity condition is the following: There must be at least one admissible execution with decision value 0, and there must be at least one admissible execution with decision value 1. Prove that there is no wait-free algorithm for this problem in an asynchronous system.

Hint: Modify the the proof of the existence of a bivalent initial configuration (Lemma 5.16).

5.17 In the *transaction commit* problem for distributed databases, each of n processors forms an independent opinion whether to commit or abort a distributed transaction. The processors must come to a consistent decision such that if even one processor's opinion is to abort, then the transaction is aborted, and if all processors' opinions are to commit, then the transaction is committed. Is this problem solvable in an asynchronous system subject to crash failures? Why or why not?

5.18 This exercise guides you through a direct proof of the impossibility of 1-resilient consensus for shared memory. Assume A is a 1-resilient consensus algorithm for n processors in shared memory.

(a) Prove that there is a bivalent initial configuration of A.

(b) Let D be a bivalent configuration of A and p_i be any processor. Using the outline given below, prove that there exists a schedule σ ending with the event i such that $\sigma(D)$ is bivalent.

Outline: Suppose, in contradiction, that there is no such schedule. Then every schedule that ends in i, when started at D, leads to a univalent configuration. Without loss of generality, assume that $i(D)$ is 0-valent.

(b.1) Show that there exists a finite schedule α, in which p_i does not take a step, and a processor p_j other than p_i, such that $i(\alpha(D))$ is 0-valent and $i(j(\alpha(D)))$ is 1-valent.

(b.2) Let $D_0 = \alpha(D)$ and $D_1 = j(\alpha(D))$. Consider the possible actions being performed by p_i and p_j in taking a step from D_0 (e.g., reading or writing) and show that a contradiction is obtained in each case.

(c) Combine (a) and (b) above to show there exists an admissible execution of A that does not satisfy the termination condition.

5.19 Consider an asynchronous shared memory system in which there are only test&set registers (as defined in Chapter 4) and two processors. Show that it is possible to solve consensus in this system even if one processor can crash.

5.20 Show that the consensus problem cannot be solved in an asynchronous system with only test&set registers and three processors, if two processors may fail by crashing. The proof may follow Section 5.3.1:

    1. Define $C \overset{\neg\{p_i,p_j\}}{\sim} C'$ to mean that C is similar to C' for all processors but p_i and p_j.

    2. Argue why Lemma 5.16 holds in this case as well.

    3. Prove Lemma 5.17 for this model. (This is where most of the work is.)

5.21 Show that consensus cannot be solved in an asynchronous shared memory system with only test&set registers, with $n > 2$ processors, two of which may fail by crashing.

5.22 Can consensus be solved in an asynchronous shared memory system with $n > 2$ processors, two of which may fail by crashing, if we allow read/write operations, in addition to test&set operations?

5.23 Argue why the restricted form of the algorithms assumed in Section 5.3.2 does not lose any generality.

5.24 Prove that Algorithm 17 correctly simulates an n-processor consensus algorithm with two processors.

5.25 Modify Algorithm 17 (and its correctness proof) so that get-read skips steps that are known to be computed (based on *lastpair*).

5.26 An alternative version of the consensus problem requires that the input value of one distinguished processor (called the *general*) be distributed to all the other processors (called the *lieutenants*); this problem is known as *single-source consensus*. In more detail, the conditions to be satisfied are:

Termination: Every nonfaulty lieutenant must eventually decide

Agreement: All the nonfaulty lieutenants must have the same decision

Validity: If the general is nonfaulty, then the common decision value is the general's input.

The difference is in the validity condition: note that if the general is faulty, then the nonfaulty processors need not decide on the general's input but they must still agree with each other. Consider the synchronous message-passing model subject to Byzantine faults. Show how to transform a solution to the consensus problem into a solution to the general's problem and vice versa. What are the message and round overheads of your transformations?

Chapter Notes

The consensus problem was introduced by Lamport, Pease, and Shostak in two papers [163, 207]. The problem was originally defined for Byzantine failures. The simple algorithm for solving consensus in the presence of crash failures presented in Section 5.1.3 is based on an algorithm of Dolev and Strong that uses authentication to handle more severe failures [99]. The lower bound on the number of rounds needed for solving consensus was originally proved by Fischer and Lynch [107] for Byzantine failures and was later extended to crash failures by Dolev and Strong [99]. Subsequent work simplified and strengthened the lower bound [101, 185, 193]. Our presentation is based on that by Aguilera and Toueg [7].

After considering crash failures, we turned to the Byzantine failure model; this is a good model for human malfeasance. It is a worst-case assumption and is also applicable to machine errors—it covers the situation when a seemingly less malicious fault happens at just the wrong time for the software, causing the most damage. If a system designer is not sure exactly how errors will be manifested, a conservative assumption is that they will be Byzantine.

The $3f + 1$ lower bound on the number of faulty processors as well as the simple exponential algorithm were first proved in [207]. Our presentation follows later formulations of these results by Fischer, Lynch, and Merritt [109] for the $3f + 1$ lower bound, and by Bar-Noy, Dolev, Dwork, and Strong [44] for the exponential algorithm of Section 5.2.4. We also presented a consensus algorithm with constant message size (Algorithm 16); this algorithm is due to Berman and Garay [50]. Garay and Moses present a consensus algorithm tolerating Byzantine failures; the algorithm sends messages with polynomial size, works in $f + 1$ rounds, and requires only that $n > 3f$ [119].

There is an efficient reduction from the consensus problem with a general to ordinary consensus by Turpin and Coan [255].

The consensus algorithms we have presented assume that all processors can directly exchange messages with each other; this means that the topology of the communication graph is a clique. For other topologies, Dolev [91] has shown that a necessary and sufficient condition for the existence of a consensus algorithm tolerating Byzantine failures is that the connectivity of the graph is at least $2f + 1$. Fischer, Lynch, and Merritt present an alternative proof for the necessity of this condition, using an argument similar to the $3f + 1$ lower bound on the number of faulty processors [109].

Exercises 5.12 through 5.14 were suggested by Neiger [196].

The impossibility of achieving consensus in an asynchronous system was first proved in a breakthrough paper by Fischer, Lynch, and Paterson [110]. Their proof dealt only with message-passing systems. Exercise 5.18 walks through their proof, adapted for shared memory. Later, the impossibility result was extended to the shared memory model by Loui and Abu-Amara [173] and (implicitly) by Dolev, Dwork, and Stockmeyer [92]. Loui and Abu-Amara [173] provide a complete direct proof of the general impossibility result for shared memory systems. Special cases of this result were also proved by Chor, Israeli, and Li [81]. Loui and Abu-Amara also studied the possibility of solving consensus by using test&set operations (see Exercises 5.19 through 5.22).

We have chosen to prove the impossibility result by first concentrating on the shared memory wait-free case and then extending it to the other cases, a single failure and message-passing systems, by reduction. Not only is the shared memory wait-free case simpler, but this also fits better with our aim of unifying models of distributed computation by showing simulations (explored in more depth in Part II of the book).

The impossibility proof for the shared memory wait-free case follows Herlihy [134], who uses the consensus problem to study the "power" of various object types, as shall be seen in Chapter 15. The simulation result for 1-resiliency is based on the algorithm of Borowsky and Gafni [58].

The simulation depends on the ability to map the inputs of the simulating processors into inputs of the simulated algorithm and then to map back the outputs of the simulated algorithm to outputs of the simulating processors. This mapping is trivial for the consensus problem but is not necessarily so for other problems; for more discussion of this issue and another description of the simulation, see the work of Borowsky, Gafni, Lynch, and Rajsbaum [59].

6

Causality and Time

Notions of causality and time play an important role in the design of distributed algorithms. It is often helpful to know the relative order in which events take place in the system. This knowledge can be achieved even in totally asynchronous systems that have no way of measuring the passage of real time, by observing the causality relations between events. In the first part of this chapter, we precisely define the causality relationships in a distributed system and study mechanisms for observing them.

In many systems, processors have access to real-time measuring devices, either in the form of hardware clocks, by tuning in to a satellite clock, or by reading the time across a communication network. Solutions to many problems in distributed systems are much simpler or more efficient if clocks are available and provide good readings of real time. Therefore, this chapter also considers the problem of getting clocks to provide good approximations of real time.

The message-passing systems considered in this chapter can have arbitrary topologies.

This is the first of three chapters that address issues of causality and time in distributed systems. Chapter 11 presents methods for running algorithms designed for one set of timing assumptions in systems that provide another set of assumptions. Chapter 13 considers the problem of maintaining synchronized clocks in the presence of drift and faults.

6.1 CAPTURING CAUSALITY

Let us now take a more careful look at the structure of executions and the relationships between events in a distributed system. We mostly address asynchronous message-passing systems, but at the end of this section, we describe how to extend the same notions to shared memory systems.

Because executions are sequences of events, they induce a total order on all the events. Because a sequence orders all events with respect to each other, this way of describing executions loses information. For example, it is possible that two computation events by different processors do not influence each other, yet they are (arbitrarily) ordered by the execution. The structure of causality between events is lost.

We start by carefully defining the notion of one computation event influencing another computation event. Then we define *logical clocks*, which are a way for assigning timestamps to computation events in a manner that captures the causality structure on them. We also present a variant of logical clocks, called *vector clocks*, which indicate whether one event does *not* influence another as well as indicating whether one event does influence another.

6.1.1 The Happens-Before Relation

We now take a more careful look at the information about the causality relations between computation events that is contained in an execution. Let us fix some execution α.

First, consider two events[1] ϕ_1 and ϕ_2 by the same processor p_i. One event ϕ_1 of p_i can causally influence another event ϕ_2 of p_i only if ϕ_1 occurs before ϕ_2 at p_i, because we assume that each processor is a sequential process. The execution respects this ordering.

Next, consider two events by different processors. The only way for one processor to influence another processor is by sending a message to the other processor. That is, an event ϕ_1 of processor p_i causally influences an event ϕ_2 of processor p_j if ϕ_1 is the event that sends message m from p_i to p_j and ϕ_2 is the event in which the message m is received by p_j. Recall that in our formal model, a processor can receive several messages and send several messages at the same (computation) event.

Finally, note that events can causally influence each other indirectly through other events. See Figure 6.1. (The figures in this chapter represent an execution as a set of sequences, one per processor, with arrows between sequences representing messages, in order to highlight the causality, or lack of causality, between events. For simplicity, we depict only one message being sent or received at each event.) In this figure, ϕ_1 influences ϕ_2 because it is an earlier event of the same processor p_0; ϕ_2 influences ϕ_{13} because the message sent by p_0 at ϕ_2 is received by p_2 in ϕ_{13}; by transitivity, ϕ_1 influences ϕ_{13}.

---

[1] For the rest of this section only, "event" means "computation event," when this should not cause confusion.

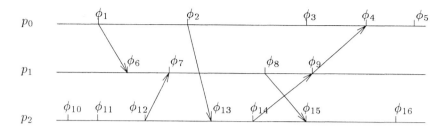

Fig. 6.1   Causal influence in an example execution.

To summarize the above discussion, the happens-before relation for execution α is formally defined as follows. Given two events ϕ_1 and ϕ_2 in α, ϕ_1 *happens before* ϕ_2, denoted $\phi_1 \overset{\alpha}{\Rightarrow} \phi_2$, if one of the following conditions holds:

1. ϕ_1 and ϕ_2 are events by the same processor p_i, and ϕ_1 occurs before ϕ_2 in α.

2. ϕ_1 is the send event of the message m from p_i to p_j, and ϕ_2 is the receive event of the message m by p_j.

3. There exists an event ϕ such that $\phi_1 \overset{\alpha}{\Rightarrow} \phi$ and $\phi \overset{\alpha}{\Rightarrow} \phi_2$.

The first condition captures the causality relation between events of the same processor, the second condition captures the causality relation between events of different processors, and the third condition induces transitivity. Obviously, $\overset{\alpha}{\Rightarrow}$ is an irreflexive partial order.

The important property of the happens-before relation is that it completely characterizes the causality relations in an execution. In particular, if the events of an execution are reordered with respect to each other but without altering the happens-before relation, the result is still an execution and it is indistinguishable to the processors.

The reorderings that can occur without affecting the happens-before relation do not change the order in which events occur at individual processors and do not cause a message to be delivered before it is sent. Other than these constraints, events at different processors can be reshuffled.

We make the following more precise definition.

Definition 6.1 *Given an execution segment $\alpha = exec(C, \sigma)$, a permutation π of a schedule σ is a* causal shuffle *of σ if*

1. for all i, $0 \leq i \leq n - 1$, $\sigma|i = \pi|i$, and

2. if a message m is sent during processor p_i's (computation) event ϕ in α, then in π, ϕ precedes the delivery of m.

See an example in Figure 6.2.

The next two lemmas follow directly from the definitions of the happens-before relation, causal shuffle, and similarity.

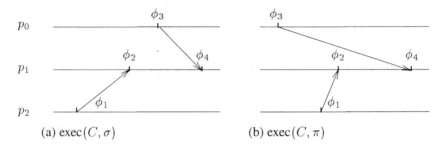

Fig. 6.2 π is a causal shuffle of σ.

Lemma 6.1 *Let $\alpha = exec(C, \sigma)$ be an execution fragment. Then any total ordering of the events in σ that is consistent with the happens-before relation of α is a causal shuffle of σ.*

Lemma 6.2 *Let $\alpha = exec(C, \sigma)$ be an execution fragment. Let π be a causal shuffle of σ. Then $\alpha' = exec(C, \pi)$ is an execution fragment and is similar to α.*

Informally, this means that if two executions have the 'same' happens-before relation, then they are similar.

6.1.2 Logical Clocks

How can processors *observe* the happens-before relation in an execution α? One possible way is to attach a tag, commonly called a *logical timestamp*, to each (computation) event. That is, with each event ϕ, we associate a timestamp, $LT(\phi)$; to capture the happens-before relation, we require an irreflexive partial order $<$ on the timestamps, such that for every pair of events, ϕ_1 and ϕ_2,

$$\text{if } \phi_1 \overset{\alpha}{\Rightarrow} \phi_2, \text{ then } LT(\phi_1) < LT(\phi_2)$$

The following simple algorithm can be used to maintain logical timestamps correctly. Each processor p_i keeps a local variable LT_i, called its *logical clock*, which is a nonnegative integer, initially 0. As part of each (computation) event, p_i increases LT_i to be one greater than the maximum of LT_i's current value and the largest timestamp on any message received in this event. Every message sent by the event is timestamped with the new value of LT_i.

The timestamp associated with an event ϕ, $LT(\phi)$, of processor p_i, is the new value LT_i computed during the event. The partial order on timestamps is the ordinary $<$ relation among integers. In Figure 6.3, we see the logical timestamps assigned by the above algorithm to the execution of Figure 6.1.

For each processor p_i, the value of LT_i is strictly increasing. Therefore, if ϕ_1 and ϕ_2 are events by the same processor p_i, and ϕ_1 occurs before ϕ_2 in p_i, then $LT(\phi_1) < LT(\phi_2)$. Furthermore, the logical timestamp of the (computation) event

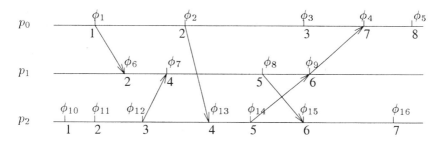

Fig. 6.3 Logical timestamps for the execution of Figure 6.1.

in which a message is received is at least one larger than the logical timestamp of the corresponding message send event. Therefore, if ϕ_1 is the send event of the message m from p_i to p_j and ϕ_2 is the receive event of the message m by p_j, then $LT(\phi_1) < LT(\phi_2)$. These facts, together with the transitivity of less than, clearly imply:

Theorem 6.3 *Let α be an execution, and let ϕ_1 and ϕ_2 be two events in α. If $\phi_1 \overset{\alpha}{\Rightarrow} \phi_2$, then $LT(\phi_1) < LT(\phi_2)$.*

6.1.3   Vector Clocks

By comparing the logical timestamps of two events in an execution α, we can tell if one of them does not causally influence the other. Specifically, if the logical timestamp of ϕ_1 is larger than or equal to the logical timestamp of ϕ_2, then ϕ_1 does not happen before ϕ_2. That is,

$$\text{if } LT(\phi_1) \geq LT(\phi_2) \text{ then } \phi_1 \overset{\alpha}{\not\Rightarrow} \phi_2$$

However, the converse is not true, that is, it is possible that $LT(\phi_1) < LT(\phi_2)$ but $\phi_1 \overset{\alpha}{\not\Rightarrow} \phi_2$. Consider, for example, the events ϕ_2 and ϕ_{12} in Figure 6.3; $LT(\phi_2) < LT(\phi_{12})$ but $\phi_2 \overset{\alpha}{\not\Rightarrow} \phi_{12}$.

The problem is that the happens-before relation is (in general) a partial order, whereas the logical timestamps are integers with the totally ordered $<$ relation. Therefore, information about non-causality is lost. We now turn our attention to logical timestamps that capture non-causality. We must choose logical timestamps from a domain that is not totally ordered; we will use vectors of integers.

First, let us define non-causality more precisely. Two events ϕ_1 and ϕ_2 are *concurrent* in execution α, denoted $\phi_1||_\alpha\phi_2$, if $\phi_1 \overset{\alpha}{\not\Rightarrow} \phi_2$ and $\phi_2 \overset{\alpha}{\not\Rightarrow} \phi_1$. (To avoid clutter, the subscript α is omitted when it should be clear from the context.) Lemmas 6.1 and 6.2 imply that if $\phi_1||_\alpha\phi_2$ then there are two executions α_1 and α_2, both indistinguishable from α, such that ϕ_1 occurs before ϕ_2 in α_1 and ϕ_2 occurs before ϕ_1 in α_2. Intuitively, processors cannot tell whether ϕ_1 occurs before ϕ_2 or vice versa, and in fact, it makes no difference which order they occur in. For example, in Figure 6.3, $\phi_8||\phi_{13}$.

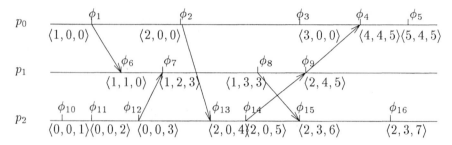

Fig. 6.4 Vector timestamps for the execution of Figure 6.1.

Vector timestamps provide a way to capture causality and non-causality, as follows. Each processor p_i keeps a local n-element array VC_i, called its *vector clock*, each element of which is a nonnegative integer, initially 0. As part of each (computation) event, p_i updates VC_i as follows. $VC_i[i]$ is incremented by one. For each $j \neq i$, $VC_i[j]$ is set equal to the maximum of its current value and the largest value for entry j among the timestamps of messages received in this event. Every message sent by the event is timestamped with the new value of VC_i.

The *vector timestamp* of an event is the value of VC at the end of the event. Figure 6.4 shows the vector timestamps assigned by the above algorithm to the execution of Figure 6.1; the reader is encouraged to compare this figure with Figure 6.3.

In a sense, for any pair of processors p_i and p_j, the value of $VC_j[i]$ is an "estimate," maintained by p_j, of $VC_i[i]$ (the number of steps taken by p_i so far). Only p_i can increase the value of the ith coordinate, and therefore:

Proposition 6.4 *For every processor p_j, in every reachable configuration, $VC_j[i] \leq VC_i[i]$, for all i, $0 \leq i \leq n - 1$.*

For logical timestamps, which are integers, we had the natural total ordering of the integers. For vector timestamps, which are vectors of integers, we now define a partial ordering. Let $\vec{v}_1$ and $\vec{v}_2$ be two vectors of n integers. Then $\vec{v}_1 \leq \vec{v}_2$ if and only if for every i, $0 \leq i \leq n - 1$, $\vec{v}_1[i] \leq \vec{v}_2[i]$; and $\vec{v}_1 < \vec{v}_2$ if and only if $\vec{v}_1 \leq \vec{v}_2$ and $\vec{v}_1 \neq \vec{v}_2$. Vectors $\vec{v}_1$ and $\vec{v}_2$ are *incomparable* if neither $\vec{v}_1 \leq \vec{v}_2$ nor $\vec{v}_2 \leq \vec{v}_1$.

Vector timestamps are said to *capture concurrency* if for any pair of events ϕ_1 and ϕ_2 in any execution, $\phi_1 \| \phi_2$ if and only if $VC(\phi_1)$ and $VC(\phi_2)$ are incomparable.

Suppose event ϕ_1 occurs at processor p_i in an execution and subsequently event ϕ_2 occurs at p_i. Each entry in VC_i is nondecreasing and furthermore, because ϕ_1 occurs before ϕ_2 at p_i, $VC_i[i](\phi_1) < VC_i[i](\phi_2)$, for every i. This implies that $VC(\phi_1) < VC(\phi_2)$.

Now consider two events in an execution, ϕ_1, the sending of a message with vector timestamp $\vec{T}$ by p_i, and ϕ_2, the receipt of the message by p_j. During ϕ_2, p_j updates each entry of its vector to be at least as large as the corresponding entry in $\vec{T}$ and then p_j increments its own entry by one. Therefore, Proposition 6.4 implies that $VC(\phi_1) < VC(\phi_2)$.

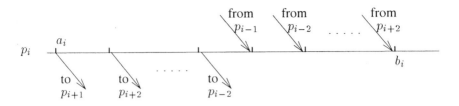

Fig. 6.5 The events of processor p_i in α.

These two facts, together with the transitivity of the less than relation for vectors, imply:

Theorem 6.5 *Let α be an execution, and let ϕ_1 and ϕ_2 be two events in α. If $\phi_1 \overset{\alpha}{\Rightarrow} \phi_2$, then $VC(\phi_1) < VC(\phi_2)$.*

Now consider two concurrent events in an execution, ϕ_1 at p_i and ϕ_2 at p_j. Obviously p_i and p_j are distinct. Suppose $VC_i[i](\phi_1)$ is ℓ. Then $VC_j[i](\phi_2)$ must be less than ℓ, implying that $VC_i(\phi_1)$ is not less than $VC_j(\phi_2)$, since the only way processor p_j can obtain a value for the ith entry of its vector that is at least ℓ is through a chain of messages originating at p_i at event ϕ_1 or later. But such a chain would imply that ϕ_1 and ϕ_2 are not concurrent. Similarly, the jth entry in $VC_i(\phi_1)$ must be less than the jth entry in $VC_j(\phi_2)$. Thus the converse of Theorem 6.5 is also true:

Theorem 6.6 *Let α be an execution, and let ϕ_1 and ϕ_2 be two events in α. If $VC(\phi_1) < VC(\phi_2)$, then $\phi_1 \overset{\alpha}{\Rightarrow} \phi_2$.*

These two theorems imply that $\phi_1 \| \phi_2$ if and only if $VC(\phi_1)$ and $VC(\phi_2)$ are incomparable. Hence, vector timestamps capture concurrency.

6.1.3.1 A Lower Bound on the Size of Vector Clocks

We have seen that vector timestamps provide a way for processors to maintain causality and concurrency information about events. However, this mechanism requires a vector of n entries to be sent with each message; this can be a very high overhead. There are certain ways to save on the size of vector timestamps (see Exercise 6.2), but as we show next, in some sense, a vector with n entries is required in order to capture concurrency.

Consider a complete network, with the execution α depicted in Figure 6.5. In this execution, each processor p_i sequentially sends a message to all the processors except p_{i-1}, in increasing order of index, starting with p_{i+1} and wrapping around if necessary; namely, p_i sends to $p_{i+1}, p_{i+2}, \ldots, p_{n-1}, p_0, \ldots, p_{i-2}$. After all the messages have been sent, each p_i sequentially receives all the messages sent to it, in decreasing order of the sender's index, starting with p_{i-1} and wrapping around; namely, p_i receives from $p_{i-1}, p_{i-2}, \ldots, p_0, p_{n-1}, \ldots, p_{i+2}$. Note that p_i does not receive a message from p_{i+1}.

For each processor p_i, denote the first send event by a_i and the last receive event by b_i. In α a processor sends all its messages before it receives any message; therefore,

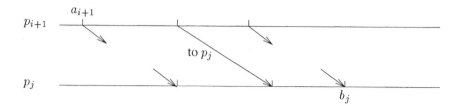

Fig. 6.6 p_{i+1} and p_j in α.

the causality relation is simple and does not include any transitively derived relations. Because no message is sent from p_{i+1} to p_i, the lack of transitivity in the message pattern of α implies:

Lemma 6.7 *For every i, $0 \le i \le n - 1$, $a_{i+1} || b_i$.*

On the other hand, for every processor p_j other than p_i, the first send event of p_{i+1} causally influences some receive event of p_j. That is:

Lemma 6.8 *For every i and j, $0 \le i \ne j \le n - 1$, $a_{i+1} \stackrel{\alpha}{\Rightarrow} b_j$.*

Proof. If $j = i + 1$, then a_{i+1} and $b_j = b_{i+1}$ occur at the same processor p_{i+1}, and therefore $a_{i+1} \stackrel{\alpha}{\Rightarrow} b_j$.

Otherwise, suppose $j \ne i + 1$. By the assumption that $j \ne i$, p_{i+1} sends a message to p_j in the execution. Since a_{i+1} is the first send by p_{i+1}, a_{i+1} is either equal to, or happens before, p_{i+1} sends to p_j. By definition, p_{i+1}'s send to p_j happens before p_j's receipt from p_{i+1}. Since b_j is the last receive by p_j, p_j's receipt from p_{i+1} is either equal to, or happens before, b_j (see Fig. 6.6). $\qquad\qquad\square$

The main theorem here claims that if we map events in α to vectors in a manner that captures concurrency, then the vectors must have n entries.

Theorem 6.9 *If VC is a function that maps each event in α to a vector in $\Re^k$ in a manner that captures concurrency, then $k \ge n$.*

Proof. Fix some i, $0 \le i \le n - 1$. By Lemma 6.7, $a_{i+1} || b_i$. Since *VC* captures concurrency, this implies that $VC(a_{i+1})$ and $VC(b_i)$ are incomparable. If for all coordinates r, $VC[r](b_i) \ge VC[r](a_{i+1})$, then $VC(b_i) \ge VC(a_{i+1})$. Therefore, there exists some coordinate r such that $VC[r](b_i) < VC[r](a_{i+1})$; denote one of these indices by $\ell(i)$.

In this manner, we have defined a function

$$\ell : \{0, \ldots, n - 1\} \to \{0, \ldots, k - 1\}$$

We prove that $k \ge n$ by showing that this function is one-to-one.

Assume, by way of contradiction, that ℓ is not one-to-one, that is, there exist two indices i and j, $i \neq j$, such that $\ell(i) = \ell(j) = r$. By the definition of the function ℓ, $VC[r](b_i) < VC[r](a_{i+1})$ and $VC[r](b_j) < VC[r](a_{j+1})$.

By Lemma 6.8, $a_{i+1} \stackrel{\alpha}{\Rightarrow} b_j$. Since VC captures concurrency, it follows that $VC(a_{i+1}) \leq VC(b_j)$. Thus

$$VC[r](b_i) < VC[r](a_{i+1}) \leq VC[r](b_j) < VC[r](a_{j+1})$$

which contradicts Lemma 6.8. □

This theorem implies that if timestamps are represented as vectors of real numbers that capture concurrency, then they must have n coordinates. The proof does not rely on the fact that vector entries are reals, just that they are all comparable. Thus, the same proof holds for vectors in S^k, where S is any (infinite) totally ordered set, and vectors are ordered lexicographically according to the ordering relation on S. This shows the optimality of the vector timestamps algorithm we described. However, at least theoretically, timestamps may be represented as other mathematical objects, potentially requiring less space and yet still capturing causality.

6.1.4 Shared Memory Systems

The happens-before relation was defined for message-passing systems in which processors influence each other by sending messages. Here we describe how to extend it to shared memory systems in which shared variables are accessed only with read and write operations.

In a shared memory system, one processor p_i influences another processor p_j by writing a value to a shared variable, which is later read by p_j. Earlier events of a processor still influence later events, just as in message-passing systems. This discussion motivates the following definition.

Given two events ϕ_1 and ϕ_2 in an execution α, ϕ_1 *happens before* ϕ_2, denoted $\phi_1 \stackrel{\alpha}{\Rightarrow} \phi_2$, if one of the following conditions holds:

1. ϕ_1 and ϕ_2 are events by the same processor p_i, and ϕ_1 occurs before ϕ_2 in α.

2. ϕ_1 and ϕ_2 are conflicting events, that is, both access the same shared variable and one of them is a write, and ϕ_1 occurs before ϕ_2 in α.

3. There exists an event ϕ such that $\phi_1 \stackrel{\alpha}{\Rightarrow} \phi$ and $\phi \stackrel{\alpha}{\Rightarrow} \phi_2$.

The notion of a causal shuffle can be adapted to the shared memory model, so that lemmas similar to Lemmas 6.1 and 6.2 can be proved (see Exercise 6.3).

6.2 EXAMPLES OF USING CAUSALITY

In this section, we present examples of using the happens-before relation to understand the behavior of a distributed system. The first example is to find consistent

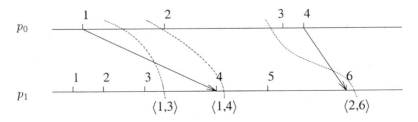

Fig. 6.7 Some consistent and inconsistent cuts.

cuts, that is, states that can be held concurrently by processors. The second uses the happens-before relation to show a separation between synchronous and asynchronous systems.

6.2.1 Consistent Cuts

In a distributed system, there is generally no omniscient observer who can record an instantaneous snapshot of the system state. Such a capability would be desirable for solving problems such as restoring the system after a crash, determining whether there is a deadlock in the system, and determining whether the computation has terminated. Instead, the components of the system themselves must cooperate to achieve an approximate snapshot. The causality relation among system events is useful for defining a meaningful static approximation to a dynamically changing system.

We make the simplifying assumption that at each computation event a processor receives at most one message. This situation can be simulated by instituting a local queue of incoming messages and handling only a single message at each step (see Exercise 6.4).

Given an execution α, we number the computation steps at each processor 1, 2, 3, etc.. A *cut* through the execution is an n-vector $\vec{k} = \langle k_0, \ldots, k_{n-1} \rangle$ of positive integers. Given a cut of an execution, one can construct a set of processor states: The state of processor p_i is its state in α immediately after its k_ith computation event.

A cut $\vec{k}$ of an execution α is *consistent* if, for all i and j, the (k_i+1)st computation event of p_i in α does not happen before the k_jth computation event of p_j in α. That is, the k_jth computation event of p_j does not depend on any action taken by another processor after the cut.[2] Consider, for example, Figure 6.7, in which cuts $\langle 1,3 \rangle$ and $\langle 1,4 \rangle$ are consistent, whereas $\langle 2,6 \rangle$ is not, because p_0's third event happens before p_1's sixth event.

For simplicity of presentation, we assume that the links deliver messages in FIFO order. (FIFO order can be implemented, if necessary, by using sequence numbers; see Chapter 8.)

---

[2]This does not imply that the k_ith event of p_i and the k_jth event of p_j are concurrent.

6.2.1.1 Finding the Maximal Consistent Cut

Given a cut $\vec{k}$ of an execution, we would like to find a consistent cut that precedes (or at least, does not follow) $\vec{k}$. In fact, we usually would like to find the most recent such consistent cut $\vec{k_1}$, where "most recent" means that there is no other consistent cut $\vec{k_2}$ where $\vec{k_1} < \vec{k_2}$ (using the relation on vectors defined in Section 6.1.3). It can be shown that there is a unique such *maximal consistent cut* preceding $\vec{k}$ (see Exercise 6.5).

We now define in more detail the problem of finding the maximal consistent cut preceding a given cut.

We assume that there is an algorithm A running in a reliable asynchronous message-passing system. At some instant, every processor is given a cut $\vec{k}$ (that is not in the future) and each processor is to compute its own entry in the maximal consistent cut preceding $\vec{k}$. The means by which the input is given to the processors is intentionally not pinned down (see the chapter notes). To achieve this task, processors are allowed to store extra information, tag algorithm A messages with extra information, and send additional messages.

We describe a method for solving this problem that requires $O(n)$ overhead on each algorithm A message but no additional messages. Algorithm A messages are tagged with vector timestamps. The vector timestamp of each computation event of a processor is stored at that processor; that is, each p_i has an (unbounded length)[3] array $store_i$ such that $store_i[m]$ holds the vector timestamp at the end of p_i's mth computation event. When p_i gets the input $\vec{k}$, it begins with $store_i[m]$, where m is p_i's entry in $\vec{k}$, and scans down $store_i$, until finding the largest m' that does not exceed m such that $store_i[m'] \leq \vec{k}$. The answer computed by p_i is m'.

It should be straightforward to see that the algorithm is correct (see Exercise 6.6).

6.2.1.2 Taking a Distributed Snapshot

A different approach to the problem of finding a recent consistent cut is, instead of being given the upper bounding cut, processors are told *when* to start finding a consistent cut. While processors are executing algorithm A, each processor in some set S of processors receives an indication that the processors are to start computing a consistent cut that includes the state of at least one processor in S at the time it received the start indication. Such a cut is a *distributed snapshot*.

There is an algorithm for this problem that sends additional messages (called *markers*) instead of adding overhead to algorithm A messages. Processing of a marker message should not affect the computation of algorithm A. Because the problem is to obtain a snapshot of the execution of algorithm A, the receipt of marker messages must not disrupt the computation of the cut. To avoid this problem, each processor keeps track of the number of algorithm A messages that it has received so far (thus excluding marker messages).

The marker messages are disseminated by using flooding, interspersed with the algorithm A messages. In more detail, each processor p_i has a local variable ans_i that is initially undefined and that at the end holds the answer (p_i's entry in the desired

---

[3]The space needed for the array can be garbage collected by using checkpoints; see the chapter notes.

Algorithm 19 Distributed snapshot algorithm:
code for processor p_i, $0 \leq i \leq n - 1$.

Initially $ans = \perp$ and $num = 0$

1: upon receiving an algorithm A message:
2:      $num := num + 1$
3:      perform algorithm A action

4: upon receiving a marker message or indication to take snapshot:
5:      if $ans = \perp$ then
6:          $ans := num$
7:          send marker to all neighbors

---

consistent cut). On receiving a marker message from a neighbor or an indication to begin the algorithm, p_i does the following. If ans_i has already been set, then p_i does nothing. Otherwise, p_i sets ans_i to the number of algorithm A messages received so far and sends a marker message to all its neighbors. The code appears in Algorithm 19.

Theorem 6.10 *Algorithm 19 computes a distributed snapshot using $O(m)$ additional messages.*

Proof. Let $\vec{k}$ be the answer computed by the algorithm. Let p_f be the first processor to receive a start indication. Since no marker messages have yet been sent, its state when the indication was received is included in $\vec{k}$. Suppose in contradiction there exist processors p_i and p_j such that the k_jth (algorithm A) computation event of p_j depends on the $(k_i + 1)$st (algorithm A) computation event of p_i. Then there is a chain of (algorithm A) messages from p_i to p_j, $m_1, m_2, \ldots, m_l$, such that m_1 is sent by p_i to some p_{i_2} after the cut at p_i, m_2 is sent by p_{i_2} to some p_{i_3} after the receipt of m_1, etc., and m_l is sent by p_{i_l} to p_j after the receipt of m_{l-1} and received by p_j before the cut.

Thus there exists some message m_h that is sent by p_{i_h} after the cut and received by $p_{i_{h+1}}$ before the cut. But since m_h is sent after the cut, p_{i_h} has already sent the marker message to $p_{i_{h+1}}$ before sending m_h. Since the links are FIFO, the marker message is received at $p_{i_{h+1}}$ before m_h is, and thus m_h is not received before the cut. $\qquad\square$

6.2.1.3 What About the Channel States?

The algorithms just discussed for finding the maximal consistent cut and a distributed snapshot ignored the contents of the message channels. One solution to this problem is to assume that the processors' local states encode which messages have been sent and received. Then the information can be inferred from the collection of processor states.

However, this is often not a practical or efficient solution. For one thing, this approach means that the size of the processor states must grow without bound. More generally, it does not allow convenient optimizations.

Luckily, the channel states can be captured in both cases without making such a strong assumption on the nature of the processor states.

The maximal consistent cut algorithm is modified as follows. Each entry in a *store* array contains the number of messages received (directly) from each neighbor so far, in addition to the vector timestamp. When the maximal consistent cut is to be computed, each processor p_i scans its *store*$_i$ array upward starting at the earliest entry, instead of downward starting at the most recent entry. As it scans upward, it "replays" the earlier computation and keeps track of the sequence of messages it is supposed to send. The procedure stops with the latest entry in *store*$_i$, say the m'th, such that the vector timestamp stored in *store*$_i[m']$ is less than or equal to $\vec{k}$, the given cut. Consider any neighbor p_j of p_i. The information recorded in *store*$_i[m']$ includes the number of messages received by p_i from p_j through p_i's m'th computation event. Let x be this number. When p_i has finished its replay, it sends x to p_j. When p_j receives the message from p_i, it waits until it has finished its own replay. Then p_j computes the state of the channel from p_j to p_i for the consistent cut to be the suffix, beginning at the $(x+1)$st, of the sequence of messages that it generated during the replay destined for p_i.

The distributed snapshot algorithm can be modified so that each processor p_i records the sequence of messages it receives from each neighbor p_j between the time that p_i recorded its own answer and the time that p_i received the marker message from p_j. Exercise 6.7 asks you to work out the details of this modification and verify that the sequence of messages recorded by p_i for neighbor p_j is the sequence of messages in transit in the configuration corresponding to the computed snapshot.

6.2.2 A Limitation of the Happens-Before Relation: The Session Problem

In this subsection, we explore an aspect of executions that cannot be captured by the happens-before relation, yet one that is important for some applications. Informally, the happens-before relation only captures dependencies inside the system, but does not take into account relationships observed from outside the system, in its interaction with the environment. We consider a problem, called the *session* problem, that can be solved quickly in the synchronous model, but requires significant time overhead in the asynchronous model, because of the necessity of explicit communication.

Intuitively, a session is a minimal length of time during which each processor performs a special action at least once. The problem has a numeric parameter, s, representing the number of sessions to be achieved.

More precisely, each processor p_i has an integer variable SA_i. During the course of execution, p_i increments SA_i every now and then. The incrementing of this variable represents the "special action" mentioned above. An execution is divided into disjoint sessions, where a *session* is a minimal length fragment of the execution in which every processor increments its *SA* variable at least once.

An algorithm for the *s*-session problem must guarantee the following conditions, in every admissible execution:

- There are at least *s* sessions

- No processor increments its *SA* variable infinitely many times (i.e., the processors eventually stop performing special actions).

The running time of an execution is the time of the last increment of an *SA* variable, using the standard asynchronous time measure from Chapter 2.

In the synchronous model, there is a simple algorithm for generating *s* sessions: Just let each processor perform *s* special actions and then cease. At each round there is a session, because each processor performs a special action. Clearly, the time is at most *s*.

In contrast, in the asynchronous model it can be shown that the time to solve the problem depends on D, the diameter of the communication network, as well as *s*. In particular, a lower bound on the time is $(s - 1) \cdot D$.

Theorem 6.11 *Let A be any s-session algorithm for an asynchronous message-passing system whose diameter is D. Then the (asynchronous) time complexity of A is greater than $(s - 1) \cdot D$.*

Proof. Suppose in contradiction there is an *s*-session algorithm A for the system with time complexity at most $(s - 1) \cdot D$.

Let α be an admissible execution of A that happens to be synchronous. That is, α consists of a series of rounds, where each round contains a deliver event for every message in transit, followed by a computation step by each processor. (Of course A must also work correctly in asynchronous executions as well as in such well-behaved ones as α.)

Let $\beta\delta$ be the schedule of α, where β ends at the end of the round containing the final special action. Thus δ contains no special actions. By the assumption on the time complexity of A and the construction of α, β consists of at most $(s - 1) \cdot D$ rounds.

We will show how to shuffle the events in β so that fewer than *s* sessions are achieved, yet processors cannot distinguish this situation from the original, and thus they will stop performing special actions prematurely. The intuition is that there is not enough time for information concerning the achievement of sessions to flow through the communication network. Yet explicit communication is the only way in an asynchronous system that processors can know whether a session has occurred. Lemma 6.12 proves a general fact about shufflings of events. Lemma 6.13 uses the general lemma to show that a specific shuffling has the desired effect.

Lemma 6.12 *Let γ be any contiguous subsequence of β consisting of at most x complete rounds, for any positive integer x. Let C be the configuration immediately preceding the first event of γ in execution α. Choose any two processors p_i and p_j.*

If $dist(p_i, p_j) \geq x$, then there exists a sequence of events $\gamma' = \gamma^1 \gamma^2$, also denoted split$(\gamma, j, i)$, *such that*

- γ^1 *is p_i-free,*

- γ^2 *is p_j-free, and*

- *exec(C, γ') is an execution fragment that is similar to exec(C, γ).*

Proof. Let ϕ_i be the first event by p_i in γ and let ϕ_j be the last event by p_j in γ. (If p_i takes no steps in γ, then let γ^1 equal γ and γ^2 be empty. Similarly, if p_j takes no steps in γ, let γ^2 equal γ and γ^1 be empty.)

We first prove that $\phi_i \not\xrightarrow{A} \phi_j$. That is, no event of p_j during γ depends on any event of p_i during γ. If there were such a dependency, then there would be a chain of messages from ϕ_i to ϕ_j in γ. The number of rounds required for this chain is at least $dist(p_i, p_j) + 1$, by the construction of α. (Remember that a computation event cannot causally influence another computation event within the same round.) But this number of rounds is at least $x + 1$, contradicting the assumption on the number of rounds in γ.

Let R be the relation consisting of the happens-before relation of α restricted to events in γ, plus the additional ordering constraint (ϕ_j, ϕ_i), namely, ϕ_j should appear before ϕ_i. By the previous lemma, $\phi_i \not\xrightarrow{A} \phi_j$, and thus R is a partial order on the events of γ.

Let γ' be any total order of the events in γ that is consistent with R. Since γ' is consistent with the constraint that ϕ_i (the first event of p_i) appear after ϕ_j (the last event of p_j), it follows that $\gamma' = \gamma^1 \gamma^2$, where γ^1 is p_i-free and γ^2 is p_j-free.

Since γ' is a causal shuffle of γ (see Exercise 6.8), Lemma 6.2 implies that $exec(C, \gamma')$ is an execution fragment and is similar to $exec(C, \gamma)$. □

Partition β into $\beta_1 \ldots \beta_{s-1}$, where each β_i consists of at most D complete rounds. (If this were not possible, then the number of rounds in β would be more than $(s - 1) \cdot D$, violating the assumption on the running time of A.)

Pick p_0 and p_1 such that $dist(p_0, p_1) = D$.

Define β'_i to be $split(\beta_i, 1, 0)$ if i is odd and to be $split(\beta_i, 0, 1)$ if i is even, $1 \leq i \leq s - 1$.

Lemma 6.13 *Let C_0 be the initial configuration of α. Then $exec(C_0, \beta'_1 \ldots \beta'_{s-1})$ is an execution of A that is similar to $exec(C_0, \beta)$.*

Proof. The lemma is proved by showing that $exec(C_0, \beta'_1 \ldots \beta'_i)$ is an execution of A that is similar to $exec(C_0, \beta_1 \ldots \beta_i)$, $1 \leq i \leq s - 1$. This is proved by induction on i.

Basis: $i = 0$. True since $C_0 = C_0$.

Induction: $i > 0$. By the inductive hypothesis, $exec(C_0, \beta'_1 \ldots \beta'_{i-1})$ is an execution of A that is similar to $exec(C_0, \beta_1 \ldots \beta_{i-1})$. Thus the two executions end in the same configuration, call it C_{i-1}. By Lemma 6.12, $exec(C_{i-1}, \beta'_i)$ is an

Fig. 6.8 The sessions in the shuffled execution α', assuming $s - 1$ is even.

execution fragment that is similar to $exec(C_{i-1}, \beta_i)$, implying that the inductive step is true. □

As a corollary to Lemma 6.13, $\alpha' = exec(C_0, \beta'_1 \ldots \beta'_{s-1}\delta)$ is an admissible execution of A.

We finish the proof by showing that there are too few sessions in α', contradicting the assumed correctness of A. Session 1 cannot end before the second part of β'_1, since p_0 takes no steps in the first part of β'_1. Session 2 cannot end before the second part of β'_2, since p_1 takes no steps after the end of session 1 until the second part of β'_2. Continuing this argument, we see that session $s - 1$ cannot end until the second part of β'_{s-1}. But the remaining part of β'_{s-1} does not comprise a complete session, since either p_0 or p_1 takes no steps (depending on whether $s - 1$ is even or odd). See Figure 6.8.

Since no special actions are performed in δ, all sessions must be included in $exec(C_0, \beta'_1 \ldots \beta'_{s-1})$, and therefore, α' contains at most $s - 1$ sessions. □

6.3 CLOCK SYNCHRONIZATION

The next part of this chapter is concerned with issues that arise when processors have access to physical clocks that provide (approximations to) the real time. First, we explain how to model such clocks. Then we define the problem of getting these clocks close together and give tight bounds on how closely such clocks can be synchronized in one simple situation, when clocks do not drift. Chapter 13 will consider in more detail the problem of maintaining synchronized clocks in the presence of drift, in addition to handling faults.

6.3.1 Modeling Physical Clocks

Recall the definition of a timed execution for asynchronous systems from Chapter 2. In the asynchronous model, the times at which events occur (called *real time*) are not available to the processors. We now consider stronger models in which the real times, or at least some approximation of them, are available to the processors. The mechanism by which such time information is made available to a processor is a *hardware clock*.

We now define the formal model for a system with hardware clocks. In each timed execution, associated with each processor p_i, there is an increasing function

HC_i from nonnegative real numbers to nonnegative real numbers. When p_i performs a computation step at real time t, the value of $HC_i(t)$ is available as part of the input to p_i's transition function. However, p_i's transition function cannot change HC_i.

At the least informative extreme, HC_i simply counts how many steps p_i has taken so far in the execution; that is, for each t such that p_i has a computation event with occurrence time t, $HC_i(t)$ equals the number of computation events by p_i so far. (Such a mechanism can be achieved with a simple counter and does not require any additional model assumptions.) At the most informative extreme, HC_i tells p_i the current real time, that is, $HC_i(t) = t$.

In this section, we will consider an intermediate situation, when HC_i reliably measures how much real time has elapsed, although its actual value is not equal to real time; that is, $HC_i(t) = t + c_i$, where c_i is some constant offset. In Chapter 13, we will consider the possibility that the rate at which HC_i increases drifts away from real time, either gaining or losing time.

Although events may happen simultaneously in a distributed system, for mathematical convenience, we have considered executions as sequences of events by imposing an arbitrary ordering on concurrent events. However, it is sometimes useful to break apart an execution into n sequences, where each sequence represents the "view" of a processor. Because processors have access to hardware clocks, we must modify the definition of view from Chapter 5:

Definition 6.2 *A view with clock values of a processor p_i (in a model with hardware clocks) consists of an initial state of p_i, a sequence of events (computation and deliver) that occur at p_i, and a hardware clock value assigned to each event. The hardware clock values must be increasing, and if the sequence of events is infinite they must increase without bound.*

Definition 6.3 *A timed view with clock values of a processor p_i (in a model with hardware clocks) is a view with clock values together with a real time assigned to each event. The assignment must be consistent with the hardware clock having the form $HC_i(t) = t + c_i$ for some constant c_i.*

Obviously, given a timed execution α, timed views with clock values can be extracted, denoted $\alpha | i$ for p_i's timed view with clock values. For the rest of this chapter, we refer to (timed and untimed) views with clock values simply as *views*.

A set of n timed views η_i, one for each p_i, $0 \leq i \leq n - 1$, can be merged as follows. Begin with the initial configuration obtained by combining the initial states of all the timed views. Then obtain a sequence of events by interleaving the events in the timed views consistently with the real times, breaking ties by ordering all deliver events at time t before any computation events at time t, and breaking any remaining ties with processor indices. Finally, apply this sequence of events in order, beginning with the initial configuration constructed, to obtain a timed execution. Denote the result merge$(\eta_0, \ldots, \eta_{n-1})$. Let the hardware clock function for p_i be any increasing function that is consistent with the real and clock times associated with each event in p_i's timed view.

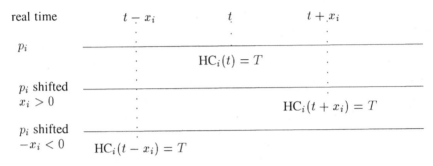

Fig. 6.9   Shifting a processor later and earlier.

Whether the resulting sequence is an execution depends on whether the timed views are "consistent." For instance, if a message is delivered to p_i from p_j at time t in η_i, but p_j does not send m to p_i before time t in η_j, then the merge of the timed views is not a timed execution. For the merge of a set of n timed views to make a timed execution, each message received must have been previously sent.

The notion of timed views is useful in proving lower bounds, when we want to start with one timed execution, modify the processors' timed views in certain ways, and then recombine the timed views to obtain another timed execution. We next give an example of such modifications. We define a notion of shifting a processor's timed view by some additive amount in an execution; the real times at which the events of the processor occur are made later (or earlier) by some fixed amount. The net result is that the processors cannot tell any difference because events still happen at the same hardware clock times, although the hardware clocks have changed. This observation is formalized in the lemma following the definition.

Definition 6.4 *Let α be a timed execution with hardware clocks and let $\vec{x}$ be a vector of n real numbers. Define* shift$(\alpha, \vec{x})$ *to be* merge$(\eta_0, \ldots, \eta_{n-1})$*, where η_i is the timed view obtained by adding x_i to the real time associated with each event in $\alpha|i$.*

See Figure 6.9 for an example of shifting a processor later and earlier. Real time is indicated at the top, increasing to the right. The first horizontal line represents p_i's timed view in which its hardware clock reads T at real time t. The second horizontal line is the result of shifting p_i's timed view by a positive amount x_i, after which p_i's hardware clock reads T at a later real time, $t + x_i$. The third horizontal line is the result of shifting p_i's timed view by a negative amount $-x_i$, after which p_i's hardware clock reads T at an earlier real time, $t - x_i$.

The result of shifting an execution is not necessarily an execution. The potential violation of the definition of execution is that a message may not be in the appropriate processor's *outbuf* variable when a deliver event occurs. This would occur if processors have been shifted relative to each other in such a way that a message is now delivered before it is sent. However, we can still make some claims about the message delays and hardware clocks concerning the result of shifting an execution.

Lemma 6.14 *Let α be a timed execution with hardware clocks HC_i, $0 \le i \le n-1$, and $\vec{x}$ be a vector of n real numbers. In* shift$(\alpha, \vec{x})$:
(a) the hardware clock of p_i, HC_i', is equal to $HC_i - x_i$, $0 \le i \le n-1$, and
(b) every message from p_i to p_j has delay $\delta - x_i + x_j$, where δ is the delay of the message in α, $0 \le i, j \le n-1$.

Proof. Let $\alpha' = $ shift$(\alpha, \vec{x})$.

(a) Suppose p_i's hardware clock reads T at real time t in α, that is, $HC_i(t) = T$. By definition, in α', p_i's hardware clock reads T at real time $t + x_i$, that is, $HC_i'(t + x_i) = T$. Thus $HC_i'(t + x_i) = HC_i(t)$. Since hardware clocks have no drift, $HC_i'(t + x_i)$ equals $HC_i'(t) + x_i$, and part (a) of the lemma follows.

(b) Consider message m sent by p_i at real time t_s and received by p_j at real time t_r in α. The delay of m in α is $\delta = t_r - t_s$. In α', the computation event of p_i that sends m occurs at $t_s + x_i$ and the computation event of p_j that receives m occurs at $t_r + x_j$. Thus the delay of m in α' is $t_r + x_j - (t_s + x_i) = \delta - x_i + x_j$, and part (b) of the lemma follows. $\qquad\qquad\square$

6.3.2 The Clock Synchronization Problem

The clock synchronization problem requires processors to bring their clocks close together, by using communication among them. Because the hardware clocks are not under the control of the processors, we assume that each processor has a special state component adj_i that it can manipulate. The *adjusted* clock of p_i is a function of p_i's hardware clock and state variable adj_i. During the process of synchronizing the clocks, p_i can change the value stored in adj_i and thus change the value of the adjusted clock.

Here we assume that hardware clocks do not drift, and hence the only compensation needed for each hardware clock is an (additive) offset. Thus the adjusted clock is defined to be the sum of the hardware clock and the current value of adj_i.

Given a timed execution, the adjusted clock of p_i can be represented as a function $AC_i(t) = HC_i(t) + adj_i(t)$, where $adj_i(t)$ is the value of adj_i in the configuration immediately before the earliest event whose occurrence time is greater than t.

In the case hardware clocks have no drift, once synchronization is achieved, no further action is required. Thus the clock synchronization problem under the assumption of no drift is defined as follows:

Definition 6.5 Achieving ϵ-Synchronized Clocks: *In every admissible[4] timed execution, there exists real time t_f such that the algorithm has terminated by real time t_f, and, for all processors p_i and p_j, and all $t \ge t_f$, $|AC_i(t) - AC_j(t)| \le \epsilon$.*

This condition states that at any given real time t, the adjusted clock values are within some ϵ, called the *skew*. Another way of looking at this is to measure how far apart in real time the clocks reach the same clock time T, called the *precision*.

---

[4] A timed execution is admissible if clocks do not drift.

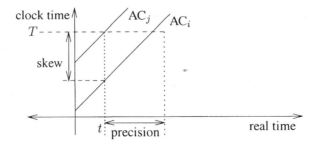

Fig. 6.10 Relationship between skew and precision for clocks with no drift.

When clocks have no drift, these are equal. (See Fig. 6.10; the skew and precision are equal because both clock functions have slope 1.) Sometimes one viewpoint is more convenient than another.

The requirement that the algorithm terminates at some point, implying that no further changes are made to the *adj* variables, is important (see Exercise 6.9).

Throughout this section, we will assume that there exist nonnegative constants d and u, $d \geq u$, such that in every admissible timed execution, every message has delay within the interval $[d - u, d]$. The value u is the *uncertainty* in the message delay. Since the delay of a message is the time between the computation event that sends the message and the computation event when the recipient processes the message, this condition has implications for the frequency of deliver and computation events—namely, if p_i sends a message m to p_j at real time t, then a deliver event for m followed by a computation step for p_j must occur no later than time $t + d$ and no sooner than time $t + d - u$.

It is possible to achieve clock synchronization when upper bounds on message delay are not known or do not exist, given an appropriately modified definition of clock synchronization. However, such algorithms are more complicated to analyze and cannot guarantee an upper bound on skew that holds for all executions (see Exercise 6.10).

6.3.3 The Two Processors Case

To obtain some intuition about the clock synchronization problem, let us consider the simple case of two processors, p_0 and p_1. The first idea is the following algorithm: Processor p_0 sets adj_0 to 0 and sends its current hardware clock value to processor p_1. On receiving the message with value T, processor p_1 sets its adjusted clock to be $T + (d - u)$ by setting adj_1 equal to $T + (d - u) - HC_1$. (In this formula, HC_1 indicates the current value of p_1's hardware clock.)

The best-case performance of the algorithm is when p_0's message actually has delay $d - u$, in which case the skew between the two processors' adjusted clocks is 0 (see Fig. 6.11(a)). On the other hand, the worst case of the algorithm is when the

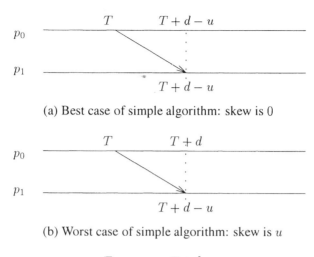

(a) Best case of simple algorithm: skew is 0

(b) Worst case of simple algorithm: skew is u

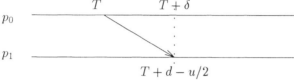

(c) Improved algorithm: skew is at most $u/2$

Fig. 6.11 Clock synchronization for two processors.

message has delay d, because the adjustment is calculated assuming that the message was delayed only $d - u$ time units. In this case, the skew is u (see Fig. 6.11(b)).

One might be tempted to calculate the adjustment assuming that the message was delayed d time units. However, in this case, the worst case of the algorithm happens when the message is delayed $d - u$ time units, again giving a skew of u.

As indicated by these two examples, the difficulty of clock synchronization is the difference between the estimated delay used for calculating the adjustment and the actual delay. As we show below, it is best to estimate the delay as $d - u/2$. That is, on receiving the message with value T, p_1 sets adj_1 to be $T + (d - u/2) - HC_1$. The skew achieved by this algorithm is at most $u/2$, because if we consider an arbitrary execution of the algorithm, and let δ be the delay of the message from p_0 to p_1, then $d - u \leq \delta \leq d$. Therefore, $|\delta - (d - u/2)| \leq u/2$, which implies the bound (see Fig. 6.11(c)).

The last algorithm assumes that d and u are known to the algorithm. The same skew $(u/2)$ can be achieved even if d and u are unknown; see Exercise 6.12.

We now argue that $u/2$ is the best skew that can be achieved in the worst case by a clock synchronization algorithm A for two processors p_0 and p_1.

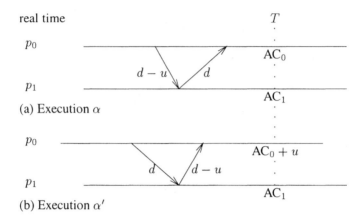

Fig. 6.12   Executions used in the proof of the lower bound for two processors.

Let α be an admissible timed execution of A in which the delay of messages from p_0 to p_1 is $d - u$ and the delay of messages from p_1 to p_0 is d (see Fig. 6.12(a)). Because we assume that hardware clocks do not drift, neither do adjusted clocks after termination, and thus the skew between adjusted clocks does not change. Let AC_0 and AC_1 be the adjusted clocks at some time T after termination. Because the algorithm has skew ϵ,

$$AC_0 \geq AC_1 - \epsilon$$

Now consider $\alpha' = \text{shift}(\alpha, \langle -u, 0 \rangle)$, the result of shifting p_0 earlier by u and not shifting p_1 (see Fig. 6.12(b)). Note that α' is an admissible timed execution, because all message delays are between $d - u$ and d, by Lemma 6.14. By the same lemma, at time T in α', the adjusted clock of p_0 is $AC_0 + u$ whereas the adjusted clock of p_1 remains AC_1. Because the algorithm has skew ϵ,

$$AC_1 \geq (AC_0 + u) - \epsilon$$

Putting these inequalities together, we get:

$$AC_0 \geq AC_0 + u - 2\epsilon$$

which after simple algebraic manipulation implies that $\epsilon \geq u/2$.

In Sections 6.3.4 and 6.3.5, we extend the above algorithm and lower bound to the general case of n processors, to show that the smallest skew that can be achieved is exactly $u(1 - \frac{1}{n})$.

6.3.4   An Upper Bound

Recall that we assume that processors are located at the nodes of a complete communication network. A very simple algorithm is to choose one of the processors as

---

Algorithm 20 A clock synchronization algorithm for n processors:
code for processor p_i, $0 \leq i \leq n - 1$.

---

initially $\textit{diff}[i] = 0$

1: at first computation step:
2:      send HC (current hardware clock value) to all other processors

3: upon receiving message T from some p_j:
4:      $\textit{diff}[j] := T + d - u/2 - HC$
5:      if a message has been received from every other processor then
6:          $adj := \frac{1}{n} \sum_{k=0}^{n-1} \textit{diff}[k]$

---

a *center*, and to apply the two-processor algorithm between any processor and the center. Because each processor is at most $u/2$ away from the clock of the center, it follows that the skew of this algorithm is u.

We next see that we can do slightly better: There is a clock synchronization algorithm with skew $u(1 - \frac{1}{n})$. The pseudocode appears in Algorithm 20. Essentially, each processor computes an estimate of the average hardware clock value and adjusts its clock to that value.

Theorem 6.15 *Algorithm 20 achieves* $u(1 - \frac{1}{n})$*-synchronization for n processors.*

Proof. Consider any admissible timed execution of the algorithm. After p_i receives the message from p_j, $\textit{diff}_i[j]$ holds p_i's approximation of the difference between HC_j and HC_i. Because of the way $\textit{diff}_i[j]$ is calculated, the error in the approximation is plus or minus $u/2$. More formally:

Lemma 6.16 *For every time t after p_i sets $\textit{diff}_i[j]$, $j \neq i$, $\textit{diff}_i[j](t) = HC_j(t) - HC_i(t) + err_{ji}$, where err_{ji} is a constant with $-u/2 \leq err_{ji} \leq u/2$.*

We now bound the difference between p_i's and p_j's adjusted clocks at any time t after the algorithm terminates. By the definition of the adjusted clocks,

$$|AC_i(t) - AC_j(t)| = \left| HC_i(t) + \frac{1}{n}\sum_{k=0}^{n-1} \textit{diff}_i[k] - HC_j(t) - \frac{1}{n}\sum_{k=0}^{n-1} \textit{diff}_j[k] \right|$$

After some algebraic manipulation, we obtain:

$$\frac{1}{n} \left| HC_i(t) - HC_j(t) + \textit{diff}_i[i] - \textit{diff}_j[i] + HC_i(t) - HC_j(t) + \textit{diff}_i[j] - \textit{diff}_j[j] \right.$$

$$\left. + \sum_{k=0, k \neq i,j}^{n-1} \left(HC_i(t) - HC_j(t) + \textit{diff}_i[k] - \textit{diff}_j[k] \right) \right|$$

By laws of absolute value and the fact that $\textit{diff}_i[i] = \textit{diff}_j[j] = 0$, this expression is at most

$$\frac{1}{n} \left(\left| HC_j(t) - HC_i(t) + \textit{diff}_j[i] \right| + \left| HC_i(t) - HC_j(t) + \textit{diff}_i[j] \right| \right.$$

$$+ \sum_{k=0, k \neq i, j}^{n-1} |HC_i(t) - HC_j(t) + \mathit{diff}_i[k] - \mathit{diff}_j[k]| \,)$$

The first term corresponds to the difference between p_i's knowledge of its own clock and p_j's estimate of p_i's clock. The second term corresponds to the difference between p_j's knowledge of its own clock and p_i's estimate of p_j's clock. Each of the remaining $n - 2$ terms corresponds to the difference between p_i's estimate of p_k's clock and p_j's estimate of p_k's clock.

By Lemma 6.16, the first term is equal to $|\mathit{err}_{ij}|$, which is at most $u/2$, and the second term is equal to $|\mathit{err}_{ji}|$, which is also at most $u/2$. Each of the remaining $n - 2$ terms, $|HC_i(t) - HC_j(t) + \mathit{diff}_i[k] - \mathit{diff}_j[k]|$, is equal to

$$|HC_i(t) - HC_j(t) + HC_k(t) - HC_i(t) + \mathit{err}_{ki} - HC_k(t) + HC_j(t) - \mathit{err}_{kj}|$$

All the terms other than err_{ki} and err_{kj} cancel, leaving a quantity that is at most $u/2 + u/2 = u$.

Thus the overall expression is at most $\frac{1}{n}(\frac{u}{2} + \frac{u}{2} + (n-2)u) = u(1 - \frac{1}{n})$. $\qquad \square$

6.3.5   A Lower Bound

We now show that $u(1 - \frac{1}{n})$ is the best skew that can be achieved by a clock synchronization algorithm for n processors connected by a complete communication network, where u is the uncertainty in the message delay.

Theorem 6.17 *For every algorithm that achieves ϵ-synchronized clocks, ϵ is at least $u(1 - \frac{1}{n})$.*

Proof.   Consider any clock synchronization algorithm A. Let α be an admissible timed execution of A with hardware clocks HC_i, $0 \leq i \leq n - 1$, and the following (fixed) message delays. For two processors p_i and p_j, $i < j$:

- The delay of every message from p_i to p_j is exactly $d - u$.

- The delay of every message from p_j to p_i is exactly d.

(See Fig. 6.13.)

Let AC_i, $0 \leq i \leq n - 1$, be the adjusted clocks in α after termination. Pick any time t after termination.

Lemma 6.18 *For each k, $1 \leq k \leq n - 1$, $AC_{k-1}(t) \leq AC_k(t) - u + \epsilon$.*

Proof.   Pick any k, $1 \leq k \leq n - 1$. Define $\alpha' = \mathrm{shift}(\alpha, \vec{x})$, where $x_i = -u$ if $0 \leq i \leq k - 1$ and $x_i = 0$ if $k \leq i \leq n - 1$ (see Figure 6.13).

By Lemma 6.14, the message delays in α' are as follows. Consider two processors p_i and p_j with $i < j$. If $j \leq k - 1$ or $k \leq i$, then the delays from p_i to p_j are $d - u$ and the delays from p_j to p_i are d. Otherwise, when $i \leq k - 1 < j$, the delays from p_i to p_j are d and the delays from p_j to p_i are $d - u$.

Fig. 6.13 Illustration for Theorem 6.17: executions α (left) and α' (right).

Thus α' is admissible and the algorithm must work correctly in it; in particular, it must achieve ϵ-synchronized clocks. Since processors are shifted earlier in real time, t is also after termination in α'. Thus $AC'_{k-1}(t) \leq AC'_k(t) + \epsilon$.

By Lemma 6.14, $AC'_{k-1}(t) = AC_{k-1}(t) + u$ and $AC'_k(t) = AC_k(t)$.

Putting all the pieces together gives $AC_{k-1}(t) \leq AC_k(t) - u + \epsilon$. ☐

Since A is presumed to achieve ϵ-synchronized clocks, $AC_{n-1}(t) \leq AC_0(t) + \epsilon$. We apply the lemma repeatedly to finish the proof, as follows.

$$
\begin{aligned}
AC_{n-1}(t) &\leq AC_0(t) + \epsilon \\
&\leq AC_1(t) - u + 2\epsilon \\
&\leq AC_2(t) - 2u + 3\epsilon \\
&\leq \cdots \\
&\leq AC_{n-1}(t) - (n-1)u + n\epsilon
\end{aligned}
$$

Thus $\epsilon \geq u(1 - \frac{1}{n})$. ☐

6.3.6 Practical Clock Synchronization: Estimating Clock Differences

Measurements of actual message delays in networks indicate that they are not uniformly distributed between a minimum and a maximum value. Instead, the distribution typically has a spike close to the minimum and then a long tail going toward infinity. One consequence is that there is not a well-defined maximum delay — delays can be arbitrarily large if we are sufficiently unlucky. However, as the probability of very large delays is very small, often this problem is dealt with by assuming some upper bound on delay that captures a large enough fraction of the messages, and any message that arrives later than that is treated as a lost message.

When mapping this reality to the abstract model presented earlier in this section, $d - u$ represents the minimum delay and d the assumed upper bound. Thus d is used as a "timeout parameter" and can trigger some action to be taken when a message is viewed as lost.

However, when d is chosen to be very large, most messages take significantly less time than d to reach their destination. Algorithms such as Algorithm 20 that assume that message delays are $d - u/2$ are thus massively overestimating the delay, which causes the resulting skew to be quite large. In other words, it is inappropriate to use the timeout interval to approximate delays of messages in the clock synchronization algorithm.

A more clever approach is to take advantage of the smaller delays that occur most of the time in practice to get improved performance for clock synchronization. To expand on this idea, let's consider a primitive that is popular in many clock synchronization algorithms: having one processor estimate the difference between its clock and that of another processor.

In Algorithm 20, processor p_j sends its current clock value to processor p_i and then p_i calculates the difference assuming that this message was in transit for $d - u/2$ time. Note that p_j just sends the message on its own initiative, not in response to something that p_i does. The resulting error in the estimate is at most $u/2$, and when d, the maximum delay, is much larger than the minimum delay $d - u$, this error is approximately $d/2$, which is still large.

An alternative is to have p_i send a query message to p_j, which p_j answers immediately with its current clock value. When p_j receives the response, it calculates the round-trip time of this pair of messages and assumes that each message took half the time. If the round-trip time is significantly less than $2d$, we have a much better clock estimate, as we now explain. Suppose the round-trip time is $2d'$, where $d' \ll d$. The error is at most half of $d' - (d - u)$, or $u/2 - (d - d')/2$, which is less than $d'/2$ and much less than $d/2$.

Note, though, that double the number of messages are required for the latter method.

What if you want to guarantee, at least with high probability, that you get a good estimate? A processor can repeatedly initiate the query-response until one occurs with a sufficiently small round-trip delay. The expected number of times that a processor will need to do so depends on the desired probability of success, the desired bound on the error, and the distribution on the message delay.

Now consider what processors can do with the improved clock difference estimates. Assume that the response to a query requires no local processing time (Exercise 6.12 addresses how to relax this assumption). The two-processor algorithm from Section 6.3.3 can be modified so that p_1 sends a query to p_0 when its hardware clock reads T_s. In response, p_0 sets adj_0 to 0 and sends the current value T of its hardware clock back to p_1. When p_1 gets the response T, at hardware clock time T_r, it sets its adjustment variable to $T + \frac{1}{2}(T_r - T_s) - HC_1$. When the round-trip delay of the query-response pair is d', the resulting worst-case skew is $u/2 - (d - d')/2$, which contrasts with the worst-case skew of $u/2$ for the original algorithm. The difference is significant if $d' \ll d$.

Exercises

6.1 Consider the execution in Figure 6.14.

(a) Assign logical timestamps to the events.

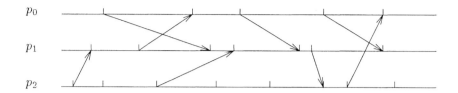

p_0

p_1

p_2

Fig. 6.14   Execution for Exercise 6.1.

(b) Assign vector timestamps to the events.

6.2 Suggest improvements in the message complexity of vector clocks.

6.3 Extend the notion of a causal shuffle and prove Lemmas 6.1 and 6.2 for the shared memory model.

6.4 Prove that there is no loss of generality in assuming that at each computation event a processor receives exactly one message.

6.5 Prove that there is a unique maximal consistent cut preceding any given cut.

6.6 Prove that the algorithm for finding a maximal consistent cut is correct.

6.7 Modify the snapshot algorithm to record the channel states as well as the processor states. Prove that your algorithm is correct.

6.8 In the proof of Theorem 6.11, verify that γ' is a causal shuffle of γ.

6.9 Show that if the requirement of termination is dropped from the definition of achieving clock synchronization, a skew of 0 is obtainable.

Hint: The adjusted clocks in this scheme are not very useful.

6.10 Devise an algorithm to synchronize clocks when there is no upper bound on message delays.

6.11 Suppose we have a distributed system whose topology is a tree instead of a clique. Assume the message delay on every link is in the range $[d - u, d]$. What is the tight bound on the skew obtainable in this case?

6.12 Explain how a processor can calculate the round-trip delay of a query-response message pair when an arbitrary amount of time can elapse between the receipt of the query and the sending of the response.

6.13 Modify Algorithm 20 for synchronizing the clocks of n processors to use the improved clock difference estimation technique in Section 6.3.6.

Analyze the worst-case skew achieved by your algorithm when the maximum message delay is some $d' \ll d$.

6.14 Suppose that p_0 has access to some external source of time, so that its adjusted clock can be considered correct and should not be altered. How can the two-processor algorithm from Section 6.3.3 be modified so that p_1 can synchronize its clock as closely as possible to that of p_0?

Chapter Notes

The first part of this chapter concentrated on the notion of causal influence between events. The happens-before relation was defined by Lamport [155], as was the algorithm for logical timestamps. Vector timestamps were defined independently by Mattern [181] and by Fidge [106]. The first applications of vectors to capture causality were for distributed database management, for example, by Strom and Yemini [247]. The lower bound on the size of vector timestamps is due to Charron-Bost [72]. Schwarz and Mattern describe several implementations and uses of logical and vector clocks in their exposition of causality and non-causality [239].

The happens-before relation is used widely in the theory and practice of distributed systems; we presented only two of its applications. Johnson and Zwaenepoel [145] proved that there is a unique maximal consistent cut below another cut (Exercise 6.5). The algorithm for finding a maximal consistent cut is from Sistla and Welch [244], who used it for crash recovery with independent logging; here, the input $\vec{k}$ contains log information provided by the processors.

The algorithm for taking a consistent snapshot (Algorithm 19) is due to Chandy and Lamport [69]. Distributed snapshots can be used to solve several problems including termination detection, scheduling, and detection of stable properties. For more information about distributed snapshots, see the papers of Chandy [68] and Lai and Yang [152], as well as the chapter by Babaoglu and Marzullo [42]. Distributed snapshots are related to the problem of taking an atomic snapshot of shared memory, which will be studied in Chapter 10.

Another important application of logical time is for debugging (using nonstable predicates), see, for example, the work of Garg and Waldecker [121]; additional applications are discussed by Mattern [181] and Morgan [191].

The results for the session problem (Section 6.2.2) are based on results of Arjomandi, Fischer, and Lynch [19] and Attiya and Mavronicolas [30].

The second part of the chapter was dedicated to clock synchronization in the no drift case (Section 6.3); our exposition is based on the results of Lundelius and Lynch [174]. Their results concern only a complete network with the same uncertainty bounds for all communication links; arbitrary topologies and arbitrary uncertainties (as well as the situation in Exercise 6.11) were investigated by Halpern, Megiddo, and Munshi [130]. The case when uncertainties are unknown or unbounded was considered by Attiya, Herzberg, and Rajsbaum [29] and Patt-Shamir and Rajsbaum [206]. Lamport [155] describes and analyzes an algorithm that tolerates drift.

Chapter 13 discusses the problem of synchronizing clocks in the presence of failures and drift.

Our definition of the clock synchronization problem only requires the adjusted clocks to be close *to each other*; this is known as *internal* clock synchronization. *External clock synchronization* requires that the adjusted clocks to be close to *real time*; external clock synchronization can be achieved only if there are sources for measuring the real time.

Practical network protocols for clock synchronization, especially Mills' *Network Time Protocol* (NTP) [186] rely on having access to a reliable and accurate time source, such as a Global Positioning System satellite; these protocols achieve external clock synchronization. Mills' paper [186] contains the solution to Exercise 6.14. The time sampling algorithm described in Section 6.3.6 was suggested by Cristian [87]. His paper expands on this idea, handling the case when clocks drift, and describes a time service that tolerates failures of processes, clocks, and communication.

Yang and Marsland edited a collection of papers on global states and time in distributed systems [263]; some of the papers mentioned above appear in this collection.

Part II

Simulations

7

A Formal Model for Simulations

In the remainder of the book, we will be studying tools and abstractions for simplifying the design of distributed algorithms. To put this work on a formal footing, we need to modify our model to handle specifications and implementations in a more general manner.

7.1 PROBLEM SPECIFICATIONS

There are various approaches to specifying a problem to be solved. So far in this book, we have taken a relatively ad hoc approach, which has served us adequately, because we have been discussing particular problems, for example, leader election, mutual exclusion, and consensus. In this ad hoc approach, we have put conditions on the states of the processors as they relate to each other and to the initial states.

Now we wish to specify problems more generally, so that we can talk about system simulations and algorithms for arbitrary problems. Instead of looking inside an algorithm, we will focus on the interface between an algorithm (equivalently, the processors) and the external world.

Formally, a *problem specification* $\mathcal{P}$ is a set of *inputs* $in(\mathcal{P})$, a set of *outputs* $out(\mathcal{P})$, and a set of *allowable sequences* $seq(\mathcal{P})$ of inputs and outputs; $in(\mathcal{P})$ and $out(\mathcal{P})$ form the *interface* for $\mathcal{P}$. Each input or output has a name and may have some data associated with it as a parameter. These are how the processors communicate with the external world, that is, with the users of the algorithm. Inputs come in to the processor from the external world, and outputs go out from the processor to the external world. The sequences specify the allowed interleavings of inputs and outputs. Thus a problem is specified at the interface between the algorithm and the external world. A problem specification might impose certain constraints on the inputs, meaning that the users must use the system "properly."

For example, the mutual exclusion problem for n processors can be specified as follows. The inputs are T_i and E_i, $0 \leq i \leq n - 1$, where T_i indicates that the ith user wishes to try to enter the critical section and E_i indicates that the ith user wishes to exit the critical section. The outputs are C_i and R_i, $0 \leq i \leq n - 1$, where C_i indicates that the ith user may now enter the critical section and R_i indicates that the ith user may now enter the remainder section. A sequence α of these inputs and outputs is in the set of allowable sequences if and only if, for each i,

1. $\alpha|i$ cycles through T_i, C_i, E_i, R_i in that order, and

2. Whenever C_i occurs, the most recent preceding input or output for any other j is not C_j

Condition 1 states that the user and the algorithm interact properly with each other. Note that condition 1 imposes some constraints on the user to behave "properly." Condition 2 states that no two users are simultaneously in the critical section. Specifying the no-lockout and no-deadlock versions of the mutual exclusion problem is left as an exercise (Exercise 7.1).

7.2 COMMUNICATION SYSTEMS

The formal model used in Part I of this book explicitly modeled the communication systems—with *inbuf* and *outbuf* state components and deliver events for message passing and with explicit shared variables as part of the configurations for shared memory.

In this part of the book, our focus is on how to provide such communication mechanisms in software, via simulations. Thus we no longer explicitly model message channels or shared variables. Instead we have a *communication system* that is interposed between the processors. Processors communicate with each other via the communication system. The communication system will be different in different situations; for instance, it has a different interface for message passing (sends and receives) than it does for shared memory (invocations and responses on shared objects), and it provides different ordering guarantees under different synchrony assumptions. It even provides different guarantees on the contents of messages, depending on the failure assumptions being made.

We will be studying how to simulate certain kinds of communication systems out of weaker ones; in particular, how to implement broadcasts in message passing (Chapter 8), how to implement shared objects either out of message passing (Chapters 9 and 10) or out of other shared objects (Chapters 10 and 15), how to implement stronger synchrony guarantees (Chapter 11), and how to implement more benign failures (Chapter 12).

Next we describe two kinds of (failure-free) asynchronous message-passing systems, one with point-to-point communication and the other with broadcast communication, by giving a problem specification for each one. At relevant points later in the book, as needed, we will provide problem specifications for shared memory, other synchrony requirements, and various failure modes.

7.2.1   Asynchronous Point-to-Point Message Passing

The interface to an asynchronous point-to-point message-passing system is with two types of events:

$send_i(M)$: an input event of the message-passing system, on behalf of processor p_i, that sends a (possibly empty) set M of messages. Each message includes an indication of the sender and recipient, there is at most one message for each recipient, and the sender-recipient pairs must be compatible with the assumed topology of the underlying system.

$recv_i(M)$: an output event of the message-passing system, on behalf of processor p_i, in which the (possibly empty) set M of messages is received. Each message in M must have p_i as its recipient.

The set of allowable sequences of inputs and outputs consists of every sequence satisfying the following. There exists a mapping κ from the set of messages appearing in all the $recv_i(M)$ events, for all i, to the set of messages appearing in $send_i(M)$ events, for all i, such that each message m in a recv event is mapped to a message with the same content appearing in an earlier send event, and

Integrity: κ is well-defined. That is, every message received was previously sent—no message is received "out of thin air." This implies there is no corruption of messages.

No Duplicates: κ is one-to-one. That is, no message is received more than once.

Liveness: κ is onto. That is, every message that is sent is received. This means there is no omission of messages.

These properties will be modified later when failures are considered.

7.2.2   Asynchronous Broadcast

Here we describe a system supporting generic broadcast communication. In Chapter 8 we define broadcasts with different service qualities.

The interface to a basic asynchronous broadcast service is with two types of events:

$bc\text{-}send_i(m)$: An input event of the broadcast service, on behalf of processor p_i, that sends a message m to all processors.

bc-recv$_i$(m, j): An output event of the broadcast service, on behalf of processor p_i, that receives the message m previously broadcast by p_j.

The set of allowable sequences of inputs and outputs consists of every sequence satisfying the following. There exists a mapping κ from each bc-recv$_i$(m,j) event to an earlier bc-send$_j$(m) event, with the following properties:

Integrity: κ is well-defined. That is, every message received was previously sent—no message is received "out of thin air."

No Duplicates: For each processor p_i, $0 \leq i \leq n - 1$, the restriction of κ to bc-recv$_i$ events is one-to-one. That is, no message is received more than once at any single processor.

Liveness: For each processor p_i, $0 \leq i \leq n-1$, the restriction of κ to bc-recv$_i$ events is onto. That is, every message that is sent is received at every processor.

As in the point-to-point case, these properties will be modified later when failures are considered.

7.3 PROCESSES

To simulate one kind of system out of another, there will be a piece of code running on each processor that implements the desired communication system. Thus it is no longer accurate to identify "the algorithm" with the processor, because there will be multiple processes running on each processor. For instance, there could be a process corresponding to an algorithm that uses the asynchronous broadcast system and a process corresponding to an algorithm that simulates the asynchronous broadcast system on top of the asynchronous point-to-point message-passing system.

We present a relatively restricted form of algorithm composition, which is sufficient for our needs in this book. We assume an ordering of processes, forming a "stack of protocols", as shown in Figure 7.1 (a). The environment, or external world, is the user (either human or software) of the system we are explicitly modeling. The communication system is the black-box entity through which the nodes ultimately communicate; its implementation is currently not of interest. Each layer in the stack communicates with the layer above through what it views as inputs and outputs to the external world. Likewise, each process uses communication primitives to interact with the layer beneath it, as if it were communicating directly with some underlying communication system. Only the top process actually communicates with the external world, and only the bottom process actually interacts with the communication system.

An input coming in either from the external world or from the communication system triggers the processes on a node to take a series of steps. For example, suppose we have a stack of processes, all of which use a message-passing paradigm for communication, and an input occurs at the top layer process. That process takes in the input and in response does a send. The next process down in the stack takes

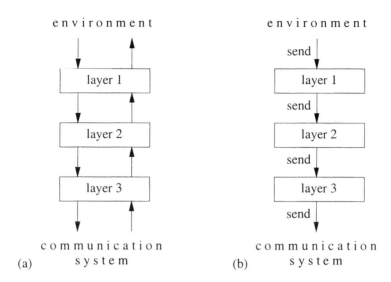

Fig. 7.1   The layered model (a) and sample propagation of events (b).

in the send as its input and does a send to the process below it. Eventually we get to whatever we are considering as the "real" communication system in this view (see Fig. 7.1 (b)).

All the events on a node that are triggered, either directly or indirectly, by one input event happen atomically with respect to events on other nodes. Thus local processing time is not taken into account. The rationale for this restriction is that studies of distributed systems are primarily concerned with the time for communication between physically dispersed nodes, not the time for local computation and intra-node communication, which is generally negligible in comparison.

We now proceed in more detail.

A *system* consists of a collection of n processors (or nodes), p_0 through p_{n-1}, a communication system C linking the nodes, and the environment $\mathcal{E}$.

The environment $\mathcal{E}$ and the communication system C are not explicitly modeled as processes. Instead, they are given as problem specifications, which impose conditions on their behavior. The reason is that we want to be as general as possible and allow all possible implementations of the environment and communication system that satisfy the specification.

A *node* is a hardware notion. Running on each node are one or more (software) *processes*. We restrict our attention to the situation in which the processes are organized into a single stack of layers and there are the same number of layers on each node. Each layer communicates with the layer above it and the layer below it. The bottom layer communicates with the communication system, and the top layer communicates with the environment.

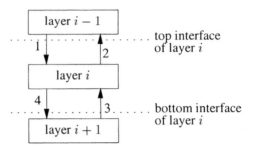

Fig. 7.2 Events at a process.

Each process is modeled as an automaton. It has a (possibly infinite) set of states, including a subset of initial states. Transitions between the states are triggered by the occurrence of events of the process. The process has four kinds of events (see Fig. 7.2):

1. Inputs coming in from the layer above (or the environment, if this is the top layer)

2. Outputs going out to the layer above

3. Inputs coming in from the layer below (or the communication system, if this is the bottom layer)

4. Outputs going out to the layer below

Events of type 1 and 2 form the *top interface* of the process, and events of type 3 and 4 form the *bottom interface* of the process.

An event is said to be *enabled* in a state of a process if there is a transition from that state labeled with that event. An event that is an *input* for a process is one over which the process has no control; formally, an input must be enabled in every state of the process. A process has control over the occurrence of an *output* event; the transition function encodes when the output can occur. Events are shared by processes; an output from one layer is an input to an adjacent layer.

Inputs from the environment and from the communication system are called *node inputs*. In asynchronous systems, we require that the processes on a single node interact in such a way that only a finite number of events (other than node inputs) are directly or indirectly enabled in response to any single node input. Each node input can cause some (finite number of) events to be enabled on that node; when each of those occurs it can cause some other events to be enabled; etc. Eventually, though, all this activity must die down. No constraints are put on the order in which enabled events must occur in the node.

A *configuration* of the system specifies a state for every process on every node. Note that, unlike the definition of configuration in the model of Part I, now a configuration does not include the state of the communication system. An *initial* configuration contains all initial states.

An *execution* of the system is a sequence $C_0\phi_1 C_1 \phi_2 C_2 \ldots$ of alternating configurations C_i and events ϕ_i, beginning with a configuration and, if it is finite, ending with a configuration, that satisfies the following conditions.

1. Configuration C_0 is an initial configuration.

2. For each $i \geq 1$, event ϕ_i is enabled in configuration C_{i-1} and configuration C_i is the result of ϕ_i acting on C_{i-1}. In more detail, every state component is the same in C_i as it is in C_{i-1}, except for the (at most two) processes for which ϕ_i is an event. The state components for those processes change according to the transition functions of those processes.

3. For each $i \geq 1$, if event ϕ_i is not a node input, then $i > 1$ and it is on the same node as event ϕ_{i-1}. Thus the first event must be a node input, and every event that is not a node input must immediately follow some other event on the same node.

4. For each $i \geq 1$, if event ϕ_i is a node input, then no event (other than a node input) is enabled in C_{i-1}. Thus a node input does not occur until all the other events have "played out" and no more are enabled.

The last two conditions specify atomicity with respect to the events on different nodes. A node is triggered into action by the occurrence of an input, either from the environment or from the communication system. The trigger causes a chain reaction of events at the same node, and this chain reaction occurs atomically until no more events are enabled, other than node inputs.

The *schedule* of an execution is the sequence of events in the execution, without the configurations.

Given execution α, we denote by $top(\alpha)$ (respectively, $bot(\alpha)$) the restriction of the schedule of α to the events of the top (respectively, bottom) interface of the top (respectively, bottom) layer.

7.4 ADMISSIBILITY

We will only require proper behavior of the system when the communication system and the environment behave "properly." These situations are captured as "admissibility" conditions on executions. Only admissible executions will be required to be correct.

An execution is *fair* if every event, other than a node input, that is continuously enabled eventually occurs. Fairness makes sure that the execution does not halt prematurely, while there is still a step to be taken.

An execution α is *user compliant for problem specification* $\mathcal{P}$ if, informally speaking, the environment satisfies the input constraints of $\mathcal{P}$ (if any). More formally, for every prefix $\alpha'\phi$ of α, where ϕ is an input from the environment, if α' is a prefix of some element of $seq(\mathcal{P})$, then so is $\alpha'\phi$. The details of the input constraints will naturally vary depending on the particular problem. For instance, in the mutual

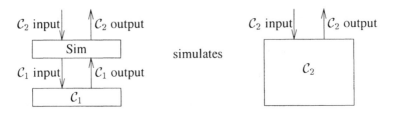

Fig. 7.3   Simulating C_2 from C_1.

exclusion problem specification the environment at a node should only indicate that it is ready to leave the critical section if it is currently in the critical section.

An execution α is *correct for communication system* C if $bot(\alpha)$ is an element of $seq(C)$. This condition states that the communication system is correct, according to the problem specification of C.

Finally, we define an execution to be (P, C)-*admissible* if it is fair, user compliant for problem specification P, and correct for communication system C. When P and C are clear from context, we simply say "admissible." Although the details of this definition of "admissible" are different than our usage of the word in Part I, the spirit is the same; admissibility captures the extra conditions over and above the basic conditions required of executions.

7.5 SIMULATIONS

We can now state our formal definitions of one system simulating another system.

Communication system C_1 *globally simulates* (or simply *simulates*) communication system C_2 if there exists a collection of processes, one for each node, called Sim (the simulation program) that satisfies the following.

1. The top interface of Sim is the interface of C_2.

2. The bottom interface of Sim is the interface of C_1.

3. For every (C_2, C_1)-admissible execution α of Sim, there exists a sequence σ in $seq(C_2)$ such that $\sigma = top(\alpha)$.

In other words, running the simulation on top of communication system C_1 produces the same appearance to the environment as does communication system C_2 (see Fig. 7.3).

We sometimes need a weaker definition of simulation, in which the users at individual nodes cannot tell the difference between running directly on system C_2 and running on top of a simulation that itself is running on top of system C_1, but an external observer, who can tell in what order events occur at different nodes, can tell the difference. This is called *local simulation*. To define it precisely, we first define weaker notions of user compliance and admissibility.

An execution α is *locally user compliant for problem specification* $\mathcal{P}$ if, informally speaking, the environment satisfies the input constraints of $\mathcal{P}$ *on a per node basis, but not necessarily globally.* More formally, for every prefix $\alpha'\phi$ of α, where ϕ is an input from the environment, if there exists σ' in $seq(\mathcal{P})$ such that if $\alpha'|i$ is a prefix of $\sigma'|i$, for all i, then there exists σ in $seq(\mathcal{P})$ such that $\alpha'\phi|i$ is a prefix of $\sigma|i$, for all i.

An execution is $(\mathcal{P}, \mathcal{C})$-*locally-admissible* if it is fair, locally user compliant for $\mathcal{P}$, and correct for the communication system $\mathcal{C}$.

The definition of local simulation is the same as global simulation except that condition 3 becomes:

3'. For every $(\mathcal{C}_2, \mathcal{C}_1)$-locally-admissible execution α of Sim, there exists a sequence σ in $seq(\mathcal{C}_2)$ such that $\sigma|i = top(\alpha)|i$ for all i, $0 \le i \le n-1$.

7.6 PSEUDOCODE CONVENTIONS

The pseudocode description of an asynchronous message-passing algorithm will consist of a list of input and output events. Each list element will begin with the name of the event and include the changes to the local state that result from the occurrence of the event; the changes will be described in typical sequential pseudocode.

Besides local state changes, the occurrence of an event causes zero or more outputs to become enabled. Most of the time, this will be indicated by simply stating "enable output X." Occasionally it is more convenient to list the conditions under which an output is enabled together with the local state changes caused by its occurrence; this is usually the case when the enabling conditions are somewhat involved.

If the result of an occurrence of an output event is simply to disable it, that is, no (additional) local state changes are made, then we will not include a separate list element for that output.

Recall that in the asynchronous systems, the order in which the enabled outputs occur in an execution is immaterial, as long as the proper atomicity for events on the same node is maintained.

Exercises

7.1 Using the model presented in this chapter, specify the no deadlock and no lockout versions of the mutual exclusion problem.

7.2 Prove that global simulation implies local simulation.

7.3 Prove that global simulation is transitive, that is, if A globally simulates B, and B globally simulates C, then A globally simulates C.

Is the same true of local simulation?

Chapter Notes

The formal model presented in this chapter is a special case of the input-output automaton (IOA) model of Lynch and Tuttle [177]. The IOA model is a very general model for describing entities that interact asynchronously through inputs and outputs. We have used IOA as an "assembly language" to describe layered systems. The first two conditions on the definition of execution are the conditions for being an execution in the IOA model. However, we have restricted our attention to a subset of executions that also satisfy the node atomicity property, with the last two conditions. Our motivation for doing so was to have a (relatively) unified treatment of both asynchronous and synchronous models; our definitions for the synchronous model appear in Chapters 11 and 12. The IOA model treats composition and fairness more generally and provides support for a number of verification methods, in particular, hierarchical proofs of correctness. Chapter 8 of the book by Lynch [175] contains additional references concerning the IOA model.

Layering is the technique that allows system designers to control the complexity of building large-scale systems. In particular, layering in communication systems is exemplified by the International Standards Organization's Open Systems Interconnection Reference Model for computer networks (cf. [251]).

Although the specification of broadcast presented here results in a message being received by all the processors, the actual topology of the system need not be a clique. Typically the broadcast will be running on top of a *network layer protocol*, which takes care of routing messages over paths of point-to-point channels for any topology (again, cf. [251]).

8

Broadcast and Multicast

In this chapter, we discuss one of the most important abstractions for designing distributed programs: communication primitives that provide broadcast and multicast with powerful semantics.

Previously, when addressing the message passing model, we assumed that processors communicate over point-to-point links, which provides *one-to-one* communication, that is, one processor sends a message on an incident link to a single other processor. However, in many cases, it is useful to send a message to several processors at the same time. Such a facility provides *one-to-all* or *one-to-many* communication, by having a *broadcast* or a *multicast* step, in which a processor sends a message either to all or to a number of processors.

Broadcast and multicast can easily be simulated by sending a number of point-to-point messages; furthermore, in certain systems, based on local area networks, the low-level communication layer provides broadcast or multicast primitives of this kind. Yet, in both cases, there is no guarantee regarding *ordering*, because messages are not necessarily received in the same order. Similarly, there is no guarantee regarding *reliability*, because failures might cause processors to receive different sets of messages.

This chapter formalizes several ordering and reliability requirements, and shows how to provide them. The first part of the chapter addresses broadcast services, which support one-to-all communication with guarantees about ordering and reliability of messages. Then we address multicast services, which provide one-to-many communication.

8.1   SPECIFICATION OF BROADCAST SERVICES

In this section, we define various broadcast services. We begin with the basic definitions. We then describe three different ordering properties that can be provided, and we finish with a definition of fault tolerance.

8.1.1   The Basic Service Specification

A broadcast service can support various properties specified, for example, by the type of ordering and by the degree of fault tolerance they provide. These properties together form the *quality of service* provided by the broadcast; several such properties are specified in Section 8.1.2. To specify the quality of service, the interface to the basic broadcast service from Chapter 7 is modified:

bc-send$_i$(m, **qos**): An input event of processor p_i, which sends a message m to all processors, containing an indication of the sender; *qos* is a parameter describing the quality of service required.

bc-recv$_i$(m, j, **qos**): An output event in which processor p_i receives the message m previously broadcast by p_j; *qos*, as above, describes the quality of service provided.

A broadcast message is also received at the sender itself. Note that the bc-send and bc-recv operations do not block, that is, the bc-send operation does not wait for the message to be received at all processors, and the bc-recv operation works in interrupt mode.

These procedures for a particular quality of service (say, X) are transparently implemented on top of some low-level communication system that provides another, usually weaker, quality of service (say, Y). The type of the low-level communication system is unimportant in the specification of the broadcast, although it can influence the design of the implementation. For each processor,[1] there is a piece of code that, by communicating with its counterparts on other nodes using the low-level communication system, provides the desired quality of service.

As defined in Section 7.2.2, the basic broadcast service specification for n processors consists of sequences of bc-send$_i$ and bc-recv$_i$ events, $0 \leq i \leq n - 1$. In these sequences, each bc-recv$_i$(m,j,basic) event is mapped to an earlier bc-send$_j$(m,basic) event, every message received was previously sent (Integrity), and every message that is sent is received once (Liveness) and only once (No Duplicates) at every processor.

The Liveness property is a strong one. When we consider the possibility of failures later, we will weaken the Liveness property.

---

[1] There can be several user processes on the same processor requiring broadcast communication; typically, a single *daemon* process interacts on behalf of all user processes with the low-level communication system. Keeping with the terminology used earlier in this book, we refer to this daemon as a *processor*.

8.1.2   Broadcast Service Qualities

Broadcast properties can be organized along two axes:

Ordering: Do processors see all messages in the same order or just see the messages from a single processor in the order they were sent? Does the order in which messages are received by the broadcast service preserve the happens-before relation?

Reliability: Do all processors see the same set of messages even if failures occur in the underlying system? Do all processors see all the messages broadcast by a nonfaulty processor?

We next explore these two axes separately.

8.1.2.1   Ordering   We consider three popular ordering requirements. The first one requires the ordering of all messages sent by the same processor. The second one requires the ordering of all messages, irrespective of sender. The final one requires the ordering of messages that are causally related.

A single-source FIFO (**ssf**) broadcast service is specified by further constraining the set of sequences defining the basic broadcast service. Using the mapping κ to disambiguate messages with the same content, we require that sequences of bc-send and bc-recv events also satisfy:[2]

Single-Source FIFO: For all messages m_1 and m_2 and all processors p_i and p_j, if p_i sends m_1 before it sends m_2, then m_2 is *not* received at p_j before m_1 is.

A totally ordered (**to**) broadcast service is specified by further constraining the set of sequences defining the basic broadcast service. Each sequence of bc-send and bc-recv events must also satisfy:

Totally Ordered: For all messages m_1 and m_2 and all processors p_i and p_j, if m_1 is received at p_i before m_2 is, then m_2 is *not* received at p_j before m_1 is.

Before defining the next ordering property, we extend the notion of one event happening before another to define what is meant by one message happening before another. We assume that all communication of the high-level application is performed by using only bc-send and bc-recv. That is, there are no "behind the scenes" messages. Given a sequence of bc-send and bc-recv events, message m_1 is said to *happen before* message m_2 if either:

- The bc-recv event for m_1 happens before (in the sense from Chapter 6) the bc-send event for m_2, or

- m_1 and m_2 are sent by the same processor and m_1 is sent before m_2

---

[2]"Send" and "recv" here refer to "bc-send" and "bc-recv" with quality of service **ssf**. Analogous shortenings are used subsequently.

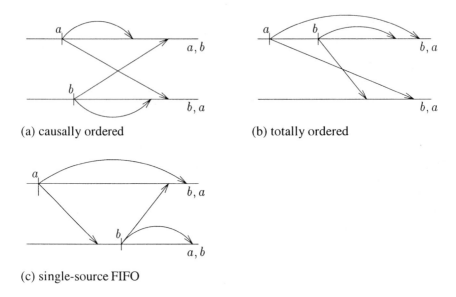

(a) causally ordered   (b) totally ordered

(c) single-source FIFO

Fig. 8.1   Scenarios demonstrating relationships among the ordering requirements.

A causally ordered (CO) broadcast service is specified by further constraining the set of sequences defining the basic broadcast service. Each sequence of bc-send and bc-recv events must also satisfy:

Causally Ordered: For all messages m_1 and m_2 and every processor p_i, if m_1 happens before m_2, then m_2 is *not* received at p_i before m_1 is.

What are the relationships between these three ordering requirements? First note that causally ordered implies single-source FIFO, because the happens-before relation on messages respects the order in which individual processors send the messages. Other than that situation, none of these ordering requirements implies any other. To see this, consider the three scenarios in Figure 8.1: (a) shows that causally ordered does not imply totally ordered, (b) shows that totally ordered does not imply causally ordered or single-source FIFO, and (c) shows that single-source FIFO does not imply causally ordered or totally ordered.

8.1.2.2   Reliability   Recall that the basic broadcast service must satisfy three properties: Integrity, No Duplicates, and Liveness. In the presence of faulty processors, the Liveness property must be weakened. The specification of a basic broadcast service that is *reliable* (in the presence of f faults) consists of all sequences of bc-send and bc-recv events that satisfy the following. There must be a partitioning of the processor indices into "faulty" and "nonfaulty" such that there are at most f faulty processors, and the mapping κ from bc-recv(m) events to bc-send(m) events (as defined in Section 7.2.2) must satisfy the following properties:

Integrity: For each processor p_i, $0 \leq i \leq n - 1$, the restriction of κ to bc-recv$_i$ events is well-defined. That is, every message received was previously sent— no message is received "out of thin air."

No Duplicates: For each processor p_i, $0 \leq i \leq n - 1$, the restriction of κ to bc-recv$_i$ events is one-to-one. That is, no message is received more than once at any single processor.

Nonfaulty Liveness: When restricted to bc-send and bc-recv events at nonfaulty processors, κ is onto. That is, all messages broadcast by a nonfaulty processor are eventually received by all nonfaulty processors.

Faulty Liveness: If one nonfaulty processor has a bc-recv event that maps to a particular bc-send event of a faulty processor, then every nonfaulty processor has a bc-recv event that maps to the same bc-send event. That is, every message sent by a faulty processor is either received by all nonfaulty processors or by none of them.

This specification is independent of the particular type of failures to be tolerated. However, we will restrict our attention in this chapter to crash failures of the processors.

These conditions give no guarantee on the messages received by faulty processors. The notes at the end of the chapter discuss why we may want to make such provisions, and how to extend the definitions accordingly.

8.1.2.3 *Discussion of Broadcast Properties* Recall that a bc-send$_i(m)$ event does not force an immediate bc-recv$_i(m)$ at p_i. That is, it is possible that the message m is received at p_i with some delay (similar to the delay it incurs before being received at other processors).

If a broadcast service provides total ordering as well as single-source FIFO ordering, then it is causally ordered. (See Exercise 8.1.)

Several combinations of broadcast service properties have proven to be useful and have been assigned their own names. *Atomic* broadcast is a reliable broadcast with total ordering; atomic broadcast is also called *total* broadcast. *FIFO atomic* broadcast is an atomic broadcast with single-source FIFO ordering. *Causal atomic* broadcast is an atomic broadcast that preserves causality (and is therefore also FIFO atomic broadcast). This implies that FIFO atomic broadcast and causal atomic broadcast are equivalent.

8.2 IMPLEMENTING A BROADCAST SERVICE

In this section, we present several implementations of broadcast services, with various qualities of service. By "implementation" we mean global simulation, as defined in Chapter 7.

We first present algorithms for providing basic broadcast and the ordering properties when there are no failures. In Section 8.2.5, we discuss implementations of reliable broadcast.

Throughout this chapter we assume that the underlying message system is asynchronous and point-to-point.

8.2.1 Basic Broadcast Service

The basic broadcast service is simple to implement on top of an asynchronous point-to-point message system with no failures. When a bc-send occurs for message m at processor p_i, p_i uses the underlying point-to-point message system to send a copy of m to all the processors. Once a processor receives the message from p_i over the underlying message system, it performs the bc-recv event for m and i. The proof that this implementation is correct is left to the reader.

8.2.2 Single-Source FIFO Ordering

Single-source FIFO ordering is probably the simplest property to implement on top of basic broadcast. Each processor assigns a sequence number to each of the messages it broadcasts; the sequence number is incremented by one whenever a new message is broadcast. The recipient of a message from p_i with sequence number T waits to perform the single-source FIFO receipt of that message until it has done so for all messages from p_i with sequence numbers less than T. More detailed pseudocode and the proof that this algorithm indeed provides single-source FIFO ordering are left to the reader (Exercise 8.3).

8.2.3 Totally Ordered Broadcast

A more difficult property to provide is total ordering. Here we describe two possible ways to do so, on top of basic broadcast. First, we outline an asymmetric algorithm that relies on a central coordinator that orders all messages; second, we describe in detail a symmetric algorithm in which processors decide together on an order for all broadcast messages. The second algorithm works on top of a single-source FIFO broadcast service.

8.2.3.1 An Asymmetric Algorithm In response to a request to send a message m in the totally ordered broadcast service, processor p_i sends m using the basic broadcast service to a unique central site at processor p_c. Processor p_c assigns a sequence number to each message and then sends it to all processors using the basic broadcast service. Processors perform the receives for the totally ordered broadcast service in the order specified by the sequence numbers on the messages, waiting if necessary to receive all messages with sequence number less than T before performing the receive for the message with sequence number T. Clearly, because all messages are assigned a number in a central site, the receives of the totally ordered broadcast service happen in the same order at all processors. A more detailed proof that this algorithm indeed provides a total ordering is left to the reader.

To spread the communication overhead, the role of the central site can rotate among processors; the central site is identified with a token, and this token circulates among the processors. Here, we do not discuss the details of this idea any further (see the notes at the end of this chapter).

8.2.3.2 A Symmetric Algorithm

The broadcast algorithm we present is based on assigning timestamps to messages. It also assumes that the underlying communication system provides single-source FIFO broadcast, for example, by using the algorithm of Section 8.2.2.

In the algorithm, each processor maintains an increasing counter, or timestamp. When the processor is supposed to broadcast a message, it tags the message with the current value of its counter before sending it out. Each processor also maintains a vector with estimates of the timestamps of all other processes. The meaning of processor p_i's entry for processor p_j in the vector is that p_i will never again receive a message from p_j with timestamp smaller than or equal to that value. Processor p_i updates its entry for p_j by using the tags on messages received from p_j and using special "timestamp update" messages sent by p_j.

Each processor maintains its own timestamp to be greater than or equal to its estimates of the timestamps of all the other processors, based on the tags of messages it receives. When a processor jumps its own timestamp up in order to ensure this condition, it sends out a timestamp update message.

Each processor maintains a set of messages that are waiting to be received (for the totally ordered broadcast). A message with timestamp T is (total order) received only when the processor is certain that all other messages with timestamp $\leq T$ have arrived at it. This is done by waiting until every entry in its vector is at least T. Then the processor handles all pending messages with timestamps less than or equal to T, in order, breaking ties using processor ids.

The pseudocode appears in Algorithm 21.

To show that this algorithm implements totally ordered broadcast, we must show that messages are received in the same order at all processors. The ordering of messages is done by timestamps, breaking ties with processor ids. The resulting sequence respects the order at each processor by construction and because of the way timestamps are assigned.

More formally, fix some fair execution α of the algorithm that is correct for the single-source FIFO communication system. (Because there are no input constraints that must be satisfied by the environment, the requirement to be user compliant can be dropped from the definition of admissible.)

The next lemma follows immediately from the code.

Lemma 8.1 *Let p_i be any processor. Then every message contained in a bc-send$_i$(m,to) event in α is given a unique timestamp, and timestamps are assigned by p_i in increasing order.*

This immediately implies:

Algorithm 21 Totally ordered broadcast algorithm: code for p_i, $0 \leq i \leq n - 1$.

Initially $ts[j] = 0, 0 \leq j \leq n - 1$, and *pending* is empty

1:   when bc-send$_i$(m,to) occurs: // quality of service to means totally ordered
2:       $ts[i] := ts[i] + 1$
3:       add $\langle m, ts[i], i \rangle$ to *pending*
4:       enable bc-send$_i$($\langle m, ts[i] \rangle$,ssf)
                                     // quality of service ssf means single-source FIFO

5:   when bc-recv$_i$($\langle m, T \rangle$,j,ssf), $j \neq i$, occurs:
                                     // j indicates sender; ignore messages from self
6:       $ts[j] := T$
7:       add $\langle m, T, j \rangle$ to *pending*
8:       if $T > ts[i]$ then
9:           $ts[i] := T$
10:          enable bc-send$_i$($\langle ts\text{-}up, T \rangle$,ssf)   // bcast timestamp update message

11: when bc-recv$_i$($\langle ts\text{-}up, T \rangle$,$j$,ssf), $j \neq i$, occurs: // ignore messages from self
12:      ts$[j] := T$

13: enable bc-recv$_i$(m,j,to) when
14:      $\langle m, T, j \rangle$ is the entry in *pending* with the smallest (T, j)
15:      $T \leq ts[k]$ for all k
16: result: remove $\langle m, T, j \rangle$ from *pending*

Lemma 8.2 *The timestamps assigned to messages in α, together with processor ids, form a total order.*

This total order is called *timestamp order*.

Theorem 8.3 *Algorithm 21 is a totally ordered broadcast algorithm.*

Proof. In order to show that the algorithm is correct, we must show the Integrity, No Duplicates, Liveness, and Total Ordering properties.

Integrity and No Duplicates hold because they hold for the underlying single-source FIFO broadcast service.

Liveness: Suppose in contradiction that some processor p_i has some entry stuck in its pending set forever. Let $\langle m, T, j \rangle$ be the entry with the smallest (T, j) among all those stuck at p_i.

Since processors assign timestamps in increasing order, eventually $\langle m, T, j \rangle$ is the smallest entry overall in p_i's pending set. Since $\langle m, T, j \rangle$ is stuck, there exists some k such that $T > ts[k]$ at p_i forever. So at some point p_i stops increasing $ts[k]$. Let T' be the largest value attained by $ts[k]$ at p_i.

Note that k cannot equal i, since p_i's timestamp never decreases. Then p_i receives no more messages from p_k (over the single-source FIFO broadcast service) after some point. Since messages from p_k are received at p_i in the order sent and since they have increasing timestamps, p_k never sends a message with timestamp larger than T'. But that means p_k never gets the message $\langle m,T,j \rangle$ from p_j, contradicting the correctness of the single-source FIFO broadcast service.

Total Ordering: Suppose p_i performs bc-recv$_i(m_1,j_1,$to) and later performs bc-recv$_i(m_2,j_2,$to). We must show that $(T_1,j_1) < (T_2,j_2)$, where (T_1,j_1) is m_1's timestamp and (T_2,j_2) is m_2's timestamp.

Case 1: Suppose $\langle m_2,T_2,j_2 \rangle$ is in p_i's pending set when bc-recv$_i(m_1,j_1,$to) occurs. Then $(T_1,j_1) < (T_2,j_2)$, since otherwise m_2 would be accepted before m_1.

Case 2: Suppose $\langle m_2,T_2,j_2 \rangle$ is not yet in p_i's pending set when bc-recv$_i(m_1,j_1,$ to) occurs. However, $T_1 \leq ts[j_2]$. Therefore p_i received some message m from p_{j_2} (over the single-source FIFO broadcast service) before this point whose timestamp T is greater than or equal to T_1. By the single-source FIFO property, p_{j_2} sends m_2 after it sends m, and thus m_2's timestamp T_2 is greater than T. Thus $T_2 > T_1$. □

8.2.4 Causality

Both totally ordered broadcast algorithms presented in Section 8.2.3 already preserve causality. The proof that the asymmetric algorithm of Section 8.2.3 provides causal receipt of messages is left to the reader; see Exercise 8.6. Here we show that the timestamp order, defined for the symmetric algorithm, Algorithm 21, extends the happens-before relation on the high-level broadcast messages.

Lemma 8.4 *The timestamp order extends the happens-before relation.*

Proof. Let p_i be any processor. Clearly, the timestamps assigned to messages broadcast by p_i are increasing. So, we only need to prove that the timestamp assigned to a message broadcast by p_i is strictly larger than the timestamp of any message previously received at p_i.

Let (T_1,j) be the timestamp of a message m_1 received at p_i and let (T_2,i) be the timestamp of a message m_2 broadcast by p_i after the receipt of m_1. Clearly, by the code of the algorithm, $T_1 < T_2$, which proves the lemma. □

Therefore, we have.

Theorem 8.5 *Algorithm 21 is a causally ordered broadcast algorithm.*

However, causality can be implemented without total ordering. Logical time can be used to add causality to a broadcast algorithm, with any quality of service. We now describe an algorithm that provides causality but not total ordering. The pseudocode appears as Algorithm 22. The algorithm uses vector timestamps, as defined in Chapter 6. Each processor maintains a vector clock and each message is tagged with a vector timestamp that is the current value of the vector clock. Before a message can be (causally) received, it has to pass through a "logical ordering" filter, which guarantees that messages are received according to the causal ordering.

Algorithm 22 Causally ordered broadcast algorithm: code for p_i, $0 \leq i \leq n - 1$.

Initially $vt[j] = 0, 0 \leq j \leq n - 1$, and *pending* is empty

1: when bc-send$_i$(m,co) occurs:
                                                // quality of service co means causally ordered
2:      $vt[i] := vt[i] + 1$
3:      enable bc-recv$_i$($\langle m \rangle$,co)   // receive the message locally
4:      enable bc-send$_i$($\langle m, vt \rangle$,basic)
                                    // quality of service basic means ordinary broadcast

5: when bc-recv$_i$($\langle m, v \rangle$,j,basic), $j \neq i$, occurs:
                                    // j indicates sender; ignore messages from self
6:      add $\langle m, v, j \rangle$ to *pending*

7: enable bc-recv$_i$(m, j, co) when:
8:      $\langle m, v, j \rangle$ is in *pending*
9:      $v[j] = vt[j] + 1$
10:     $v[k] \leq vt[k]$ for all $k \neq i$
11: result: remove $\langle m, v, j \rangle$ from *pending*
12:     $vt[j] := vt[j] + 1$

Recall that the value of the kth coordinate of the vector clock at processor p_j indicates how many messages from p_k were (causally) received by p_j. Assume that a message m tagged with vector timestamp v arrives at p_j from p_i (using the basic broadcast service); when can p_j (causally) receive m? Clearly, p_j must first (causally) receive all previous messages from p_i; their number is indicated by $v[i] - 1$. For all other processors p_k, p_j must first (causally) receive all messages (causally) received by p_i before sending m; their number is indicated by $v[k]$. As we argue below, when these conditions are satisfied, p_j has already (causally) received all messages that happen before m. Therefore, p_j can (causally) receive m.

Figure 8.2 presents an example execution of Algorithm 22. In this execution, two messages are delayed: First, the message $\langle 0, 2, 0 \rangle$ is delayed until the previous message from p_1, $\langle 0, 1, 0 \rangle$, arrives; later, the message $\langle 1, 3, 0 \rangle$ from p_0 is delayed until the message $\langle 0, 3, 0 \rangle$ from p_1 (which happens before it) arrives.

The precondition in Line 9 for performing the causal receive guarantees that, in Line 12, p_i assigns the maximum of $vt_i[k]$ and v to $vt_i[k]$, for every k. This implies the following lemma, whose proof is left to the reader (Exercise 8.6):

Lemma 8.6 *vt_i is a vector clock.*

Intuitively, this lemma implies that messages are received in causal order and justifies the immediate (causal) receipt of messages to self, as shown in the proof of Theorem 8.7.

Theorem 8.7 *Algorithm 22 is a causally ordered broadcast algorithm.*

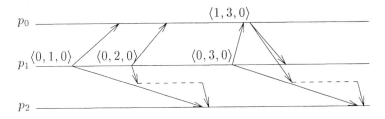

Fig. 8.2 Illustration for the behavior of Algorithm 22.

Proof. Integrity and No Duplicates hold because they hold for the underlying basic broadcast service.

Liveness: Suppose, in contradiction that some processor p_i has some entry stuck in its *pending* set forever. Let $\langle m, v, j \rangle$ be the entry with the smallest vector timestamp (in the lexicographic ordering on vector timestamps) among all those stuck at p_i.

Since $\langle m, v, j \rangle$ is stuck, either $v[j]$ is never equal to $vt_i[j] + 1$ or $v[k]$ is always greater than $vt_i[k]$, for some k. First, consider the former case. Since $vt_i[j]$ is always incremented by one, it gets stuck at some value less than $v[j] - 1$. This means that some message m' sent by p_i before m has not been (causally) received by p_j, and in the latter case, some message m' (causally) received at p_i before sending m, has not been (causally) received by p_j. In both cases, by the Liveness properties of the underlying broadcast service, m' must be stuck in p_j's *pending* set. Clearly, the vector timestamp of m' is smaller than v, but this contradicts the minimality of m.

Causally Ordered: Assume a message m from p_j is (causally) received at p_i, and let v be its vector timestamp. Let m' be a message that happens before m, with vector timestamp v'. By Lemma 8.6, $v' < v$, and by the condition in Lines 9–10, p_i receives m' before m. $\qquad \Box$

This algorithm is more efficient than the totally ordered broadcast algorithm (Algorithm 21). For example, messages are locally received immediately; however, the tags are n times as big. Another important advantage of this algorithm is that causal ordering can be provided even in the presence of failures, whereas total ordering cannot, as we shall see in Section 8.2.5.2.

8.2.5 Reliability

We now turn to the problem of implementing reliable broadcast on top of an asynchronous point-to-point message passing system subject to f processor crashes. Here we need to define more precisely the interface to the underlying point-to-point system on which reliable broadcast is implemented; in this system, messages sent by faulty processors may not be received.

The inputs are $send_i(M)$ and the outputs are $recv_j(M)$, where i indicates the sending processor, j indicates the receiving processor, and M is a set of messages (each message includes an indication of the sender and recipient). A sequence of

---

Algorithm 23 Reliable broadcast algorithm: code for p_i, $0 \leq i \leq n - 1$.

1:   when bc-send$_i$(m,reliable) occurs:
2:      enable bc-send$_i$($\langle m,i \rangle$,basic)   // message includes id of original sender
                              // quality of service basic means ordinary broadcast

3:   when bc-recv$_i$($\langle m,k \rangle$,j,basic) occurs:
4:      if m was not already received then
5:         enable bc-send$_i$($\langle m,k \rangle$,basic)
                              // quality of service basic means ordinary broadcast
6:         enable bc-recv$_i$(m,k,reliable)

---

inputs and outputs is in the allowable set if it satisfies the following: There exists a partitioning of processor indices into faulty and nonfaulty, with at most f being faulty, satisfying the following properties.

Integrity: Every message received by any processor p_i was previously sent to p_i by some processor.

No Duplicates: No message sent is received more than once.

Nonfaulty Liveness: Every message sent by a nonfaulty processor to any nonfaulty processor is eventually received.

In the above definition, no restrictions are placed on the messages received by faulty processors; see the chapter notes for further discussion of the problems this might cause.

8.2.5.1 *Reliable Basic Broadcast*

The following simple "message diffusion" algorithm provides reliable broadcast in the presence of crash failures. The algorithm is simple: When a processor is supposed to perform the reliable broadcast send for a message, it sends the message to all the processors. When a processor receives a message for the first time (from the underlying message system), it sends this message to all its neighbors and then performs the reliable broadcast receive for it. The pseudocode appears in Algorithm 23.

Theorem 8.8 *Algorithm 23 is a reliable broadcast algorithm.*

Proof. We need to prove that the algorithm satisfies the four properties for reliable broadcast.

Integrity and No Duplicates: They follow immediately from the analogous properties of the underlying point-to-point communication system.

Nonfaulty Liveness: Clearly, if a nonfaulty processor broadcasts a message then it sends it to all processors (including itself). By the Nonfaulty Liveness property of the underlying communication system, all nonfaulty processors receive this message and, by the code, perform the reliable bc-recv for it.

Faulty Liveness: Assume that some nonfaulty processor performs the reliable bc-recv for a message m. Before doing so, the processor forwards the message to all processors. By the Nonfaulty Liveness property of the underlying communication system, all processors receive this message and perform the reliable bc-recv for it, if they have not done so already. □

8.2.5.2 *Reliable Broadcast with Ordering Properties*

Adding single-source FIFO to reliable broadcast can be achieved exactly as in the failure-free case discussed above.

Totally ordered reliable broadcast cannot be achieved in the presence of crash failures when the underlying communication system is asynchronous. This is true because totally ordered reliable broadcast can be used to solve consensus (Exercise 8.10), and as we saw in Chapter 5, consensus cannot be solved in an asynchronous system subject to crash failures. In Section 8.4, we discuss strengthenings of the model that permit totally ordered reliable broadcast to be implemented.

In contrast, causally ordered broadcast can be achieved in the presence of crash failures. In particular, using Algorithm 22 with a reliable broadcast service instead of a basic broadcast service provides a reliable causally ordered broadcast service. The proof of correctness is similar to the proof of Theorem 8.7 and is left to the reader. Messages sent by nonfaulty processors are delivered rather quickly, because of the underlying message diffusion algorithm used to achieve reliability.

8.3 MULTICAST IN GROUPS

So far in this chapter, we have assumed that messages are broadcast to all the processors. However, in many realistic situations, a message need only get to a subset of the processors. For example, in the replicated database application we present in Section 8.4, it is expected that only a (small) number of processors will be servers. It is not desirable to replicate the data in all processors, for reasons of efficiency, security, maintenance, and so on. In this case, we need only send a message to a subset of the processors, that is, we desire *one-to-many* communication.

A *group* is a collection of processors that act together, as specified by the system or by an application. A processor can belong to several groups, depending on its functionality. We would like to enable processors to view groups of processors as a single entity and to provide the illusion that information can be sent to the whole group as one. We formalize this by extending the notions developed for broadcast services.

At this point, we sidestep the issues of managing the groups by assuming that groups are static and well-defined. That is, the groups are specified in advance, and no new groups are formed during the execution of the system. Furthermore, groups are identified by a *group id*, and it is known which processors belong to which group. The chapter notes discuss how groups are managed.

8.3.1   Specification

A multicast service, like the broadcast services discussed in Section 8.1.2, will satisfy various reliability and ordering properties, modified to be with respect to the relevant group. An additional property we require is that messages should be ordered across groups.

In more detail, the interface to a basic multicast system is with two events:

mc-send$_i$(m,G, **qos**): An input event of processor p_i, which sends a message m to all processors in group G, where *qos* is a parameter describing the quality of service required.

mc-recv$_i$(m,j, **qos**): An output event in which processor p_i receives a message m previously multicast by p_j, where *qos*, as above, describes the quality of service provided.

A sequence of inputs and outputs is in the set of allowable sequences for a basic multicast systems if there exists a mapping, κ, from each mc-recv$_i$(m, j) event in the sequence to an earlier mc-send$_j$(m, G) event such that $p_j \in G$. That is, no message is received by a processor that is not in the group to which the message was multicast. The mapping κ must also satisfy the same Integrity and No Duplicates properties as for broadcast (Section 7.2.2), and a slightly modified Liveness condition; the modification is that every message sent is received at every processor *in the group to which it was directed.*

The definition of a reliable multicast extends the notion of reliable broadcast in the obvious manner. A multicast service is *reliable* if the mapping κ satisfies the following properties:

Integrity: Every message received by a processor was previously sent to the group containing that processor.

No Duplicates: No message is received more than once at the same processor.

Nonfaulty Liveness: If a mc-recv(m) event at a nonfaulty processor is mapped by κ to some mc-send(m,G) event, then every nonfaulty processor in G has an mc-recv(m) event that is mapped by κ to the same mc-send event. That is, every message sent by a nonfaulty processor is received by every nonfaulty processor in the target group.

Faulty Liveness: Every message sent by a faulty processor is either received by all nonfaulty processors in the target group or by none of them.

The definition of an ordered multicast also extends the definition for ordered broadcast. Once again, we distinguish between total ordering and single-source FIFO ordering; here, in addition, we require the same order of receipt only for two messages that were multicast to the *same* group by arbitrary senders (in the totally ordered case) or by the same sender (in the single-source FIFO case).

We also have a stronger condition, defined as follows:

Multiple-Group Ordering: Let m_1 and m_2 be messages. For any pair of processors p_i and p_j, if the events mc-recv$_i(m_1)$ and mc-recv$_i(m_2)$ occur at p_i and p_j, then they occur in the same order.

This condition implies that m_1 and m_2 were either sent to the same group or to groups whose intersection contains p_i and p_j.

Finally, we modify the causality property along the same lines. A multicast service is *causally ordered* if for any pair of messages m_1 and m_2, if m_1 happens before m_2, then for any processor p_i, if the event mc-recv(m_2) occurs at p_i, the event mc-recv(m_1) occurs at p_i earlier.

8.3.2 Implementation

A simple technique to implement multicast is to impose it on top of a broadcast service. To each message, we attach the id of the group to which it is addressed. The multicast algorithm filters the messages received by the broadcast service and delivers only the messages addressed to groups to which the processor belongs. Different service qualities are achieved by employing an underlying broadcast service with the corresponding qualities. This correspondence is obvious for all qualities, except for Multiple-Group Ordering. Yet, if the underlying broadcast algorithm supports Total Ordering, then we also have Multiple-Group Ordering (see Exercise 8.11). This method is not very efficient—it employs a heavy broadcast mechanism, even if groups are small, and enforces global ordering, even if groups are disjoint.

An alternative approach extends the asymmetric algorithm for total ordering (of Section 8.2.3.1). Instead of a single central site, we have a number of coordinator sites; in particular, a single processor in each multicast group is designated as the *primary destination*. We assume that each processor can communicate with each other processor and that messages between them are received in FIFO order.

We pick a primary destination for each multicast group and organize *all* processors into a *message propagation forest*, so that the following properties are guaranteed:

- The primary destination of a group G is an ancestor of all processors in G.

- If two multicast groups intersect, then the primary destination of one group is an ancestor of the primary destination of the other group.

The second property implies that the primary destinations of intersecting multicast groups are in the same tree in the message propagation forest.

For example, Figure 8.3 presents a possible message propagation forest (in this case, a tree) for a system with eight processors and seven multicast groups. In this example, p_3 is the primary destination for $\{p_2, p_3\}$, $\{p_1, p_2, p_3, p_4\}$, $\{p_3, p_4, p_5\}$, and $\{p_3, p_7\}$.

To send a message to group G, a processor sends it to the primary destination of G; the message is then propagated down the tree until it reaches all the processors in group G. In the example of Figure 8.3, a message to the group $\{p_0, p_1, p_2\}$ is sent to p_2 and is propagated to p_0 and p_1; a message to the group $\{p_2, p_3\}$ is sent to p_3 and is

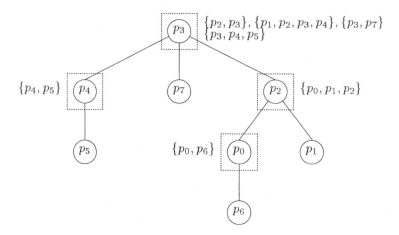

Fig. 8.3   A message propagation forest with a single tree; the primary destinations are marked with boxes, and the groups are indicated next to them.

propagated to p_2; and a message to the group $\{p_4, p_5\}$ is sent to p_4 and is propagated to p_5.

Messages to intersecting groups get ordered as they are funneled through the common ancestor in the the message propagation forest. For example, the messages to the intersecting groups $\{p_0, p_1, p_2\}$ and $\{p_2, p_3\}$ are both funneled through p_2, where they are ordered. This order is preserved because messages sent over the lower layer are received in FIFO order.

Note that because p_4 and p_2 are primary destinations for non-intersecting multicast groups, neither of them is an ancestor of the other. In fact, processors in a disjoint set of multicast groups can be placed in a separate tree in the message propagation forest.

The details of this algorithm, as well as heuristics for constructing a message propagation forest with minimal depth, are not discussed any further; the chapter notes indicate the source of this algorithm.

Another important issue is what happens when groups are dynamic, either because processors leave and join groups or because processors fail and recover. The question is, How are messages ordered with respect to the new groups? For example, is it guaranteed that a processor joining a group will receive all messages previously received by the group, or will it start receiving messages from a particular point onward?

Special *group membership change* events occur when the membership of a multi-cast group changes, for any of the above reasons. *Virtual synchrony* is the property that group membership change events are ordered together with ordinary messages. This ensures that multicast messages are received completely and if needed, in order, to the group according to its new membership. If two processors stay in the same group after a change in membership, they will receive the same messages (and in the same order, according to the ordering constraint required). Virtual synchrony places no restriction on the behavior of faulty processors or on processors that become detached from the majority of processors because of communication failures.

8.4 AN APPLICATION: REPLICATION

8.4.1 Replicated Database

Here we describe a highly simplified example of the utility of a broadcast facility, with different qualities of service. The example is the implementation of a replicated database.

In this application, a database is replicated in a number of sites. Replication increases availability of the data because the data is available even when some of the replicas fail and improves performance by allowing data to be retrieved from the least loaded or "nearest" replica.

For simplicity, we assume the database is replicated in all processors. To guarantee the consistency of the database, it is required that the same set of updates is applied to all copies of the database that are situated at nonfaulty processors and that the updates are applied in the same order.

Assume that updates are sent with an atomic broadcast, which is reliable and supports total ordering. Then applying the updates in the order in which the corresponding messages are received immediately ensures the consistency of the database.

FIFO atomic broadcast (or multicast) is useful when updates may depend on each other. Consider, for example, a database that contains data on bank accounts, and a customer that first deposits money to an account and then withdraws money from the same account (counting on the money just deposited). Assume that the order of these transactions is reversed. Then it is possible that the account will show a negative balance, or even that the withdrawal will not be approved.

8.4.2 The State Machine Approach

The database example is generalized by the *state machine approach*, a general methodology for handling replicated data as part of an implementation of a fault-tolerant service, which is used by a number of *client* processors. The service is conceptually provided by a *state machine*.

A state machine consists of some internal variables and responds to various requests from clients. A request may cause changes to the internal variables and may cause some outputs. An output may be directed to the client that invoked the request or may be directed to other entities in the system. Two important assumptions made in the state machine approach are (1) requests are processed by a state machine in causal order and (2) outputs are completely determined by the sequence of requests processed and by nothing else.

To make the service that is being provided fault tolerant, the state machine is replicated at a number of processors. Client interactions with the state machine replicas must be carefully coordinated. In particular, we must ensure that every replica receives the same sequence of requests.[3] This condition can be achieved by a totally ordered broadcast mechanism. As we discussed above, such a broadcast cannot be achieved in an asynchronous system subject to (unannounced) crash failures.

We now discuss three ways to achieve a totally ordered broadcast in two stronger models.

We first consider a type of processor failure that is even more benign than crash failures, called *failstop*. In the failstop model, processors have some method for correctly detecting whether another processor has failed. (See the chapter notes for a discussion of some such methods.)

Second, we consider a stronger model in which there are known upper bounds on message delay and processor step time. In this model, we can tolerate unannounced crash failures.

Each of the three methods is based on the idea of assigning timestamps to requests and processing the requests in timestamp order. The trick is to figure out when a request can be processed; we have to be sure that no request with higher priority (lower timestamp) will be received later, that is, we have to be sure that the first request is *stable*.

Method 1: In the asynchronous system with failstop processors, FIFO channels are implemented. Logical clocks are used as the timestamps by the clients, and every client is required to invoke a request infinitely often (a request can be null). The client sends the request (and its timestamp) using reliable broadcast. A request is *stable* at a state machine replica if the replica has received a request with a larger timestamp from every nonfaulty client. The failstop assumption is crucial for determining which clients are faulty.

Method 2: In the system with bounded message delay d and crash failures, we implement synchronized clocks. (Chapter 13 discusses fault-tolerant clock synchronization algorithms for such systems.) Each client assigns its request a timestamp consisting of the current value of its synchronized clocks and its id (to break ties). The synchronized clocks must ensure that every request from the same client has a different clock time, and that the clock skew, ϵ, is less than the minimum message delay, $d - u$. These conditions are needed to make sure that the timestamps are consistent with causality. A client sends a request (and its timestamp) using reliable broadcast. The request is *stable* at a state machine replica once the replica's clock time is at least $2d + \epsilon$ larger than the timestamp on the request. At this time, every request with a smaller timestamp will have been received already. The reason is that any other request reaches a nonfaulty processor within d time, and that processor relays the request, as part of the reliable broadcast, so that all nonfaulty processors receive the request within another d time. The ϵ term takes care of the clock skew.

Method 3: We assume the same kind of system as for Method 2; however, the clocks need not be synchronized. In this method, the timestamps are assigned by the

---

[3]This requirement can be weakened in special cases. For instance, a read-only request need not go to all replicas, and two requests that commute can be processed in either order.

replicas, not the clients. Clients send requests (without timestamps) using reliable broadcast. The replicas determine the timestamps as follows. There are two kinds of timestamps, *candidate* and *final*. When the replica at processor p_i receives a request, it assigns a candidate timestamp to it whose value is $i + 1$ more than the maximum of the largest timestamp, either candidate or final, assigned by p_i so far. After p_i has waited $2d$ time, it has received the candidate timestamp for that request from all nonfaulty replicas. Then p_i assigns the maximum candidate timestamp received as the final timestamp. A request r is *stable* at replica p_i if it has been assigned a final timestamp by p_i and there is no other request r' for which p_i has proposed a candidate timestamp smaller than r's final timestamp. Thus there is no possibility that the final timestamp for r' will be earlier than that of r.

Exercises

8.1 Prove that if a broadcast service provides both single-source FIFO ordering and total ordering, then it is also causal.

8.2 Write pseudocode for the basic broadcast algorithm described in Section 8.2.1; prove its correctness.

8.3 Write pseudocode for the single-source FIFO broadcast algorithm described in Section 8.2.2; prove its correctness.

8.4 Extend the asymmetric algorithm of Section 8.2.3 to provide FIFO ordering.

Hint: Force a FIFO order on the messages from each processor to the central site.

8.5 Show that the symmetric algorithm of Section 8.2.3.2 (Algorithm 21) provides FIFO ordering.

8.6 Show that Algorithm 21 provides the causal ordering property, if each point-to-point link delivers messages in FIFO order.

8.7 Prove Lemma 8.6.

8.8 Can the vector timestamps used in Algorithm 22 be replaced with ordinary (scalar) timestamps?

8.9 Show that Algorithm 22 does not provide total ordering, by explicitly constructing an execution in which (concurrent) messages are not received in the same order by all processors.

8.10 Prove that totally ordered reliable broadcast cannot be implemented on top of an asynchronous point-to-point message system.

Hint: Use reduction to the consensus problem.

8.11 Show that broadcast with total ordering implies multiple-group ordering.

Chapter Notes

Broadcast and multicast are the cornerstones of many distributed systems. A few of them provide only reliability, for example, SIFT [261], whereas others provide ordering and/or causality, in addition to reliability, for example, Amoeba [146], Delta-4 [218], Isis [55], Psync [215], Transis [11], Totem [183], and Horus [256]. Besides supporting different service qualities, different systems rely on different implementations. There has been work comparing the performance of different implementations of atomic broadcast (cf. [86]).

Atomic broadcast implementations were first suggested by Chang and Maxemchuk [71], by Schneider, Gries, and Schlichting [236], and by Cristian, Aghili, Dolev, and Strong [88]. Cheriton and Zwaenepoel suggested process groups as an abstraction in the V system [77]. Birman and Joseph were the first to connect the ordering and reliability concepts suggested for broadcast with the notion of process groups [53].

This chapter started with definitions of several qualities of service that could be provided by a broadcast simulation; our definitions build on the work of Garcia-Molina and Spauster [120] as well as Hadzilacos and Toueg [129].

Next, several simulations of broadcast with various qualities of service were described. The algorithm for FIFO ordering is folklore. The asymmetric algorithm of Section 8.2.3.1 is due to Chang and Maxemchuk [71], who also describe mechanisms for rotating the coordinator's job. In this algorithm, a message is sent to the coordinator via point-to-point transmission, and then it is broadcast to all processors. An alternative algorithm is to broadcast the message to all processors and then have the coordinator send ordering information; this alternative is beneficial when the message body is large. The symmetric algorithm (Algorithm 21) is based on the ideas of Lamport [154] and Schneider [238]. Our treatment follows Attiya and Welch [34], as corrected by Higham and Warpechowska-Gruca [138]. Other algorithms can be found in [9, 10, 53, 54, 120, 129, 146, 183].

The causal broadcast algorithm (Algorithm 22) is based on algorithms of Schiper, Eggli, and Sandoz [235] and of Raynal, Schiper, and Toueg [227]; Schwarz and Mattern describe this algorithm in the general context of causality [239].

Algorithm 23, the implementation of reliable broadcast by message diffusion, is from Cristian, Aghili, Dolev, and Strong [88]; this paper also contains implementations that can withstand Byzantine failures.

The propagation forest algorithm for providing multi-group ordering (described in Section 8.3) is by Garcia-Molina and Spauster [120].

There is a wide body of algorithms that build broadcast or multicast over hardware that provides unreliable broadcast, for example, Amoeba [146], Psync [215], Transis [11], and Totem [183].

Handling dynamic groups is typically studied in the context of *group communication* systems. The April 1996 issue of the *Communications of the ACM* is dedicated to this topic, and among others, it includes papers describing the Totem, the Transis, and the Horus systems. Virtual synchrony was originally defined for Isis (see Birman and van Renesse [55]). *Extended virtual synchrony* specifies how group membership events are reported to processors that recover and to processors that are detached from the majority of processors. It was defined for Totem by Moser, Amir, Melliar-Smith, and Agrawal [192]. An alternative specification extending virtual synchrony to apply when the network partitions was implemented in Transis (see Dolev, Malki, and Strong [97]).

The Rampart toolkit built by Reiter [228] supports secure group membership changes and reliable atomic group multicasts, in the presence of Byzantine failure.

The state machine approach (described in Section 8.4.2) was suggested by Lamport [155] for failure-free systems; it was extended to failstop processors by Schneider [237] and to Byzantine failures by Lamport [157]. Schneider [238] gives a survey of the state machine approach. A different way to realize the state-machine approach is described in Chapter 17.

The failstop algorithm for totally ordered broadcast (Method 1 in Section 8.4.2) is from Schneider [237]. The totally ordered broadcast algorithm using synchronized clocks (Method 2 in Section 8.4.2) is due to Cristian, Aghili, Strong and Dolev [88]; they also discuss algorithms for more severe fault models. The other totally ordered broadcast algorithm (Method 3 in Section 8.4.2) is essentially the ABCAST algorithm in ISIS [53].

The ordering and reliability properties we have specified for broadcasts put no restrictions on messages received by faulty processors. For example, it is possible that a faulty processor receives a certain message and nonfaulty processors do not receive this message. Alternatively, it is possible that messages are received by a faulty processor in an order that does not obey the requirements placed on nonfaulty processors. Even worse, nonfaulty processors may receive the first message broadcast by a faulty processor, then fail to receive the second one, then receive the third one, etc.

We may require the properties to hold *uniformly*, for both nonfaulty and faulty processors. For example, *uniform integrity* requires that every processor (nonfaulty or faulty) receives a message only if it was previously sent. The notion of uniformity was introduced by Neiger and Toueg [199]; it is discussed at length in Hadzilacos and Toueg [129].

Even when broadcast properties are uniform, it is not trivial to avoid *contamination* of the information in the system. For example, assume that atomic broadcast is used to keep consistent multiple copies of some data. It is possible that a faulty processor will skip the receipt of one atomic broadcast message, including some update to the data; this processor later operates correctly and replies to queries based on the incorrect data it has. To avoid contamination, a processor can refuse to receive any message that reflects the receipt of a series of messages not compatible with the messages received so far by the processor. Gopal and Toueg [124] discuss contamination and how to avoid it.

Group communication systems have been a lively research topic in recent years, with numerous implementations and almost as many specifications. One reason for this proliferation is that fault-tolerant group communication systems inherently require agreement among failure-prone processors: on a sequence of message deliveries, on the membership of a multicast group, or on the order of processor crashes and recoveries. The natural specification of these mechanisms cannot be satisfied when the system is asynchronous, because agreement is not possible in such systems (as was shown in Chapter 5).

An abundance of specifications have tried to cope with this impossibility either by weakening the problem specification or by making stronger environment assumptions. Chockler, Keidar and Vitenberg [79] present a comprehensive description of these specifications and discuss related implementations.

9

Distributed Shared Memory

Distributed shared memory (DSM) is a model for interprocess communication that provides the illusion of a shared memory on top of a message passing system. In this model, processes running on separate nodes can access a shared memory address space, provided by the underlying DSM system, through familiar read and write operations. Thus, by avoiding the programming complexities of message passing, it has become a convenient model for programmers. Such systems are becoming quite common in practical distributed systems (see the notes at the end of this chapter).

In terms of our model in Chapter 7, a DSM is a (global) simulation of an asynchronous shared memory model by the asynchronous message passing model. We call the simulation program, which runs on top of the message system providing the illusion of shared memory, the *memory consistency system* (MCS). The MCS consists of local MCS processes at each processor p_i, which use local memory (e.g., caches) and communicate with each other using a message-passing communication system (see Fig. 9.1). We are not considering faults (see the notes for Chapter 10 for pointers to papers concerning fault-tolerant DSMs).

This chapter focuses on shared memory systems in which all the shared objects are read/write registers. The exercises and chapter notes mention implementations of other data types.

We start this chapter with specifications of the two asynchronous shared memory communication systems to be simulated, introducing the notions of *linearizability* and *sequential consistency*. Next, we present implementations of distributed shared memory, both for linearizability and for sequential consistency. It turns out that sequential consistency has implementations with local operations. In contrast, we show that no such implementations exist for linearizability. By "local" we mean that

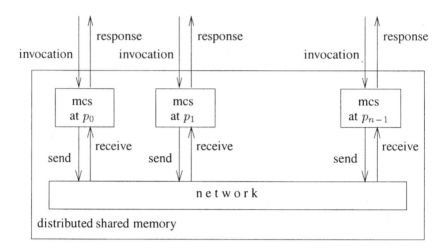

Fig. 9.1   A memory consistency system.

the MCS can decide on the response to an invocation using local computation and need not wait for the result of any communication.

9.1 LINEARIZABLE SHARED MEMORY

Every shared object is assumed to have a sequential specification, which indicates the desired behavior of the object in the absence of concurrency. The object supports *operations*, which are pairs of invocations and matching responses. A *sequential specification* consists of a set of operations and a set of sequences of operations. The latter set comprises the *legal* operation sequences.

For example, a read/write object X supports read and write operations. The invocation for a read is $read_i(X)$ and responses are $return_i(X, v)$, where i indicates the node and v the return value. The invocations for a write have the form $write_i(X, v)$, where v is the value to be written, and the response is $ack_i(X)$. A sequence of operations is legal if each read returns the value of the most recent preceding write, if there is one, and otherwise returns the initial value.

We can now specify a linearizable shared memory communication system. Its inputs are invocations on the shared objects, and its outputs are responses from the shared objects.

For a sequence σ to be in the allowable set, the following properties must be satisfied:

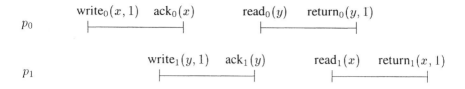

Fig. 9.2 A linearizable execution σ_1.

Correct interaction: For each p_i, $\sigma|i$ consists of alternating invocations and matching responses, beginning with an invocation.[1] This condition imposes constraints on the inputs.

The correct interaction property applies to all objects simultaneously, implying that a processor has to wait for a response from one object before submitting an invocation on another object; this prohibits processors from *pipelining* operations on shared objects.

Liveness: Every invocation has a matching response.

Linearizability: There exists a permutation π of all the operations in σ such that

1. For each object O, $\pi|O$ is legal[2] (i.e., is in the sequential specification of O); and

2. If the response of operation o_1 occurs in σ before the invocation of operation o_2, then o_1 appears before o_2 in π.

In other words, a sequence is linearizable if there is a way to reorder the operations in the sequence that (1) respects the semantics of the objects, as expressed in their sequential specifications, and (2) respects the real-time ordering of events among all the nodes.

For instance, suppose we have two shared registers x and y, both initially 0. The sequence

$$\sigma_1 = \text{write}_0(x, 1)\ \text{write}_1(y, 1)\ \text{ack}_0(x)\ \text{ack}_1(y)$$
$$\text{read}_0(y)\ \text{read}_1(x)\ \text{return}_0(y, 1)\ \text{return}_1(x, 1)$$

(see Fig. 9.2) is linearizable, because $\pi_1 = w_0 w_1 r_0 r_1$ is the desired permutation, where w_i indicates the (complete) write operation by p_i and r_i the (complete) read operation by p_i.

Suppose that r_0 returns 0 instead of 1. The resulting sequence

---

[1]The notation $\sigma|i$ indicates the subsequence of σ consisting of all invocations and responses that are performed by p_i.
[2]The notation $\pi|O$ indicates the subsequence of π consisting of all invocations and responses that are performed on object O.

$$\sigma_2 = \text{write}_0(x, 1) \text{ write}_1(y, 1) \text{ ack}_0(x) \text{ ack}_1(y)$$
$$\text{read}_0(y) \text{ read}_1(x) \text{ return}_0(y, 0) \text{ return}_1(x, 1)$$

is not linearizable. To respect the semantics of y, r_0 (which returns 0 from y) must precede w_1 (which writes 1 to y). But this would violate the real-time ordering, because w_1 precedes r_0 in σ_2.

9.2 SEQUENTIALLY CONSISTENT SHARED MEMORY

However, as we have seen before in this book, in many situations the relative order of events at *different* nodes is irrelevant. The consistency condition called sequential consistency exploits this idea. Formally, a sequence σ of invocations and responses (satisfying the same correct interaction and liveness properties as for linearizable shared memory) is *sequentially consistent* if there exists a permutation π of the operations in σ such that

1. For every object O, $\pi|O$ is legal, according to the sequential specification of O; and

2. If the response for operation o_1 at node p_i occurs in σ before the invocation for operation o_2 at node p_i, then o_1 appears before o_2 in π.

The first condition, requiring the permutation to be legal, is the same as for linearizability. The second condition has been weakened; instead of having to preserve the order of all non overlapping operations at all nodes, it is only required for operations at the same node. The second condition is equivalently written $\sigma|i = \pi|i$, for all i.

The sequence σ_2 is sequentially consistent; $w_0 r_0 w_1 r_1$ is the desired permutation. The read by p_0 has been moved before the write by p_1.

Linearizability is a strictly stronger condition than sequential consistency, that is, every sequence that is linearizable is also sequentially consistent, but the reverse is not true (for example, σ_2). As we shall see below, this difference between sequential consistency and linearizability imposes a difference in the cost of implementing them.

There exist sequences that are not sequentially consistent. For example, suppose r_1 also returns 0 instead of 1, resulting in the sequence

$$\sigma_3 = \text{write}_0(x, 1) \text{ write}_1(y, 1) \text{ ack}_0(x) \text{ ack}_1(y)$$
$$\text{read}_0(y) \text{ read}_1(x) \text{ return}_0(y, 0) \text{ return}_1(x, 0)$$

This sequence is not sequentially consistent. To respect the semantics of x and y, r_0 must precede w_1 and r_1 must precede w_0. To respect the order of events at p_1, w_1 must precede r_1. Yet, by transitivity, these constraints would require r_0 to precede w_0, which violates the order of events at p_0.

Both linearizability and sequential consistency are considered *strong* consistency conditions. In a strong consistency condition, it is required that all processes agree on the same view of the order in which operations occur.

9.3 ALGORITHMS

In this section we present one algorithm for a DSM that provides linearizability and two algorithms that provide sequential consistency.

The design and correctness proofs of the algorithms are greatly simplified by assuming that the underlying message-passing communication system supports totally ordered broadcast, as discussed in Chapter 8. In fact, some form of reliable broadcast is probably embedded in most implementations of distributed shared memory. Therefore, it is helpful to decouple the broadcast component when designing and verifying the implementation; later, it is possible to optimize the broadcast implementation for this specific usage. This also provides an interesting application, demonstrating the usefulness of ordered broadcast.

In this chapter, we use the shorthand notation tbc-send$_i(m)$ to mean bc-send$_i(m,$to$)$ and tbc-recv$_i(m)$ to mean bc-recv$_i(m,$to$)$; that is, a broadcast send and receive with the quality of service required to be totally ordered.

All of our algorithms use complete replication; there is a local copy of every shared object in the state of the MCS process at every node. See the chapter notes for references to algorithms that are more space efficient.

9.3.1 Linearizability

When a request to read or write a shared object is received by the MCS process at a node, it sends a broadcast message containing the request and waits to receive its own message back. When the message arrives, it performs the response for the pending operation, returning the value of its copy of the object for a read and performing an ack for a write. Furthermore, whenever an MCS process receives a broadcast message for a write, it updates its copy of the object accordingly.

Theorem 9.1 *The linearizable shared memory system is simulated by the totally ordered broadcast system.*

Proof. Let α be an admissible execution of the algorithm (i.e., it is fair, user compliant for the shared memory system, and correct for the totally ordered broadcast communication system). We must show that $top(\alpha)$ is linearizable.

Let $\sigma = top(\alpha)$. Order the operations in σ according to the total order provided in α for their broadcasts, to create the desired permutation π.

We now check that π respects the semantics of the objects. Let x be a read/write object. $\pi|x$ is the sequence of operations that access x. Since the broadcasts are totally ordered, every MCS process receives the messages for the operations on x in the same order, which is the order of π, and manages its copy of x correctly.

We now check that π respects the real time ordering of operations in α. Suppose operation o_1 finishes in α before operation o_2 begins. Then o_1's broadcast has been received at its initiator before o_2's broadcast is sent by its initiator. Obviously, o_2's broadcast is ordered after o_1's. Thus o_1 appears in π before o_2. $\qquad\square$

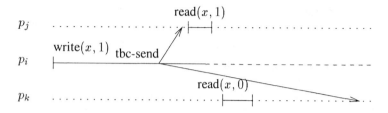

Fig. 9.3 A nonlinearizable execution.

Since the totally ordered broadcast system is simulated by the (point-to-point) message passing system (cf. Chapter 8), we have as a corollary:

Theorem 9.2 *The linearizable shared memory system is simulated by the (point-to-point) message passing system.*

The linearizability algorithm requires every operation, whether a read or a write, to wait until the initiator receives its own broadcast message back. Measured in terms of broadcast operations, the linearizability algorithm is quite efficient—each operation completes within a constant number of broadcast operations. However, a more accurate way to measure the algorithm is in terms of basic point-to-point communication; such analysis depends on the complexities of the underlying totally ordered broadcast algorithm, which are quite high.

Let's try to optimize this algorithm. Note that no copies are changed as a result of receiving the broadcast message for a read. One might think, Why bother to send it? Why not just return the value of your own copy right away?

The problem is that the resulting algorithm does not guarantee linearizability. Consider an execution in which the initial value of x is 0. Processor p_i experiences an invocation to write 1 to x and performs the tbc-send for the write. The broadcast message arrives at processor p_j, which updates its local copy of x to be 1, subsequently does a read on x, and returns the new value 1. Consider a third processor p_k, which has not yet received p_i's broadcast message and still has its local copy of x equal to 0. Suppose that after p_j's read but before receiving p_i's broadcast message, p_k does a read on x, returning the old value 0 (see Fig. 9.3).

No permutation of these three operations can both conform to the read/write specification and preserve the relative real-time orderings of all non overlapping operations.

However, as we show next, this algorithm does provide sequential consistency.

9.3.2 Sequential Consistency

9.3.2.1 Local Read Algorithm In the algorithm, each processor keeps a local copy of every object. A read returns the value of the local copy immediately. When a write comes in to p_i, p_i sends a totally ordered broadcast containing the name of the

---

Algorithm 24 Sequentially consistent local read algorithm:
code for processor p_i, $0 \le i \le n - 1$.

Initially $copy[x]$ holds the initial value of shared object x, for all x

1: when $read_i(x)$ occurs:
2:      enable $return_i(x, copy[x])$

3: when $write_i(x, v)$ occurs:
4:      enable $tbc\text{-}send_i(x, v)$

5: when $tbc\text{-}recv_i(x, v)$ from p_j occurs:
6:      $copy[x] := v$
7:      if $j = i$ then enable $ack_i(x)$

---

object to be updated and the value to be written; but it does not yet generate an ack for the write operation. When p_i receives an update message, it writes the new value to its local copy of the object. If the update message was originated by p_i, then p_i generates an ack and the (unique pending) write operation returns. The pseudocode appears as Algorithm 24.

To prove the correctness of the algorithm, we first show two lemmas that hold for every admissible execution α.

Lemma 9.3 *For every processor p_i, p_i's local copies take on all the values contained in write operations, all updates occur in the same order at each processor, and this order preserves the order of write operations on a per-processor basis.*

Proof. By the code, a tbc-send is done exactly once for each write operation. By the guarantees of the totally ordered broadcast, each processor receives exactly one message for each write operation, these messages are received in the same order at each processor, and this order respects the order of sending on a per-processor basis. □

Call the total order of Lemma 9.3 the *tbcast order*. Lemma 9.4 is true because a write does not end until its update is performed at its initiator and no other operation has begun at the initiator in the meantime.

Lemma 9.4 *For every processor p_i and all shared objects x and y, if read r of object y follows write w to object x in $top(\alpha)|i$, then r's read of p_i's local copy of y follows w's write of p_i's local copy of x.*

Theorem 9.5 *Algorithm 24 implements a sequentially consistent shared memory with local reads.*

Proof. Clearly the reads are local. The rest of the proof shows that $top(\alpha)$ satisfies sequential consistency for any admissible execution α.

Define the permutation π of operations in $top(\alpha)$ as follows. Order the writes in π in tbcast order. Now we explain where to insert the reads. We consider each read in order starting at the beginning of α. Read r by p_i on x is placed immediately after the later (in π) of (1) the previous (in α) operation for p_i (either read or write, on any object) and (2) the write that caused the latest update of p_i's local copy of x preceding the point when r's return was enabled. Break ties using processor ids (e.g., if every processor reads some object before any processor writes any object, then π begins with p_0's read, followed by p_1's read, etc.).

We must show $top(\alpha)|i = \pi|i$ for all processors p_i. Fix some processor p_i. The relative ordering of two reads in $top(\alpha)|i$ is the same as in $\pi|i$, by the definition of π. The relative ordering of two writes in $top(\alpha)|i$ is the same in $\pi|i$, by Lemma 9.3. Suppose in $top(\alpha)|i$ that read r follows write w. By the definition of π, r comes after w in π.

Suppose in $top(\alpha)|i$ that read r precedes write w. Suppose in contradiction that r comes after w in π. Then in π there is some read r' by p_i that reads v from x and some write w' by some p_j that writes v to x such that (1) r' equals r or occurs before r in α, (2) w' equals w or follows w in the tbcast order, and (3) w' causes the latest update to p_i's copy of x that precedes the enabling of the return event for r'. But in α, r' finishes before w starts. Since updates are performed in α in tbcast order (Lemma 9.3), r' cannot see the update of w', a contradiction.

We must show π is legal. Consider read r by p_i that reads v from x in π. Let w be the write in α that causes the latest update to p_i's copy of x preceding r's read of p_i's copy of x. Suppose w is performed by p_j. (If there is no such w, then consider an imaginary "initializing" write at the beginning of α.) By the definition of π, r follows w in π. We must show that no other write to x falls in between w and r in π. Suppose in contradiction that w' does, where w' is a write of v' to x by some p_k. Then by Lemma 9.3, the update for w' follows the update for w at every processor in α.

Case 1: $k = i$. Since π preserves the order of operations at p_i, w' precedes r in α. Since the update for w' follows the update for w in α, r sees the update belonging to w', not w, contradicting the choice of w.

Case 2: $k \neq i$. By Condition 1 of the definition of π, there is some operation in $top(\alpha)|i$ that, in π, precedes r and follows w' (otherwise r would not follow w'). Let o be the first such operation.

Suppose o is a write to some object y. By Lemma 9.4, o's update to p_i's copy of y precedes r's read of p_i's copy of x. Since updates are done in tbcast order, the update for w' occurs at p_i before the update for o, and thus before r's read, contradicting the choice of w.

Suppose o is a read. By the definition of π, o is a read of x, and the update of p_i's copy of x due to w' is the latest one preceding o's read (otherwise o would not follow w'). Since updates are done in tbcast order, the value from w' supersedes the value from w, contradicting the choice of w.   □

Algorithm 25 Sequentially consistent local write algorithm:
code for processor p_i, $0 \leq i \leq n - 1$.

Initially $copy[x]$ holds the initial value of shared object x, for all x, and $num = 0$

1: when $read_i(x)$ occurs:
2:      if $num = 0$ then enable $return_i(x, copy[x])$

3: when $write_i(x, v)$ occurs:
4:      $num := num + 1$
5:      enable $tbc\text{-}send_i(x, v)$
6:      enable $ack_i(x)$

7: when $tbc\text{-}recv_i(x, v)$ from p_j occurs:
8:      $copy[x] := v$
9:      if $j = i$ then
10:         $num := num - 1$
11:         if $num = 0$ and a read on x is pending then
12:             enable $return_i(x, copy[x])$

9.3.2.2 Local Write Algorithm

It is possible to reverse which operation is local and which is slow in the previous algorithm. The next algorithm we present has local writes and slow reads.

When a $write(x)$ comes in to p_i, a broadcast message is sent as in the previous algorithm; however, it is acked immediately. When a $read(x)$ comes in to p_i, if p_i has no pending updates (to any object, not just to x), then it returns the current value of its copy of x. Otherwise, it waits to receive the broadcast message for all writes that it initiated itself and then returns. This is done by maintaining a count of its self-initiated pending write broadcasts and waiting until this count is zero. Effectively, the algorithm pipelines write updates generated at the same processor. The pseudocode appears as Algorithm 25.

Theorem 9.6 *Algorithm 25 implements a sequentially consistent shared memory with local writes.*

Proof. Clearly every write is local. The structure of the proof of sequential consistency is identical to that in the proof of Theorem 9.5. We just need a new proof for Lemma 9.4. Lemma 9.4 is still true for this algorithm because when a read occurs at p_i, if any update initiated by p_i is still waiting, then the return is delayed until the latest such update is performed. □

An explicit scenario can be constructed to show that this algorithm does not provide linearizability (see Exercise 9.5).

Thus neither of these two algorithms for sequential consistency can guarantee linearizability. This is true even if the algorithms run on top of a message system that provides more stringent timing guarantees than in the asynchronous case. As we will show below, reads and writes for linearizability cannot be local as long as there is any uncertainty in the message delay.

9.4 LOWER BOUNDS

In this section we show some lower bounds on the time to perform operations in DSM implementations. The lower bounds assume that the underlying communication system is the (asynchronous) point-to-point message passing system, and not the totally ordered broadcast system.

First, we show that the trade-off hinted at by the existence of the local read and local write algorithms for sequential consistency is inherent. We show that the sum of the worst-case times for read and write must be at least the maximum message delay, in any sequentially consistent implementation.

Then we show that the worst-case times of both reads and writes for linearizability are at least a constant fraction of the uncertainty in the message delay.

To make these claims precise, we must add provisions for time and clocks to our new layered model of computation.

9.4.1 Adding Time and Clocks to the Layered Model

We adapt the definitions from Part I, in particular, the notion of a timed execution from Chapter 2 and the notions of hardware clocks and shifting from Chapter 6.

The only change needed to the definition of a timed execution is that only node input events are assigned times. The time of an event that is not a node input is "inherited" from the node input event that (directly or indirectly) triggered it.

Hardware clocks are modeled as in Chapter 6. The lower bounds shown in this chapter assume that the hardware clocks run at the same rate as real time but are not initially synchronized.

The notions of a processor's view and timed view (with clock values) and the merge operation on timed views are the same.

The definition of shifting executions is the same, and Lemma 6.14 is still valid.

In this section, the definition of an admissible timed execution will include the following additional constraint:

- Every message delay is in the range $[d - u, d]$, for some nonnegative constants d and u, with $u \leq d$.

Given a particular MCS, we will let t_{op} be the worst-case time, over all admissible executions, for an operation of type "op."[3] (The *time* for an operation is the difference

---

[3]Technically, an operation consists of a specific invocation and its matching specific response. However, it is often convenient to group together a number of "similar" operations into a single operation *type*; for instance, operation type "write" includes [write(x, v), ack], for all x and v.

between the real time when the response occurs and the real time when the invocation occurs.)

9.4.2 Sequential Consistency

Theorem 9.7 *For any sequentially consistent memory consistency system that provides two read/write objects, $t_{read} + t_{write} \geq d$.*

Proof. Fix a sequentially consistent MCS that provides two shared objects x and y, both initially 0.

Assume by way of contradiction that $t_{read} + t_{write} < d$.

There exists an admissible execution α_0 of the MCS such that

$$top(\alpha_0) = \text{write}_0(x, 1)\ \text{ack}_0(x)\ \text{read}_0(y)\ \text{return}_0(y, 0)$$

and the write begins at time 0 and the read returns before time d. Assume further that every message sent in α_0 has delay d. Thus no messages have been received by any node at the time when the read returns.

Similarly, there exists an admissible execution α_1 of the MCS such that

$$top(\alpha_1) = \text{write}_1(y, 1)\ \text{ack}_1(y)\ \text{read}_1(x)\ \text{return}_1(x, 0)$$

and the write begins at time 0 and the read returns before time d. Assume further that every message sent in α_1 has delay d. Thus no messages have been received by any node at the time when the read returns.

Informally, the final step of the proof is to create a new execution α that combines the behavior of p_0 in α_0, in which p_0 writes x and reads y, with the behavior of p_1 in α_1, in which p_1 writes y and reads x. Because both operations of each processor complete before time d, p_0 does not know about p_1's operations and vice versa. Thus the processors return the same values in α as they do in α_0 (or α_1). After time d in α, we allow any pending messages to be delivered, but it is too late for them to affect the values returned earlier. And the values that were returned are inconsistent with sequential consistency.

We proceed more formally. Recall from Chapter 6 that, for $i = 0, 1$, $\alpha_i|i$ denotes the timed history of p_i in α_i. (Recall that the timed history consists of the initial state and the sequence of events that occur at p_i together with the real times and the clock times.) Let η_i be the prefix of $\alpha_i|i$ ending just before time d. Let α' be merge(η_0, η_1). The result is a prefix of an admissible execution α. Because α is admissible, it is supposed to satisfy sequential consistency. But $top(\alpha)$ is the sequence σ_3, which we showed in Section 9.2 is not sequentially consistent. $\qquad\square$

9.4.3 Linearizability

The lower bound of d just shown for sequential consistency on the sum of the worst-case times for a read and a write also holds for linearizability, because linearizability is a stronger condition.

For linearizability, we can show additional lower bounds on the worst-case times for reads and writes. In particular, under reasonable assumptions about the pattern of sharing, in any linearizable implementation of an object, the worst-case time for a write is $u/2$ and the worst-case time for a read is $u/4$. Thus it is not possible to have local read or local write algorithms for linearizability, as it was for sequential consistency.

Note that if $u = 0$, then the lower bounds for linearizability become 0. In fact, this bound is tight in that case; if $u = 0$, then local read and local write algorithms are possible for linearizability (see Exercise 9.7).

Theorem 9.8 *For any linearizable memory consistency system that provides a read/write object written by two processors and read by a third, $t_{\text{write}} \geq \frac{u}{2}$.*

Proof. Fix a linearizable MCS that provides a shared object x, initially 0, that is read by p_0 and written by p_1 and p_2.

Assume by way of contradiction that $t_{\text{write}} < \frac{u}{2}$.

We construct an execution of the MCS that, because of the shortness of the writes, can be shifted without violating the message delay constraints so as to violate linearizability. In the original execution p_1 writes 1 to x, then p_2 writes 2 to x, and then p_0 reads x, returning 2. After shifting p_1 and p_2 so that their writes have exchanged places, the result is no longer linearizable, since p_0 should return 1 instead of 2. The details follow.

There exists an admissible execution α of the MCS such that (see Fig. 9.4(a)):

- $top(\alpha)$ is $\text{write}_1(x, 1)$ $\text{ack}_1(x)$ $\text{write}_2(x, 2)$ $\text{ack}_2(x)$ $\text{read}_0(x)$ $\text{return}_0(x, 2)$;

- The $\text{write}_1(x, 1)$ occurs at time 0, the $\text{write}_2(x, 2)$ occurs at time $\frac{u}{2}$, and the $\text{read}_0(x)$ occurs at time u; and

- The message delays in α are d from p_1 to p_2, $d - u$ from p_2 to p_1, and $d - \frac{u}{2}$ for all other ordered pairs of processors.

Let $\beta = \text{shift}(\alpha, \langle 0, \frac{u}{2}, -\frac{u}{2} \rangle)$; that is, we shift p_1 later by $\frac{u}{2}$ and p_2 earlier by $\frac{u}{2}$ (see Fig. 9.4(b)). The result is still admissible, since by Lemma 6.14 the delay of a message either from p_1 or to p_2 becomes $d - u$, the delay of a message from p_2 or to p_1 becomes d, and all other delays are unchanged.

But $top(\beta)$ is

$$\text{write}_2(x, 2) \ \text{ack}_2(x) \ \text{write}_1(x, 1) \ \text{ack}_1(x) \ \text{read}_0(x) \ \text{return}_0(x, 2)$$

which violates linearizability, because p_0's read should return 1, not 2.   □

Now we show the lower bound for reads.

Theorem 9.9 *For any linearizable memory consistency system that provides a read/write object x read by two processors and written by a third, $t_{\text{read}} \geq \frac{u}{4}$.*

Proof. Fix a linearizable MCS that provides a shared object x, initially 0, that is written by p_0 and read by p_1 and p_2.

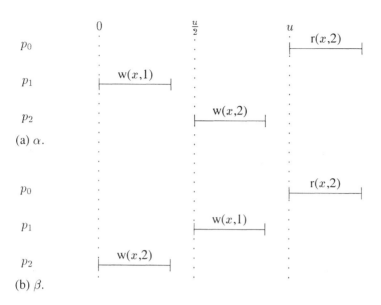

Fig. 9.4 Illustration for the proof of Theorem 9.8; important time points are marked at the top.

Assume by way of contradiction that $t_{read} < \frac{u}{4}$.

As in the previous proof, we construct an execution of the MCS that, because of the shortness of the reads, can be shifted without violating the message delay constraints so as to violate linearizability. In the original execution, p_1 reads 0 from x, then p_1 and p_2 alternate reading x while p_0 concurrently writes 1 to x, and then p_2 reads 1 from x. Thus there exists a read r_1, say by p_1, that returns 0 and is immediately followed by a read r_2 by p_2 that returns 1. After shifting p_2 so that adjacent reads by p_1 and p_2 have exchanged places, and in particular r_2 precedes r_1, the result is no longer linearizable, since r_2 returns the new value 1 and r_1 returns the old value 0. The details follow.

Let $k = \lceil t_{write}/u \rceil$. There exists an admissible execution α of the MCS in which all message delays are $d - \frac{u}{2}$, containing the following events (see Fig. 9.5(a)).

- At time $\frac{u}{4}$, p_0 does a $write_0(x, 1)$.

- At some time between $\frac{u}{4}$ and $(4k + 1) \cdot \frac{u}{4}$, p_0 does an $ack_0(x)$. (By definition of k, $(4k + 1) \cdot \frac{u}{4} \geq \frac{u}{4} + t_{write}$, and thus p_0's write operation is guaranteed to finish in this interval.)

- At time $2i \cdot \frac{u}{4}$, p_1 does a $read_1(x)$, $0 \leq i \leq 2k$.

- At some time between $2i \cdot \frac{u}{4}$ and $(2i + 1) \cdot \frac{u}{4}$, p_1 does a $return_1(x, v_{2i})$, $0 \leq i \leq 2k$.

- At time $(2i + 1) \cdot \frac{u}{4}$, p_2 does a $read_2(x)$, $0 \leq i \leq 2k$.

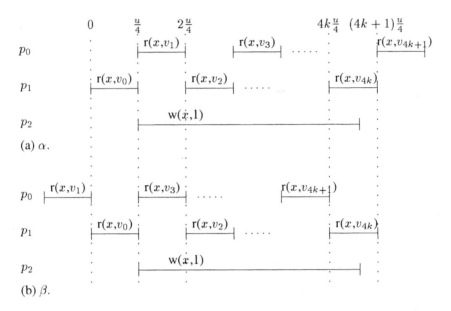

Fig. 9.5 Illustration for the proof of Theorem 9.9; important time points are marked at the top.

- At some time between $(2i+1) \cdot \frac{u}{4}$ and $(2i+2) \cdot \frac{u}{4}$, p_2 does a $\text{return}_2(x, v_{2i+1})$, $0 \le i \le 2k$.

Thus in $top(\alpha)$, p_1's read of v_0 precedes p_0's write, p_2's read of v_{4k+1} follows p_0's write, no two read operations overlap, and the order of the values read from x is $v_0, v_1, v_2, \ldots, v_{4k+1}$. By linearizability, $v_0 = 0$ and $v_{4k+1} = 1$. Thus there exists some j, $0 \le j \le 4k$, such that $v_j = 0$ and $v_{j+1} = 1$. Without loss of generality, assume that j is even, so that v_j is the result of a read by p_1.

Define $\beta = \text{shift}(\alpha, \langle 0, 0, -\frac{u}{2} \rangle)$; that is, we shift p_2 earlier by $\frac{u}{2}$ (see Fig. 9.5(b)). The result is admissible, since by Lemma 6.14 the message delays to p_2 become $d - u$, the message delays from p_2 become d, and the remaining message delays are unchanged.

As a result of the shifting, we have reordered read operations with respect to each other at p_1 and p_2. Specifically, in $top(\beta)$, the order of the values read from x is v_1, $v_0, v_3, v_2, \ldots, v_{j+1}, v_j, \ldots$. Thus in $top(\beta)$ we now have $v_{j+1} = 1$ being read before $v_j = 0$, which violates linearizability. $\qquad \square$

Exercises

9.1 Prove that an algorithm that locally simulates a linearizable shared memory provides sequential consistency.

9.2 Prove that linearizability is local, that is, if we compose separate implementations of linearizable shared variables x and y, the result is also linearizable.

9.3 Prove that sequential consistency is not composable. That is, present a schedule that is not sequentially consistent but whose projection on each object *is* sequentially consistent.

9.4 Prove that the response time of the totally ordered broadcast algorithm of Section 8.2.3.2 (Algorithm 21) is $2d$.

9.5 Present a schedule of the local writes algorithm (Algorithm 25) that is sequentially consistent but is not linearizable.

9.6 For each ϵ between 0 and u, describe an algorithm for sequential consistency in which reads take time $d - \epsilon$ and writes take time ϵ.

9.7 Show that if $u = 0$, then local read and local write algorithms are possible for linearizability.

9.8 What happens to Theorem 9.8 if the assumption about the number of distinct readers and writers is removed?

9.9 Develop a linearizable algorithm for implementing shared objects of other data types besides read/write registers, for instance, stacks and queues. Try to get the best time complexity for operations that you can.

9.10 This exercise asks you to generalize the proof of Theorem 9.8 that $t_{\text{write}} \geq \frac{u}{2}$.

(a) Consider a shared object (data type) specification with the following property. There exists a sequence ρ of operations and two operations op^1 and op^2 that are both of type op such that (1) $\rho \, op^1 \, op^2$ and $\rho \, op^2 \, op^1$ are both legal and (2) there exists a sequence γ of operations such that $\rho \, op^1 \, op^2 \, \gamma$ is legal but $\rho \, op^2 \, op^1 \, \gamma$ is not. Suppose at least two processors can perform operations of type op and there is a third processor that can perform the operations in ρ and γ. Prove that in any linearizable implementation of this data type, $t_{\text{op}} \geq \frac{u}{2}$.

(b) What does this result imply about the worst-case time for linearizable implementations of stacks and queues?

9.11 (a) An operation of a data type is called an *accessor* if, informally speaking, it does not change the "state" of the object. Make a formal definition of accessor using the notion of legal sequences of operations.

(b) Consider a shared object (data type) specification that satisfies the following property. There exists a sequence ρ of operations, two operations aop^1 and aop^2 that are both of type aop, an accessor, and there exists an operation op such that (1) $\rho \, aop^1$ and $\rho \, op \, aop^2$ are legal, but (2) $\rho \, aop^2$ and $\rho \, op \, aop^1$ are not legal. Suppose at least two processors can perform operations of type aop and a third can perform op. Prove that in any linearizable implementation of this data type, $t_{\text{aop}} \geq \frac{u}{2}$.

(c) What does this result imply about the worst-case time for linearizable implementations of read/write registers and of augmented stacks and queues? (An *augmented* stack or queue provides an additional peek operation that returns the value at the top of the stack or head of the queue but does not change the data structure.)

Chapter Notes

In the shared memory model presented in this chapter, there is no obvious way to determine the state of a shared object in a configuration, if an operation on that object is pending. An alternative characterization of linearizability is that each operation, which actually takes some amount of time to complete (between the invocation and response) can be condensed to occur at a single point, so that no other events appear to occur in between. This point is called the *linearization point* of the operation. Because these two definitions are equivalent, the type of model used in Part I, in which the current values of the shared objects are explicitly part of configurations, is valid. For proving properties of shared memory algorithms, it is usually more convenient to use the approach from Part I. The new style of definition is more useful for showing how to implement shared objects, either out of other kinds of shared objects or on top of message passing.

The defining characteristic of a DSM is providing the illusion of physically shared memory in a system in which each node has its own local memory. Both hardware and software systems have been built that implement various consistency conditions. The types of systems have ranged from tightly coupled multiprocessors to collections of homogeneous machines on an Ethernet, and even include heterogeneous distributed systems. Although many of the specification questions are the same in these different types of systems, implementation issues are different. Survey papers on DSM systems include those by Nitzberg and Lo [201] and by Protic et al. [221].

Representative software systems include, in rough chronological order, Ivy by Li and Hudak [166, 167], Munin by Bennett et al. [49], Orca by Bal et al. [43], and TreadMarks by Amza et al. [12]. On the hardware side, several multiprocessors supporting DSM have been described, including Dash by Gharachorloo et al. [122] and Plus by Bisiani and Ravishankar [56].

As mentioned in the survey paper by Nitzberg and Lo [201], many of the issues involved in building a DSM have arisen in other contexts, such as multiprocessor caches, networked file systems, and distributed database management systems. These issues include the consistency condition to be provided, the structure of the shared data (i.e., whether associative addressing is used, whether the data is object oriented), the size of the unit of sharing, the handling of heterogeneous hardware, and interactions with the system's synchronization primitives and memory management schemes. In this chapter we have focused on the consistency condition to be provided.

Sequential consistency and linearizability are "strong" consistency conditions, both requiring the existence of a single view held by all the processors of the order in which operations occur. The term sequential consistency was first proposed by

Lamport in [156]. Lamport also formalized the notion of linearizability [159] for read/write registers, although he called it "atomicity"; the term "linearizability" was coined by Herlihy and Wing [135], who extended atomicity to arbitrary data types and explored the issue of composition (cf. Exercise 9.3).

The style of specification for consistency conditions in this chaper is taken from Attiya and Welch [34] and follows that of Herlihy and Wing [135]. Afek, Brown and Merritt [4] specify sequential consistency differently, by describing an explicit state machine and requiring a particular relationship between the executions of the state machine and those of any algorithm that is to provide sequential consistency.

We described some simple algorithms for linearizability and sequential consistency that rely on full replication and a broadcast primitive. The local-read and local-write algorithms for sequential consistency are taken from [34]; the Orca distributed programming language [43] is implemented with a similar style algorithm for sequential consistency. A similar algorithm for linearizability, but with improved response time, is described by Mavronicolas and Roth [182] and by Chaudhuri et al. [74].

In many situations, full replication of each shared data item is not desirable. Solutions more along the lines of caching algorithms, where the locations of copies can change dynamically, have been proposed. Afek et al. [4] have described an algorithm for sequential consistency that does not rely on full replication. A linearizable algorithm that incorporates replica management is described by Poulakidas and Singh [217].

The lower bounds presented in this chapter were taken from [34]. The lower bound for sequential consistency was originally proved by Lipton and Sandberg [170]. An improved lower bound on the time for linearizable reads appears in the paper by Mavronicolas and Roth [182] (as does the solution to Exercise 9.6 for read/write objects).

Separation results between sequential consistency and linearizability for other data types besides read/write registers have been shown for stacks and queues by Attiya and Welch [34] and for several classes of arbitrary data types by Kosa [149]. The latter paper contains the solutions to Exercises 9.10 and 9.11.

We have seen in this chapter that implementing sequential consistency or linearizability requires significant time overhead. "Weak" consistency conditions overcome this drawback. In weak conditions, there is no common (global) view of the order in which all the operations occur; rather, each processor has its own view of the order of operations. Different weak conditions are distinguished from each other by the subset of operations on which views should agree. The research on weak conditions was spearheaded in the computer architecture community. Early papers include those by Dubois and Scheurich [100], Adve and Hill [2], and Gharachorloo et al. [122]. A formal treatment of weak conditions within a framework similar to the one in this chapter can be found in [28, 112, 113]. These papers include a good description of related definitions, as well as examples and comparisons with other frameworks for specifying consistency conditions.

Protic, Tomasevic, and Milutinovic edited a collection of papers on distributed shared memory [222]; some of the papers mentioned above appear in this collection.

10

Fault-Tolerant Simulations of Read/Write Objects

In preceding chapters, we have seen several types of shared objects, differing both in their sharing patterns (i.e., how many processors can access an object) and in their semantics (i.e., what type of operations can be applied to the object). A natural question concerns the relative power of these objects, that is, do different types of shared objects admit solutions to different problems?

One way to compare the power of shared object types is to simulate a shared object of one type, the high-level type, using shared objects of another type, the low-level type. Such a simulation implies that any algorithm that uses objects of the high-level type will also work using objects of the low-level type, allowing one to design algorithms assuming the more convenient high-level objects, but to run it in a system that provides only the low-level objects, which might be a more realistic assumption. The existence of such a simulation indicates that, at least theoretically, the low-level type allows solutions to the same problems that the high-level type does.

A traditional method of simulating shared objects using low-level objects is to use critical sections (cf. Chapter 4). In this method, access to the low-level objects in the simulation of the high-level object is guarded by a critical section and the objects are updated in mutual exclusion. Although simple, this solution is very sensitive to processor failures and slowdowns. A failed or slow processor that is inside the critical section can block or delay the progress of all processors and prohibit them from accessing the simulated shared object. Therefore, we are interested in simulations that are *wait-free*, that is, such that each processor can complete an access to the high-level object using a finite number of accesses to the low-level objects, without depending on other processors. (A more precise definition appears below.)

This chapter is the first of two chapters that discuss the relationships between various types of shared objects. In this chapter, we restrict our attention to a few kinds of objects that can be wait-free simulated from read/write registers. Chapter 15 addresses arbitrary data types.

Throughout this chapter we are concerned solely with linearizable objects.

10.1   FAULT-TOLERANT SHARED MEMORY SIMULATIONS

In this chapter, we study how to simulate shared memory systems both on top of other kinds of shared memory and on top of an asynchronous message-passing system, in the presence of crash failures. We consider two ways to formalize such simulations. In the first, we define a failure-prone version of linearizable shared memory and require the existence of a global simulation as defined in Chapter 7. In the second, we place an additional constraint on the definition of the simulation but keep the original (failure free) definition of linearizable shared memory.

The definition of an (asynchronous) shared memory system that is subject to crash failures differs from the failure-free definition in Chapter 9 (Section 9.1) in two ways. First, the liveness condition is weakened to require responses only for invocations by nonfaulty processors. Second, the linearizability condition must be modified. Consider the situation in which a processor has done all the work to implement a high-level operation but fails just before it completes the operation. Subsequent reads will observe the result of the operation, even though it is not complete. Thus the definition of linearizability must require that there is a permutation of all the completed operations *and some subset of the pending operations* satisfying the same properties.

Here is the definition of an *f-resilient shared memory system*. Inputs are invocations on the shared object, and outputs are responses from the shared object. For a sequence of events σ to be in the allowable set, there must be a partitioning of the processor indices into "faulty" and "nonfaulty" such that there are at most f faulty processors and the following properties are satisfied:

Correct Interaction: For each processor p_i, $\sigma|i$ consists of alternating invocations and matching responses, beginning with an invocation. This condition imposes constraints on the inputs.

Nonfaulty Liveness: Every invocation by a nonfaulty processor has a matching response.

Extended Linearizability: There exists a permutation π of all the completed operations in σ and some subset of the pending operations such that

1. For each object O, $\pi|O$ is legal, that is, it is in the sequential specification of O; and

2. If the response of operation o_1 occurs in σ before the invocation of operation o_2, then o_1 appears before o_2 in π

We will be studying whether communication system C_1 can simulate communication system C_2, where C_2 is a shared memory system consisting of certain types of objects and subject to f processor crashes and C_1 is a communication system (either shared memory or message passing) that is also subject to f processor crashes.

Throughout most of this chapter, we will be studying the wait-free case, that is, when $f = n - 1$. For this case, there is an alternative definition of a simulation of an f-resilient shared memory system. (Exercise 10.2 asks you to show that the two definitions are equivalent.)

Intuitively, we want the simulation not to delay faster processors on account of slower ones. Thus we define a *wait-free simulation* to be a (global) simulation of one (failure free) shared memory system by another (failure free) shared memory system with the following additional property:

- Let α be any admissible execution of the simulation program. Let α' be any finite prefix of α in which some processor p_i has a pending high-level operation, that is, there is an invocation from the environment at p_i without a matching response. Then there must exist an extension of α' consisting solely of events by p_i in which the pending operation is completed.

Another way of stating the wait-free property is that every operation is able to complete on its own, from any point, without assistance from other processors.

Usually we will use the wait-free simulation definition when $f = n - 1$.

By the definition of linearizability, there exists a single point, called the *linearization point*, somewhere between the invocation and response of the operation at which the operation appears to take effect. One strategy for showing that an execution is linearizable is to explicitly assign a candidate for the linearization point of every simulated operation, somewhere between its invocation and response. Clearly, the order implied by the sequence of linearization points preserves the order of non-overlapping operations. If we show, in addition, that every read operation returns the value of the write operation with the latest linearization point that precedes the linearization point of the read operation, then we have shown the desired linearization of the execution. Linearization points correspond to our intuition that each operation "appears" to execute atomically at some point during its execution interval.

10.2   SIMPLE READ/WRITE REGISTER SIMULATIONS

In Chapter 4, we mentioned different types of read/write registers, depending on the manner in which processors access them: single-reader or multi-reader, single-writer or multi-writer. Registers can be further classified depending on the number of values that can be written to them; they may be *binary*, with only two possible values, or *multi-valued*, with any finite number of possible values.

In this section, we show that registers that may seem more complicated, namely, multi-writer multi-reader multi-valued registers, have a wait-free simulation using simpler registers, that is, single-writer single-reader binary registers. This simulation is incremental, going through several stages in which the versatility of accesses

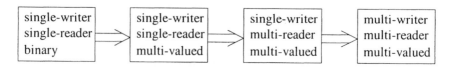

Fig. 10.1 Chain of constructions presented in this chapter.

increases. Figure 10.1 depicts the stages of this simulation. In this figure, an arrow stands for a simulation of a register type from a simpler (more restricted) register type. Actually, the binary to multi-valued construction requires that the multi-valued register being simulated take on only a bounded number of different values. In contrast, the other constructions depend on using building block registers that can take on unbounded values. However, it is possible to transform these unbounded value simulation algorithms into algorithms that only use bounded values (see the chapter notes).

10.2.1 Multi-Valued from Binary

The basic object we consider is a single-writer, single-reader binary register. For each register, there is a single processor (the writer) that can write to it and a single processor (the reader) that can read from it. Only binary values can be written to a register of this type, that is, its value is either 0 or 1.

We describe how to simulate a K-valued single-writer single-reader register from a binary single-writer single-reader register for $K > 2$. For simplicity, we talk about a single register R, and two well-defined processors, a (single) reader and a (single) writer. Such simulations can be combined to simulate multiple registers; see Exercise 9.2.

We consider a simple approach in which values are represented in unary; that is, to simulate the K-valued single-writer single-reader register R, we use an array of K binary single-writer single-reader registers, $B[0 \ldots K-1]$. The value i is represented by a 1 in the ith entry and 0 in all other entries. Thus the possible values of R are $\{0, 1, \ldots, K-1\}$.

When read and write operations do not overlap, it is simple to perform operations: A read operation scans the array beginning with index 0 until it finds a 1 in some entry and returns the index of this entry. A write operation writes the value v, by writing the value 1 in the entry whose index is v and clearing (setting to 0) the entry corresponding to the previous value, if different from v.

This simple algorithm is correct if we are guaranteed that read and write operations do not overlap, but it returns incorrect responses when read and write operations may overlap. Consider, for example, the scenario depicted in Figure 10.2 in which R initially holds the value 3, and thus $B[3] = 1$ while $B[2] = B[1] = B[0] = 0$. In response to a request to read the multi-valued register, the reader reads $B[0]$ and observes 0, then reads $B[1]$ and observes 0, and then reads $B[2]$. While the reader

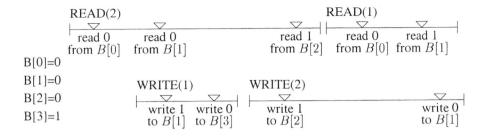

Fig. 10.2 A counterexample to simple multi-valued algorithm; the triangular markers indicate the linearization points of the low-level operations.

is waiting to get the response from $B[2]$, the writer performs a high-level write of 1, during which it sets $B[1]$ to 1 and clears $B[3]$. Then the writer begins a high-level write of 2 and begins writing 1 to $B[2]$. Finally the reader gets the response from $B[2]$, with value 1. Now the reader returns 2 as the value of the multi-valued register. Subsequently, the reader begins a second read on the multi-valued register; it reads $B[0]$ and observes 0, then reads $B[1]$ and observes 1. Thus the reader returns 1 as the value of the multi-valued register. Finally the writer receives the ack for its write to $B[2]$, and clears $B[1]$.[1]

That is, the operations by the reader are

$$\text{read}(R, 2), \text{read}(R, 1)$$

in this order, whereas the operations by the writer are

$$\text{write}(R, 1), \text{write}(R, 2)$$

Any linearization of these operations must preserve the order between the read operations as well as the order between the write operations. However, to preserve the semantics of the register R, write$(R, 2)$ must appear before read$(R, 2)$, while write$(R, 1)$ must appear before read$(R, 1)$ and after read$(R, 2)$. Thus, either the order between the read operations or the order between write operations should be reversed.

To avoid this problem of "new-old" inversion of values, two changes are made: (1) a write operation clears *only* the entries whose indices are smaller than the value it is writing, and (2) a read operation does not stop when it finds the first 1 but makes sure there are still zeroes in all lower indices. Specifically, the reader scans from the low values toward the high values until it finds the first 1; then it reverses direction and scans back down to the beginning, keeping track of the smallest index observed

---

[1] This scenario suggests another problem: if no write follows the first write, then the reader will run off the end of the array in the first read, as it will observe zeroes in all the binary registers, causing the high-level read to be undefined.

Algorithm 26 Simulating a multi-valued register R from binary registers: code for reader and writer.

Initially the shared registers $B[0]$ through $B[K-1]$ are all 0, except $B[i] = 1$, where i is the initial value of R

```
1:   when read(R) occurs:                            // the reader reads from register R
2:       i := 0
3:       while B[i] = 0 do i := i + 1                 // upward scan
4:       up, v := i
5:       for i = up - 1 downto 0 do                   // downward scan
6:           if B[i] = 1 then v := i
7:       return(R, v)

8:   when write(R, v) occurs:        // the writer writes the value v to register R
9:       B[v] := 1
10:      for i := v - 1 downto 0 do B[i] := 0
11:      ack(R)
```

---

to contain a 1 during the downward scan. This is the value returned. The pseudocode appears as Algorithm 26.

Clearly, the algorithm is wait-free: Each write executes at most K low-level write operations, whereas each read executes at most $2K - 1$ low-level read operations. To show that the algorithm is correct, we need to show that each of its admissible executions is linearizable, that is, there is permutation of the high-level operations that preserves the order of non-overlapping operations, and in which every read returns the value of the latest preceding write. The proof technique is to explicitly describe an ordering of the operations that satisfies the semantics and then show that it respects the order of operations; a similar approach was used in the proof of Theorem 9.5 in Chapter 9.

Consider any admissible execution α of the algorithm and fix a linearization of the operations on the low-level binary registers. Such a linearization exists because α is admissible.

In the rest of this section, high-level operations are capitalized (e.g., Read), whereas low-level operations are not (e.g., read). We say that a (low-level) read r of any $B[v]$ in α *reads from* a (low-level) write w to $B[v]$ if w is the latest write to $B[v]$ that precedes r in the linearization of the operations on $B[v]$. We say that a (high-level) Read R in α *reads from* a (high-level) Write W if R returns v and W contains the write to $B[v]$ that R's last read of $B[v]$ reads from. Note that W writes the value v, by writing a 1 in $B[v]$, and thus a Read that returns v reads from a Write that writes v.

Construct a permutation π of the high-level operations in α as follows. First, place all the Writes in the order in which they occur in α; because there is only one writer, this order is well-defined.

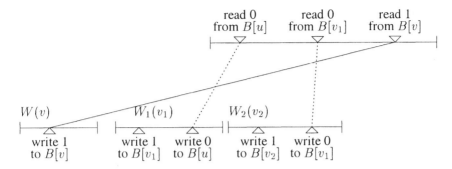

Fig. 10.3 Scenario for proof of Lemma 10.1; dotted lines indicate low-level reads-from relationships, and solid line indicates high-level reads-from relationship.

Consider the Reads in the order in which they occur in α; because there is only one reader, this order is well-defined. For each Read R, let W be the Write that R reads from. Place R in π immediately before the Write in π just following W. The purpose is to place R after W and after all previous Reads that also read from W (which have already been placed after W).

We must show that π is a linearization of α. First note that π satisfies the sequential specification of a read write register by construction. Now we show that the real-time ordering of operations in α is preserved in π. For any pair of Writes, this is preserved by construction. If a Read R finishes in α before Write W begins, then clearly R precedes W in π, because R cannot read from a Write that starts after R ends.

To argue the two other cases, we use Lemma 10.1, which constrains the Writes that a Read can read from in certain situations.

Lemma 10.1 *Consider two values u and v with $u < v$. If Read R returns v and R's read of $B[u]$ during its upward scan reads from a write contained in Write W_1, then R does not read from any Write that precedes W_1.*

Proof. Suppose in contradiction that R reads from a Write W that precedes W_1 (see Fig. 10.3). Let v_1 be the value written by W_1. Since W_1 writes a 1 to $B[v_1]$ and then does a downward scan, $v_1 > u$. Also, $v_1 < v$, since otherwise W_1 would overwrite W's write to v, contradicting the fact that R reads from W.

Thus in R's upward scan, it reads $B[v_1]$ after $B[u]$ and before $B[v]$. R must read a 0 in $B[v_1]$ since otherwise it would not return v. Consequently there must be another write W_2, after W_1, that writes 0 in $B[v_1]$ before R's read of $B[v_1]$. Let v_2 be the value written by W_2. Note that v_2 must be less than v_1 for the same reason that v_1 is less than v.

Similarly, W_2 must be followed by a Write W_3 that writes v_3, with $v_2 < v_3 < v$, and so on.

Thus there exists an infinite increasing sequence of integers $v_1, v_2, v_3, \ldots$, all of which are less than v. This is a contradiction. $\qquad\square$

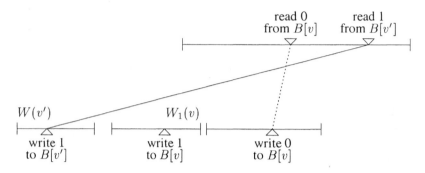

Fig. 10.4 Scenario for the Write-before-Read case.

We now return to verifying that π, the permutation defined above, respects the ordering of non-overlapping high-level operations in the execution α.

Case 1: Write before Read: Suppose in contradiction that Write W finishes in α before Read R begins but in π, R is placed before W. Then R reads from some Write W' that precedes W. Let W write v and W' write v'. Thus the value of R is v'.

First, assume $v' \leq v$. Then W overwrites the write to $B[v']$ by W' before R begins, and R cannot read from W'.

Now consider the case $v' > v$ (see Fig. 10.4). W writes a 1 in $B[v]$. Since R does not see this 1 and stop at $B[v]$ during its upward scan, there must be a Write after W containing a write of 0 to $B[v]$ that R's read of $B[v]$ reads from. Then, by Lemma 10.1, R cannot read from W'.

Case 2: Read before Read: Suppose in contradiction that Read R_1 precedes Read R_2 in α but follows R_2 in π. This inversion implies that R_1 reads from a Write $W_1(v_1)$ that follows the Write $W_2(v_2)$ that R_2 reads from.

First, consider the case where $v_1 = v_2$. Then when W_1 writes 1 to $B[v_1]$, it overwrites the 1 that W_2 wrote to $B[v_2]$ earlier. To be consistent with real time, the operations on $B[v_1]$ must be linearized in the order: W_2's write, W_1's write, R_1's last read, R_2's last read. This contradicts the assumption that R_2 reads from W_2.

Since v_1 and v_2 must therefore be distinct, we next consider the case where $v_1 > v_2$ (see Fig. 10.5). Since R_2 reads from W_2, no write to $B[v_2]$ is linearized between W_2's write of 1 to $B[v_2]$ and R_2's last read of $B[v_2]$. Since R_1 reads from W_1, W_1's write of 1 to $B[v_1]$ precedes R_1's last read of $B[v_1]$. So $B[v_2]$ has the value 1 starting before R_1 does its last read of $B[v_1]$ and ending after R_2 does its last read of $B[v_2]$. But then R_1's read of $B[v_2]$ during its downward scan would return 1, not 0, a contradiction since R_1 returns v_1, which is larger than v_2.

Finally, we consider the case where $v_1 < v_2$ (see Figure 10.6). Since R_1 reads from W_1, W_1's write of 1 to $B[v_1]$ precedes R_1's last read of $B[v_1]$. Since R_2 returns $v_2 > v_1$, R_2's first read of $B[v_1]$ must return 0. So there must be another Write after W_1 containing a write of 0 to $B[v_1]$ that R_2's read of $B[v_1]$ reads from. Then, by Lemma 10.1, R cannot read from W'.

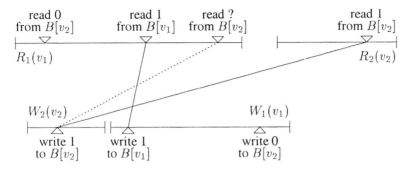

Fig. 10.5 Scenario for the Read-before-Read case when $v_1 > v_2$.

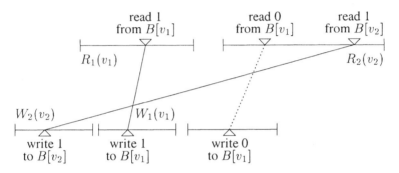

Fig. 10.6 Scenario for the Read-before-Read case when $v_1 < v_2$.

Thus π is a linearization of α and we have:

Theorem 10.2 *There exists a wait-free simulation of a K-valued register using K binary registers in which each high-level operation performs $O(K)$ low-level operations.*

10.2.2 Multi-Reader from Single-Reader

The next step we take in the simulation of general read/write registers is to allow several processors to read from the same register; we still allow only one processor to write the register. That is, we use single-writer single-reader registers to build a wait-free simulation of a single-writer *multi*-reader register.

Let n be the number of reading processors to be supported by the multi-reader register. A simple idea for this simulation is to use a collection of n shared single-writer single-reader registers, *Val*[i], $i = 1, \ldots, n$, one for each reader. In a write operation, the writer stores the new value in the registers, one after the other. In a read operation, the read returns the value in its register. The simulation is clearly wait-free. However, it is incorrect, that is, it has executions that are not linearizable.

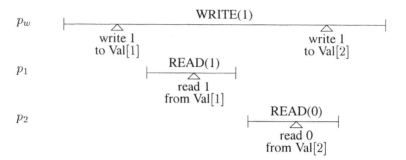

Fig. 10.7 A counterexample to the multi-reader algorithm.

Consider for example the following execution in which a new-old inversion of values happens, that is, a later read operation returns the value of an earlier write.

Assume that the initial value of the register is 0 and that the writer, p_w, wishes to write 1 to the register. Consider the following sequence of operations (see Fig. 10.7):

- p_w starts the write operation and begins writing 1 to *Val*[1].

- p_1 reads the value 1 from *Val*[1] and returns 1.

- p_2 reads the value 0 from *Val*[2] and returns 0.

- p_w finally receives the ack for its write to *Val*[1], writes 1 to *Val*[2], and returns.

This execution cannot be linearized because the read of p_1 should be ordered after the write of p_w and the read of p_2 should be ordered before the write of p_w; therefore, the read of p_1 should be ordered after the read of p_2; however, the read of p_1 occurs strictly before the read of p_2.

One might be tempted to require the readers to read again and again, to use more registers, or to require the writer to write more values. None of these fixes is correct (see Exercise 10.3 for an example), as shown by Theorem 10.3.

Theorem 10.3 *In any wait-free simulation of a single-writer multi-reader register from any number of single-writer single-reader registers, at least one reader must write.*

Proof. Suppose in contradiction there exists such a simulation for a register R in which the readers do not write. Let p_w be the writer and p_1 and p_2 the readers of R. Suppose the initial value of R is 0.

Since the readers do not write, the execution of the writer is unaffected by concurrent reading.

Since the registers used by the simulation are single-reader, they can be partitioned into two sets, S_1 and S_2, such that only the reader p_1 reads the registers in S_1 and only the reader p_2 reads the registers in S_2.

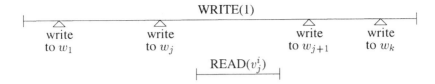

Fig. 10.8 Illustration of α_j^i in the proof of Theorem 10.3.

Consider the execution α of a high-level write of 1 to R, starting in the initial configuration. The writer p_w performs a series of low-level writes, $w_1, \ldots, w_k$, on the single-reader registers. Each w_i involves a register in either S_1 or S_2.

For each $i = 1, 2$, and each $j = 0, \ldots, k$, define an alternative execution α_j^i obtained from α by interposing a high-level read operation by p_i after the linearization point of w_j (if this write exists) and before the linearization point of w_{j+1} (if this write exists). Let v_j^i be the value returned by this high-level read (see Fig. 10.8). That is, we check to see what value would be returned by each reader after each low-level write.

Since the simulation guarantees linearizability, for each $i = 1, 2$, there exists j_i between 1 and k such that $v_j^i = 0$ for all $j < j_i$ and $v_j^i = 1$ for all $j \geq j_i$. That is, there is a single low-level write operation that causes p_i to observe the simulated register as having changed its value from 0 to 1.

It is crucial to realize that j_1 cannot equal j_2. The reason is that w_{j_1} writes some register in S_1, the set of registers that p_1 can read. (See Exercise 10.4.) Similarly, w_{j_2} writes some register in S_2, the set of registers that p_2 can read. Since S_1 and S_2 are disjoint, j_1 cannot equal j_2.

Without loss of generality, assume $j_1 < j_2$. Let α' be an execution obtained from α by inserting a read by p_1 followed by a read by p_2 after w_{j_1} and before w_{j_1+1}.

By definition of j_1 and j_2 and the assumption that $j_1 < j_2$, p_1's read returns 1 and p_2's read returns 0 in α'. But this contradicts the assumption that the simulation guarantees linearizability, since p_1's read precedes p_2's, yet sees the newer value. $\square$

To avoid the ordering problem described above, the readers write to each other (through additional registers), creating an ordering among them. Before a reader returns from a read operation, it announces the value it has decided to return. A reader reads not only the value written for it by the writer, but also the values announced by the other readers. It then chooses the most recent value among the values it has read.

Crucial to this algorithm is the ability to compare different values and choose the most recent one among them. We assume that registers can take on an unbounded number of values. Therefore, the writer chooses a nonnegative integer to associate as a *sequence number*, or *timestamp*, with each value it writes. The writer increments the sequence number each time it wishes to write a new value. Clearly, the value associated with the largest sequence number among a set of values is the one written by the most recent write.

Algorithm 27 Simulating a multi-reader register R from single-reader registers: code for readers and writer.

Initially $Report[i, j] = Val[i] = (v_0, 0), 1 \leq i, j \leq n$,
where v_0 is the initial value of R

1: when $read_r(R)$ occurs: // reader p_r reads from register R
2:      $(v[0], s[0]) := Val[r]$ // most recent value reported to p_r by writer
3:      for $i := 1$ to n do
         $(v[i], s[i]) := Report[i, r]$ // most recent value reported to p_r by reader p_i
4:      let j be such that $s[j] = \max\{s[0], s[1], \ldots, s[n]\}$
5:      for $i := 1$ to n do $Report[r, i] := (v[j], s[j])$ // p_r reports to each reader p_i
6:      $return_r(R, v[j])$

7: when $write(R, v)$ occurs: // the writer writes v to register R
8:      $seq := seq + 1$ // local variable $seq = 0$ initially
9:      for $i := 1$ to n do $Val[i] := (v, seq)$
10:     $ack(R)$

In the rest of this section, we refer to a *value* as a pair containing a value of the high-level register and a sequence number.

The pseudocode for a register supporting one writer p_w and n readers $p_1, \ldots, p_n$ appears in Algorithm 27; it uses the following shared arrays of single-writer single-reader read/write registers:

Val[i]: The value written by p_w for each reader p_i, $1 \leq i \leq n$.

Report[i, j]: The value returned by the most recent read operation performed by p_i; written by p_i and read by p_j, $1 \leq i, j \leq n$.

Each processor has two local arrays, v and s, each of which is an $(n + 1)$-element array, that hold the values and corresponding sequence numbers respectively reported most recently by the writer and n readers.

The algorithm is clearly wait-free: Each simulated operation performs a fixed number of low-level operations—n for a write operation and $2n + 1$ for a read operation. To prove that the simulation is correct it remains to show that every admissible execution is linearizable.

Consider any admissible execution α. To show that α is linearizable, we have to show that there is a permutation π of the high-level operations in α that preserves the order of non-overlapping operations, and in which every read operation returns the value of the latest preceding write.

For this algorithm, we prove linearizability by explicitly constructing π, as was done in Section 10.2.1. We construct π in two steps.

First, we put in π all the write operations according to the order in which they occur in α; because write operations are executed sequentially by the unique writer, this sequence is well-defined. Note that this order is consistent with that of the timestamps associated with the values written.

Next, we add the read operations to π. We consider the reads one by one, in the order of their responses in α. A read operation that returns a value with timestamp T is placed immediately before the write that follows (in π) the write operation that generated timestamp T. (If there is no such write, then it goes at the end.)

By the defined placement of each read, every read returns the value of the latest preceding write and therefore π is legal.

Lemma 10.4 shows that π preserves the real-time order of non-overlapping operations.

Lemma 10.4 *Let op_1 and op_2 be two high-level operations in α such that op_1 ends before op_2 begins. Then op_1 precedes op_2 in π.*

Proof. By construction, the real-time order of write operations is preserved.

Consider some read operation r by p_i that returns a value associated with time-stamp T.

Consider a write w that follows r in α. Suppose in contradiction that read r is placed after write w in π. Then the write w' that generates timestamp T must be either w or a later write, implying that w' occurs after r in α, which is a contradiction.

Consider a write w that precedes r in α. Since r occurs after w, r reads from *Val[i]* the value written by w or a later write, by the linearizability of *Val[i]*. By the semantics of max on integers and because timestamps are increasing, r returns a value whose associated timestamp is generated by w or a later write. Thus r is not placed before w in π.

Consider a read r' by p_j that follows r in α. By linearizability, p_j obtains a timestamp from *Report[i]* during r' that is written during r or later. Since the timestamps are increasing integers, no timestamp written to *Report[i]* after r was generated before T was generated. Thus the max in r' returns a timestamp that was generated at least as recently as T, and thus r' will not be placed before r. □

Note that the simulation of a single register requires n low-level (single-reader) registers for communication from the writer to the readers and $n(n-1)$ low-level registers for communication among the n readers.

Thus we have:

Theorem 10.5 *There exists a wait-free simulation of an n-reader register using $O(n^2)$ single-reader registers in which each high-level operation performs $O(n)$ low-level operations.*

10.2.3 Multi-Writer from Single-Writer

The final step we make in this section is to construct a multi-writer multi-reader read/write register from single-writer multi-reader registers. As for the previous simulation, we assume here that the registers can hold an unbounded number of values.

The idea of the algorithm is to have each writer announce each value it desires to write to all the readers, by writing it in its own (single-writer multi-reader) register; each reader reads all the values written by the writers and picks the most recent one among them.

Once again, the crucial issue is to find a way to compare the values written by the writes and find the most recent one among them. To achieve this, we assign a timestamp to each value written. Unlike the previous algorithm, in this one the timestamps are not generated by a single processor (the single writer), but by several processors (all possible writers). The most important requirement of the timestamps is that they be totally ordered. Furthermore, the timestamps should reflect the order of non-overlapping operations; that is, if a write operation completely precedes another write operation then the first operation should get a lower timestamp.

Interestingly, we have already seen a method for creating such timestamps, in the context of vector clocks (Chapter 6). Recall that these timestamps are vectors of length m, where m is the number of writers, and that the algorithm for picking a timestamp is as follows: The new timestamp of a processor is the vector consisting of the local timestamps read from all other processors, with its local timestamp increased by 1.

We apply lexicographic order to the vectors of timestamps; that is, two vectors are ordered according to the relative order of the values in the first coordinate in which the vectors differ. This is a total order extending the partial order defined for vector timestamps in Chapter 6 (Section 6.1.3).

The m writers are $p_0, \ldots, p_{m-1}$, and all of the processors, $p_0, \ldots, p_{n-1}$, are the readers. The pseudocode appears in Algorithm 28. It uses the following shared arrays of single-writer multi-reader read/write registers:

TS[i]: The vector timestamp of writer p_i, $0 \leq i \leq m - 1$. It is written by p_i and read by all writers.

Val[i]: The latest value written by writer p_i, $0 \leq i \leq m - 1$, together with the vector timestamp associated with that value. It is written by p_i and read by all readers.

Clearly, the algorithm is wait-free because any simulated operation requires a linear number of low-level operations.

To prove that the simulation is correct we have to show that every admissible execution is linearizable. The proof is very similar to the linearizability proof of the previous simulation.

Consider any admissible execution α. To show α is linearizable, we have to show that there is a permutation π of the high-level operations in α that preserves the order of non-overlapping operations, and in which every read operation returns the value of the latest preceding write.

The key to the proof is the lexicographic order on timestamps. The proof of Lemma 10.6 is left as an exercise to the reader (Exercise 10.6).

Lemma 10.6 *The lexicographic order of the timestamps is a total order consistent with the partial order in which they are generated.*

Algorithm 28 Simulating a multi-writer register R from single-writer registers: code for readers and writers.

Initially $TS[i] = \langle 0, \ldots, 0 \rangle$ and
$Val[i]$ equals the desired initial value of R, $0 \le i \le m - 1$

```
1:   when read_r(R) occurs:              // reader p_r reads from register R, 0 ≤ r < n
2:       for i := 0 to m − 1 do (v[i], t[i]) := Val[i]        // v and t are local
3:       let j be such that t[j] = max{t[0], ..., t[m − 1]}    // lexicographic max
4:       return_r(R, v[j])

5:   when write_w(R, v) occurs:  // writer p_w writes v to register R, 0 ≤ w ≤ m − 1
6:       ts := NewCTS()                                        // ts is local
7:       Val[w] := (v, ts)                              // write to shared register
8:       ack_w(R)

9:   procedure NewCTS_w():           // writer p_w obtains a new vector timestamp
10:      for i := 0 to m − 1 do
11:          lts[i] := TS[i].[i]            // extract the ith entry from TS of ith writer
12:          lts[w] := lts[w] + 1                              // increment own entry
13:      TS[w] := lts                                   // write to shared register
14:      return lts
```

Inspection of the pseudocode reveals that the values written to each TS variable are written in nondecreasing lexicographic order, and therefore we have the following lemma:

Lemma 10.7 *For each i, if vector timestamp VT_1 is written to $Val[i]$ and later vector timestamp VT_2 is written to $Val[i]$, then $VT_1 \le VT_2$.*

The candidate linearization order π is defined in two steps, in a manner similar to that in Section 10.2.2.

First, we put into π all the write operations according to the lexicographic ordering on the timestamps associated with the values they write. Second, we consider each read operation in turn, in the order in which its response occurs in α. A read operation that returns a value associated with timestamp VT is placed immediately before the write operation that follows (in π) the write operation that generated VT.

By the defined placement of each read, π is legal, since each read returns the value of the latest preceding write.

Lemma 10.8 shows that π preserves the real-time order of non-overlapping operations.

Lemma 10.8 *Let op_1 and op_2 be two high-level operations in α such that op_1 ends before op_2 begins. Then op_1 precedes op_2 in π.*

Proof. By construction and Lemma 10.6, the real-time order of write operations is preserved.

Consider a read operation, r, by p_i that returns a value associated with timestamp VT.

Consider a write w that follows r in α. Suppose in contradiction that read r is placed after write w in π. Then the write w' that generates timestamp VT must be either w or a later write, implying that w' occurs in α after r, a contradiction.

Consider a write w by p_j that precedes r in α. Since r occurs after w, r reads from $Val[j]$ the value written by w or a later write, by the linearizability of $Val[j]$. By the semantics of max on vectors of integers and Lemma 10.6, r returns a value whose associated timestamp is generated by w or a later write. Thus r is not placed before w in π.

Consider a read r' by p_j that follows r in α. During r, p_i reads all Val variables and returns the value whose associated timestamp is the lexicographic maximum. Later, during r', p_j does the same thing. By Lemma 10.7, the timestamps appearing in each Val variable are in non-decreasing lexicographic order, and thus by Lemma 10.6 the timestamps are in non-decreasing order of when they were generated. Thus r' obtains timestamps from the Val variables that are at least as recent as those obtained by r. By the semantics of max on vectors of integers, the timestamp associated with the value returned by r' is at least as recent as the timestamp associated with the value returned by r. Thus r' is not placed before r in π. $\qquad\square$

Note that the construction of a single register requires $O(m)$ low-level (single-writer) registers, where m is the number of writers.

Thus we have:

Theorem 10.9 *There exists a wait-free simulation of an m-writer register using $O(m)$ single-writer registers in which each high-level operation performs $O(m)$ low-level operations.*

10.3 ATOMIC SNAPSHOT OBJECTS

The shared objects we have seen so far in this chapter allow only a single data item to be accessed in a memory operation, although they allow several processors to access it (for reading, writing, or both). We now turn to atomic snapshot objects—shared objects partitioned into segments. Each segment belongs to a different processor and is written separately, but all segments can be read at once by any processor. In this section, we present a wait-free simulation of an atomic snapshot object from bounded-size read/write registers.

As we shall see (e.g., in Chapter 16), the ability to read all segments atomically can simplify the design and verification of shared memory algorithms. Because they can be simulated from read/write registers, there is no loss of generality in assuming the existence of atomic snapshot objects.

The sequential specification of an *atomic snapshot object* provides two kinds of operations for each user i, $0 \leq i \leq n - 1$:

- A scan$_i$ invocation whose response is return$_i(V)$, where V is an n-element vector called a *view* (with a value for each segment), and

- An update$_i(d)$ invocation whose response is ack$_i$, where d is the data to be written to p_i's segment

A sequence of scan and update operations is in the allowable set if and only if, for each V returned by a scan operation, $V[i]$ equals the parameter of the latest preceding update$_i$ operation, for all i. If there is no preceding update$_i$ operation, then $V[i]$ equals the initial value of p_i's segment of the object.

We describe a simulation of an atomic snapshot object from single-reader, single-writer read/write registers of bounded size.

The main idea of the scan is to collect (i.e., read) all the segments twice; this is called a *double collect*. If no segment is updated during the double collect, then the result of each collect is clearly a snapshot, as no updates occur in between the two collects. When a successful double collect occurs, the scan can return; this is the crux of the algorithm. There are two difficulties in implementing this idea: how to tell if the segments have been updated and what to do if the segments have been updated.

A simple way to solve the first problem is to include an (unbounded) sequence number with the data item in each segment (see the chapter notes). A more space-efficient solution is to employ a *handshaking mechanism*. The handshaking mechanism is not powerful enough to indicate precisely how many changes have been made; instead, it can indicate whether at least one change has been made to a segment or whether at most one change has been made.

To solve the problem of what to do if a change to a segment is observed, we show that if a scanner observes several changes in the segment of a specific updater then the updater has performed a complete update during the scan. We embed a scan operation at the beginning of the update; the view obtained in this scan is written with the data. The scanner returns the view obtained in the last collect. As we prove below, this view is an allowed response for this scan.

10.3.1 Handshaking Procedures

We now describe the general method of handshaking that provides two properties that are crucial to the correct operation of the atomic snapshot algorithm.

Consider a fixed ordered pair of distinct processors (p_i, p_j). Four procedures are defined for this ordered pair[2]: tryHS$_i$, tryHS$_j$, checkHS$_i$, and checkHS$_j$. The procedures interact via two shared single-reader, single-writer binary read/write registers, called the *handshaking bits*: h_i, which is written by p_i and read by p_j, and h_j, which is written by p_j and read by p_i. Processor p_i tries to handshake by modifying its own bit to make the two bits equal, whereas p_j tries to make the bits unequal. Then p_i checks whether a handshake occurred (informally, whether p_j tries to handshake

---

[2]The atomic snapshot algorithm only uses three of the procedures; for generality we include the fourth one.

Algorithm 29 Handshaking procedures for the ordered pair of processors (p_i, p_j).

1: procedure tryHS$_i$():	// p_i tries to handshake
2: $h_i := h_j$	// by trying to make the bits equal
3: return	
4: procedure tryHS$_j$():	// p_j tries to handshake
5: $h_j := \neg h_i$	// by trying to make the bits unequal
6: return	
7: procedure checkHS$_i$():	// p_i checks whether a handshake occurred
8: return $(h_i \neq h_j)$	
9: procedure checkHS$_j$():	// p_j checks whether a handshake occurred
10: return $(h_j = h_i)$	

---

between the time of p_i's last handshake try and the check) by testing whether the bits are unequal. To check whether a handshake occurs, p_j tests whether the bits are equal.

The pseudocode for the handshaking procedures appears in Algorithm 29. To make the code more readable, it appears as if both processors read each bit, but because each bit is single-writer, the writer can simply remember in a local variable what it last wrote to the bit.

Consider an admissible execution containing multiple calls to the handshaking procedures and a fixed linearization of the read and write operations embedded in the procedures. In the sequel we refer to these operations as occurring before, after, or between other operations with respect to this linearization. The properties we wish to have are (cf. Fig. 10.9):

Handshaking Property 1: If a checkHS$_i$ returns true, then there exists a tryHS$_j$ whose write occurs between the read of the previous tryHS$_i$ and the read of the checkHS$_i$. The same is also true with i and j reversed.

Handshaking Property 2: If a checkHS$_i$ returns false, then there is no tryHS$_j$ whose read and write occur between the write of the previous tryHS$_i$ and the read of the checkHS$_i$. The same is also true with i and j reversed.

Note that Handshaking Property 2 is not quite the negation of Handshaking Property 1; this uncertainty is the weakness mentioned earlier in our discussion of the mechanism.

The following theorem proves that the handshaking properties above are ensured by the procedures of Algorithm 29.

Theorem 10.10 *Consider any execution of the handshaking procedures that is correct for the read/write registers communication system, in which only the handshaking procedures alter the handshaking bits. Then the procedures satisfy the handshaking properties.*

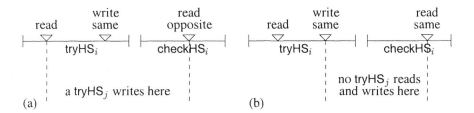

Fig. 10.9 Demonstrations for Handshaking Properties 1 (a) and 2 (b): Triangles indicate linearization points of low-level operations.

Proof. We prove the handshaking properties as stated; the proofs when i and j are reversed are left as an exercise (cf. Exercise 10.7).

Handshaking Property 1: Suppose a call to checkHS$_i$ returns true. Then p_i observes the bits to be unequal, that is, its read of h_j returns the opposite of what was written to h_i in the preceding tryHS$_i$. Without loss of generality, suppose p_i reads h_j to be 1 in the checkHS$_i$, while h_i is 0. Then in the preceding tryHS$_i$, p_i wrote a 0 to h_i because it observed h_j to be 0. Thus there must be a call to tryHS$_j$ whose write to h_j (changing it from 0 to 1) is linearized between the specified points.

Handshaking Property 2: Suppose a call to checkHS$_i$ returns false. Then p_i observes the bits to be equal, that is, its read of h_j returns the same value that was written to h_i in the preceding tryHS$_i$. Without loss of generality, suppose this value is 0. Suppose in contradiction there is a call to tryHS$_j$ whose read and write occur between the specified points. In particular, the read of h_i in tryHS$_j$ follows the prior tryHS$_i$, and will return 0; hence, 1 will be written to h_j in tryHS$_j$. Any subsequent calls to tryHS$_j$ in that interval will do the same. But then the read of h_j in checkHS$_i$ returns 1, not 0, a contradiction. □

10.3.2 A Bounded Memory Simulation

For each processor p_i acting as a scanner and each (distinct) processor p_j acting as an updater, we have a separate handshaking mechanism in the atomic snapshot simulation, denoted by the ordered pair (p_i, p_j). The first entry in the pair indicates the scanner, and the second indicates the updater. Thus we need a way to distinguish the procedure names and the variable names so that, for instance, the variables for the pair (p_i, p_j) will be distinct from those for (p_j, p_i) and so that the procedure names will not be confused. We will use the superscript (i, j) on the procedure and variable names for the ordered pair (p_i, p_j), for example, $h_i^{(i,j)}$ and checkHS$_i^{(i,j)}$.

A scanner tries to handshake with all the other processors, then does the double collect, and then checks the handshakes with all the other processors. Because handshaking and collecting, on the scanner's side, and writing and handshaking, on the updater's side, are done in separate operations, an update to some segment may not be observed (see Fig. 10.10). To differentiate two consecutive updates to the

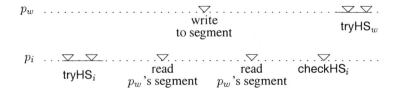

Fig. 10.10   Why toggle bits are needed.

same segment, we include a bit with the data of each segment, which the updater toggles in each update.

The scanner, p_i, repeatedly tries to handshake, double collects, and checks for handshakes until it observes three changes in the segment of some processor p_j. The implication of observing three changes in p_j's segment is that p_j has performed a complete update during p_i's scan. We alter the update code to first perform a scan and then include the view returned by the scan with the data and toggle bit. The scanner p_i returns the view obtained from p_j in the last collect.

The pseudocode appears as Algorithm 30. Each processor p_i has a local array $shook[0 \ldots n-1]$, which counts, for each updater p_j, the number of times p_j was observed by p_i to have tried to handshake with p_i.

The following lemmas are with respect to an admissible execution α of Algorithm 30. When we refer to a scan execution, we mean the execution of the procedure scan inside either a scan or an update operation.

Lemma 10.11 explains how the condition in Line 15 "catches" an intervening update operation.

Lemma 10.11 *If, during some execution by p_i of Line 15 in the* scan *procedure, the condition returns true for some j, then p_j executes either Line 6 or the write of the handshake with p_i in Line 7 between the previous execution in Line 12 of the read of* $\text{tryHS}_i^{(i,j)}$ *and this execution of Line 15.*

Proof.   The condition in Line 15 is true for j either because $a[j].toggle \neq b[j].toggle$ or because $\text{checkHS}_i^{(i,j)}$ returns true. In the first case, p_j writes to $Segment[j]$ (Line 6) during p_i's double collect (Lines 13–14). In the second case, Handshaking Property 1 implies that there has been a write of $\text{tryHS}_j^{(i,j)}$ (Line 7) since the read of the previous $\text{tryHS}_i^{(i,j)}$ (Line 12).   □

Note that a scan execution can either return a view in Line 18, in which case it is called a *direct* scan, or borrow a view, in Line 16, in which case it is called an *indirect* scan. Lemma 10.12 indicates why it is reasonable for an indirect scan to borrow the view returned by another scan.

Lemma 10.12 *An indirect* scan *returns the view of a direct* scan *whose execution is enclosed within the execution of the indirect* scan.

Algorithm 30 Wait-free atomic snapshot object simulation from read/write registers: code for processor p_i, $0 \le i \le n - 1$.

Initially $Segment[i].data = v_i$, $Segment[i].view$ equals $\langle v_0, \ldots, v_{n-1} \rangle$,
where v_j is the initial value of p_j's segment,
and (local) $shook[j] = 0$, for all j

```
1:   when scan_i() occurs:                                    // scan_i is an input event
2:       view := scan()                                  // scan is a procedure; view is local
3:       return_i(view)                                       // return_i is an output event

4:   when update_i(d) occurs:           // processor p_i updates its segment to hold d
5:       view := scan()
6:       Segment[i] := (d, view, ¬Segment[i].toggle)               // flip the toggle bit
7:       for all j ≠ i do tryHS_i^{(j,i)}()                   // handshake with all scanners
8:       ack_i

9:   procedure scan() :
10:      for all j ≠ i do shook[j] := 0                              // shook is local
11:      while true do
12:          for all j ≠ i do tryHS_i^{(i,j)}()             // handshake with all updaters
13:          for all j ≠ i do a[j] := Segment[j]                      // first collect
14:          for all j ≠ i do b[j] := Segment[j]                     // second collect
15:          if, for some j ≠ i, checkHS_i^{(i,j)}()
                 or (a[j].toggle ≠ b[j].toggle) then            // update progress observed
16:              if shook[j] = 2 then return(b[j].view)              // indirect scan
17:              else shook[j] := shook[j] + 1
18:          else return(⟨b[0].data, . . . , b[n − 1].data⟩)              // direct scan
```

Proof. Let p_i be the processor that executes the indirect scan. Assume that the indirect scan borrows a view to return from processor p_j. Thus p_i's indirect scan evaluates the condition in Line 15 to be true for j three times. By Lemma 10.11, p_j performs Line 6 or Line 7 in three distinct intervals; hence, p_j performs Line 6 or Line 7 three different times. It follows that the third execution by p_j of Line 6 or 7 is part of an update$_j$ operation that starts after p_i's scan starts. The reason is that a single update operation can cause the condition in Line 15 to be true twice, first in Line 6 and then in Line 7. Thus the scan embedded in that update$_j$ operation, which provides the borrowed view, is enclosed within the execution of the indirect scan of p_i.

If that embedded scan is direct, we are done. If not, then this argument can be applied inductively, noting that there can be at most n concurrent operations in the system. Hence, eventually the embedded scan is direct, and the result follows by the transitivity of containment of the embedded scan intervals. $\qquad\square$

Because the execution α is correct for the read/write registers communication system, the reads and writes on the *Segment*[i] shared registers are linearizable. For each configuration C_k in α, define the *actual value of the snapshot object* to be the vector $\langle d_0, \ldots, d_{n-1} \rangle$, where d_i is the first parameter of the latest write by processor p_i to *Segment*[i] (in Line 6) that is linearized before C_k. If there is no such write, then d_i is the initial value of *Segment*[i].*data*.

A direct scan has a successful double collect when the test in Line 15 is false for all j. That is, no processor is observed to make progress in between the two collects in Lines 13 and 14. Lemma 10.13 proves that the values returned by a direct scan constitute a "snapshot" after the first collect of the successful double collect.

Lemma 10.13 *A direct* scan *in* α *returns the actual value of the atomic snapshot object in the configuration immediately following the last read in the first collect of the successful double collect.*

Proof.   Suppose p_i performs a direct scan. Let p_j be any other processor.

Consider the behavior of p_i during the final execution of the while loop (Lines 11–18). Let s_i be the tryHS$_i^{(i,j)}$ execution in Line 12. Let r_1 be the linearization point of the last read in the first collect (Line 13). Let r_2 be the linearization point of the read of *Segment*[j] in the second collect (Line 14). Let c_i be the checkHS$_i^{(i,j)}$ execution in Line 15.

Since the direct scan returns the value read at r_2, we must show that no write to *Segment*[j] is linearized in between r_1 and r_2.

Since c_i returns false, Handshaking Property 2 implies that there is no complete tryHS$_j$ execution between the point of s_i and the point of c_i. Thus at most one write to *Segment*[j] can take place in that interval. If there were one such write, and it took place between r_1 and r_2, then it would cause the toggle bit to change between the reads of *Segment*[j] in the two collects. This contradicts the fact that the if condition in Line 15 was false. ☐

To prove linearizability, we identify a linearization point for each operation, inside its interval, in a way that preserves the semantics of the snapshot object. The proposed linearization for the scan and update operations in α is the result of ordering the operations according to these linearization points.

A scan operation whose embedded call to procedure scan is direct is linearized immediately after the last read of the first collect in the successful double collect. A scan operation whose embedded call to procedure scan is indirect is linearized at the same point as the direct scan whose view is borrowed. Lemma 10.12 guarantees that such a direct scan exists and is entirely contained in the interval of the scan operation. Thus all scan operations are linearized inside their intervals. Furthermore, Lemma 10.13 implies:

Lemma 10.14 *Every scan operation returns a view that is the actual value of the atomic snapshot object at the linearization point of the scan.*

An update operation by p_i is linearized at the same point in the execution as its embedded write to *Segment*[i]. By Lemma 10.14, data values returned by a scan operation are simultaneously held in all the registers at the linearization point of the operation. Therefore, each scan operation returns the value for the ith segment written by the latest update operation by p_i that precedes it in the linearization.

This completes the proof of linearizability, and leaves only the wait-free requirement. Each unsuccessful double collect by p_i can be attributed to some j, for which the condition in Line 15 holds. By the pigeonhole principle, in $2n + 1$ unsuccessful double collects three are attributed to the same j. Two of these double collects will increment $shook_i[j]$ to 1 and then 2 (in Line 17), and the third will borrow an indirect view from p_j (in Line 16).

Hence scan operations are wait-free, because the tryHS and checkHS procedures are wait-free. This, in turn, implies that update operations are wait-free. The same argument shows that each high-level operation performs $O(n^2)$ low-level operations.

Theorem 10.15 *There exists a wait-free simulation of an atomic snapshot object using read/write registers.*

10.4 SIMULATING SHARED REGISTERS IN MESSAGE-PASSING SYSTEMS

The last simulation we present in this chapter shows how to take algorithms designed for shared memory systems and run them in asynchronous message-passing systems. If we are not concerned with failures or slowdowns of processors, then the methods of Chapter 9 can be used to simulate read/write registers (e.g., the algorithm of Section 9.3.1). However, these methods are based on waiting for acknowledgments (in the underlying total broadcast algorithm) and hence are not resilient to failures.

We describe a simulation of a single-reader single-writer read/write register by n processors, in the presence of f failures, where $f < n/2$. The simulated register satisfies the definition of f-resilient shared memory. The simulation can be replicated to provide multiple shared registers.

When there are failures in a message-passing system, a processor cannot be sure that another processor will receive a message sent to it. Moreover, it cannot wait for an acknowledgment from the receiver, because the receiver may fail. To provide tolerance to $f < n/2$ failures, we use all the processors, not just the designated reader and writer of the register, as extra storage to help with the simulation of each shared register. In order to be able to pick the latest value among those stored at various processors, the values are accompanied by a sequence number.

Consider a particular simulated register. When the writer wants to write a value to this register, it increments a local counter to produce a sequence number and sends a ⟨*newval*⟩ message containing the new value and the sequence number to all the processors. Each recipient updates its local copy of the register with the information, if the sequence number is larger than what it currently has; in any event, the recipient sends back an ⟨*ack*⟩ message. Once the writer receives an ⟨*ack*⟩ from at least $\lfloor \frac{n}{2} \rfloor + 1$ processors, it finishes the write. Because $n > 2f$, it follows that $\lfloor \frac{n}{2} \rfloor + 1 < n - f$, and thus, the writer is guaranteed to receive responses from at least that many processors.

When the reader wants to read the register, it sends a $\langle request \rangle$ message to all the processors. Each recipient sends back a $\langle value \rangle$ message containing the information it currently has. Once the reader receives a $\langle value \rangle$ message from at least $\lfloor \frac{n}{2} \rfloor +$ 1 processors, it returns the value with the largest sequence number among those received.

Each read and write operation communicates with a set of at least $\lfloor \frac{n}{2} \rfloor + 1$ processors, which is a majority of the processors. Thus there is at least one processor in the intersection of the subsets for each read and write operation. This intersection property guarantees that the latest value written will be obtained by each read.

To overcome potential problems caused by the asynchrony of the underlying message system, both the reader and writer maintain a local array $status[0..n-1]$, to manage the communication; $status[j]$ contains one of the following values:

***not_sent*:** The message for the most recent operation has not yet been sent to p_j (because p_j has not acknowledged a previous message).

***not_acked*:** The message for the most recent operation has been sent to p_j but not yet acknowledged by p_j.

***acked*:** The message for the most recent operation has been acknowledged by p_j.

In addition, an integer counter, *num_acks*, counts the number of responses received so far during the current operation.

The pseudocode for the writer and reader appear as Algorithms 31 and 32, respectively; the code common to all processors appears as Algorithm 33. To avoid cluttering the code, the register name is not explicitly included; however, we do need a separate copy of all the local variables for each simulated register, and the register name should be a parameter to the high-level event names.

To prove the correctness of the algorithm, consider an arbitrary admissible execution of the algorithm. The next two lemmas show that the *status* variables ensure that the responses received were indeed sent in reply to the message sent during the current read or write operation.

Lemma 10.16 *When a write operation completes, at least $\lfloor \frac{n}{2} \rfloor + 1$ processors store a value in their copy of the variable last whose sequence number equals the sequence number of the write.*

Proof. Choose any processor p_j. The following facts about the writer p_w's $status[j]$ variable can be verified by induction.

- If $status[j]$ equals *acked*, then no message is in transit from p_w to p_j or vice versa.

- If $status[j]$ equals *not_acked*, then exactly one message is in transit from p_w to p_j or vice versa, either $\langle newval \rangle$ or $\langle ack \rangle$. Furthermore, if it is $\langle newval \rangle$, then the data in the message is for p_w's most recent write.

Algorithm 31 Read/write register simulation by message passing:
code for processor p_w, the (unique) writer of the simulated register.

Initially $status[j]$ equals $acked$ for all j, seq equals 0, and $pending$ equals $false$

1:   when $write_w(v)$ occurs: // processor p_w writes v to the register
2:       $pending := true$
3:       $seq := seq + 1$
4:       $num\_acks := 0$
5:       for all j do
6:          if $status[j] = acked$ then   // got response for previous operation
7:             enable $send_w \langle newval, (v, seq) \rangle$ to p_j
8:             $status[j] := not\_acked$
9:          else $status[j] := not\_sent$

10: when $\langle ack \rangle$ is received from p_j:
11:      if not $pending$ then $status[j] := acked$ // no operation in progress
12:      else if $status[j] = not\_sent$ then   // response to a previous message
13:          enable $send_w \langle newval, (v, seq) \rangle$ to p_j
14:          $status[j] := not\_acked$
15:      else   // response for the current operation
16:          $status[j] := acked$
17:          $num\_acks := num\_acks + 1$
18:          if $num\_acks \geq \lfloor \frac{n}{2} \rfloor + 1$ then   // acks received from majority
19:             $pending := false$
20:             enable ack_w

- If $status[j]$ equals not_sent, then exactly one message is in transit from p_w to p_j or vice versa, either $\langle newval \rangle$ or $\langle ack \rangle$. Furthermore, if it is $\langle newval \rangle$, then the data in the message is for a write prior to the most recent one.

Then num_acks correctly counts the number of acks received for the current write, and each one indicates that the sending processor has set its variable $last$ to the data for the current write. □

Lemma 10.17 can be proved in a very similar way (see Exercise 10.8).

Lemma 10.17 *When a read operation completes, the reader has received a $\langle value \rangle$ message from at least $\lfloor \frac{n}{2} \rfloor + 1$ processors containing the value of the sender's variable last at some point since the read began.*

Lemma 10.18 deals with the ordering of the value returned by a read operation and the value written by a write operation that completely precedes it.

Lemma 10.18 *If write operation w completes before read operation r starts, then the sequence number assigned to w (in Line 3) is less than or equal to the sequence number associated with the value returned by r (cf. Line 15).*

Algorithm 32 Read/write register simulation by message passing:
code for processor p_r, the (unique) reader of the simulated register.

Initially *status*[j] equals *acked* for all j, *seq* equals 0, and *pending* equals *false*

1:	when read$_r$() occurs:	// processor p_r reads from the register
2:	*pending* := *true*	
3:	*num_acks* := 0	
4:	for all j do	
5:	if *status*[j] = *acked* then	// got response for previous operation
6:	enable send$_r$ ⟨*request*⟩ to p_j	
7:	*status*[j] := *not_acked*	
8:	else *status*[j] := *not_sent*	
9:	when ⟨*value*,(v, s)⟩ is received from p_j:	
10:	if not *pending* then *status*[j] := *acked*	// no operation in progress
11:	else if *status*[j] = *not_sent* then	// response to a previous message
12:	enable send$_r$ ⟨*request*⟩ to p_j	
13:	*status*[j] := *not_acked*	
14:	else	// response for the current operation
15:	if $s > seq$ then { $val := v$; $seq := s$ }	// more recent value
16:	*status*[j] := *acked*	
17:	*num_acks* := *num_acks* + 1	
18:	if *num_acks* $\geq \lfloor \frac{n}{2} \rfloor + 1$ then	// acks received from majority
19:	*pending* := *false*	
20:	enable return$_r$ (*val*)	

Proof. Let x be the sequence number of w. By Lemma 10.16, when w ends, at least $\lfloor \frac{n}{2} \rfloor + 1$ processors store data in their copies of the variable *last* with sequence number x. Call this set of processors S_w. By Lemma 10.17, when r ends, it has received at least $\lfloor \frac{n}{2} \rfloor + 1$ messages from processors containing the values of their copies of the variable *last* at some point since r began. Call this set of processors S_r. Since n is the total number of processors, S_w and S_r have a nonempty intersection. See Figure 10.11.

Let p_j be some processor in their intersection. Since the sequence number in p_j's variable *last$_j$* never decreases, the sequence number reported by p_j to the read r is at least x, and the lemma follows.   □

Obviously, each read returns a value written by some write that began before the read ended. Since the sequence numbers of writes are strictly increasing, we have:

Lemma 10.19 *If write operation w starts after the completion of read operation r, then the sequence number assigned to w is greater than the sequence number associated with the value returned by r.*

Finally, we can prove (see Exercise 10.9):

Algorithm 33 Read/write register simulation by message passing:
code for every processor p_i, $0 \leq i \leq n - 1$, including p_w and p_r.

Initially *last* equals $(v_0, 0)$, where v_0 is the initial value of the simulated register

1:   when $\langle newval, (v, s) \rangle$ is received from p_w:
                                                           // v is more recent than current value
2:         *last* := (v, s)
3:         enable send$_i$ $\langle ack \rangle$ to p_w

4:   when $\langle request \rangle$ is received from p_r:
5:         enable send$_i$ $\langle value, last \rangle$ to p_r

---

Lemma 10.20 *If read operation r_1 occurs before read operation r_2, then the sequence number associated with the value returned by r_1 is less than or equal to the sequence number associated with the value returned by r_2.*

These three lemmas prove that the algorithm is correct (see Exercise 10.10). Each invocation of a read or write operation requires sending one message to a majority of the processors and receiving their responses. Clearly, at most $2n$ messages are sent as the result of each invocation of an operation. Moreover, if each message takes at most one time unit, then the existence of a nonfaulty majority implies that the time complexity is $O(1)$.

Theorem 10.21 *If $f < n/2$, then there exists a simulation of a single-reader single-writer read/write register for n processors using asynchronous message passing, in the presence of f crash failures. Each register operation requires $O(n)$ messages and $O(1)$ time.*

What happens if we have multiple readers? It can be shown that new-old inversions, similar to those described in Section 10.2.2, can occur when there are concurrent read operations (Exercise 10.11). One solution is to employ Algorithm 27 (see Exercise 10.12). However, this requires another layer of sequence numbers and increases the time and message complexity.

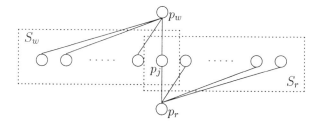

Fig. 10.11 Illustration for the proof of Lemma 10.18.

An alternative, more optimized, approach is to piggyback on the sequence numbers already used in our algorithm. The only modification we need to make is to have a reader communicate the value it is about to return to a majority of the processors (in a manner similar to the algorithm performed by the writer). This way, any read operation that starts later will observe a larger timestamp and return a later value.

Once we have multi-reader registers, we can then use Algorithm 28 to build multi-writer registers in the message passing model. We can also simulate atomic snapshot objects in message passing.

We conclude this section by proving that the requirement that $f < n/2$ is necessary, that is, if more than half the processors may fail then read/write registers cannot be simulated in message passing.

Theorem 10.22 *In any simulation of a single-reader single-writer read/write register for n processors using asynchronous message passing, the number of failures f must be less than $n/2$.*

Proof.   Suppose in contradiction there is such a simulation A with $n \leq 2f$. Partition the set of processors into two sets S_0 and S_1, with $|S_0| = \lceil n/2 \rceil$ and $|S_1| = \lfloor n/2 \rfloor$. Note that both sets have size at most f.

Consider an admissible execution α_0 of A in which the initial value of the simulated register is 0, all processors in S_0 are nonfaulty, and all processors in S_1 crash initially. Suppose processor p_0 in S_0 invokes a write operation with value 1 at time 0 and no other operations are invoked. Since the algorithm must tolerate up to f failures, p_0's write operation will eventually finish at some time t_0.

Consider a second admissible execution α_1 of A in which the initial value of the simulated register is 0, all processors in S_0 crash initially, and all processors in S_1 are nonfaulty. Suppose processor p_1 in S_1 invokes a read operation at time $t_0 + 1$ and no other operations are invoked. Since the algorithm must tolerate up to f failures, p_1's read operation will eventually finish at some time t_1 and, by linearizability, will return the value 0.

Finally, consider an admissible execution β of A that is a "merger" of α_0 and α_1. In more detail, processors in S_0 experience the same sequence of events up through time t_1 as they do in α_0, while processors in S_1 experience the same sequence of events up through time t_1 as they do in α_1. There are no failures in β, but messages that are sent between the two groups have their delivery delayed until after time t_1. Since p_1 cannot distinguish between α_1 and β, it still returns 0 for its read. However, this violates linearizability, since the latest preceding write (the write by p_0) has the value 1. $\qquad\square$

Exercises

10.1 Expand on the critical section idea for simulating shared memory (in a non-fault-tolerant way).

10.2 Show that the two definitions of wait-free simulation discussed in Section 10.1 are equivalent.

10.3 Suppose we attempt to fix the straw man multi-reader algorithm of Section 10.2.2 without having the readers write, by having each reader read the array B twice. Show a counterexample to this algorithm.

10.4 In the proof of Theorem 10.3, show that w_{j_i} must be a write to a register in S_i, for $i = 1, 2$.

10.5 Does there exist a wait-free simulation of an n-reader register from single-reader registers in which only one reader writes, when $n > 2$?

Does there exist such a simulation for $n > 2$ readers in which only $n - 1$ readers write?

10.6 Prove Lemma 10.6.

10.7 Prove the properties in Theorem 10.10 when i and j are reversed.

10.8 Prove Lemma 10.17.

10.9 Prove Lemma 10.20.

10.10 Prove Theorem 10.21.

10.11 Construct an execution in which multiple readers run the simulation of a single-writer single-reader register in the message-passing model (Section 10.4) and experience a new-old inversion.

10.12 Show how to combine Algorithm 27 and the simulation of a single-writer single-reader register from message passing (Section 10.4) to obtain a simulation of a single-writer multi-reader read/write register in a message-passing system with f failures, $f < 2n$. What are the message and time complexities of the resulting algorithm?

10.13 Show a direct simulation of a single-writer multi-reader register from message passing extending the algorithm of Section 10.4, without using an extra layer of sequence numbers. Prove the correctness of this algorithm.

Chapter Notes

This chapter concentrated on the simulation of read/write objects from other, lower-level, read/write objects and from asynchronous message passing.

The original definitions of different types of registers based on their sharing patterns were proposed by Lamport [158, 159]. Lamport also defined weaker types of registers, called *safe* and *regular*. Loosely speaking, safe registers are guaranteed to return correct values only for read operations that do not overlap write operations;

regular registers guarantee that a read operation returns a "current" value but do not prohibit new-old inversions between reads.

The general notion of linearizability was extended to wait-free algorithms by Herlihy [134]. Algorithm 26, the simulation of the multi-valued register from binary registers, is due to Vidyasankar [257]. Algorithm 27, the unbounded multi-reader algorithm, is due to Israeli and Li [140]. Algorithm 28, the unbounded multi-writer algorithm, is due to Vitányi and Awerbuch [258].

The unbounded timestamps used in the algorithms for simulating multi-reader registers and multi-writer registers can be replaced with bounded timestamps using ideas of Dolev and Shavit [98] and Dwork and Waarts [102]; see Chapter 16 of [35] for details.

Other simulations of multi-valued registers from binary ones appear in Chaudhuri, Kosa, and Welch [76]. Bounded simulations of multi-reader registers were given by Singh, Anderson, and Gouda [243]. Li, Tromp, and Vitányi [168] presented a bounded simulation of multi-writer multi-reader registers from single-writer single-reader registers.

The atomic snapshot problem was defined using three different specification methods by Afek et al. [3], by Anderson [13], and by Aspnes and Herlihy [22]; these papers also presented simulations of atomic snapshots from registers.

The simulation we presented is based on the algorithm of Afek et al. [3]. This algorithm uses $O(n^2)$ read and write operations for each snapshot operations; the best algorithm to date, using $O(n \log n)$ operations, was given by Attiya and Rachman [31]. The handshaking bits were first used by Peterson [213] and by Lamport [159].

We have specified *single-writer* atomic snapshot objects, which allow only one processor to write to each segment; *multi-writer* snapshot objects were defined by Anderson [14], who also showed how they can be simulated using *single-writer* snapshot objects and multi-writer read/write registers.

Atomic snapshots resemble distributed snapshots, studied in Chapter 6, in requiring an instantaneous view of many system components. An atomic snapshot gives the effect of reading several memory segments at once; a distributed snapshot records the local states of several processors. One difference is in the specification: atomic snapshots order the views obtained by scanners, whereas distributed snapshots do not provide any guarantee about the consistent cuts obtained in different invocations. Another difference is in the simulations: the atomic snapshot algorithm is wait-free and can tolerate processor failures, whereas the distributed snapshot algorithm does not tolerate failures.

The simulation of read/write registers from message passing is due to Attiya, Bar-Noy, and Dolev [25]. It requires integer sequence numbers, and thus the size of messages is unbounded. To bound the message size, Attiya, Bar-Noy, and Dolev used bounded timestamps. An alternative simulation with bounded messages was given by Attiya [24]. The shared memory simulation uses a particular kind of *quorum system*, the majority quorum system, to ensure that each read obtains the value of the most recent write. This idea has been generalized to other quorum systems, including those that can tolerate Byzantine failures [179].

The simulation in Section 10.4 provides a distributed shared memory that is fault tolerant, in contrast to the distributed shared memory algorithms of Chapter 9, which were not fault tolerant. The fault tolerance provided here ensures that the data in the shared objects remains available to correct processors, despite the failures of some processors. Processors that fail are no longer of interest, and no guarantees are made about them. One-resilient algorithms for the same notion of fault-tolerant distributed shared memory were presented by Stumm and Zhou [248].

DSMs that can tolerate processor failures and recoveries have been a subject of recent interest. Many sequentially consistent DSM systems that are tolerant of processors that crash and recover have been described in the literature (e.g., [248, 262, 229, 147]). There has also been work on recoverable DSMs that support weaker consistency conditions (e.g., [143, 148, 200]). In these papers, techniques including checkpoints of consistent cuts and logging information to stable storage are employed to reintegrate recovered processors.

11

Simulating Synchrony

As we have seen in previous chapters, the possible behaviors of a synchronous system are more restricted than the possible behaviors of an asynchronous system. Thus it is easier to design and understand algorithms for synchronous systems. However, most real systems are at least somewhat asynchronous. In Chapter 6, we have seen ways to observe the causality structure of events in executions. In this chapter, we show how they can be employed to run algorithms designed under strict synchronization assumptions, in systems that provide weaker synchronization guarantees.

Throughout this chapter, we only consider message-passing systems in which there are no failures. The topology of the communication system can be arbitrary and, as always, the only (direct) communication is between nodes that are neighbors in the topology.

We begin the chapter by specifying synchronous message-passing systems in our layered model of computation.

Then we show how a small modification to the logical clocks from Chapter 6, called *logical buffering*, can be used to provide the illusion that the processors take steps in lockstep, when in reality they are totally asynchronous. Thus logical buffering is a way to simulate a system in which processors are synchronous and messages are asynchronous with a (totally) asynchronous system. Another way to view this simulation is that asynchronous processors can simulate processors with the most powerful kind of hardware clocks, those that always equal real time, as long as message delay remains asynchronous.

The second synchrony simulation we study in this chapter is one to simulate the synchronous system with the asynchronous system. Logical buffering can be used to simulate synchronous *processors*, but it does not ensure any bounds on message delay. To create the illusion of synchronous message delay, more effort is required. A simulation from the synchronous system to the asynchronous system is called a *synchronizer*. We present a simple synchronizer in this chapter.

Both simulations are *local*, not *global*. We conclude the chapter by discussing some implications of this fact.

11.1   SYNCHRONOUS MESSAGE-PASSING SPECIFICATION

In this section, we give a problem specification of the communication system we wish to simulate, a synchronous message-passing system. The key difference from the asynchronous case is that send and recv events at different processors must be interleaved in a regular way to achieve the lockstep rounds that characterize the synchronous model.

Formally, the inputs and outputs are the same as for asynchronous message passing, defined in Chapter 7, that is, the inputs are of the form $send_i(M)$ and the outputs are of the form $recv_i(M)$, where i indicates a processor and M is a set of messages (including possibly the empty set).

As in the model used in Part I, a round for a processor consists of sending messages, receiving messages sent in that round, and performing local computation, which will determine what messages to send in the next round. Conceptually, each round occurs concurrently at all the processors. Because our notion of execution is a sequence of events, we must choose some (arbitrary) total order of events that is consistent with the partial order. There are a number of total orders that will work. We choose a particular total order here that is consistent with our requirement, from Chapter 7, that all enabled events take place on a node before any event on another node can take place. This total order is embodied in the Round-Robin property below that is placed on allowable sequences of the synchronous message passing model. According to the Round-Robin property, all the round 1 send events take place. Then the receipts of the round 1 messages occur. Because of the node atomicity requirement, when a processor receives a message, the very next event must be the send that is triggered by that receipt, which in this case is the send for round 2. Because the receive for round 1 cannot be separated from the send for round 2, we have a series of recv-send pairs, one for each processor, in which messages for round 1 are received and messages for round 2 are sent. Then we have another series of recv-send pairs, in which messages for round 2 are received and messages for round 3 are sent.

Formally, every sequence in the allowable set must conform to the following "round" structure:

Round-Robin: The sequence is infinite and consists of a series of subsequences, where the first subsequence has the form $send_0$, ..., $send_{n-1}$, and each later subsequence has the form $recv_0$, $send_0$, $recv_1$, $send_1$, ..., $recv_{n-1}$, $send_{n-1}$. The kth $send_i$ and the kth $recv_i$ events form *round* k for processor p_i.

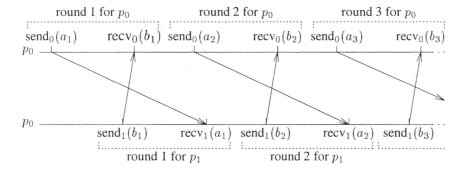

Fig. 11.1 How rounds overlap.

The Round-Robin property imposes constraints on the inputs (the send events) from the environment; they must occur in Round-Robin order and be properly interleaved with the outputs (the recv events).

As an example, consider three rounds of a system consisting of two processors p_0 and p_1, which are directly connected:

$$\text{send}_0(a_1), \text{send}_1(b_1), \text{recv}_0(b_1), \text{send}_0(a_2), \text{recv}_1(a_1), \text{send}_1(b_2),$$
$$\text{recv}_0(b_2), \text{send}_0(a_3), \text{recv}_1(a_2), \text{send}_1(b_3), \text{recv}_0(b_3), \ldots$$

(See Fig. 11.1.)

The sets of messages sent and received must satisfy the following conditions:

Integrity: Every message received by processor p_i from processor p_j in round k was sent in round k by p_j.

No Duplicates: No message is received more than once. Thus each recv event contains at most one message from each neighbor.

Liveness: Every message sent in round k is received in round k.

The environment (that is, the algorithm using the synchronous message-passing system) decides unilaterally what should be sent in the first round for each processor. In later rounds, the environment can decide based on what it has previously received.

11.2 SIMULATING SYNCHRONOUS PROCESSORS

In this section, we consider two systems with asynchronous communication (i.e., unbounded message delays), one with synchronous (lockstep) processors, called SynchP, and one with asynchronous processors, called Asynch. We will show that Asynch can locally simulate SynchP.

Asynch is the standard asynchronous message-passing communication system. SynchP is a weakening of the standard synchronous message-passing communication

---

Algorithm 34 Logical buffering to simulate synchronous processors:
code for p_i, $0 \leq i \leq n - 1$.

Initially *round* $= 0$ and *buffer* $= \emptyset$

1: when SynchP-send$_i(S)$ occurs:
2:    *round* $:=$ *round* $+ 1$
3:    enable Asynch-send$_i(\{\langle m, round \rangle : m \in S\})$

4: when Asynch-recv$_i(M)$ occurs:
5:    add M to *buffer*
6:    *ready* $:= \{m : \langle m, tag \rangle \in buffer$ and $tag \leq round\}$
7:    remove from *buffer* every element that contributed to *ready*
8:    enable SynchP-recv$_i(ready)$

---

system; an allowable sequence is still an infinite series of rounds, but there is no longer the requirement that every message sent in round k be received in round k. Instead, every message sent in round k must be received in round k or later. Messages need not be delivered in FIFO order, but no message is delivered more than once.

The only situation observable to the processors that can happen in Asynch but not in SynchP is for a message that was sent at the sender's kth send step to be received at the recipient's jth recv step, where $j < k$. If this situation were to occur when processors take steps in lockstep, it would mean that the message is received before it is sent. To avoid this situation, the simulation employs *logical buffering*; each processor keeps a round counter that counts how many send steps it has taken, each message is tagged with the sender's round count, and the recipient delays processing of a message until its round count equals or exceeds that on the message.

Logical buffering provides properties similar to those of logical clocks; however, with logical clocks some logical times may be skipped, but not with logical buffering. Skipping some logical times may have drawbacks, for instance, if certain actions are scheduled to occur at certain logical times. With logical buffering, the round counts themselves are consistent with the happens-before relation.

The pseudocode is presented in Algorithm 34. SynchP-send indicates the send for system SynchP and is an input to the logical buffering algorithm. SynchP-recv indicates the receive for system SynchP and is an output of the logical buffering algorithm. Asynch-send and Asynch-recv are the communication primitives used by the logical buffering processes to communicate with each other over the asynchronous communication system. The result of the occurrence of Asynch-send$_i$ and SynchP-recv$_i$ is simply to disable that event, as explained in Section 7.6. There must be an infinite number of SynchP-send$_i$ events, for each i; however, the empty set of messages is an allowable parameter for SynchP-send$_i$.

Theorem 11.1 *System Asynch locally simulates system SynchP.*

Proof. Consider the logical buffering algorithm, Algorithm 34. Obviously, it has the correct top and bottom interfaces.

Let α be an execution of the logical buffering algorithm that is locally admissible for (SynchP,Asynch). Locally user compliant for SynchP means that each node alternates sends and receives, but the sends and receives at different nodes are not necessarily interleaved regularly as they would be in the actual SynchP system. We must show that there exists a sequence σ in seq(SynchP) such that $\sigma|i = top(\alpha)|i$, for all i, $0 \leq i \leq n - 1$.

Define σ to be the result of taking the n sequences $top(\alpha)|i$, $0 \leq i \leq n - 1$, and interleaving them so as to conform to the Round-Robin property of the synchronous system.

To verify that σ is in seq(SynchP), we only need to check that every message sent in some round is eventually received in the same or a later round and is not received twice. No message is delivered too early, since messages are tagged and held in buffer variables in execution α. Every message is eventually delivered, since the round counter increments without bound because of the infinite number of SynchP-$send_i$ events, and the tags do not change in α. No message is received twice since messages are removed from *buffer* once they become ready. $\qquad\square$

Thus logical buffering can provide the illusion that processors possess more synchrony than they already do, going from totally asynchronous to lockstep. However, the level of synchrony of the communication is not improved.

11.3 SIMULATING SYNCHRONOUS PROCESSORS AND SYNCHRONOUS COMMUNICATION

Previously in this chapter, we have seen how to (locally) simulate synchronous processors with asynchronous processors. In this section we show how to (locally) simulate the fully synchronous message-passing communication system, denoted Synch, with Asynch, the fully asynchronous message-passing communication system. Such a simulation is called a *synchronizer*.

In addition to having synchronous processors, the synchronous system guarantees that in the kth round of each processor it receives all the messages that were sent to it by its neighbors in their kth round.[*] In this section, we show how to achieve this property, by using a synchronizer and thus locally simulating the synchronous system by the asynchronous system.

The main difficulty in ensuring the above property is that a node does not usually know which of its neighbors have sent a message to it in the current round. Because there is no bound on the delay a message can incur in the asynchronous system, simply waiting long enough before generating the (synchronous) receive event does not suffice; additional messages have to be sent in order to achieve synchronization.

11.3.1 A Simple Synchronizer

In this section, we present a simple synchronizer called ALPHA. Synchronizer ALPHA is efficient in terms of time but inefficient in terms of messages; the chapter notes

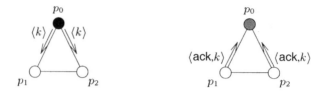

Fig. 11.2 Processor p_0 sends round k messages to its neighbors (left) and then receives $\langle \text{ack} \rangle$ messages (right).

discuss another synchronizer that provides a trade-off between time complexity and message complexity.

Before generating the receive for round k, the synchronizer at a node p_i must know that it has received all the round k messages that were sent to this node. The idea is to have the neighbors of p_i check whether all their messages were received and have them notify p_i. It is simple for a node to know whether all its messages were received, if we require each node to send an acknowledgment for every message (of the original synchronous algorithm) received. If all round k messages sent by a node have been acknowledged, then the node is said to be *safe* for round k. Observe that the acknowledgments only double the number of messages sent by the original algorithm. Also observe that each node detects that it is safe for round k a constant time after it generates the synchronous send for round k (using the method of measuring time complexity for asynchronous algorithms from Chapter 2).

Figure 11.2 presents a simple execution in which p_0 sends messages to its neighbors and receives acknowledgments; at this point, p_0 is safe. In this figure and Figure 11.3, a black node represents a processor just starting a round and a gray node represents a safe processor; otherwise, the node is white.

A node can generate its next synchronous receive once all its neighbors are safe. Most synchronizers use the same mechanism of acknowledgments to detect that nodes are safe; they differ in the mechanism by which nodes notify their neighbors that they are safe. In synchronizer ALPHA, a safe node directly informs all its neighbors by sending them messages. When node p_i has been informed that all its neighbors are safe for round k, p_i knows that all round k messages sent to it have arrived, and it generates the synchronous receive for round k.

Figure 11.3 presents the extension of the execution in Figure 11.2: p_0 and p_2 indicate they are safe, allowing p_1 to do its round k receive and the move on to send its round $k+1$ messages.

The pseudocode appears in Algorithm 35. Synch-send and Synch-recv indicate the events of the synchronous system, whereas Asynch-send and Asynch-recv indicate those of the asynchronous system. This version of the code uses unbounded space for simplicity. An exercise is to reduce the space usage (Exercise 11.3). As we did in Chapter 2, we describe the algorithm as if each message of the underlying asynchronous system is received separately. Similar arguments justify this simplification.

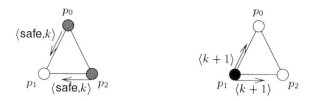

Fig. 11.3 Processors p_0 and p_2 send $\langle$safe$\rangle$ messages for round k (left) and then p_1 sends round $k + 1$ message (right).

Theorem 11.2 *Asynch locally simulates Synch.*

Proof. Consider synchronizer ALPHA of Algorithm 35. Obviously, it has the correct top and bottom interfaces.

Let α be any execution of synchronizer ALPHA that is (Synch,Asynch)-locally-admissible. We must show that there exists a sequence σ in seq(Synch) such that $\sigma|i = top(\alpha)|i$, for all i, $0 \leq i \leq n - 1$.

Define σ to be the result of taking the n sequences $top(\alpha)|i$, $0 \leq i \leq n - 1$, and interleaving them so as to conform to the Round-Robin property of the synchronous system.

To verify that σ is in seq(Synch), we prove three lemmas. Lemma 11.3 states that the Synch-recv events at p_j are done in the correct order, that is, that if p_j performs Synch-recv for round r, then the previous Synch-recv performed by p_j was for round $r - 1$. Lemma 11.4 states that if processor p_j performs Synch-recv for round r, then $buffer[r]$ consists exactly of all round r messages sent to p_j. Lemma 11.5 states that p_j performs an infinite number of Synch-recv events.

The proof of Lemma 11.3 is left as an exercise (Exercise 11.4).

Lemma 11.3 *If p_j performs Synch-recv for round r in α, then the previous Synch-recv performed by p_j is for round $r - 1$.*

Lemma 11.4 *If p_j performs Synch-recv for round r, then $buffer[r]$ consists of all round r messages sent to p_j in α.*

Proof. The use of the round tag and the separate variables for each round ensure that no extraneous messages are in $buffer[r]$.

Let m be a message Synch-sent by p_i to p_j in round r. After the Synch-send, p_i Asynch-sends m to p_j. On its arrival, p_j puts it in $buffer[r]$. Suppose in contradiction p_j has already done Synch-recv for round r. Then $safe_j[r]$ must have included i at the time when p_j performed the Synch-recv. So p_j received a $\langle$safe,$r\rangle$ message from p_i. But then p_i would have already received an $\langle$ack,$r\rangle$ message from p_j for this message, which it has not sent yet, a contradiction. $\square$

Lemma 11.5 *Each processor performs a Synch-recv event for round r, for every $r \geq 1$.*

Algorithm 35 Simple synchronizer ALPHA with unbounded space:
code for p_i, $0 \leq i \leq n - 1$.

Initially *round* = 0 and
buffer[r], *safe*[r], and *ack-missing*[r] are empty, for all $r \geq 1$

1: when Synch-send$_i(S)$ occurs:
2:     *round* := *round* + 1
3:     *ack-missing*[*round*] := $\{j : p_j$ is a recipient of a message in $S\}$
4:     enable Asynch-send$_i(\langle m, round\rangle)$ to p_j, for each $m \in S$ with recipient p_j

5: when Asynch-recv$_i(\langle m, r\rangle)$ from p_j occurs:
6:     add (m, j) to *buffer*[r]
7:     enable Asynch-send$_i(\langle \text{ack}, r\rangle)$ to p_j // acknowledge

8: when Asynch-recv$_i(\langle \text{ack}, r\rangle)$ from p_j occurs:
9:     remove j from *ack-missing*[r]
10:   if *ack-missing*[r] = $\emptyset$ then   // all neighbors have acknowledged
11:       enable Asynch-send$_i(\langle \text{safe}, r\rangle)$ to all neighbors   // p_i is safe

12: when Asynch-recv$_i(\langle \text{safe}, r\rangle)$ from p_j occurs:
13:   add j to *safe*[r]
14:   if *safe*[r] includes all neighbors then   // all neighbors are safe
15:       enable Synch-recv$_i(buffer[r])$ // for round r

Proof. Suppose in contradiction that the lemma is false. Let r be the smallest round number such that some processor p_i never performs Synch-recv for round r.

First we argue that Synch-send for round r occurs at every node. If $r = 1$, then the Synch-sends occur because α is locally user compliant for Synch. If $r > 1$, then every processor performs Synch-recv for round $r - 1$ by choice of r, and so Synch-send for round r occurs at every node because α is locally user compliant for Synch.

Thus every neighbor p_j of p_i experiences Synch-send for round r. Then p_j does Asynch-send to the appropriate neighbors, gets back the $\langle \text{ack} \rangle$ messages, becomes safe, and sends $\langle \text{safe} \rangle$ messages to all neighbors, including p_i.

Thus p_i receives $\langle \text{safe} \rangle$ messages from all neighbors and performs Synch-recv for round r, a contradiction.   □

These three lemmas show that Asynch locally simulates Synch using ALPHA.   □

The total complexity of the resulting algorithm depends on the overhead introduced by the synchronizer and, of course, on the time and message complexity of the synchronous algorithm.

Clearly, the time overhead of ALPHA is $O(1)$ per round. Because two additional messages per edge are sent (one in each direction), the message overhead of ALPHA

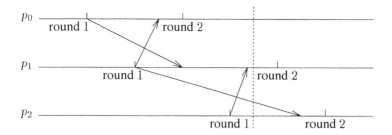

Fig. 11.4 Example execution of a synchronizer.

is $O(|E|)$ per round. Note that $O(|E|)$ messages are sent per round, regardless of the number of original messages sent during this round. The chapter notes discuss another synchronizer that exhibits a tradeoff between time and message overhead.

11.3.2 Application: Constructing a Breadth-First Search Tree

To see the usefulness of a synchronizer, we consider a problem that is much easier to solve in a synchronous system than an asynchronous one—construction of a breadth-first search (BFS) tree of a network (with arbitrary topology). Recall that the modified flooding algorithm of Chapter 2 (Algorithm 2) solves the BFS tree problem in synchronous systems, given a particular node to serve as the root of the tree. On the other hand, in an asynchronous system, the spanning tree constructed by the algorithm is not necessarily a BFS tree.

This problem is one of the prime examples for the utility of the synchronizer concept; in fact, the most efficient known asynchronous solutions for this problem were achieved by applying a synchronizer to a synchronous algorithm.

Consider now an execution of the synchronous BFS tree algorithm (Algorithm 2), on top of synchronizer ALPHA. The composition forms a BFS tree algorithm for the asynchronous case. Because its time complexity in the synchronous system is $O(D)$, where D is the diameter of the communication graph, it follows that in the asynchronous system, its time complexity is $O(D)$ and its message complexity is $O(D \cdot |E|)$.

11.4 LOCAL VS. GLOBAL SIMULATIONS

Consider an asynchronous message-passing system in which three nodes are arranged in a chain: There is a link from p_0 to p_1 and from p_1 to p_2. There is an execution of the synchronizer in this system in which the following events take place (see Fig. 11.4):

- p_0 simulates round 1;

- p_1 simulates round 1;

- p_0 simulates round 2, receiving p_1's round 1 message;

- p_2 simulates round 1;

- p_1 simulates round 2, receiving p_0's and p_2's round 1 messages;

- p_2 simulates round 2, receiving p_1's round 1 message.

Suppose the synchronous algorithm running on top of the synchronizer solves the session problem from Chapter 6 in the synchronous system, for two sessions, by having each processor perform special actions at rounds 1 and 2. Unfortunately, the transformed algorithm is not correct, because there is only one session in the execution described above, not two.

This scenario indicates the limitations of local simulations as opposed to global simulations. In the synchronous system, the rounds of the processors are guaranteed to be correctly interleaved so as to achieve two sessions. But the synchronizer, although it mimics the same execution on a per-node basis, cannot achieve the same interleaving of events at different nodes.

Informally speaking, local simulations preserve correctness for *internal* problems, those whose specifications do not depend on the real time at which events occur. The existence of a synchronizer implies that there is no difference in what can be computed in the synchronous and asynchronous systems, as long as we restrict our attention to internal problems in the absence of failures.

The lower bound on the running time for the session problem presented in Chapter 6 implies that any simulation of the synchronous system by the asynchronous system that preserves the relative order of events across nodes will require time overhead of a factor of the diameter of the communication network, roughly. The reason is that such a general simulation would transform the synchronous algorithm for the session problem into an algorithm for the asynchronous system, which by this lower bound must incur the stated overhead.

Exercises

11.1 Does logical buffering work for simulating system SynchP by system AsynchP in the presence of crash failures? If so, why? If not, then modify it to do so. What about Byzantine failures?

11.2 Is wait-free consensus possible in the system SynchP? What if there is at most one failure?

Hint: Think about Exercise 11.1.

11.3 Show how to bound the space complexity of synchronizer ALPHA.

11.4 Prove Lemma 11.3.

11.5 What are the worst-case time and message complexities of the asynchronous BFS tree algorithm that results from applying synchronizer ALPHA? What network topology exhibits this worst-case behavior?

11.6 Apply synchronizer ALPHA to both of the synchronous leader election algorithms in Chapter 3. What are the resulting time and message complexities? How do they compare to the lower bounds for asynchronous leader election?

11.7 Is mutual exclusion an internal problem?

11.8 If a specification is not internal, does that mean it cannot be implemented in an asynchronous system?

Chapter Notes

This chapter described two methods for simulating synchrony: logical buffering and synchronizers.

Logical buffering was independently developed by Neiger and Toueg [199] and by Welch [259]. Neiger and Toueg's paper defined the class of internal problems for which the translation is valid and applied it to systems with synchronized clocks, as well as other situations. Welch's paper gave fault-tolerant implementations of logical buffering in the asynchronous case. The latter paper contains the answer to Exercise 11.1, as well as to Exercise 11.2. An alternative answer to Exercise 11.2 can be found in Dolev, Dwork, and Stockmeyer [92].

Synchronizers were introduced by Awerbuch [36], who also suggested ALPHA (Algorithm 35) and the application to BFS tree construction; additional applications appear in [38]. Awerbuch [36] also describes two other synchronizers, BETA, with low message overhead, and GAMMA, which provides a trade-off between message and time overhead. Chapter 18 of [35] describes synchronizer ZETA, having the same trade-off as GAMMA.

Awerbuch [36] proved that the trade-off given by GAMMA is essentially optimal, if the synchronizer must simulate one round after the other. Some improved synchronizers have been suggested under various restrictions, for example on the network topology (Peleg and Ullman [209]). Awerbuch and Peleg [40] showed that if a synchronizer is not required to work in a round-by-round manner then the above trade-off is not inherent. Peleg's book [208] includes a thorough discussion of these topics.

12

Improving the Fault Tolerance of Algorithms

In Chapter 11, we saw examples of simulating a more well-behaved situation (namely, a synchronous system) with a less well-behaved situation (namely, an asynchronous system). The advantage of such simulations is that often algorithms can be developed for the more well-behaved case with less effort and complexity and then automatically translated to work in the less well-behaved case.

The same idea can be applied in the realm of fault tolerance. As we have seen in Chapter 5, more benign types of faults, such as crash failures, are easier to handle than more severe types of faults, such as Byzantine failures. In particular, more benign types of faults can often be tolerated with simpler algorithms. In this chapter, we explore methods that automatically translate algorithms designed to tolerate more benign faults into algorithms that can tolerate more severe faults. This chapter deals only with message-passing systems, because usually only crash failures are considered in the context of shared memory systems. We also extend the layered model of computation to handle synchronous processors.

12.1 OVERVIEW

The bulk of this chapter presents a simulation that makes Byzantine failures appear to be crash failures in the synchronous case. Although it is possible to achieve this in one step (see the notes at the end of the chapter), it is conceptually easier to break this task down into subtasks, each one focusing on masking a particular aspect of Byzantine failures.

There are three problematic aspects of Byzantine behavior. The first is that a faulty processor can send messages with different contents to different processors in the same round. The second is that a faulty processor can send messages with arbitrary content (even if it sends the same message to all processors). The third is that this type of bad behavior can persist over many rounds.

Our approach to designing the overall simulation is to tackle each problem in isolation, designing three fault model simulations. The first simulation is from Byzantine to "identical Byzantine" (like Byzantine, but where faulty processors are restricted so that each one sends either nothing or the same message to all processors at each round). The second simulation is from identical Byzantine to "omission" (faulty processors send messages with correct contents but may fail to receive or send some messages). The third simulation is from omission to crash. More precise definitions of the communication system in the presence of these types of faults are given below.

In going from Byzantine to identical Byzantine, we must prevent faulty processors from sending conflicting messages. This can be done by having processors echo to each other the messages received over the lower level and then receiving at the higher level only those messages for which sufficiently many echoes were received. By setting this threshold high enough and assuming enough processors are nonfaulty, this scheme will ensure that no conflicting messages are received.

In going from identical Byzantine to omission, the contents of the messages received must be validated as being consistent with the high level algorithm A being run on top of the omission system. This is achieved by sending along with each message of the algorithm A the set of messages received by the algorithm at the previous simulated round, as justification for the sending of this message.

In going from omission to crash, once a processor exhibits a failure, we must ensure that it takes no more steps. This is accomplished by having processors echo to each other the messages received over the lower level. If a processor does not receive enough echoes of its own message, then it halts (crashes itself).

However, there is a problem with this approach. In order to validate messages in going from identical Byzantine to omission, a processor must have more information about messages sent by faulty processors than that described above. It is possible that a faulty processor p_k's message at some round will be received at one processor, p_i, but not at another, p_j. However, for p_j to correctly validate later messages from p_i, it needs to know that p_i received p_k's message.

As a result, the interface of the identical Byzantine model is slightly different than the other interfaces. Each message includes a round tag, meaning that the message was originally sent in the round indicated by the tag. The identical Byzantine model guarantees that if one nonfaulty processor receives a message from a faulty processor, then *eventually* every nonfaulty processor receives that message, although not necessarily in the same round.

After describing the modifications to the formal model in Section 12.2, we start in Section 12.3 with a simulation of the identical Byzantine model on top of Byzantine failures (Fig. 12.1(a)). This simulation masks inconsistent messages of faulty processors, but doubles the number of rounds.

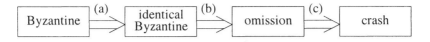

Fig. 12.1 Summary of simulations for the synchronous case.

Next, in Section 12.4 we show a simulation of omission failures on top of the identical Byzantine model (Fig. 12.1(b)). This simulation is based on validating the messages of faulty processors to make sure they are consistent with the application program; it has no overhead in rounds.

Finally, in Section 12.5 we show a simulation of crash failures on top of omission failures (Fig. 12.1(c)). This simulation is based on having processors crash themselves if they perform an omission failure; it doubles the number of rounds.

Throughout this chapter, f is the upper bound on the number of faulty processors.

The faulty behavior in all cases is pushed into the communication system. Thus in the formal model, the processes always change state correctly (according to what information they receive from the communication system). The communication system decides to stop delivering some processor's message, or to corrupt the contents, etc. (Exercise 12.2 asks you to prove that this model is equivalent to the previous definition.)

We assume that the topology of the message-passing system is fully connected, and that each processor sends the same message to all the processors at each round, that is, the processor is actually doing a broadcast.

When we consider a particular simulation from one model to another, we sometimes call the high level send event *broadcast* and the high-level receive event *accept*, to distinguish them from the low-level send and receive events.

12.2   MODELING SYNCHRONOUS PROCESSORS AND BYZANTINE FAILURES

In Chapter 11, we gave a specification of a synchronous message-passing communication system and showed how to locally simulate it with asynchronous systems. We now consider the other side of the coin: how to *use* a synchronous message-passing communication system to solve some other problem. In this section, we describe restrictions on the behavior of synchronous processors in our layered model.

In the synchronous message-passing system, we impose a more structured requirement on the interaction of processes at a node. The transition function of each process must satisfy the following: When an input from the layer below occurs at a process, at most one output is enabled, either to the layer above or the layer below. When an input from the layer above occurs at a process, at most one output is enabled and it must be to the layer below. The resulting behavior of all the processes on a node is that activity propagates down the process stack, or propagates up the process stack, or propagates up the stack and turns around and propagates down. The reason for the

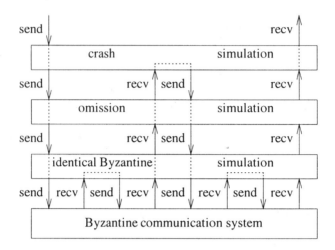

Fig. 12.2 Sample execution of all layers at one node; a single round of the environment with Byzantine failures is two rounds of the crash failure simulation and the omission failure simulation and is four rounds of the identical Byzantine failures simulation.

asymmetry is that we want to model the response to receiving a set of messages as happening atomically with the receipt, but the response to an environment input will have to wait (generally, for some communication).

In the synchronous message-passing model, in addition to the four conditions specified at the end of Section 7.3, an execution must satisfy the following:

5. The first event at each node is an input from the environment. Each output to the environment at a node, except for the last one for that node, is immediately followed by an input from the environment at the same node.

This condition places restrictions on the behavior of the environment and ensures that environment events and communication system events are interleaved properly.

Figure 12.2 shows node steps and rounds in the fault tolerance simulations; in the figure, dotted lines link together events that happen atomically at the node.

In pseudocode descriptions of algorithms for synchronous message-passing systems, the order in which all the events triggered by a node input occur must be specified carefully. In this case, the triggered events must conform to a specific pattern (e.g., going up from the bottom layer, then turning around and coming back down). Instead of stating that output X has become enabled (and being rather loose about when it should occur), we will have a line of code with the name of the output, meaning that the output must actually occur before proceeding.

Next, we define the synchronous message-passing model subject to Byzantine processor failures.

The inputs are of the form Byz-send$_i(m)$ and the outputs are of the form Byz-recv$_i(M)$, where i indicates a processor, m is a message (to be sent to all the processors), and M is a set of messages, at most one coming from each processor.

A sequence is in the allowable set if it conforms to the standard synchronous round structure described in Chapter 7.

Furthermore, there must be a partitioning of the processor ids into faulty and nonfaulty, with at most f faulty, satisfying the following conditions (here and in the rest of the chapter, we assume that variables range over the appropriate values):

Nonfaulty Integrity: If nonfaulty processor p_i receives message m from nonfaulty processor p_j in round k, then p_j sends m in round k.

Nonfaulty Liveness: If nonfaulty processor p_i sends m in round k, then nonfaulty processor p_j receives m from p_i in round k.

Note that there are no requirements on the messages received from or by faulty processors.

When there is the potential for confusion, "send" is replaced with "Byz-send" and "recv" with "Byz-recv."

12.3 SIMULATING IDENTICAL BYZANTINE FAILURES ON TOP OF BYZANTINE FAILURES

In this section we specify a communication system model called *identical Byzantine* that restricts the power of Byzantine processors. The basic idea is that faulty processors can still send arbitrary messages, but all processors that receive a message from a faulty processor receive the same message. We start with a precise definition of the identical Byzantine fault model and then describe how to simulate it in the presence of (unrestricted) Byzantine failures.

12.3.1 Definition of Identical Byzantine

The formal definition of a synchronous message-passing communication system subject to identical Byzantine failures is the same as for (unrestricted) Byzantine failures with these changes. Each message received has the format (m, k), where m is the content of the message and k is a positive integer (the *round tag*); and the conditions to be satisfied are the following:

Nonfaulty Integrity: If nonfaulty processor p_i receives (m, k) from nonfaulty processor p_j, then p_j sends m in round k.

Faulty Integrity (Identical Contents): If nonfaulty processor p_i receives (m, k) from p_h and nonfaulty processor p_j receives (m', k) from p_h, then $m = m'$.

No Duplicates: Nonfaulty processor p_i receives only one message with tag k from p_j.

Nonfaulty Liveness: If nonfaulty processor p_i sends m in round k, then nonfaulty processor p_j receives (m, k) in round k.

Faulty Liveness (Relay): If nonfaulty processor p_i receives (m, k) from (faulty) processor p_h in round r, then nonfaulty processor p_j receives (m, k) from p_h by round $r + 1$.

When there is the potential for confusion, "send" is replaced with "id-send" and "recv" with "id-recv."

12.3.2 Simulating Identical Byzantine

We now present a simulation of the identical Byzantine failure model in the Byzantine failure model. Intuitively, to successfully broadcast a message, a processor has to obtain a set of "witnesses" for this message. A nonfaulty processor accepts a message only when it knows that there are enough witnesses for this broadcast. The simulation uses two rounds of the underlying Byzantine system to simulate each round of the identical Byzantine system and requires that $n > 4f$.

Round k of the identical Byzantine system is simulated by rounds $2k - 1$ and $2k$ of the underlying Byzantine system, which are also denoted $(k, 1)$ and $(k, 2)$.

To broadcast m in simulated round k, the sender, p_i, sends a message $\langle \text{init}, m, k \rangle$ to all[1] processors in round $(k, 1)$. When a processor receives the first init message of p_i for round k, it acts as witness for this broadcast and sends a message $\langle \text{echo}, m, k, i \rangle$ to all processors in round $(k, 2)$. When a processor receives $n - 2f$ echo messages in a single round, it becomes a witness to the broadcast and sends its own echo message to all processors; at this point, it knows that at least one nonfaulty processor is already a witness to this message. When a processor receives $n - f$ echo messages in a single round, it accepts that message, if it has not already accepted a message from p_i for simulated round k.

The pseudocode appears in Algorithm 36. The function first-accept(k', j) returns true if and only if the processor has not already accepted a message from p_j for round k'.

We now prove that this algorithm simulates identical Byzantine failures on top of Byzantine failures, according to the definition of (global) simulation in Chapter 7.

Theorem 12.1 *In any execution of Algorithm 36 that is admissible (i.e., fair, user compliant for the identical Byzantine specification, and correct for the Byzantine communication system), the five conditions defining identical Byzantine are satisfied.*

Proof. Since α is correct for the Byzantine communication system, $bot(\alpha)$ is in the allowable set of sequences for that specification. In particular, there is a partitioning of the processor ids into faulty and nonfaulty, with at most f faulty. Throughout this proof, this partitioning is what defines which processors are faulty and which are nonfaulty.

Nonfaulty Integrity: Suppose nonfaulty processor p_i accepts (m, k) from nonfaulty processor p_j. Then (m, k) with sender p_j is in p_i's accepted set in round

---

[1] Throughout this chapter, this means including itself.

Algorithm 36 Simulating round $k \geq 1$ of the identical Byzantine fault model: code for processor p_i, $0 \leq i \leq n - 1$.

Initially $S = \emptyset$ and *accepted* $= \emptyset$

```
1:   round (k, 1): in response to id-send_i(m):
2:       Byz-send_i(S ∪ {⟨init,m,k⟩})
3:       Byz-recv_i(R)
4:       S := { ⟨echo,m',k,j⟩ : there is a single ⟨init,m',k⟩ in R with sender p_j }
5:       S := S ∪ { ⟨echo,m',k',j⟩ : k' < k and
                 m' is the only message for which at least n − 2f
                 ⟨echo,m',k',j⟩ messages have been received in this round }
6:       accepted := {(m', k') with sender p_j : at least n − f ⟨echo,m',k',j⟩
                 messages have been received in this round and first-accept(k', j)}

7:   round (k, 2):
8:       Byz-send_i(S)
9:       Byz-recv_i(R)
10:      S := { ⟨echo,m',k',j⟩ : k' ≤ k and
                 m' is the only message for which at least n − 2f
                 ⟨echo,m',k',j⟩ messages have been received in this round }
11:      accepted := accepted ∪{(m', k') with sender p_j : at least n − f
                 ⟨echo,m',k',j⟩ messages have been received in this round
                 and first-accept(k', j)}
12:      id-recv_i(accepted)
```

$(r, 2)$, for some r. Thus p_i receives at least $n - f$ $\langle \text{echo},m,k,j \rangle$ messages in round $(r, 2)$. Consequently, at least $n - 2f$ nonfaulty processors sent $\langle \text{echo},m,k,j \rangle$ in round $(r, 2)$. Let p_h be among the first nonfaulty processors to send $\langle \text{echo},m,k,j \rangle$ (in any round). Since the threshold for sending an echo due to the receipt of many echoes is $n - 2f > f$, and since only faulty processors have sent $\langle \text{echo},m,k,j \rangle$ in earlier rounds, p_h sends $\langle \text{echo},m,k,j \rangle$ due to the receipt of $\langle \text{init},m,k \rangle$ from p_j in round $(k, 1)$ (see Line 4 of the code). Since p_j is nonfaulty, p_i broadcasts m in simulated round k.

Note that this proof only requires that $n > 3f$; however, a later property, Faulty Liveness, requires that $n > 4f$.

No Duplicates: This condition holds because of the first-accept check performed in Lines 6 and 11.

Nonfaulty Liveness: This condition follows in a straightforward way from the code.

Faulty Liveness (Relay): Suppose nonfaulty processor p_i accepts (m, k) from processor p_h in simulated round r. Then there are at least $n - 2f$ nonfaulty processors that send $\langle \text{echo},m,k,h \rangle$ for some h, say, in round $(r, 2)$.

Thus every nonfaulty processor p_j receives at least $n - 2f$ $\langle \text{echo},m,k,h \rangle$ messages in round $(r, 2)$. The number of additional $\langle \text{echo},*,k,h \rangle$ messages received by p_j in round $(r, 2)$ is at most $2f$; since $n > 4f$, this number is smaller than $n - 2f$, and thus p_j cannot send a different $\langle \text{echo}, *, k, h \rangle$ message. So p_j sends $\langle \text{echo}, m, k, h \rangle$ in round $(r + 1, 1)$. Consequently, every nonfaulty processor receives at least $n - f$ $\langle \text{echo}, m, k, h \rangle$ messages in round $(r + 1, 1)$ and accepts (m, k) from p_h by simulated round $r + 1$.

Faulty Integrity: Suppose nonfaulty processor p_i accepts (m, k) from processor p_h in round r and and nonfaulty processor p_j accepts (m', k) from p_h in round r'. Toward a contradiction, assume $m \neq m'$. If $r < r'$, then by Faulty Liveness, p_j accepts (m, k) from p_h, and by No Duplicates, it cannot accept (m', k) later; the same argument holds if $r' < r$. Thus it suffices to consider the case in which p_i accepts (m, k) from p_h and p_j accepts (m', k) from p_h in the same round.

As argued above for Nonfaulty Integrity, there are at least $n - 2f$ nonfaulty processors that send $\langle \text{echo}, m, k, h \rangle$ in this round, and at least $n - 2f$ nonfaulty processors that send $\langle \text{echo}, m', k, h \rangle$ in this round. Since each nonfaulty processor only sends one $\langle \text{echo}, *, k, h \rangle$ message in each round, these sets of nonfaulty processors are disjoint. Thus the total number of nonfaulty processors, $n - f$, is at least $2(n - 2f)$. This implies that $n \leq 3f$, a contradiction. $\qquad\square$

What are the costs of this simulation? Clearly, the simulation doubles the number of rounds.

As specified, the algorithm requires processors to echo messages in all rounds after they are originally sent. Yet, once a processor accepts a message, Faulty and Nonfaulty Integrity guarantee that all processors accept this message within at most a single round. Thus we can modify the simulation so that a processor stops echoing a message one round after it accepts it.

We now calculate the maximum number of bits sent in messages by nonfaulty processors. Consider message m broadcast in round k by a nonfaulty processor p_i. As a result, p_i sends $\langle \text{init}, m, k \rangle$ to all processors, and then all nonfaulty processors exchange $\langle \text{echo}, m, k, i \rangle$ messages. The total number of bits sent due to m is $O(n^2(s + \log n + \log k))$, where s is the size of m in bits.

Theorem 12.2 *Using Algorithm 36, the Byzantine model simulates the identical Byzantine model, if $n > 4f$. Every simulated round requires two rounds, and the number of message bits sent by all nonfaulty processors for each simulated round k message m from a nonfaulty processor is $O(n^2(s + \log n + \log k))$, where s is the size of m in bits.*

12.4 SIMULATING OMISSION FAILURES ON TOP OF IDENTICAL BYZANTINE FAILURES

The *omission* model of failure is intermediate between the more benign model of crash failures and the more malicious model of Byzantine failures. In this model, a faulty processor does not fabricate messages that are not according to the algorithm;

however, it may omit to send or receive some messages, send a message to some processors and not to others, etc.

After defining the model more precisely, we describe a simulation of omission failures on top of identical Byzantine failures.

12.4.1 Definition of Omission

The formal definition of a synchronous message-passing communication system subject to omission failures is the same as for the Byzantine case, except that the conditions to be satisfied are the following:

Integrity: Every message received by processor p_i from processor p_j in round k was sent in round k by p_j.

Nonfaulty Liveness: The message sent in round k by nonfaulty processor p_i is received by *nonfaulty* processor p_j in round k.

Note that a faulty processor may fail to receive messages sent by some nonfaulty processors, and messages sent by a faulty processor may fail to be received at some processors.

When there is the potential for confusion, "send" is replaced with "om-send" and "recv" with "om-recv."

The omission failure model is a special case of the Byzantine failure model. However, the omission failure model does not allow the full range of faulty behavior that Byzantine failures can exhibit; for instance, the contents of messages cannot be arbitrary. Thus omission failures are strictly weaker than Byzantine failures.

12.4.2 Simulating Omission

The identical Byzantine fault model gives us some of the properties of omission failures. That is, if two nonfaulty processors receive a message in some round from another processor, faulty or nonfaulty, then it must be the same message. Yet, the identical Byzantine model still allows a nonfaulty processor to send incorrect messages, not according to the protocol, for example, claiming it received a message that was never sent to it.

To circumvent this problem, we apply a *validation* procedure, exploiting the fact that the same messages should be received by all processors in the identical Byzantine model, although possibly with a one round lag. Thus, whenever a processor p_i sends a message m, it also sends its *support* set, i.e., the messages that cause p_i to generate m. If p_i generated this message correctly, then the receiver of m has also received the support messages, and the receiver can check the validity of generating m.

Unlike the other simulations we have seen, this one requires knowledge of the application program A, i.e., the environment that is using the communication system being simulated.

The pseudocode for the simulation appears in Algorithm 37. We assume, without loss of generality, that the message to be sent in round k of A by a processor is the

---

Algorithm 37 Round k of the simulation of omission failures:
code for processor p_i, $0 \leq i \leq n - 1$.

Initially $valid = \emptyset$, $accepted = \emptyset$, and $pending = \emptyset$

1: In response to om-send$_i(m)$:
2:      id-send$_i(\langle m, accepted \rangle)$
3:      id-recv$_i(R)$
4:      add R to $pending$
5:      validate($pending$)
6:      $accepted := \{m'$ with sender $p_j : (m', j, k) \in valid\}$
7:      om-recv$_i(accepted)$

8: procedure validate($pending$):
9:      for each $\langle m', support, k' \rangle \in pending$ with sender p_j,
            in increasing order of k', do
10:         if $k' = 1$ then
11:             if m' is an initial state of the A process on p_j then
12:                 add $(m', j, 1)$ to $valid$ and remove it from $pending$
13:         else   // $k' > 1$
14:             if $(m'', h, k' - 1) \in valid$ for each $m'' \in support$ with sender p_h
                    and $(v, j, k' - 1) \in valid$ for some v
                    and $m' = \text{transition}_A(j, v, support)$
15:             then add (m', j, k') to $valid$ and remove it from $pending$

---

current state of that processor. The function $\text{transition}_A(i, s, R)$ returns the state of p_i resulting from applying algorithm A's transition function when p_i is in state s (which encodes the round number) and accepts the set R of messages.

We would like to show that Algorithm 37 allows the identical Byzantine failure model to simulate the omission failure model. Recall that the definition of simulation from Chapter 7 is the following: For every execution α of the algorithm that is admissible (i.e., fair, user compliant for the omission failures specification, and correct for the identical Byzantine communication system), the restriction of α to the omission failure interface satisfies the conditions of the omission failure model. However, the omission failure model places an integrity condition on messages received by faulty processes, as well as nonfaulty: Any message received must have been sent. Yet the identical Byzantine model has no such condition: Messages received by faulty processors can have arbitrary content. Thus there is no way to guarantee for *all* the processes the illusion of the omission failure model in the presence of identical Byzantine failures. Instead we weaken the definition of simulation so that it only places restrictions on the views of the *nonfaulty* processes.

Communication system C_1 *simulates* communication system C_2 *with respect to the nonfaulty processors when the environment algorithm is known* if, for every algorithm A whose bottom interface is the interface of C_2, there exists a collection of processes,

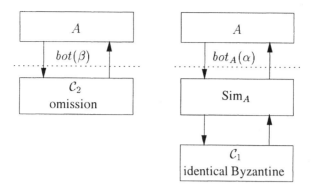

Fig. 12.3 Illustration for the definition of simulating with respect to the nonfaulty processors; identical Byzantine simulates omission failures with respect to the nonfaulty processors.

one for each node, called Sim_A (the simulation program) that satisfies the following (see Fig. 12.3):

1. The top interface of Sim is the interface of C_2.

2. The bottom interface of Sim is the interface of C_1.

3. Let α be any execution of the system in which A is layered on top of Sim_A that is correct for communication system C_1. There must exist an execution β of A that is correct for communication system C_2 such that, informally speaking, the nonfaulty algorithm A processes have the same views in β as they do in α. More formally, $bot(\beta)|P_{\text{NF}} = bot_A(\alpha)|P_{\text{NF}}$, where P_{NF} is the set of processors that are nonfaulty in α and $bot_A(\alpha)$ is the restriction of α to the events of the bottom interface of A.

We define execution β of A as follows. We have the same nonfaulty processors in β as in α. The execution β has the standard synchronous rounds structure.

The initial state of processor p_j in β is the content of any round 1 message from p_j that is validated by a nonfaulty processor in α. If no nonfaulty processor ever does so, then p_j's initial state is arbitrary. By the definition of identical Byzantine, the initial state of p_j is well-defined—no two nonfaulty processors will validate different round 1 messages from p_j.

In round k of β, processor p_j broadcasts its current state and changes state according to A depending on its current state and the messages accepted.

In round k of β, processor p_j accepts message m from processor p_i if and only if, in α, some nonfaulty processor validates p_j's round $k + 1$ message claiming that p_j accepted m from p_i in round k. Although it may seem counter-intuitive, a message from p_j is defined to be received in β only if some nonfaulty processor validates it in the next round of α; later, we prove that messages sent by nonfaulty processors are always received.

First, we show that if a nonfaulty processor validates another processor's round r message in α, then by the next round every nonfaulty processor has done so, and the contents of the message are consistent with the algorithm A state in β.

Lemma 12.3 *If nonfaulty processor p_i validates processor p_j's round r message m in round k of α, then*

1. *Every nonfaulty processor validates p_j's round r message m by round $k + 1$ of α, and*

2. *m is the state of the algorithm A process at p_j at the beginning of round r in β.*

Proof.   First we prove Part 1.

Suppose nonfaulty processor p_i validates processor p_j's round r message m in round k of α. Then p_i validates all messages in the support set of p_j's round r message by round k. Furthermore, p_i validates p_j's round $r - 1$ message v by round k. Finally, $m = \mathsf{transition}_A(j, v, support)$.

Processor p_i is able to validate all these messages because it has received some set S of messages. By the identical Byzantine Nonfaulty and Faulty Liveness conditions, every nonfaulty processor receives all the messages in S by round $k + 1$, and validates p_j's round r message.

We prove Part 2 by induction on k.

Basis: $k = 1$. Suppose nonfaulty processor p_i validates processor p_j's round r message m in round 1 of α. Then $r = 1$, m is an initial state of p_j in A, and p_i receives m as p_j's round 1 message in round 1. By definition, m is the state of p_j at the beginning of round 1 in β.

Induction: $k > 1$. Suppose nonfaulty processor p_i validates processor p_j's round r message m in round k of α. Then p_i validates all messages in the support set of p_j's round r message by round k. Furthermore, p_i validates p_j's round $r - 1$ message v by round k. Finally, $m = \mathsf{transition}_A(j, v, support)$.

By the inductive hypothesis for Part 2, v is the state of p_j at the beginning of round $r - 1$ in β. By the construction of β, $support$ is the set of messages received by p_j in round $r - 1$ of β. Therefore, m is the state of p_j at the beginning of round r of β.   □

Lemma 12.4 states that if a nonfaulty processor broadcasts a message in α, then all the nonfaulty processors validate that message in the same round and the message content is consistent with the algorithm A state in α. The proof relies on Lemma 12.3.

Lemma 12.4 *If nonfaulty processor p_j sends m as its round k message in α, then*

1. *Every nonfaulty processor validates p_j's round k message in round k of α, and*

2. *m is the state of the algorithm A process at p_j at the beginning of round k in α.*

Proof.   We prove this lemma by induction on k.

Basis: $k = 1$. Suppose nonfaulty processor p_j sends m as its round 1 message in α. Part 2: Since A is running on top of the simulation, the round 1 message for p_j is an initial state of p_j in A. Part 1: By the identical Byzantine Nonfaulty Liveness condition, p_i receives p_j's round 1 message in round 1 and validates it.

Induction: $k > 1$. Suppose the lemma is true for $k - 1$. Suppose nonfaulty processor p_j sends m as its round k message in α.

Part 1: By the inductive hypothesis for Part 1, nonfaulty processor p_i validates p_j's round $k - 1$ message v in round $k - 1$. By Lemma 12.3, Part 1, p_i validates all the messages in the support set for p_j's round k message by round k (since they are validated by p_j by round $k - 1$).

Finally, $m = \text{transition}_A(j, v, support)$ and p_i validates p_j's round k message. The reason is that v is the state of the algorithm A process at p_j at the beginning of round $k - 1$ in α, by the inductive hypothesis for Part 2, and *support* is the set of messages accepted by p_j in round $k - 1$.

Part 2 follows from the previous paragraph. □

Lemma 12.5 uses the last two lemmas to show that β satisfies the omission conditions.

Lemma 12.5 *The execution β satisfies the definition of the omission model.*

Proof. *Integrity:* Suppose p_i accepts m from p_j in round k of β. Then in α, some nonfaulty processor p_h validates p_i's round $k + 1$ message claiming p_i accepted m from p_j in round k. We must show that p_j broadcast m in round k of β.

Since p_h validates p_i's round $k + 1$ message, it validates all the messages in the support set for p_i's round $k + 1$ message, including p_j's round k message containing m. Since p_h validates p_j's round k message, by Lemma 12.3, Part 2, m is the state of p_j at the beginning of round k in β. Thus p_j broadcasts m in round k of β.

Nonfaulty Liveness: Suppose nonfaulty processor p_i broadcasts message m in round k of β. Let p_j be any nonfaulty processor. We must show that, in α, some nonfaulty processor p_h validates p_j's round $k + 1$ message claiming that p_j accepted m from p_i in round k.

By Lemma 12.4, Part 2, the algorithm A process at p_i in α is in state m at the beginning of round k. Thus p_i broadcasts m in round k of α. Thus p_i sends m and its support set to all processors in round k of α.

By Lemma 12.4, Part 1, p_j validates p_i's round k message in round k of α. Thus p_j's round $k + 1$ message m' includes p_i's round k message m in its support set.

By Lemma 12.3, Part 1, p_h validates all the supporting messages for p_j's round $k + 1$ message by round $k + 1$ of α. By Lemma 12.4, Part 1, p_h validates p_j's round k message v in round k. Finally, p_h validates p_j's round $k + 1$ message m', since $m' = \text{transition}_A(j, v, support)$. The reason is that the following three facts are true: v is the state of the algorithm A process at p_j at the beginning of round k in α (by Lemma 12.4, Part 2); *support* is the set of messages accepted by p_j in round k; and m' is the message broadcast by p_j in round k of α. □

We finish by showing that the application A processes on nonfaulty nodes have the same views in α and β.

Lemma 12.6 $bot(\beta)|P_{\mathrm{NF}} = bot_A(\alpha)|P_{\mathrm{NF}}$.

Proof. Let p_j be a nonfaulty processor. We must show that in each round, the messages it receives from the underlying omission communication system in β are the same as the messages it accepts in α. Suppose p_j receives message m from processor p_i in round k of β. By the definition of β, some nonfaulty processor p_h validates p_j's round $k + 1$ message in α, claiming that p_j accepted m from p_i in round k. By the identical Byzantine Nonfaulty Integrity condition, p_j really did send this message to p_h, and thus p_j did accept m from p_i in round k. $\qquad\square$

The simulation has no overhead in rounds over the identical Byzantine—it just requires some additional tests at the end of each round. However, the messages sent by the simulation are significantly longer than messages sent by the identical Byzantine simulation, because each message is accompanied by its support set. In the worst case, the support set includes n messages, one from each processor, and thus each message requires $O(n \cdot s)$ bits, where s is the maximum size of an algorithm A message in bits.

We summarize this section with the following theorem:

Theorem 12.7 *Using Algorithm 37, the identical Byzantine failure model simulates the omission failure model with respect to the nonfaulty processors, when the environment algorithm of the omission system is known. The simulation adds no additional rounds and multiplies the number of message bits (sent by a nonfaulty processor) by n.*

12.5 SIMULATING CRASH FAILURES ON TOP OF OMISSION FAILURES

In this section, we make an additional step and show how to simulate crash failures in a system with omission failures with respect to nonfaulty processors. The environment algorithm need not be known. By combining this simulation with the simulations described in the Sections 12.3 and 12.4, we can simulate crash failures with respect to the nonfaulty processors in a system with Byzantine failures, when the environment algorithm is known. (See Exercise 12.13.)

12.5.1 Definition of Crash

The formal definition of a synchronous message-passing communication system subject to crash failures is the same as for the omission case, except that the conditions to be satisfied are the following:

Integrity: Every message received by processor p_i from processor p_j in round k was sent in round k by p_j.

Nonfaulty Liveness: The message sent in round k by nonfaulty processor p_i is received by (faulty or nonfaulty) processor p_j in round k.

Faulty Liveness: If processor p_i fails to receive (faulty) processor p_j's round k message, then no processor receives any message from p_j in round $k + 1$.

The Faulty Liveness condition implies that a faulty processor works correctly, sending and receiving the correct messages, up to some round. The faulty processor might succeed in delivering only some of its messages for that round. Subsequently, no processor ever hears from it again.

When there is the potential for confusion, "send" is replaced with "crash-send" and "recv" with "crash-recv."

12.5.2 Simulating Crash

In both crash and omission failure models, processors fail by not sending (or receiving) some of the messages. However, in the crash failure model, once a processor omits to send a message it does not send any further messages, whereas in the omission failure model, a processor may omit to send a message in one round, and then resume sending messages in later rounds.

Our approach for simulating crash failures is by having a processor p_i "crash" itself if it omits a message. A processor crashes itself by sending a special ⟨crashed⟩ message, with empty content, in every subsequent round, which is ignored by the recipients.

How can processor p_i detect that it has omitted to send a message? We require processors to echo messages they receive; then, if some processor, say, p_j, does not echo p_i's message, then either p_i omitted to send this message, or p_j omitted to receive this message. If p_i receives less than $n - f$ echoes of its message, then it blames itself for not sending the message and crashes itself; otherwise, it blames p_j (and the other processors who did not echo the message) and continues.

Unfortunately, it is possible that p_i is faulty and omits to send a message only to a single nonfaulty processor, p_j; it is also possible that p_j will not even know this has happened. (See Exercise 12.5.) To get around this problem, we require that $n > 2f$. In this case, if p_i decides not to crash itself, that is, if it sees at least $n - f$ echoes of its own message, then, because $n - f > f$, at least one nonfaulty processor echoes p_i's message. Processors accept any echoed message they receive, even if they did not receive it directly. (See Exercise 12.6.)

Thus each round k of the crash failure model translates into two rounds of the omission failure model, $2k - 1$ and $2k$, also denoted $(k, 1)$ and $(k, 2)$.

In the first round, a processor sends to all processors the message it is supposed to broadcast. In the second round, processors echo the messages they have received. If a processor receives an echo of its own message from less than $n - f$ processors, then it crashes itself (i.e., sends special crash messages in subsequent rounds). If a processor receives an echo of a message it did not receive directly, it accepts it. The pseudocode for the simulation appears in Algorithm 38.

Algorithm 38 Simulating round $k \geq 1$ for crash failures on top of omission failures: code for processor p_i, $0 \leq i \leq n - 1$.

1:   round $(k, 1)$: in response to crash-send$_i(m)$:
2:       om-send$_i(\langle \text{init}, m \rangle)$
3:       om-recv$_i(R)$
4:       $S := \{ \langle \text{echo}, m', j \rangle : \langle \text{init}, m' \rangle$ with sender p_j is in $R \}$

5:   round $(k, 2)$:
6:       om-send$_i(S)$
7:       om-recv$_i(R)$
8:       if $< n - f$ messages in R contain $\langle \text{echo}, m, i \rangle$ then crash self
9:       crash-recv$_i$ ($\{m'$ with sender $p_j : \langle \text{echo}, m', j \rangle$ is contained in
                                      a message in $R\}$)

We will prove that this algorithm enables the omission failure model to simulate the crash failure model with respect to the nonfaulty processors. We cannot show that the omission failure model simulates the crash model for *all* processors. The reason is that the crash Nonfaulty Liveness condition states that even faulty processors must receive every message sent be a nonfaulty processor; yet in the omission model, the faulty processors can experience receive omissions. However, unlike Section 12.4, the environment algorithm need not be known. The definition of *simulating with respect to the nonfaulty processors* is the same as the definition of (globally) simulating, from Section 7.5, except that condition 3 becomes:

$3'$. For every execution α of Sim that is (C_2, C_1)-admissible, there exists a sequence $\sigma \in seq(C_2)$ such that $\sigma | P_{\text{NF}} = top(\alpha) | P_{\text{NF}}$, where P_{NF} is the set of processors identified as nonfaulty by the partition that exists since σ is in $seq(C_2)$.

Fix an admissible execution α of Algorithm 38 (i.e., it is fair, user compliant for the crash specification, and correct for the omission communication system).

We will define a sequence σ of crash events and then show that σ satisfies the specification of the crash system and that nonfaulty processors have the same views in α and σ.

The sequence σ conforms to the basic round structure required by the definition of the crash system. The message in the round k crash-send$_j$ event in σ is the same as the message in the round k crash-send$_j$ event in α, for all k and j. The set of messages in the round k crash-recv$_j$ event in σ contains message m from p_i if and only if p_i broadcasts m in round $(k, 1)$ of α and either p_i has not crashed by the end of round $(k, 2)$ of α or p_j accepts a message from p_i in round $(k, 2)$ of α.

We first show, in Lemma 12.8, that nonfaulty processors never crash themselves in α. Then we show, in Lemma 12.9, that the same messages are accepted at each round in α and σ by processors that have not yet crashed themselves in α. These two lemmas are used to show, in Lemma 12.10, that σ satisfies the crash properties. Finally, Lemma 12.11 states that the application processes on nonfaulty nodes have the same views in α and σ.

Lemma 12.8 *If processor p_i is nonfaulty, then p_i never crashes itself in α.*

Proof. We prove by induction on k that p_i has not crashed by the beginning of round $(k, 1)$.

The basis, $k = 1$, follows because processes are initialized to be not yet crashed.

Suppose $k > 1$. By the inductive hypothesis, p_i has not crashed by the beginning of round $(k - 1, 1)$. Thus it sends an $\langle \text{init} \rangle$ message to all processors in round $(k - 1, 1)$. All nonfaulty processors receive p_i's $\langle \text{init} \rangle$ message, because of the omission Nonfaulty Liveness condition, and echo it. Thus p_i receives at least $n - f$ echoes for its own round $k - 1$ message and does not crash itself by the beginning of round $(k, 1)$. $\qquad\square$

Lemma 12.9 *For all $k \geq 1$, and every processor p_i that has not crashed by the beginning of round $(k, 1)$ in α, the messages that p_i accepts in round $(k - 1, 2)$ of α are the same as the messages received by p_i in round $k - 1$ of σ.*

Proof. Suppose p_i has not crashed itself by the beginning of round $(k, 1)$. We will show that the messages accepted by p_i in round $(k - 1, 2)$ of α are the same as those accepted in round $k - 1$ of σ. Consider processor p_j. It broadcasts m' in round $(k - 1, 2)$, and thus, by construction of σ, it broadcasts m' in round $k - 1$ of σ. By the definition of σ, p_i receives m' from p_j in round $k - 1$ of σ if and only if p_j has not crashed by the end of round $(k, 2)$ or p_i accepted a message from p_j in round $(k, 2)$ of α.

The only potential discrepancy between α and σ is if p_i does not accept the message from p_j in round $(k - 1, 2)$ of α, yet p_j does not crash by the end of round $(k - 1, 2)$. Since p_j does not crash, it receives at least $n - f$ echoes for its own round $k - 1$ message. Since, by assumption, p_i does not yet crash either, it gets at least $n - f$ echoes for its own round $k - 1$ message. Since p_i does not accept p_j's round $k - 1$ message, these echoes are from processors distinct from the processors that echoed p_j's round $k - 1$ message.

Thus n, the total number of processors, must be at least $2(n - f)$, implying that $n \leq 2f$, a contradiction. $\qquad\square$

Lemma 12.10 *The sequence σ satisfies the definition of the crash model.*

Proof. *Integrity.* Suppose p_j accepts m from p_i in round k of σ. By the definition of σ, p_i broadcasts m in round $(k, 1)$ of α. By construction, p_i broadcasts m in round k of σ.

Nonfaulty Liveness. Suppose nonfaulty processor p_i broadcasts m in round k of σ. By construction of σ, p_i broadcasts m in round $(k, 1)$ of α. Since p_i is nonfaulty, by Lemma 12.8 p_i has not yet crashed itself, and thus it sends $\langle \text{init}, m \rangle$ in round $(k, 1)$ of α. By the definition of σ, p_j accepts m from p_i in round k of σ.

Faulty Liveness. Suppose p_j fails to accept p_i's round k message in σ. Then by the definition of σ, p_i has crashed itself by the end of round $(k, 2)$ of α. Thus p_i sends only special crashed messages in round $(k + 1, 1)$ of α, and no processor accepts a message from p_i in round $k + 1$ of σ. $\qquad\square$

Finally, we must show that the nonfaulty processors have the same views in α as in σ. We must show that the messages a nonfaulty processor receives in each round of σ are the same as the messages it accepts in the corresponding simulated round of α. This is true because of Lemmas 12.8 and 12.9.

Lemma 12.11 $\sigma|P_{\text{NF}} = top(\alpha)|P_{\text{NF}}$.

Similarly to Algorithm 36, the number of message bits sent by a nonfaulty processor is $O(n^2(s + \log n))$, where s is the maximum size of an environment message in bits. This implies the following simulation result.

Theorem 12.12 *Using Algorithm 38, the omission failure model simulates the crash failure model with respect to the nonfaulty processors, if $n > 2f$. Every simulated round requires two rounds, and the number of message bits sent by a nonfaulty processor is $O(n^2(s + \log n))$, where s is the maximum size of an environment message in bits.*

By combining Theorem 12.12 with Theorems 12.2 and 12.7, we obtain the following important simulation result.

Theorem 12.13 *If $n > 4f$, the Byzantine failure model simulates the crash model with respect to the nonfaulty processors when the environment algorithm is known. Every simulated round requires four rounds, and the number of message bits sent by a nonfaulty processor for simulated round k is $O(n^5(s + \log n + \log k)(s + \log n))$, where s is the maximum size of an environment message in bits.*

12.6 APPLICATION: CONSENSUS IN THE PRESENCE OF BYZANTINE FAILURES

As a simple example, we apply the simulations developed in this chapter to derive an algorithm for solving consensus in the presence of Byzantine failures. Recall the very simple consensus algorithm that tolerates crash failures from Chapter 5 (Algorithm 15). This algorithm requires $f + 1$ rounds and messages of size $n \log |V|$ bits, where $|V|$ is the number of input values. We can run this algorithm together with the simulation of crash failures in a system with Byzantine failures. By appealing to Theorem 12.13, we have:

Theorem 12.14 *If $n > 4f$, then there exists an algorithm that solves the consensus problem in the presence of f Byzantine failures. The algorithm requires $4(f + 1)$ rounds and messages of size $O(n^5(n|V| + \log n + \log f)(n \log |V| + \log n))$.*

Note that this algorithm is inferior to Algorithm 16, which requires $2(f+1)$ rounds and one-bit messages. (This algorithm also requires that $n > 4f$.) A simple way to reduce the number of rounds required is to note that Algorithm 15 also tolerates omission failures (see Exercise 12.7). Therefore, we can employ the simulation of omission failures, which has smaller overhead (Theorems 12.2 and 12.7), to get:

Theorem 12.15 *If $n > 4f$, then there exists an algorithm that solves the consensus problem in the presence of f Byzantine failures. The algorithm requires $2(f + 1)$ rounds and messages of size $O(n^3(n \log |V| + \log n + \log f))$.*

There is a simulation of identical Byzantine failures that requires only that $n > 3f$ (Exercise 12.11); this implies a simulation of crash failures in a system with Byzantine failures that only requires that $n > 3f$. This, in turn, implies:

Theorem 12.16 *If $n > 3f$, then there exists an algorithm that solves the consensus problem in the presence of f Byzantine failures. The algorithm requires $3(f + 1)$ rounds and messages of size $O(n^3(n \log |V| + \log n + \log f))$.*

12.7 ASYNCHRONOUS IDENTICAL BYZANTINE ON TOP OF BYZANTINE FAILURES

We have seen simulations of crash failures in a system with more severe failures—omissions or even Byzantine failures. These simulations applied to the synchronous model; similar simulations exist also for the asynchronous model, but they are fairly restricted and can only be applied to deterministic algorithms. Because many interesting problems, for example, consensus, have only non-deterministic fault-tolerant solutions in asynchronous systems, even in the presence of the most benign failures, the benefit of such simulations is rather limited. More useful is the asynchronous version of Algorithm 36, which simulates identical Byzantine failures in the presence of Byzantine failures. This simulation works for any algorithm and is not restricted to deterministic algorithms; as we shall see later (in Chapters 13 and 14), this makes it particularly helpful in designing clock synchronization algorithms for Byzantine failures and randomized asynchronous algorithms for consensus in the presence of Byzantine failures.

12.7.1 Definition of Asynchronous Identical Byzantine

The definition of the identical Byzantine fault model for the synchronous case in Section 12.3.1 refers explicitly to round numbers, and therefore, it has to be altered in order to fit the asynchronous model. We replace the reference to specific rounds with the requirement for *eventual* delivery.

In the synchronous model, processors could broadcast different messages at different rounds. It was guaranteed that, for each round, at most one message is accepted from each processor. In the asynchronous model, there is no similar notion of round. Instead, we assume that each processor assigns distinguishing tags to the messages it broadcasts.

The definition of asynchronous identical Byzantine is the same as for the asynchronous crash point-to-point system in Chapter 8, except that the event names are id-send and id-recv; each message sent and received has the format (m, k), where

m is the message content and k is the tag, and the conditions to be satisfied are the following:

Uniqueness: There is at most one id-send$_i(*, k)$ event, for each i and k. This is a restriction on the inputs from the environment.

Nonfaulty Integrity: If nonfaulty processor p_i receives (m, k) from nonfaulty processor p_j, then p_j sent (m, k).

Faulty Integrity (Identical Contents): If nonfaulty processor p_i receives (m, k) from processor p_h and nonfaulty processor p_j receives (m', k) from p_h, then $m = m'$.

No Duplicates: Nonfaulty processor p_i receives only one message with tag k from p_j.

Nonfaulty Liveness: If nonfaulty processor p_i sends (m, k), then nonfaulty processor p_j receives (m, k) from p_i.

Faulty Liveness (Relay): If nonfaulty processor p_i receives (m, k) from (faulty) processor p_h, then nonfaulty processor p_j receives (m, k) from p_h.

These latter five conditions are analogous to those in the synchronous case (cf. Section 12.3), but with no reference to rounds.

12.7.2   Definition of Asynchronous Byzantine

We want to simulate the asynchronous identical Byzantine fault model specified in Section 12.7.1 in an asynchronous point-to-point system subject to (unrestricted) Byzantine failures. In this subsection we define the implementation system.

The definition of the asynchronous Byzantine model is the same as for the asynchronous crash point-to-point system in Chapter 8, except that the conditions to be satisfied are the following:

Nonfaulty Integrity: If nonfaulty processor p_i receives m from nonfaulty processor p_j, then p_j sent m to p_i.

No Duplicates: No message sent is received more than once.

Nonfaulty Liveness: If nonfaulty processor p_i sends m to nonfaulty processor p_j, then p_j receives m from p_i.

When there is the potential for confusion, "send" is replaced with "Byz-send" and "recv" with "Byz-recv."

12.7.3   Simulating Asynchronous Identical Byzantine

The synchronous algorithm for simulating identical Byzantine failures (Algorithm 36) can be modified to work in the asynchronous case; this simulation also assumes that

---

Algorithm 39 The asynchronous identical Byzantine simulation:
code for processor p_i, $0 \leq i \leq n - 1$.

1:   when id-send$_i(m, k)$ occurs:
2:      enable Byz-send$_i(\langle \text{init}, m, k \rangle)$ to all processors

3:   when Byz-recv$_i(\langle \text{init}, m, k \rangle)$ from p_j occurs:
4:      if first-echo(k, j) then enable Byz-send$_i(\langle \text{echo}, m, k, j \rangle)$ to all processors

5:   when Byz-recv$_i(\langle \text{echo}, m, k, j \rangle)$ occurs:
6:      $num :=$ number of copies of $\langle \text{echo}, m, k, j \rangle$ received so far
        from distinct processors
7:      if $num \geq n - f$ and first-ready(k, j) then
8:        enable Byz-send$_i(\langle \text{ready}, m, k, j \rangle)$ to all processors

9:   when Byz-recv$_i(\langle \text{ready}, m, k, j \rangle)$ occurs:
10:     $num :=$ number of copies of $\langle \text{ready}, m, k, j \rangle$ received so far
        from distinct processors
11:     if $num \geq n - 2f$ and first-ready(k, j) then
12:       enable Byz-send$_i(\langle \text{ready}, m, k, j \rangle)$ to all processors
13:     if $num \geq n - f$ and first-accept(k, j) then
14:       enable id-recv$_i(m, k)$ from p_j

$n > 4f$. We do not present this simulation here, and leave it as an exercise to the reader (Exercise 12.10). Instead, we present another simulation that only requires that $n > 3f$, but uses three types of messages. Interestingly, this implementation can be modified to work in the synchronous model (Exercise 12.11).

To broadcast a high-level message (m, k), the sender, p_i, sends a message $\langle \text{init}, m, k \rangle$ to all processors (including itself). Processors receiving this init message act as witnesses for this broadcast and send a message $\langle \text{echo}, m, k, i \rangle$ to all processors. Once a processor receives $n - f$ echo messages, it notifies the other processors it is about to accept (m, k) from p_i, by sending a $\langle \text{ready}, m, k, i \rangle$ message. Once a processor receives $n - f$ $\langle \text{ready}, m, k, i \rangle$ messages, it accepts (m, k) from p_i. In addition, if a processor receives $n - 2f$ ready messages, it also sends a ready message.

The pseudocode appears in Algorithm 39. The function first-echo(k, j) returns true if and only if the processor has not already sent an echo message with tag k for p_j; first-ready(k, j) returns true if and only if the processor has not already sent a ready message with tag k for p_j; first-accept(k, j) returns true if and only if the processor has not yet accepted a message from p_j with tag k.

We now show that the latter five properties of asynchronous identical Byzantine faults are satisfied by this algorithm. The following lemma and theorem are with respect to an arbitrary admissible execution α (i.e., it is fair, user compliant for the asynchronous identical Byzantine specification, and correct for the asynchronous Byzantine communication system).

Lemma 12.17 *If one nonfaulty processor sends* $\langle ready,m,k,h \rangle$ *and another non-faulty processor sends* $\langle ready,m',k,h' \rangle$*, then m must equal m'.*

Proof. Suppose in contradiction $m \neq m'$. Let p_i be the first nonfaulty processor to send $\langle ready,m,k,h \rangle$. Since p_i can only receive ready messages from the f faulty processors up till this point and f is less than $n - 2f$, p_i received at least $n - f$ $\langle echo,m,k,h \rangle$ messages. At least $n - 2f$ of these are from nonfaulty processors.

Similarly, p_j, the first nonfaulty processor to send $\langle ready,m',k,h \rangle$, received at least $n - 2f$ $\langle echo,m',k,h \rangle$ messages from nonfaulty processors.

Since each nonfaulty processor sends only one echo message for k and h, the total number of nonfaulty processors, $n - f$, must be at least $2(n - 2f)$, implying $n \leq 3f$, a contradiction. $\qquad\square$

Theorem 12.18 *The latter five conditions for asynchronous identical Byzantine are satisfied.*

Proof. *Nonfaulty Integrity:* Suppose nonfaulty processor p_i accepts (m, k) from nonfaulty processor p_j. Thus p_i receives at least $n - f$ $\langle ready,m,k,j \rangle$ messages, at least $n - 2f$ of which are from nonfaulty processors. Let p_h be the first nonfaulty processor to send $\langle ready,m,k,j \rangle$. Then p_h cannot have received $n - 2f$ ready messages already, since $n - 2f > f$ (recall that $n > 3f$) and up till now only faulty processors have sent $\langle ready,m,k,j \rangle$. Thus p_h receives at least $n - f$ $\langle echo,m,k,j \rangle$ messages, at least $n - 2f$ of which are from nonfaulty processors. A nonfaulty processor only sends $\langle echo,m,k,j \rangle$ if it receives $\langle init,m,k \rangle$ from p_j. Since p_j is nonfaulty, p_j did broadcast (m, k).

Faulty Integrity (Identical Contents): Suppose nonfaulty processor p_i accepts (m, k) from processor p_h and nonfaulty processor p_j accepts (m', k) from p_h. Assume for contradiction that $m \neq m'$. Thus p_i receives at least $n - f$ $\langle ready,m,k,h \rangle$ messages, at least $n - 2f$ of which are from nonfaulty processors. Similarly, p_j receives at least $n - f$ $\langle ready,m',k,h \rangle$ messages, at least $n - 2f$ of which are from nonfaulty processors. But this violates Lemma 12.17.

No Duplicates: This condition is ensured by the first-accept check in the code.

Nonfaulty Liveness: Suppose nonfaulty processor p_i broadcasts (m, k). Then p_i sends $\langle init,m,k \rangle$ to all processors and every nonfaulty processor p_j receives $\langle init,m,k \rangle$. This is the first $\langle init,*,k \rangle$ message that p_j has received from p_i by the uniqueness condition. Thus p_j sends $\langle echo,m,k,i \rangle$ to all processors.

Every nonfaulty processor p_j receives at least $n - f$ $\langle echo,m,k,i \rangle$ messages. So p_j receives at most f $\langle echo,m',k,i \rangle$ messages for any $m' \neq m$. Since $f < n - f$ (recall $n > 3f$), p_j sends $\langle ready,m,k,i \rangle$.

Every nonfaulty processor p_j receives at least $n - f$ $\langle ready,m,k,i \rangle$ messages, so p_j receives at most f $\langle ready,m',k,i \rangle$ messages for any $m' \neq m$. Since $f < n - f$, p_j accepts (m, k) from p_i.

Faulty Liveness (Relay): Suppose nonfaulty processor p_i accepts (m, k) from p_h. Then p_i receives at least $n - f$ $\langle$ready,$m,k,h\rangle$ messages, meaning that at least $n - 2f$ nonfaulty processors send $\langle$ready,$m,k,h\rangle$. Thus every nonfaulty processor p_j receives at least $n - 2f$ $\langle$ready,$m,k,h\rangle$ messages. By Lemma 12.17, p_j does not send $\langle$ready,$m',k,h\rangle$, with $m' \neq m$, and therefore, p_j sends $\langle$ready,$m,k,h\rangle$. Thus every nonfaulty processor receives at least $n - f$ $\langle$ready,$m,k,h\rangle$ messages and accepts (m, k) from p_h. $\qquad\square$

It is easy to calculate the number of messages sent by nonfaulty processors. When a nonfaulty processor p_i broadcasts m, each nonfaulty processor sends one echo message to every processor, and then each nonfaulty processor sends one ready message to every processor. Hence, the simulation requires nonfaulty processors to send a total of $O(n^2)$ point-to-point messages per original broadcast message. The total number of bits is calculated as for Algorithm 36. We leave the time complexity analysis as an exercise to the reader (Exercise 12.12). To summarize:

Theorem 12.19 *The asynchronous Byzantine failures model simulates the asynchronous identical Byzantine failures model, if $n > 3f$. The number of messages sent by nonfaulty processors for each broadcast is $O(n^2)$ and the total number of bits is $O(n^2(s + \log n + \log k))$, where s is the size of m in bits. A message broadcast by a nonfaulty processor is accepted within $O(1)$ time.*

Exercises

12.1 Show that there is no loss of generality in assuming that at each round a processor sends the same message to all processors.

12.2 Show that assuming processors are nonfaulty and the network corrupts messages is equivalent to assuming processors are faulty and the network does not corrupt messages.

12.3 Explain why the following synchronous algorithm does not solve the consensus problem: Each processor broadcasts its input using Algorithm 36. Each processor waits for two rounds and then decides on the minimum value received.

12.4 Show how to reduce the size of messages in the synchronous simulation of identical Byzantine failures (Algorithm 36).

12.5 What happens in the simulation of crash failures on omission failures (Section 12.5) if $n \leq 2f$?

12.6 In the simulation of crash failures on omission failures (Section 12.5), why do we need processors to accept messages echoed by other processors?

12.7 Prove that the algorithm for consensus in the presence of crash failures (Algorithm 15) is correct even in the presence of omission failures.

12.8 Show a simulation of crash failures on top of *send omission* failures that assumes only that $n > f$. (Informally speaking, in the send omission failure model, a faulty processor can either crash permanently at some round or at intermittent rounds, the message it sends can fail to be delivered to some of the other processors.)

12.9 Show how to avoid validation of messages and use the simulation of identical Byzantine on top of Byzantine to get a simulation of Algorithm 15 with smaller messages.

Hint: Note that in this algorithm, messages include a sequence of processor identifiers and the support are messages with prefixes of this sequence.

12.10 Modify the algorithm of Section 12.3.2 to simulate asynchronous identical Byzantine faults using only two types of messages. Assume $n > 4f$. What is the asynchronous time complexity of this algorithm?

12.11 Modify the algorithm of Section 12.7.3 to simulate synchronous identical Byzantine faults assuming $n > 3f$ and using three rounds for each simulated round.

12.12 Show that the time complexity of Algorithm 39 is $O(1)$. That is, a message broadcast by a nonfaulty processor is received by all nonfaulty processors within $O(1)$ time.

12.13 (a) Show that if A can simulate B, then A can simulate B with respect to the nonfaulty processors.

(b) Show that if A can simulate B with respect to the nonfaulty processors, then A can simulate B with respect to the nonfaulty processors when the environment algorithm is known.

(c) Show that if A can simulate B according to one definition and B can simulate C according to another definition, then A can simulate C according to the weaker of the two definitions.

Chapter Notes

The identical Byzantine model is a variant on *authenticated broadcast* of Srikanth and Toueg [246]. Our simulation of the identical Byzantine model, which assumes $n > 4f$, as well as the validated broadcast and the simulation of omission failures on top of crash failures, are all based on the work of Neiger and Toueg [198]. The asynchronous simulation of identical Byzantine was first introduced by Bracha [60], which is also the source of the simulation presented here.

For the synchronous model, the first simulation of the type considered in this chapter, of crash failures on top of *send* omission failures, was given by Hadzilacos [128]. However, this simulation is not completely general and relies on certain assumptions on the behavior of faulty processors. The best (in terms of message and time complexity) simulations of crash failures on top of Byzantine failures are due to Bazzi and Neiger [47, 46]. Their work contains a thorough study of the cost of such simulations, including lower bounds and trade-offs, in terms of the rounds overhead and the ratio of faulty processors tolerated.

Omission failures of the type considered here are sometimes called *general* omission failures, defined by Perry and Toueg [210]. Two specific types of omission failures—*send omission*, in which faulty processors only fail to send messages, and *receive omission*, in which faulty processors only fail to receive messages—have been suggested by Hadzilacos [128].

For the asynchronous model, a general simulation of crash failures on top of Byzantine failures was given by Coan [84]. It applies only to deterministic algorithms in a restricted form. One of Coan's contributions is an asynchronous simulation of identical Byzantine failures, assuming $n > 4f$; this is the origin of Neiger and Toueg's synchronous simulation we presented here (Algorithm 36); the paper [84] contains the solution to Exercise 12.10.

13

Fault-Tolerant Clock Synchronization

We now consider the problem of keeping real-time clocks synchronized in a distributed system when processors may fail. This problem is tantalizingly similar to the consensus problem, but no straightforward reductions are known between the problems.

In this chapter, we assume that hardware clocks are subject to drift. Therefore, the software clocks may drift apart as time elapses and subsequent periodic resynchronization is necessary. Now the clock synchronization problem has two parts: getting the clocks close together initially and keeping them close together.

In this chapter we focus on the problem of keeping the clocks close together, assuming that they are initially close. First, we show that, as for consensus, to solve the problem, the total number of processors, n, must be more than $3f$, where f is the maximum number of faulty processors. Then we present an algorithm for solving the problem in the presence of Byzantine failures. The algorithm is first described for a simpler fault model, and then fault-tolerant simulations from Chapter 12 are applied.

13.1 PROBLEM DEFINITION

As in Chapter 5, we have n processors in a fully connected network, in which the message delays are always in the range $[d - u, d]$, for some constants d and u. Each processor p_i has hardware clock $HC_i(t)$, adjustment variable adj_i, and adjusted clock $AC_i(t) = HC_i(t) + adj_i(t)$.

However, we now allow the possibility that up to f of the processors may exhibit Byzantine failures.

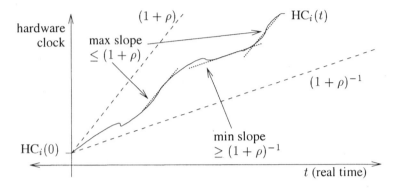

Fig. 13.1 Drift of a hardware clock.

We also consider the complications introduced when the hardware clocks can drift from real time. We assume that hardware clocks stay within a *linear envelope* of the real time; that is, there exists a positive constant ρ (the *drift*) such that each hardware clock HC_i satisfies the following property (see Fig. 13.1):

Bounded Drift: For all times t_1 and t_2, $t_2 > t_1$,

$$(1+\rho)^{-1}(t_2 - t_1) \leq HC_i(t_2) - HC_i(t_1) \leq (1+\rho)(t_2 - t_1).$$

The difference between hardware clocks of nonfaulty processors grows at a rate which is bounded by $\rho(2 + \rho)(1 + \rho)^{-1}$ (see Exercise 13.1).

Because hardware clocks can drift away from real time, either by gaining or losing time (or both), processors must continually resynchronize their clocks in order to keep them close. In this chapter we focus on the problem of keeping the clocks close together, assuming they begin close together. (Contrast this with the problem studied in Chapter 6, which was to get the clocks close together in the first place.)

We wish to guarantee that processors' clocks stay close to each other, assuming that they begin close to each other. To formalize the initialization assumption, we put an additional restriction on the definition of admissible execution, stating that at real time 0, the adjusted clocks of nonfaulty processors are within some bound B of each other. The amount B can be considered a parameter to the definition of admissible; the closeness of synchronization achievable may depend on B, the initial closeness. We require the following:

Clock Agreement: There exists a constant ϵ such that in every admissible timed execution, for all times t and all nonfaulty processors p_i and p_j,

$$|AC_i(t) - AC_j(t)| \leq \epsilon$$

A trivial solution would be to set all adjusted clocks to 0; to rule this out, we require that clocks stay within a linear envelope of their hardware clocks; formally this is stated as:

Clock Validity: There exists a positive constant γ such that in every admissible timed execution, for all times t and every nonfaulty processor p_i,

$$(1 + \gamma)^{-1}(HC_i(t) - HC_i(0)) \leq AC_i(t) - AC_i(0) \leq (1 + \gamma)(HC_i(t) - HC_i(0))$$

The clock validity condition states that the change in the adjusted clock since the beginning of the execution must be within a linear envelope of the change in the hardware clock since the beginning of the execution. Notice the difference from the hardware clock drift condition, which was a constraint on the instantaneous rate: The adjusted clock can change discontinuously, and therefore we can bound the change only over a long period. The clock validity condition is stated with respect to the hardware clocks, not real time. However, as Exercise 13.2 asks you to show, if the adjusted clock is within a linear envelope of the hardware clock and the hardware clock is within a linear envelope of real time, then the adjusted clock is within a linear envelope of real time, albeit a larger envelope.

The goal is to achieve clock agreement and validity with ϵ and γ that are as small as possible. Intuitively, the validity parameter, γ, cannot be smaller than the validity of the hardware clocks captured by ρ.

An algorithm for maintaining synchronized clocks will instruct processors to take actions periodically. A mechanism is needed for a processor to program itself to take a step when its hardware clock reaches a certain value. This ability is modeled by assuming that each processor p_i has a special state component *timer$_i$* that it can set. For an execution to be admissible, each processor must take a step once its hardware clock reaches the current value of its timer.

13.2 THE RATIO OF FAULTY PROCESSORS

In this section, we show that there can be no algorithm to satisfy clock agreement and clock validity if $n \leq 3f$; this result holds for any constants ϵ and γ, regardless of their specific values.

We will prove this result using ideas similar to two we have already seen, namely, shifting of executions (used to prove the lower bound on closeness of synchronization in Chapter 6) and specifying faulty behavior with a big ring (used to prove the $n > 3f$ lower bound for consensus in Chapter 5).

Before proving the lower bound, we need a result similar to one we used to show the lower bound on the closeness of synchronization; if both hardware clocks and message delays are altered appropriately, processors cannot tell the difference. In Chapter 6, the alteration was to add certain quantities to the real times of occurrences, resulting in a shifted execution. Here we will multiply the real times by a certain quantity, resulting in a scaled execution.

Definition 13.1 *Let α be a timed execution with hardware clocks and let s be a real number. Define* scale(α, s) *to be the execution obtained by multiplying by s the real time associated with each event in α.*

Lemma 13.1 states the relationships between the clocks and between the message delays in a timed execution and its scaled version.

Lemma 13.1 *If α is a timed execution then in $\alpha' = \mathrm{scale}(\alpha, s)$,*

(a) *$HC_i'(t) = HC_i(t/s)$ for all times t, where HC_i is p_i's hardware clock in α and HC_i' is p_i's hardware clock in α', and*

(b) *$AC_i'(t) = AC_i(t/s)$ for all times t, where AC_i is p_i's adjusted clock in α and AC_i' is p_i's adjusted clock in α', and*

(c) *If a message has delay δ in α, then it has delay $s \cdot \delta$ in α'*

Proof. The first two properties follow directly from the definition of scaling. For the last property, consider message m sent at real time t_s and received at real time t_r in α. Then in α' it is sent at real time $s \cdot t_s$ and received at real time $s \cdot t_r$. Thus its delay in α' is $s \cdot (t_r - t_s)$. $\square$

If HC_i is a linear function, then the factor of $1/s$ can be brought out of the argument to the function, and we have $HC_i'(t) = HC_i(t)/s$.

If s is larger than 1, then the hardware clocks slow down and message delays increase. If s is smaller than 1, then the hardware clocks speed up and message delays decrease. The scaled execution may or may not be admissible, because message delays and drifts may be too large or too small; however, we still have the following result:

Lemma 13.2 *If a timed execution α satisfies the clock agreement condition with parameter ϵ or the clock validity condition with parameter γ for a set of processors, then the same is true in $\alpha' = \mathrm{scale}(\alpha, s)$, for any $s > 0$.*

Proof. Suppose α satisfies the clock agreement condition for processors p_i and p_j. Denote p_i's adjusted clock in α by AC_i and p_i's adjusted clock in α' by AC_i'. By Lemma 13.1 (b), for any time t:

$$|AC_i'(t) - AC_j'(t)| = |AC_i(t/s) - AC_j(t/s)|$$

Since the adjusted clocks of p_i and p_j satisfy the clock agreement condition in α, AC_i and AC_j are within ϵ for every argument, including t/s, and the result follows.

Next, suppose α satisfies the clock validity condition for processor p_i. By Lemma 13.1 (b), for all times t:

$$AC_i'(t) - AC_i'(0) = AC_i(t/s) - AC_i(0/s)$$

Since the adjusted clock of p_i satisfies the clock validity condition in α,

$$AC_i(t/s) - AC_i(0/s) \leq (1 + \gamma)(HC_i(t/s) - HC_i(0/s))$$

which by Lemma 13.1 (a) is equal to

$$(1 + \gamma)(HC_i'(t) - HC_i'(0))$$

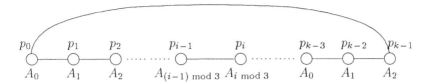

Fig. 13.2 Assignment of local algorithms in the big ring in the proof of Theorem 13.3.

The lower bound on $AC_i'(t) - AC_i'(0)$ is proved analogously.   □

The main result of this section is that no algorithm can guarantee clock agreement and clock validity, if $n \leq 3f$. We only prove the special case when $f = 1$, and leave the general case as an exercise.

The proof requires that u, the uncertainty in the message delay, not be too small; specifically, u must be at least $d(1 - (1 + \rho)^{-4})$. It is probably not clear at this point why this assumption is necessary, but it enables certain calculations to work out in the proof. Because typically ρ is on the order of 10^{-6}, this assumption is reasonable.

Theorem 13.3 *No algorithm can guarantee clock agreement and clock validity for* $f = 1$ *and* $n = 3$, *if* $u \geq d(1 - (1 + \rho)^{-4})$.

Proof.   Suppose in contradiction there is such an algorithm for $n = 3$ and $f = 1$, guaranteeing clock agreement and validity with constants ϵ and γ. Let A_i be the (local) algorithm run by p_i, for $i = 0, 1, 2$. Choose a constant k such that

1. k is a multiple of 3 and

2. $(1 + \gamma)^{-1} (1 + \rho)^{2(k-1)} > 1 + \gamma$

The reasons for these conditions on k will be pointed out as they arise.

Consider a ring network of k processors, p_0 through p_{k-1}, in which for each i, $0 \leq i \leq k - 1$, p_i runs local algorithm $A_{i \bmod 3}$ (see Figure 13.2). Here is where we use the fact that k is a multiple of 3.

We now specify a timed execution β of this ring. In β, for each i, $0 \leq i \leq k - 1$ (see Fig. 13.3):

- The hardware clock of p_i is $HC_i(t) = t(1 + \rho)^{1 - 2i}$

- The adjusted clock of p_i equals 0 at time 0, i.e., $AC_i(0) = 0$ and

- The delay of every message between p_i and $p_{(i-1) \bmod k}$ (in both directions) is $d(1 + \rho)^{2i-4}$, for $0 \leq i \leq k - 1$

We cannot claim that β satisfies the clock synchronization properties because the network has more than three processors and is not fully connected; moreover, the hardware clock drifts and message delays are not all admissible. However, we will be able to make some deductions about the behavior of β, by showing that pieces

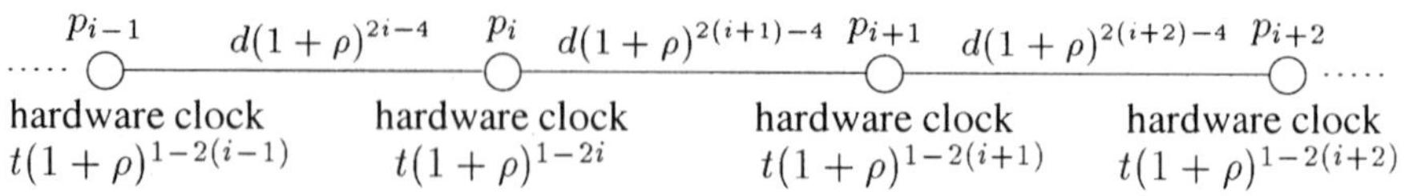

$$\underset{\underset{\substack{\text{hardware clock}\\ t(1+\rho)^{1-2(i-1)}}}{\overset{p_{i-1}}{\underset{\cdots\cdots}{\bigcirc}}}}{} \xrightarrow{d(1+\rho)^{2i-4}} \underset{\underset{\substack{\text{hardware clock}\\ t(1+\rho)^{1-2i}}}{\overset{p_i}{\bigcirc}}}{} \xrightarrow{d(1+\rho)^{2(i+1)-4}} \underset{\underset{\substack{\text{hardware clock}\\ t(1+\rho)^{1-2(i+1)}}}{\overset{p_{i+1}}{\bigcirc}}}{} \xrightarrow{d(1+\rho)^{2(i+2)-4}} \underset{\underset{\substack{\text{hardware clock}\\ t(1+\rho)^{1-2(i+2)}}}{\overset{p_{i+2}}{\bigcirc}}}{\cdots\cdots}$$

Fig. 13.3   Timed execution β of the big ring in the proof of Theorem 13.3.

of the ring "look like" certain systems in which the algorithm *is* supposed to behave properly.

Lemma 13.4 states that the adjusted clocks of two adjacent processors in the timed execution β of the ring satisfy the clock agreement condition and each adjusted clock in β satisfies the clock validity condition. The statement of the clock validity condition is simplified because the hardware clocks and adjusted clocks are all initially 0.

Lemma 13.4 *For all times t:*

(a) $|AC_i(t) - AC_{i+1}(t)| \leq \epsilon$, *for all i, $0 \leq i \leq k-2$ and*

(b) $(1+\gamma)^{-1} HC_i(t) \leq AC_i(t) \leq (1+\gamma) HC_i(t)$, *for all i, $0 \leq i \leq k-1$*

Proof.   Fix i, $0 \leq i \leq k-2$. Take processors p_i and p_{i+1} from the big ring and put them in a three-processor ring (which is also fully connected) with a third processor that is faulty in such a way that it acts like p_{i-1} from the big ring toward p_i and acts like p_{i+2} from the big ring toward p_{i+1} (see Fig. 13.4). The hardware clock times of p_i and p_{i+1} and the message delays for messages to and from p_i and p_{i+1} are the same as in the big ring's timed execution β. Call the resulting timed execution α.

As was done in the proof of Theorem 5.7, a simple induction can be used to show that p_i and p_{i+1} have the same views in α as they do in the timed execution of the big ring and thus they have the same adjusted clocks.

Let $\alpha' = \text{scale}(\alpha, (1+\rho)^{-2i})$ (see Fig. 13.5).

We will now verify that α' is admissible. By Lemma 13.1 (a), p_i's hardware clock in α' is

$$HC_i'(t) = HC_i(t(1+\rho)^{2i}) = t(1+\rho)$$

By Lemma 13.1 (a), p_{i+1}'s hardware clock in α' is

$$HC_{i+1}'(t) = HC_{i+1}(t(1+\rho)^{2i}) = t(1+\rho)^{-1}$$

By Lemma 13.1 (c), the message delays between the faulty processor and p_{i+1} are $d(1+\rho)^{-2i}(1+\rho)^{2(i+2)-4}$, which equals d. Similarly, the message delays between p_{i+1} and p_i are $d(1+\rho)^{-2}$, and the message delays between p_i and the faulty processor are $d(1+\rho)^{-4}$. The assumption that $u \geq d(1 - (1+\rho)^{-4})$ ensures that all message delays are between $d - u$ and d.

Since α' is admissible, the clock agreement and clock validity conditions hold for the adjusted clocks of p_i and p_{i+1} in α'. Lemma 13.2 implies that these conditions

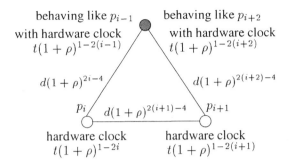

Fig. 13.4 A triangle based on the ring, for the proof of Lemma 13.4; gray node is faulty.

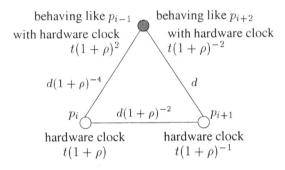

Fig. 13.5 Scaling the triangle by $(1 + \rho)^{-2i}$.

also hold in α. Since p_i and p_{i+1} have the same adjusted clocks in α as in β, the lemma follows. □

We can now complete the main proof. Repeated application of Lemma 13.4 (a), implies the following inequalities:

$$
\begin{aligned}
AC_0(t) \;&\leq\; AC_1(t) + \epsilon \\
&\leq\; AC_2(t) + 2\epsilon \\
&\leq\; \cdots \\
&\leq\; AC_{k-1}(t) + (k-1)\epsilon
\end{aligned}
$$

Rearranging the terms produces:

$$AC_{k-1}(t) \geq AC_0(t) - (k-1)\epsilon$$

Lemma 13.4 (b) implies that $AC_0(t) \geq (1+\gamma)^{-1}HC_0(t)$, and the definition of β implies that $HC_0(t) = (1+\rho)^{2(k-1)}HC_{k-1}(t)$. Thus

$$AC_{k-1}(t) \geq (1+\gamma)^{-1}(1+\rho)^{2(k-1)}HC_{k-1}(t) - (k-1)\epsilon$$

Lemma 13.4 (b) implies that

$$AC_{k-1}(t) \leq (1 + \gamma)HC_{k-1}(t)$$

The last two inequalities are combined to show:

$$(1 + \gamma)^{-1}(1 + \rho)^{2(k-1)}HC_{k-1}(t) - (k - 1)\epsilon \leq (1 + \gamma)HC_{k-1}(t)$$

Rearranging produces:

$$((1 + \gamma)^{-1}(1 + \rho)^{2(k-1)} - (1 + \gamma))HC_{k-1}(t) \leq (k - 1)\epsilon$$

HC_{k-1} increases without bound as t grows, and by choice of k, $(1 + \gamma)^{-1}(1 + \rho)^{2(k-1)} - (1 + \gamma)$ is positive. (This is where we need the second condition in the definition of k.) Thus the left-hand side of the inequality increases without bound. Yet the right-hand side, $(k - 1)\epsilon$, is a constant, which is a contradiction. $\qquad\square$

The case when $f > 1$ is proved by reduction to this theorem, as was done in Theorem 5.8; the details are left to an exercise.

13.3 A CLOCK SYNCHRONIZATION ALGORITHM

We start with an algorithm tolerating f *timing* failures, in which nonfaulty processors fail either by crashing or by having hardware clocks whose drift exceeds the bounds given in the Bounded Drift condition and thus run faster or slower; the algorithm requires $n > 2f$. Later, we discuss how to modify the algorithm to handle identical Byzantine failures. Finally, the simulation of identical Byzantine failures in a totally asynchronous system, from Chapter 12, is used. The latter simulation requires $n > 3f$, matching the bound proved in Section 13.2.

13.3.1 Timing Failures

The algorithm proceeds in synchronization *epochs*. A processor starts the kth synchronization epoch by broadcasting a message of the form $\langle k \rangle$, when the value of its adjusted clock is $k \cdot P$, for some constant P that will be specified below. P will be chosen to ensure that the start of the $(k + 1)$st synchronization epoch is still in the future, according to the newly adjusted clock. When a processor receives $f + 1$ messages of the form $\langle k \rangle$, it sets its adjusted clock to be $k \cdot P + x$. The value of x will be specified and explained shortly; its value will ensure that the adjusted clocks are never set backwards.

We assume that the adjusted clocks are initialized so that at time 0, the adjusted clock of every nonfaulty processor is between x and $x + d(1 + \rho)$. Thus the initial closeness of synchronization must be at most $d(1 + \rho)$ in every admissible execution.

Assume we have picked $P > x + d(1 + \rho)$.

The pseudocode appears in Algorithm 40; it uses the basic reliable broadcast algorithm of Chapter 8 (Algorithm 23).

Algorithm 40 A clock synchronization algorithm for drift and timing failures: code for processor p_i, $0 \leq i \leq n - 1$.

Initially $k = 1$ and $count[r] = 0$, for all r

when $AC = k \cdot P$ // time for kth synchronization epoch
1:   bc-send($\langle k \rangle$,reliable)

when bc-recv($\langle r \rangle$,j,reliable) occurs
2:   $count[r] := count[r] + 1$
3:   if $count[k] \geq f + 1$ then
4:      $AC := k \cdot P + x$ // modify *adj* to accomplish this
5:      $k := k + 1$

Because $P > x + d(1 + \rho)$ and k is initialized to 1, the nonfaulty processors' adjusted clocks at the beginning of an admissible execution have not yet reached the time to perform Line 1.

To prove that the algorithm satisfies agreement and validity with some constants ϵ and γ, which will be determined below, we look at the times processors broadcast their $\langle k \rangle$ messages.

The following real times are defined for all $k \geq 1$:

- $ready_k$ denotes the first time a nonfaulty processor broadcasts a $\langle k \rangle$ message, starting the kth synchronization epoch

- $begin_k$ denotes the first time a nonfaulty processor evaluates the condition in Line 3 to be true and sets its adjusted clock to $k \cdot P + x$ in Line 4

- end_k denotes the last time a nonfaulty processor evaluates the condition in Line 3 to be true and sets its adjusted clock to $k \cdot P + x$ in Line 4.

Let $end_0 = 0$ (see Fig. 13.6).

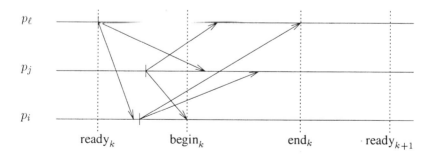

Fig. 13.6 Synchronization epochs.

The Faulty and Nonfaulty Liveness properties of reliable broadcast ensure that if one nonfaulty processor receives $f+1$ messages of the form $\langle k \rangle$, then eventually every nonfaulty processor will receive those $f+1$ messages of the form $\langle k \rangle$. Because the liveness properties are ensured in the simulation of reliable broadcast (Algorithm 23) by relaying messages immediately, those $f+1$ messages of the form $\langle k \rangle$ will be received within d time of when the first nonfaulty processor receives them. Thus we have the following lemma:

Lemma 13.5 *For all $k \geq 1$, $end_k \leq begin_k + d$.*

Let p_i be the first nonfaulty processor to start its kth synchronization epoch, and set its adjusted clock to $k \cdot P + x$. By Lemma 13.5, all nonfaulty processors set their adjusted clock to the same value at most d time later. During this time p_i's adjusted clock gains at most $d(1 + \rho)$, implying the following lemma:

Lemma 13.6 *For all $k \geq 1$ and for any pair of nonfaulty processors, p_i and p_j, $|AC_i(end_k) - AC_j(end_k)| \leq d(1 + \rho)$.*

Note that the above lemma is true by the initialization assumption for $k = 0$.

A nonfaulty processor broadcasts $\langle k \rangle$ at time $k \cdot P$ on its adjusted clock, that is, $P - x$ time on its clock after it has started the $(k-1)$st epoch. Thus all nonfaulty processors broadcast $\langle k \rangle$ messages at most $(P - x)(1 + \rho)$ real time after end_{k-1}. Because $n > 2f$, all nonfaulty processors will get $f + 1$ messages of the form $\langle k \rangle$ at most d real time later, and will start their next synchronization epoch. Therefore, we have the following lemma:

Lemma 13.7 *For all $k \geq 1$, $end_k \leq end_{k-1} + (P - x)(1 + \rho) + d$.*

Because of the lower bound on P, we can prove that the start of the next synchronization epoch is still in the future:

Lemma 13.8 *For all $k \geq 1$, $end_{k-1} < ready_k \leq begin_k$.*

Proof. By Lemma 13.6, the maximum value of a nonfaulty adjusted clock at end_{k-1} is $(k-1)P + x + d(1 + \rho)$, which, by the constraint on P, is less than $(k-1)P + P = kP$. Since $ready_k$ is the earliest real time when a nonfaulty adjusted clock reaches kP, $end_{k-1} < ready_k$.

To prove the second inequality, note that a nonfaulty processor starts the kth epoch only after receiving $\langle k \rangle$ messages from at least $f + 1$ processors, at least one of which is nonfaulty. □

Choose $x = \rho P(2 + \rho) + 2d$.

Together with the lower bound on P stated above, this implies that

$$P > (3d + \rho d)(1 - 2\rho - \rho^2)^{-1}$$

Lemma 13.9 shows that the adjusted clock of a nonfaulty processor is never set backwards, because x is chosen large enough.

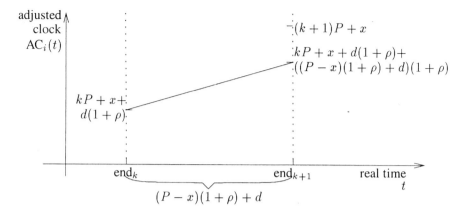

Fig. 13.7 p_i's adjusted clock is not set backwards.

Lemma 13.9 *For each nonfaulty processor p_i, $AC_i(t)$ is a nondecreasing function of t.*

Proof. The only situation in which this lemma might be violated is in the execution of Line 5. Let t be the real time at which p_i executes Line 5 to begin epoch $k + 1$. The value of processor p_i's epoch k adjusted clock at time t is maximized if it has the maximum value $kP + x + d(1 + \rho)$ at time end_k, p_i runs at the maximum rate $1 + \rho$ until time end_{k+1}, and end_{k+1} occurs as late as possible (see Fig. 13.7). Thus the maximum value of p_i's epoch k adjusted clock at time t is $kP + x + ((P - x)(1 + \rho) + 2d)(1 + \rho)$. At time t, p_i's epoch $k + 1$ clock is set to $(k + 1)P + x$.

To check that

$$kP + x + ((P - x)(1 + \rho) + 2d)(1 + \rho) \leq (k + 1)P + x$$

it is sufficient to show that

$$((P - x)(1 + \rho) + 2d)(1 + \rho) \leq P$$

By the choice of x, $((P - x)(1 + \rho) + 2d)(1 + \rho)$ is equal to

$$((P - (\rho P(2 + \rho) + 2d))(1 + \rho) + 2d)(1 + \rho)$$

which is less than

$$((P - (\rho P(2 + \rho)(1 + \rho)^{-2} + 2d))(1 + \rho) + 2d)(1 + \rho)$$

which is less than P. $\qquad\square$

We now prove clock agreement, for $\epsilon = d(1 + \rho) + x(1 + \rho) - d$. Given the definition of x, ϵ is equal to $2d + 3\rho d + 2\rho P$ plus terms of order ρ^2. (When ρ has

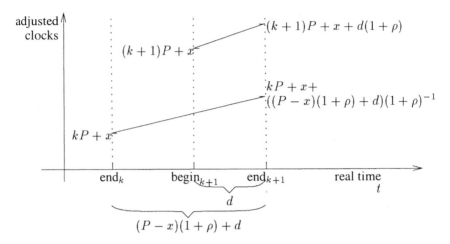

Fig. 13.8 Proof of Lemma 13.10: Epoch k clock and epoch $k + 1$ clock.

a typical value of 10^{-6}, terms of order ρ^2 are negligible.) To minimize ϵ, P must be chosen to be as small as possible; in this case, ϵ is slightly more than $2d + 9\rho d$ plus terms of order ρ^2, when ρ is small. However, there are some disadvantages associated with making P very small—in particular, more resources are taken up by the clock synchronization procedure, because resynchronization messages are sent more often.

Lemma 13.10 (clock agreement) *For any time $t \geq 0$ and any two nonfaulty processors p_i and p_j, $|AC_i(t) - AC_j(t)| \leq \epsilon$.*

Proof. We partition time into intervals between *end* points and prove the lemma for any time t, $0 \leq t \leq end_k$, by induction on k.

Since clocks are initially synchronized, the lemma holds for the base case, $k = 0$, that is, for time 0. So, assume the lemma holds for k, that is, for any time t, $0 \leq t \leq end_k$.

First, we consider the case when both processors, p_i and p_j, have already done the $(k + 1)$st synchronization; that is, AC_i and AC_j are both epoch $k + 1$ clocks. By Lemma 13.6, their difference is at most $d(1 + \rho)$, which is less than ϵ.

Next we consider the case when one processor, say, p_j, has already done the $(k + 1)$st synchronization, but the other, p_i, has not; that is, AC_i is an epoch k clock and AC_j is an epoch $k + 1$ clock. Since clocks are never set backward by Lemma 13.9, the difference between them is maximized at real time end_{k+1} if AC_j is set to $(k + 1)P + x$ at $begin_{k+1}$ and has the maximum rate, AC_i is set to $kP + x$ at end_k and has the minimum rate, and end_{k+1} occurs as late as possible (see Fig. 13.8). Exercise 13.6 asks you to verify that the difference between the clocks is at most ϵ.

Last we consider the case when both processors, p_i and p_j, have yet not done the $(k + 1)$st synchronization; that is, AC_i and AC_j are both epoch k clocks. They are

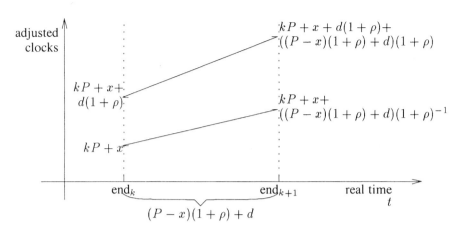

Fig. 13.9 Proof of Lemma 13.10: Epoch k clocks.

maximally far apart at real time end_{k+1} if AC_i has the minimum value $kP + x$ at real time end_k and has the minimum rate $(1 + \rho)^{-1}$, AC_j has the maximum value $kP + x + d(1 + \rho)$ at end_k and has the maximum rate $(1 + \rho)$, and end_{k+1} occurs as late as possible (see Figure 13.9). Exercise 13.7 asks you to verify that the difference between the clocks is at most ϵ. $\qquad\square$

We now show the clock validity condition, namely, that the adjusted clocks do not deviate too much from the hardware clocks. Let $\gamma = P(1 + \rho)^2(P - x)^{-1} - 1$. Simple algebraic manipulations show that

$$\gamma = \frac{1}{c} - 1 + 2\rho + \rho^2$$

where $c = 1 - \rho(2 + \rho) - 2d/P$. In the common case when ρ is small and P is large relative to d, c is slightly less than 1, and thus $\frac{1}{c} - 1$ is close to 0. Because ρ^2 is also extremely small, γ is approximately 2ρ. The rate of the adjusted clocks with respect to real time is approximately $(1 + 2\rho)(1 + \rho)$, which is roughly $1 + 3\rho$, ignoring terms of order ρ^2. Thus the drift of the adjusted clocks is roughly three times that of the hardware clocks.

Lemma 13.11 (clock validity) *For all times t and every nonfaulty processor p_i,*

$$(1 + \gamma)^{-1}(HC_i(t) - HC_i(0)) \leq AC_i(t) - AC_i(0) \leq (1 + \gamma)(HC_i(t) - HC_i(0))$$

Proof. AC_i runs at the same rate as HC_i except for when Line 5 is executed.

By Lemma 13.9, AC_i is never set backwards. Thus the change in AC_i during the real time interval $[0, t]$ is always at least equal to the change in the corresponding hardware clock HC_i, and clearly

$$(1 + \gamma)^{-1}(HC_i(t) - HC_i(0)) \leq AC_i(t) - AC_i(0)$$

(This condition holds for any $\gamma > -1$.)

We now have to consider how much faster AC_i can go than HC_i. Consider the real time t when AC_i is set to $kP + x$, for any k. The change in AC_i during the real time interval $[0, t]$ is at most $kP + x - x = kP$. That is,

$$AC_i(t) - AC_i(0) \leq kP$$

The change in HC_i during the same real time interval is minimized if we assume that each of the k resynchronization epochs takes the minimum amount of real time, $(P - x)(1 + \rho)^{-1}$, and HC_i has the slowest rate, $(1 + \rho)^{-1}$. Thus the change in HC_i is at least $k(P - x)(1 + \rho)^{-2}$. That is,

$$k(P - x)(1 + \rho)^{-2} \leq HC_i(t) - HC_i(0)$$

Therefore, to show that

$$AC_i(t) - AC_i(0) \leq (1 + \gamma)(HC_i(t) - HC_i(0))$$

it suffices to show that,

$$kP \leq (1 + \gamma)k(P - x)(1 + \rho)^{-2}$$

which follows by simple algebraic manipulations (see Exercise 13.8). □

To summarize, we have:

Theorem 13.12 *Algorithm 40 satisfies the clock agreement and clock validity conditions with*

$$\epsilon = d(1 + \rho) + (\rho P(2 + \rho) + 2d)(1 + \rho) - d$$

and

$$\gamma = P(1 + \rho)^2(P - (\rho P(2 + \rho) + 2d))^{-1} - 1$$

as long as $P > (3d + \rho d)(1 - 2\rho - \rho^2)^{-1}$, in the presence of $f < n/2$ timing failures.

13.3.2 Byzantine Failures

In the algorithm just presented, all communication between processors is via the reliable broadcast primitive. The particular simulation that we assumed in Section 13.3.1, Algorithm 23, works for asynchronous crash failures, and thus it works for timing failures. However, it does not work for Byzantine failures.

To get a clock synchronization algorithm that tolerates Byzantine failures, we can develop a simulation of reliable broadcast that tolerates Byzantine failures and use it in Algorithm 40. We will develop this simulation in two steps (a similar development appears in Chapter 14, for the randomized consensus algorithm in the presence of Byzantine failures).

First, to go from identical Byzantine failures to the timing failure model, we can employ a validation procedure as in Chapter 12. The validation makes the messages longer and causes some additional local computation, but these changes do not affect the performance analysis of the clock synchronization algorithm.

Second, to go from Byzantine failures to identical Byzantine failures we use the asynchronous simulation (Algorithm 39) from Chapter 12. This simulation affects the performance of the clock synchronization algorithm in two ways. One impact is that the number of processors, n, must now be greater than $3f$, instead of only greater than $2f$. The other impact is that in the definitions of ϵ and γ for the clock agreement and validity conditions, every occurrence of d must be replaced by $3d$. The reason is that three "rounds" of communication are required in Algorithm 39 for each simulated "round."

13.4 PRACTICAL CLOCK SYNCHRONIZATION: IDENTIFYING FAULTY CLOCKS

The Internet standard Network Time Protocol (NTP) provides synchronized clocks. Certain nodes in the system are identified as time servers. Time servers are classified as primary or secondary — primaries get their time from a reference source, such as a satellite, whereas secondaries get their clock times from either a primary or other secondaries. Time servers are organized conceptually into a hierarchy based on how many hops they are away from a primary server; this distance is called the *stratum* of the server. When a path goes down between two time servers, the strata, or shortest path distances from a primary, are recalculated.

Time servers exchange timestamped messages periodically in order to estimate round trip delays, clock offsets, and error (cf. Section 6.3.6); filtering is applied to reduce timing noise. When a node wants to update its local clock, it selects an appropriate subset of its neighboring time servers; the choice of subset is made by an algorithm that has been carefully optimized on the basis of experimental data and depends on the strata of the neighbors, among other things. Finally, the offsets estimated for this subset are combined to calculate a new value for the local clock. The algorithms in NTP have been carefully tailored to work well with the statistical behavior of links in the Internet.

One of the interesting algorithms in NTP is that for choosing which set of clock values will be combined to compute a clock update. Like the algorithm presented in this chapter, the possibility of Byzantine failures (i.e., processors with arbitrarily faulty clocks) is considered. When a processor p_i obtains an estimate of the difference between its clock and that of another processor p_j, it actually gets an *interval* in which the difference lies. Given a set of m such time intervals, up to f of which might represent values of faulty clocks, the processor must choose a subset of time intervals to use in the combining step. The time intervals that are discarded when the subset is chosen should be those that have (relatively) bad data, that is, that came from processors with faulty clocks. The assumption is that nonfaulty clocks are close to real time, and thus their time intervals will be relatively close to each other. As a result, one way to identify bad time intervals is to see which ones are not sufficiently close to enough other time intervals. In particular, the NTP algorithm finds the smallest interval I that contains the midpoint of at least $m - f$ time intervals. The time intervals that intersect the interval I are then used in the combining stage.

Exercises

13.1 Prove that the rate at which two hardware clocks of nonfaulty processors drift from each other is $\rho(2 + \rho)(1 + \rho)^{-1}$; that is, prove:

$$\max_{i,j} \frac{|HC_i(\Delta t) - HC_j(\Delta t)|}{\Delta t} \leq \rho(2 + \rho)(1 + \rho)^{-1}$$

13.2 Show that if the hardware clock is within a linear envelope of real time and the adjusted clock is within a linear envelope of the hardware clock, then the adjusted clock is within a linear envelope of real time.

Calculate the validity parameter of the adjusted clocks with respect to real time, as a function of ρ and γ.

13.3 What happens to Theorem 13.3 if there is no drift?

What happens to the result? That is, if there is no drift but there are Byzantine failures, do we need $n > 3f$ to keep the adjusted clocks synchronized?

13.4 Prove that if $\alpha' = \text{scale}(\alpha, s)$, then $\alpha = \text{scale}(\alpha', \frac{1}{s})$.

13.5 In the text it was shown that clock synchronization is impossible for three processors, one of which can be Byzantine. Extend this result to show that n must be larger than $3f$, for any value of f (not just $f = 1$).

Hint: Do not try to modify the previous proof. Instead use a reduction, as in the proof of Theorem 5.8.

13.6 Complete the second case in the proof of Lemma 13.10 by showing that the difference between a nonfaulty epoch k clock and a nonfaulty epoch $k + 1$ clock is never more than ϵ.

13.7 Complete the third case in the proof of Lemma 13.10 by showing that the difference between two nonfaulty epoch $k + 1$ clocks is never more than ϵ.

13.8 Complete the algebra in the proof of Lemma 13.11 by showing that

$$kP \leq (1 + \gamma)k(P - x)(1 + \rho)^{-2}$$

13.9 Show that the reliable broadcast simulation of Algorithm 23 does not work in the presence of Byzantine failures.

13.10 Work out the details sketched at the end of Section 13.3.2 for handling Byzantine failures in the clock synchronization algorithm and the effect on the performance.

Try to find ways to reduce the cost of validating the messages of this algorithm.

Chapter Notes

The problem of synchronizing clocks in the presence of Byzantine faults was first posed by Lamport and Melliar-Smith [162]. The lower bound on the number of processors, shown in Section 13.2, was first proved by Dolev, Halpern and Strong [94]. The proof presented here was developed by Fischer, Lynch and Merritt [109], who also proved that the connectivity of the topology graph must be at least $2f + 1$.

The clock synchronization algorithm presented in Section 13.3 is based on an algorithm of Srikanth and Toueg [245], which uses authenticated broadcast. It is similar in flavor to the algorithm of Dolev et al. [93]. Srikanth and Toueg also prove that that the clock validity parameter, γ, must be larger than or equal to hardware clocks' drift bound, ρ; they show how to modify the algorithm to get $\gamma = \rho$. The clock agreement parameter, ϵ, obtained in the algorithm of Dolev et al. is smaller than the parameter obtained in the algorithm of Srikanth and Toueg, presented here.

Welch and Lynch [260] and Mahaney and Schneider [178] designed algorithms based on approximate agreement, a problem defined in Chapter 16. In their seminal paper, Lamport and Melliar-Smith [162] presented algorithms based on using algorithms for consensus.

For some applications, discontinuities in the adjusted clock are undesirable; for instance, jobs that are supposed to begin automatically at certain times might be skipped when the clock is set forward. If adjusted clocks can be set backwards, as is the case in some algorithms, then some activities might be done twice, or a later event might be timestamped before an earlier one. These problems can be eliminated by amortizing the necessary adjustment over an interval of time, as suggested by Lamport and Melliar-Smith [162].

Solutions to the problem of achieving synchronization initially in the presence of faults are presented in [93, 245, 260]. Some of the literature on clock synchronization is described in the survey of Simons, Welch, and Lynch [242]. Other papers appear in the collection edited by Yang and Marsland [263].

The Network Time Protocol, described in Section 13.4, was developed by Mills [186, 187]. Marzullo and Owicki [180] proposed the idea of intersecting time intervals to discard faulty clock values.

Part III

Advanced Topics

14

Randomization

Previous chapters concentrated on specific problems (Part I) or on simulations between specific models of computation (Part II); this chapter concentrates on a specific type of distributed algorithms, which employ *randomization*. Randomization has proved to be a very powerful tool for designing distributed algorithms (as for many other areas). Randomization often simplifies algorithms and, more importantly, allows us to solve problems in situations where they cannot be solved by deterministic algorithms, or with fewer resources than the best deterministic algorithm.

This chapter extends the formal model to include randomization and describes randomized algorithms for three basic problems: leader election, mutual exclusion, and consensus.

For all three problems, randomization allows us to overcome impossibility results and lower bounds, by relaxing the termination conditions or the individual liveness properties (in the case of mutual exclusion).

14.1 LEADER ELECTION: A CASE STUDY

This section has the dual purpose of demonstrating a simple but powerful application of randomization and developing the formal definitions relating to randomization.

14.1.1 Weakening the Problem Definition

A *randomized* algorithm is an algorithm that has access to some source of random information, such as that provided by flipping a coin or rolling dice. More formally, we extend the transition function of a processor to take as an additional input a random number, drawn from a bounded range under some fixed distribution. The assumption of a fixed distribution suffices for all algorithms we present in this chapter. Many other probability distributions can be implemented using this type of coin (by appropriate mappings).

The addition of random information alone typically will not affect the existence of impossibility results or worst-case bounds. For instance, even if processors have access to random numbers, they will not be able to elect a leader in an anonymous ring or solve consensus in fewer than $f + 1$ rounds in *all* (admissible) executions.

However, randomization in conjunction with a judicious *weakening* of the problem statement is a powerful tool for overcoming limitations. Usually the weakening involves the termination condition (for instance, a leader must be elected with a certain probability) while the other conditions are not changed (for instance, it should never be the case that two leaders are elected).

Randomization differs from average case analysis of a deterministic algorithm. In average case analysis, there are several choices as to what is being averaged over. One natural choice is the inputs. (Other possibilities in systems that have some degree of uncertainty are the interleavings of processor steps, the message delays, and the occurrences of failures.) There are two difficulties with this approach. One is that determining an accurate probability distribution on the inputs (not to mention the processor scheduling, the message delays, or the failure events) is often not practical. Another drawback is that, even if such distributions can be chosen with some degree of confidence, very little is guaranteed about the behavior of the algorithm on a particular input. For instance, even if the *average* running time over all inputs is determined to be small, there still could be some inputs for which the running time is enormous.

In the randomized approach, more stringent guarantees can be made. Because the random numbers introduce another dimension of variability even for the same inputs, there are many different executions for the same input. A good randomized algorithm will guarantee good performance with some probability for each individual input. Typically the performance of a randomized algorithm is defined to be the *worst-case* probability over all inputs.

The simplest use of randomization is to create initial asymmetry in situations that are inherently symmetric. One such situation is anonymous rings (studied in Chapter 3). Recall that in anonymous rings, where processors do not have distinct identifiers, it is impossible to elect a unique leader (Theorem 3.2). This impossibility result holds even for randomized algorithms. However, a randomized algorithm *can* ensure that a leader is elected *with some probability*. Thus we can solve a variant of the leader election problem that relaxes the condition that eventually a leader must be elected in every admissible execution.

The relaxed version of the leader election problem requires:

Safety: In every configuration of every admissible execution, at most one processor is in an elected state.

Liveness: At least one processor is elected with some nonzero probability.

The safety property has to hold with certainty; that is, the algorithm should never elect two leaders. The liveness condition is relaxed, and the algorithm need not *always* terminate with a leader, rather, it is required to do so *with nonzero probability*. (We will spend some time exploring exactly how to define this probabilistic condition.)

An algorithm that satisfies this weakened liveness condition can fail to elect a leader either by not terminating at all or by terminating without a leader. As demonstrated below, these two ways to express liveness are typically related, and one can be traded off against the other.

14.1.2 Synchronous One-Shot Algorithm

First, let us consider synchronous rings. There is only one admissible execution on an anonymous synchronous ring for a deterministic algorithm. For a randomized algorithm, however, there can be many different executions, depending on the random choices.

The approach we will use to devising a randomized leader election algorithm is to use randomization to create asymmetry by having processors choose random *pseudo*-identifiers, drawn from some range, and then execute a deterministic leader election algorithm.

Not every deterministic leader election algorithm can be employed. Regardless of the method used for generating the pseudo-identifiers, there is always a chance that they are not distinct. The deterministic leader election algorithm must guarantee that at most a single processor terminates as a leader even in this case. Also, it is important that the algorithm does not freeze when all processors choose the same pseudo-identifier. Finally, it is helpful if the deterministic leader election algorithm detects that no leader was elected.

A simple deterministic leader election algorithm with these properties is the following. Each processor sends a message around the ring to collect all pseudo-identifiers. When the message returns (after collecting n pseudo-identifiers), a processor knows whether it is a unique maximum or not.

The pseudocode appears in Algorithm 41.

In this algorithm, the pseudo-identifier is chosen to be 2 with probability $1/n$ and 1 with probability $(1 - 1/n)$, where n is the number of processors on the ring. Thus each processor makes use of its source of randomness exactly once, and the random numbers are drawn from the range $[1..2]$.

The set of all possible admissible executions of this algorithm for fixed ring size n contains exactly one execution for each element of the set $\mathcal{R} = \{1, 2\}^n$. That is, by specifying which random number, 1 or 2, is obtained by each of the n processors in its first step, we have completely determined the execution. Given an element R of $\mathcal{R}$, we will denote the corresponding execution by $exec(R)$.

We would like to make some claims about the probabilistic behavior of this algorithm. These claims reduce to claims about the random choices.

Algorithm 41 Randomized leader election in an anonymous ring:
code for processor p_i, $0 \leq i \leq n - 1$.

1:   initially   // spontaneously or upon receiving the first message

2:        $id_i := \begin{cases} 1 & \text{with probability } 1 - \frac{1}{n} \\ 2 & \text{with probability } \frac{1}{n} \end{cases}$ // choose pseudo-identifier

3:        send $\langle id_i \rangle$ to left

4:   upon receiving $\langle S \rangle$ from right
5:        if $|S| = n$ then   // your message is back
6:             if id_i is the unique maximum of S then become *elected*   // the leader
7:             else become *non-elected*   // a nonleader
8:        else   // concatenate your id to the message and forward
9:             send $\langle S \cdot id_i \rangle$ to left

Let P be some predicate on executions, for example, at least one leader is elected. Then $\Pr[P]$ is the probability of the event

$$\{R \in \mathcal{R} : exec(R) \text{ satisfies } P\}$$

When does the randomized leader election algorithm terminate with a leader? This happens when a single processor has the maximum identifier, 2. The probability that a single processor draws 2 is the probability that $n-1$ processors draw 1, and one processor draws 2, times the number of possible choices for the processor drawing 2, that is,

$$\binom{n}{1} \frac{1}{n} \left(1 - \frac{1}{n}\right)^{n-1} = \left(1 - \frac{1}{n}\right)^{n-1} = c$$

The probability c is greater than $(1 - \frac{1}{n})^n$, which converges from above to e^{-1} as n increases, where e is the constant $\approx 2.71...$.

It is simple to show that every processor terminates after sending exactly n messages (Exercise 14.1); moreover, at most one processor terminates in an elected state (Exercise 14.2). In some executions, for example, when two processors choose the pseudo-identifier 2, no processor terminates as a leader. However, the above analysis shows that this happens with probability less than $1 - 1/e$. We have shown the following theorem:

Theorem 14.1 *There is a randomized algorithm that, with probability $c > 1/e$, elects a leader in a synchronous ring; the algorithm sends $O(n^2)$ messages.*

14.1.3   Synchronous Iterated Algorithm and Expectation

It is pleasing that the probability of termination in Algorithm 41 does not decrease with the ring size n. However, we may wish to increase the probability of termination, at the expense of more time and messages.

The algorithm can be modified so that each processor receiving a message with n pseudo-identifiers checks whether a unique leader exists (in Lines 5–7). If not, the processor chooses a new pseudo-identifier and iterates the algorithm. We will show that this approach amplifies the probability of success.

We can either have the algorithm terminate after some number of iterations and experience a nonzero probability of not electing a leader or iterate until a leader is found and risk that the algorithm does not terminate.

Let us consider the second option in more detail. In order to repeat Algorithm 41, each processor will need to access the random number source multiple times, in fact, potentially infinitely often. To completely specify an execution of the algorithm, we will need to specify, for each processor, the *sequence* of random numbers that it obtains. Thus $\mathcal{R}$ now becomes the set of all n-tuples, each element of which is a possibly infinite sequence over $\{1, 2\}$.

For the iterated algorithm, the probability that the algorithm terminates at the end of the kth iteration is equal to the probability that the algorithm fails to terminate in the first $k - 1$ iterations and succeeds in terminating in the kth iteration. The analysis in Section 14.1.2 shows that the probability of success in a single iteration is $c > 1/e$. Because the probability of success or failure in each iteration is independent, the desired probability is

$$(1 - c)^{k-1} c$$

This probability tends to 0 as k tends to ∞; thus the probability that the algorithm terminates with an elected leader is 1.

We would now like to measure the time complexity of the iterated algorithm. Clearly, a worst-case analysis is not informative, since in the worst case the required number of iterations is infinite. Instead, we will measure the *expected* number of iterations. The number of iterations until termination is a geometric random variable whose expected value is $c^{-1} < e$. Thus the expected number of iterations is less than three.

In general, the expected value of any complexity measure is defined as follows. Let T be a random variable that, for a given execution, is the value of the complexity measure of interest for that run (for instance, the number of iterations until termination). Let $E[T]$ be the expected value of T, taken over all $R \in \mathcal{R}$. That is,

$$E[T] = \sum_{x \text{ is a value of } T} x \cdot \Pr[T = x]$$

Note that by the definition of $\Pr[P]$ above, this is ultimately taking probabilities over $\mathcal{R}$.

With this definition, we have the following theorem:

Theorem 14.2 *There is a randomized algorithm that elects a leader in a synchronous ring with probability 1 in $(1/c) \cdot n < e \cdot n$ expected rounds; the algorithm sends $O(n^2)$ expected messages.*

14.1.4 Asynchronous Systems and Adversaries

Now suppose we would like to find a randomized leader election algorithm for asynchronous anonymous rings. Even without the random choices, there are many executions of the algorithm, depending on when processors take steps and when messages arrive. To be able to calculate probabilities, we need a way to factor out the variations due to causes other than the random choices. That is, we need a way to group the executions of interest so that each group differs only in the random choices; then we can perform probabilistic calculations separately for each group and then combine those results in some fashion.

The concept used to account for all the variability other than the random choices is an adversary. An *adversary* is a function that takes an execution segment and returns the next event that is to occur, namely, which processor receives which pending messages in the next step. The adversary must satisfy the admissibility conditions for the asynchronous message-passing communication system: Every processor must take an infinite number of steps and every message must eventually be received. The adversary can also control the occurrence of failures in the execution, subject to the relevant admissibility conditions.

An execution of a specific anonymous leader election algorithm is uniquely determined by an adversary $\mathcal{A}$ and an element $R \in \mathcal{R}$; it is denoted $exec(\mathcal{A}, R)$.

We need to generalize the definitions of $\Pr[P]$ and $E[T]$ from the previous subsections. Given a particular adversary $\mathcal{A}$, $\Pr_{\mathcal{A}}[P]$ is the probability of the event $\{R \in \mathcal{R} : exec(\mathcal{A}, R) \text{ satisfies } P\}$. Similarly,

$$E_{\mathcal{A}}[T] = \sum_{x \text{ is a value of } T} x \cdot \Pr_{\mathcal{A}}[T = x]$$

The performance of the algorithm overall is taken to be the worst over all possible adversaries. Thus the liveness condition for leader election is that there is a nonzero probability of termination, for every adversary:

Liveness: There exists $c > 0$ such that $\Pr_{\mathcal{A}}[\text{a leader is elected}] \geq c$, for every (admissible) adversary $\mathcal{A}$.

Similarly, the expected number of iterations until termination taken by the algorithm over all possible adversaries is defined to be

$$E[T] = \max_{\mathcal{A}} E_{\mathcal{A}}[T]$$

where T is the number of iterations. $E[T]$ is a "worst-case average."

Exercise 14.4 asks you to verify that both the one-shot and the iterated synchronous leader election algorithms have the same performance in the asynchronous case as they do in the synchronous case. The reason is that the adversaries actually cannot affect the termination of these algorithms. Once the pseudo-identifiers are chosen, the ability of the algorithm to terminate in that iteration is completely unaffected by the message delays or processor step times.

However, in most situations the adversary can have a great deal of impact on the workings of a randomized algorithm. As we shall see below, the interaction among the adversary, the algorithm, and the random choices can be extremely delicate.

Sometimes it is necessary to restrict the power of the adversary in order to be able to solve the problem. Formally, this is done by defining the input to the function modeling the adversary to be something less than the entire execution so far.

For example, in message-passing systems, a *weak* adversary cannot look at the contents of messages; it is defined as a function that takes as input the message pattern (indicating who sent messages to whom so far and when they were received, but not including the contents of the messages).

In shared memory systems, where the output of the adversary is just which processor takes the next step, a *weak* adversary cannot observe the local states of processors or the contents of the shared memory. (Such an adversary is sometimes called *oblivious*.)

14.1.5 Impossibility of Uniform Algorithms

The randomized leader election algorithms considered so far have all been nonuniform, that is, they depend on n, the number of processors in the ring. Theorem 14.3 states that knowing n is necessary for electing a leader in an anonymous ring, even for a randomized algorithm. In fact, this impossibility result holds even if the algorithm only needs to guarantee termination in a single situation.

Theorem 14.3 *There is no uniform randomized algorithm for leader election in a synchronous anonymous ring that terminates in even a single execution for a single ring size.*

We only sketch the proof of this theorem. Assume there exists such a uniform randomized leader election algorithm A. Consider some execution, α, of A on an anonymous ring with n processors, $q_0, \ldots, q_{n-1}$, in which processor q_l is elected as leader. Such an execution exists by assumption. Note that (the description of) the execution includes the outcomes of the random choices of the processors.

Now consider another execution, β, of A on an anonymous ring with $2n$ processors, $p_0, \ldots, p_{2n-1}$, which is a "doubling" of α. That is, for any $i = 0, \ldots, n - 1$, the events of p_i and p_{n+i} in β are the events of q_i in α, including the random choices, with the same interleaving (see Fig. 14.1, for $n = 4$). The execution β is possible because processors are anonymous, so we can have p_i and p_{n+i} take the same steps. However, in β, both p_l and p_{n+l} are elected as leaders. This violates the requirement that only a single leader is elected.

14.1.6 Summary of Probabilistic Definitions

In this subsection, we finish generalizing our definitions and summarize them all.

Our running example so far has been leader election in anonymous rings. Because any anonymous ring algorithm has a single initial configuration, we have seen no

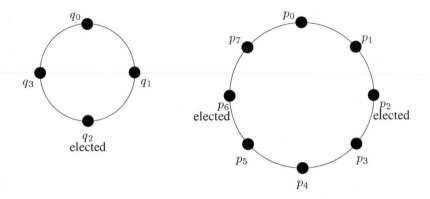

Fig. 14.1 Illustration for the proof of Theorem 14.3; $n = 4$.

impact of the initial configuration on the behavior of randomized algorithm. In the general case, though, an algorithm can have multiple initial configurations. The initial configuration is a third source of variability in the behavior of a randomized algorithm, in addition to the random choices and the adversary.

An execution of a specific algorithm is uniquely determined by an adversary $\mathcal{A}$, an initial configuration C_0, and an element $R \in \mathcal{R}$; it is denoted $exec(\mathcal{A}, C_0, R)$. ($\mathcal{R}$ is determined by the domain from which the random choices of the algorithm are drawn.)

Let P be some predicate on executions. For fixed adversary $\mathcal{A}$ and initial configuration C_0, $\Pr_{\mathcal{A},C_0}[P]$ is the probability of the event $\{R \in \mathcal{R} : exec(\mathcal{A}, C_0, R)$ satisfies $P\}$. $\mathcal{A}$ and C_0 may be omitted when they are clear from the context.

The expected value of any complexity measure is defined as follows. Let T be a random variable that, for a given execution, is the value of the complexity measure of interest for that run. For a fixed admissible adversary $\mathcal{A}$ and initial configuration C_0, let $E_{\mathcal{A},C_0}[T]$ be the expected value of T, taken over all $R \in \mathcal{R}$. That is,

$$E_{\mathcal{A},C_0}[T] = \sum_{x \text{ is a value of } T} x \cdot \Pr_{\mathcal{A},C_0}[T = x]$$

Sometimes, we are interested in the probability that a complexity measure (especially the time complexity) is smaller than some quantity, that is, in $\Pr_{\mathcal{A},C_0}[T \leq x]$. In many cases (depending on the distribution of T), this quantity and the expected value of T are related.

Define the expected value of a complexity measure for an algorithm, $E[T]$, to be the maximum, over all admissible adversaries $\mathcal{A}$ and initial configurations C_0, of $E_{\mathcal{A},C_0}[T]$. Because the maximum is taken over all initial configurations, we get to pick the worst inputs for the algorithm for each adversary.

14.2 MUTUAL EXCLUSION WITH SMALL SHARED VARIABLES

In Chapter 4, we have seen that any deterministic mutual exclusion algorithm for n processors with k-bounded waiting requires a shared variable with at least $\Omega(\log n)$ bits (Theorem 4.4). A randomized algorithm can reduce the number of shared bits required for mutual exclusion while still being fair to all processors, by guaranteeing that a processor has probability $\Theta(1/n)$ of succeeding in each attempt to enter the critical section; the algorithm uses only a constant-size shared variable. The number of attempts is measured in terms of the number of steps a processor takes after moving into the entry section and until entering the critical section. This section outlines this algorithm and points out its intricacies, demonstrating the delicate interplay between the adversary and the algorithm's random choices.

The adversary does not have access to the contents of the shared variable or to the local states of the processors, but it can observe the interaction of the algorithm with the environment. That is, the adversary can tell which of the four sections, entry, critical, exit, or remainder, each processor is currently in.

The algorithm consists of phases, each happening between successive entries to the critical section. Each phase is partitioned into two stages, which determine which processor will enter the critical section next. While the critical section is not free, there is a *drawing* stage, during which each processor wishing to enter the critical section draws a ticket. The *winner* of the lottery in the drawing stage is the processor that draws the highest ticket; if more than one processor draws the highest lottery ticket, then the first one to draw this ticket (by the actual time of the drawing) is the winner. When the critical section becomes free, the winner of the lottery is discovered in a *notification* stage. The winning processor enters the critical section, and the drawing stage of the next phase begins.

Assume that each contending processor draws a ticket according to the lottery used in the previous section (for leader election): 1 with probability $1 - \frac{1}{n}$ and 2 with probability $\frac{1}{n}$. A calculation similar to the one in the previous section shows that the probability that a *specific* processor p_i is the only one that draws the maximal ticket is at least $\frac{c}{n}$, for the same constant $c > 0$. This fact can be used to bound the number of attempts a processor needs to execute until entering the critical section. Clearly, the range of lottery tickets is constant (independent of n), and the maximal ticket drawn so far can be kept in a shared variable of constant size.

It is possible that several processors see themselves as candidates; in particular, if 1 is drawn before 2 is drawn, then the first processor to draw 1 and the first processor to draw 2 are both candidates. The notification stage is used to pick the winner among candidates.

The argument bounding the chances of a specific processor to enter the critical section depends on having each processor draw a ticket at most once in each phase. One way to guarantee this property is to keep the phase number in the shared variable and have the winner of the phase (the processor entering the critical section) increment it. Then, a processor can limit itself to draw at most one ticket in each phase by drawing a ticket only if the current phase is larger than the previous phase in which it participated. A processor can remember this phase number in a local variable.

The problem with this solution is that phase numbers are unbounded and cannot be kept in a constant-size shared variable. Instead, we employ a single random *phase bit*. This bit is set by the processor entering the critical section to be either 0 or 1 with equal probability. We modify the lottery scheme described above, so that only processors whose previous phase bit is not equal to the shared phase bit may draw a ticket. In the new lottery:

$$\Pr[p_i \text{ wins}] = \Pr[p_i \text{ wins} \mid p_i \text{ draws a ticket}] \cdot \Pr[p_i \text{ draws a ticket}]$$

and by the above argument,

$$\Pr[p_i \text{ wins}] \geq \frac{c}{n} \cdot \frac{1}{2}$$

for the same constant $c > 0$. Therefore, the probability that a processor p_i is the only processor that draws the maximal ticket is at least $\frac{c'}{n}$, for some constant $c' > 0$.

We can now suggest an algorithm that uses a shared read-modify-write variable with the following components:

Free: A flag indicating whether there is a processor in the critical section

Phase: The shared phase bit

Max: A two-bit variable containing the maximum ticket drawn (so far) in the current lottery: 0, 1 or 2.

In addition, each processor p_i has the following local variables:

last$_i$: The bit of the last phase the processor participated in

ticket$_i$: The last ticket the processor has drawn

The pseudocode appears in Algorithm 42. Processors use read-modify-write operations, which are executed atomically and without interference from other processors. Lines 1–10 are executed as a single atomic read-modify-write, in which a processor first decides whether to execute the drawing or the notification stage and then performs all the necessary assignments. When entering the critical section, a processor marks the critical section as not free, sets the phase bit and resets the maximal ticket for the next lottery, and initializes its own ticket (Lines 11–14).

Mutual exclusion is guaranteed by the *Free* component of the shared variable, which serves as a lock on the critical section (similarly to the shared variable V in Algorithm 7).

It may seem that there are at most two candidates in each phase (the first processor that draws 1 and the first processor that draws 2). However, because the algorithm uses only a single bit for the phase number and because losers are not always notified, there may be more than two candidates in a phase. Consider, for example, the following execution:

Algorithm 42 Mutual exclusion algorithm with small shared variables:
code for processor p_i, $0 \leq i \leq n - 1$.

$\langle$Entry$\rangle$:   // drawing stage
1:   if *last* $\neq$ *Phase* then   // didn't participate in this phase

2:       $ticket := \begin{cases} 1 & \text{with probability } 1 - \frac{1}{n} \\ 2 & \text{with probability } \frac{1}{n} \end{cases}$ // draw a ticket

3:   *last* := *Phase*   // remember this phase number
4:   if (*ticket* > *Max*) then   // p_i is a candidate in this phase
5:       *Max* := *ticket*
6:   else *ticket* := 0   // p_i lost
                                                              // notification stage

7:   wait until *Free* = true
8:   if *ticket* $\neq$ *Max* then   // p_i lost the lottery
9:       *ticket* := 0
10:      goto Line 1   // try again
                                      // have the critical section, but clean up first

11: *Free* := false

12: *Phase* := $\begin{cases} 0 & \text{with probability } \frac{1}{2} \\ 1 & \text{with probability } \frac{1}{2} \end{cases}$

13: *Max* := 0
14: *ticket* := 0
$\langle$Critical Section$\rangle$
$\langle$Exit$\rangle$:
15: *Free* := true

In some phase with bit 0, p_i is the first to draw a 1 ticket and p_j is the first to draw a 2 ticket. In the notification stage, p_j is scheduled first, initializes a new phase, and enters the critical section. When p_j is scheduled next, the phase bit is again 0, and the critical section is free. If no processor drew a 2 ticket so far in this phase, then p_i will execute its notification stage and observes that its ticket is equal to *max*; therefore, p_i enters the critical section.

Although this kind of behavior is unpredictable, it does not violate the expected bounded waiting property. Scenarios of the type described before affect only phases in which the highest ticket drawn is 1; however, the analysis of the lottery considered only the case where the winner draws 2. Thus the behavior of a winner with a 1 ticket does not influence the above analysis.

There is, however, a possibility that the adversary can make the algorithm violate the bounded waiting property. If the adversary wishes to bias against some processor p_k, it can let p_k take steps only in phases in which there are processors with high lottery values. This decreases p_k's probability of winning the lottery and violates the bounded waiting property. The adversary could easily have done this if it had full knowledge of the execution so far, including the local states of processors and the contents of the shared register. Surprisingly, even without this knowledge, the adversary can make deductions about information "hidden" from it; the adversary can "learn" whether a processor p_i has a high lottery value by observing the external behavior of other processors that participate with this processor in the lottery. The adversary can learn about the lottery value of a processor by a small "experiment":

The adversary waits for the critical section to be free. Then it schedules one step of processor p_i, then two steps of some other processor p_j, $j \neq i$, and then observes whether p_j enters the critical section or not. If p_j does not enter the critical section after these two steps, then p_j's lottery value must be 1 and p_i's lottery value is 2. Note that if p_j enters the critical section, the adversary waits for it to exit the critical section.

If the phase bit of p_j happens to be equal to the phase bit of p_k, then when p_k is scheduled to take its steps together with p_j, it has no chance of entering the critical section. Similar tricks can be used by the adversary to learn the exact phase bits, but this is slightly more complicated. Instead, note that the adversary can repeat the experiment, with other processors, and accumulate a set of processors, P, with lottery value 2, namely, the processors that play the role of p_i when p_j does not enter the critical section after two steps, in the scenario just described.

Note that the phase bits are random, so, with high probability, these processors have the same phase bit as p_k. Once we have this set of processors at our disposal, we can let p_k take steps always with processors with lottery value 2. Thus, p_k's probability of entering the critical section can be made very small.

This counterexample shows that arguing about the ability of an adversary is a delicate task. In this case, the adversary can deduce the values of the local variables and the shared variable, by scheduling processors and observing their interface with the environment.

This problem can be avoided by hiding the results of the lottery: The winner of the current lottery does not enter the critical section immediately, but waits for the next phase. The winner of the lottery in the previous phase enters the critical section in the current phase. In each phase, the algorithm executes the drawing stage of the current lottery, together with the notification stage of the previous lottery. Thus the behavior of the processors (as observed in the interface) does not indicate the results of the drawing stage in the current phase. The details of the implementation of this idea, as well as its correctness proof, are left out; the chapter notes discuss the relevant literature.

14.3 CONSENSUS

Our last, and perhaps most important, example of the utility of randomization in distributed computing is the consensus problem. For this problem, randomization allows us to circumvent inherent limitations—it allows us to solve consensus in asynchronous systems, and it allows us to achieve consensus in synchronous systems in fewer than $f + 1$ rounds, in the presence of f failures.

The randomized consensus problem is to achieve the following conditions:

Agreement: Nonfaulty processors do not decide on conflicting values.

Validity: If all the processors have the same input, then any value decided upon must be that common input.

Termination: All nonfaulty processors decide with some nonzero probability.

Agreement and Validity are the usual safety conditions (cf. the definition of the consensus problem for crash failures in Chapter 5). The Termination condition has been weakened; ideally, we would like to have termination with probability 1.

We present a randomized asynchronous algorithm for reaching randomized consensus that tolerates f crash failures, under the assumption $n \geq 2f + 1$. The algorithm has constant expected time complexity. This result does not contradict the impossibility result proved in Chapter 5 (Theorem 5.25), because the randomized algorithm has executions in which processors do not terminate; however, these executions occur with zero probability. In addition, if it is used in a synchronous system, the randomized algorithm is faster, on average, than the lower bound on the number of rounds proved in Chapter 5 (Theorem 5.3), for every set of inputs and pattern of failures.

The proof for Theorem 10.22 can be modified to show that $n \geq 2f + 1$ is a necessary condition for solving randomized consensus in an asynchronous systems, in the presence of f crash failures (Exercise 14.9). Thus the algorithm we present is optimal in the number of processors.

The algorithm has two parts: the first is a general phase-based voting scheme using individual processors' preferences to reach agreement (when possible), and the second is a common coin procedure used to break ties among these preferences. As described later, the general scheme can be adapted to tolerate Byzantine failures by using the asynchronous simulation of identical Byzantine failures (Algorithm 39). We also describe a simple common coin procedure that can tolerate Byzantine failures, which gives exponential expected time complexity.

Randomized consensus algorithms have been the subject of extensive research; some of the wide literature in this area is mentioned in the chapter notes.

14.3.1 The General Algorithm Scheme

The core of the algorithm is a phase-based *voting* scheme: In each phase, a processor votes on its (binary) preference for this phase by sending a message containing its preference. It calculates the outcome of the vote as the majority of all the preferences received; different processors may see different outcomes. If a processor sees a unanimous vote for some preference, it decides on this preference. In case some processors were not able to reach a decision by this point in the phase, processors exchange their outcomes from the vote. If all outcomes reported to a particular processor are the same, the processor sets its preference for the next phase to be this value; otherwise, it obtains its preference for the next phase by "flipping" a *common coin*.

Intuitively, a common coin procedure imitates the public tossing of a biased coin such that all processors see the coin landing on side v with probability at least ρ, for every v; there is a possibility that processors will not see the coin landing on the same value. Formally, an *f-resilient common coin* with *bias* ρ is a procedure (with no input) that returns a binary output. For every admissible adversary and initial configuration, all nonfaulty processors executing the procedure output v with probability at least ρ, for any value $v \in \{0, 1\}$.

A simple f-resilient common coin procedure for any $f < n$ is to have each processor output a random bit with uniform distribution; the bias of this common coin is small, 2^{-n}. Later, we present a common coin procedure with constant bias. As we shall see below, a larger bias decreases the expected number of rounds until processors decide.

The voting mechanism and the common coin procedure employ a simple information exchange procedure called get-core. This procedure guarantees the existence of a *core* set of $n - f$ processors whose values are observed by all (nonfaulty) processors; the procedure relies on the assumption that $n > 2f$ and that all processors execute it.

Algorithm 43 presents procedure get-core, which has three asynchronous phases; in every phase, a processor broadcasts to all processors and then collects information from $n - f$ processors. The algorithm relies on basic broadcast, which involves only sending a message to all processors and can be implemented in $O(1)$ time.

We first prove the properties of procedure get-core. The next lemma, whose proof is left to Exercise 14.10, shows that each nonfaulty processor eventually terminates its invocation of get-core. Recall that we assume that all $n > 2f$ processes execute get-core.

Lemma 14.4 *If processor p_i is nonfaulty, then p_i eventually returns from* get-core.

Next, we prove the existence of a large *core* group of processors whose values are seen by all nonfaulty processors.

Lemma 14.5 *There exists a set of processors, C, such that $|C| > \frac{n}{2}$ and, for every processor $p_i \in C$ and every processor p_j that returns V_j from* get-core, *V_j contains p_i's argument to* get-core.

Proof. Define a table T with n rows and n columns. For each i and j between 0 and $n - 1$, entry $T[i, j]$ contains a one if processor p_i receives a $\langle$second$\rangle$ message from p_j before sending its $\langle$third$\rangle$ message and a zero otherwise. If p_i never sends a $\langle$third$\rangle$ message, then $T[i, j]$ contains a one if and only if p_j sends its $\langle$second$\rangle$ message.

Each row contains at least $n - f$ ones, since a processor that sends a $\langle$third$\rangle$ message waits for $n - f$ $\langle$second$\rangle$ messages before doing so, and a processor that does not send a $\langle$third$\rangle$ message is the recipient of a $\langle$second$\rangle$ message from each of the $n - f$ (or more) nonfaulty processors. Thus the total number of ones in the table is at least $n(n - f)$. Since there are n columns it follows that some column ℓ contains at least $n - f$ ones. This means that the set P' of processors not receiving a $\langle$second$\rangle$ message from p_ℓ before sending their $\langle$third$\rangle$ message, contains at most f processors.

Algorithm 43 Procedure get-core: code for processor p_i, $0 \leq i \leq n-1$.

Initially *first-set, second-set, third-set* $= \emptyset$; *values*$[j] = \perp, 0 \leq j \leq n-1$

1:   when get-core(val) is invoked:
2:      $values[i] := val$
3:      bc-send($\langle$first, $val\rangle$,basic)

4:   when $\langle$first, $v\rangle$ is received from p_j:
5:      $values[j] := v$
6:      add j to *first-set*   // track the senders of $\langle$first$\rangle$ messages
7:      if $|first\text{-}set| = n - f$ then
            bc-send($\langle$second, $values\rangle$,basic)

8:   when $\langle$second, $V\rangle$ is received from p_j:
9:      if $values[k] = \perp$ then $values[k] := V[k], 0 \leq k \leq n-1$
                                             // merge with p_j's values
10:     add j to *second-set*   // track the senders of $\langle$second$\rangle$ messages
11:     if $|second\text{-}set| = n - f$ then
            bc-send($\langle$third, $values\rangle$,basic)

12:   when $\langle$third, $V'\rangle$ is received from p_j:
13:     if $values[k] = \perp$ then $values[k] := V'[k], 0 \leq k \leq n-1$
                                             // merge with p_j's values
14:     add j to *third-set*   // track the senders of $\langle$third$\rangle$ messages
15:     if $|third\text{-}set| = n - f$ then return *values*

Let W be the set of values sent by p_ℓ in its $\langle$second$\rangle$ message. By the algorithm, $|W| \geq n - f > n/2$, that is, W contains the values of at least $n - f$ processors (the "core" processors).

Since $n - f > f$, every processor receives at least one $\langle$third$\rangle$ message from a processor not in P' before completing procedure get-core. This $\langle$third$\rangle$ message clearly includes W, the values of the core processors. This implies the lemma. $\square$

The voting mechanism appears in Algorithm 44. It is deterministic—all the randomization is embedded in the common coin procedure.

Fix some admissible execution α of the algorithm. We say that processor p_i *prefers* v *in phase* r if *prefer$_i$* equals v in Lines 1–5 of phase r. For phase 1 the preference is the input. For any phase $r > 1$, the preference for phase r is assigned either in Line 6 or in Line 7 of the previous phase; if the assignment is in Line 6 then p_i *deterministically prefers* v *in phase* r.

If all processors prefer v in some phase r, then they all vote for v in phase r. Therefore, all processors that reach Line 4 of phase r obtain $n - f$ votes for v and decide on v. This implies:

Algorithm 44 The consensus algorithm: code for processor p_i, $0 \leq i \leq n - 1$.

Initially $r = 1$ and *prefer* = p_i's input x_i

```
1:   while true do                                              // phase r
2:       votes := get-core(⟨vote, prefer, r⟩)
3:       let v be the majority of phase r votes          // default if no majority
4:       if all phase r votes are v then y := v                 // decide v
                                    // do not terminate, continue with the algorithm
5:       outcomes := get-core(⟨outcome, v, r⟩)
6:       if all phase r outcome values received are w then prefer := w
7:       else prefer := common-coin()
8:       r := r + 1
```

Lemma 14.6 *For any $r \geq 1$, if all processors reaching phase r prefer v in phase r, then all nonfaulty processors decide on v no later than phase r.*

This lemma already shows that the algorithm has the validity property; if all processors start with the same input v, then they all prefer v in the first phase and, therefore, decide on v in the first phase. To prove agreement, we show that if a processor decides on some value in some phase, then all other processors prefer this value in later phases. In particular, this implies that once a processor decides on v, it continues to prefer v in later phases.

For any binary value v, let $\bar{v}$ denote $1 - v$.

Lemma 14.7 *For any $r \geq 1$, if some processor decides on v in phase r, then all nonfaulty processors either decide on v in phase r or deterministically prefer v in phase $r + 1$.*

Proof. Assume that some processor p_i decides on v in phase r. This implies that p_i obtains only votes for v in phase r. By Lemma 14.5, every other processor obtains at least $n - f$ votes for v and at most f votes for $\bar{v}$, in phase r. Since $n \geq 2f + 1$, $n - f$ has majority over f, and thus all processors see a majority vote for v in phase r. Thus a processor either decides v or has outcome v in phase r. Since all ⟨outcome⟩ messages in round r have value v, every processor sets its *prefer* variable to v at the end of round r. $\square$

The next lemma shows that if processors' preferences were picked deterministically then they agree.

Lemma 14.8 *For any $r \geq 1$, if some processor deterministically prefers v in phase $r + 1$, then no processor decides on $\bar{v}$ in phase r or deterministically prefers $\bar{v}$ in phase $r + 1$.*

Proof. Assume that some processor p_i deterministically prefers v in phase $r + 1$. By Lemma 14.7, no processor decides on $\bar{v}$ in phase r.

Assume, by way of contradiction, that some processor p_j deterministically prefers $\bar{v}$ in phase $r + 1$. But then p_i sees $n - f$ processors with outcome value v, and p_j sees $n - f$ processors with outcome value $\bar{v}$. However, $2(n - f) > n$, since $n \geq 2f + 1$; thus, some processor sent $\langle \mathsf{outcome} \rangle$ messages for both v and $\bar{v}$, which is a contradiction. $\qquad\square$

Assume that r_0 is the earliest phase in which some processor, say p_i, decides on some value, say v. By Lemma 14.8, no nonfaulty processor decides on $\bar{v}$ in phase r_0; by the minimality of r_0, no nonfaulty processor decides on $\bar{v}$ in any earlier phase. Lemma 14.7 implies that all nonfaulty processors prefer v in round $r_0 + 1$, and finally, Lemma 14.6 implies that all nonfaulty processors decide on v no later than round $r_0 + 1$. Thus the algorithm satisfies the *agreement* condition:

Lemma 14.9 *If some processor decides on v then all nonfaulty processors eventually decide on v.*

In fact, all nonfaulty processors decide on v no later than one phase later. The algorithm, as presented so far, requires processors to continue even after they decide; however, the last observation implies that a processor need only participate in the algorithm for one more phase after deciding. (See Exercise 14.12.)

To bound the expected time complexity of the algorithm, we prove that the probability of deciding in a certain phase is at least ρ, the bias of the common coin.

Lemma 14.10 *For any $r \geq 1$, the probability that all nonfaulty processors decide by phase r is at least ρ.*

Proof. We consider two cases.

Case 1: All nonfaulty processors set their preference for phase r to the return value of the common coin. The probability that all nonfaulty processors obtain the same value from the common coin is at least 2ρ—with probability ρ they all obtain 0 and with probability ρ they all obtain 1, and these two events are disjoint. In this case, all processors prefer v in phase r, so they decide at the end of phase r, by Lemma 14.6.

Case 2: Some processor deterministically prefers v in phase r. Then no processor deterministically prefers $\bar{v}$ in phase r, by Lemma 14.8. Thus each processor that reaches phase r either decides on v in phase $r - 1$, or deterministically prefers v in phase r, or uses the common coin to set its preference for phase r. In the latter case, with probability at least ρ, the return value of the common coin of phase r is v for all processors. Thus, with probability at least ρ, all processors that reach phase r prefer v in phase r, and, by Lemma 14.6, all nonfaulty processors decide on v in phase r. $\qquad\square$

Theorem 14.11 *If Algorithm 44 uses a common coin procedure with bias ρ, whose expected time complexity is T, then the expected time complexity of Algorithm 44 is $O(\rho^{-1}T)$.*

Algorithm 45 Procedure common-coin: code for processor p_i, $0 \leq i \leq n-1$.

1: when common-coin() is invoked:

2: $\quad c := \begin{cases} 0 & \text{with probability } \frac{1}{n} \\ 1 & \text{with probability } 1 - \frac{1}{n} \end{cases}$

3: $\quad$ $coins := \mathsf{get\text{-}core}(\langle \mathsf{flip}, c \rangle)$

4: $\quad$ if there exists j such that $coins[j] = 0$ then return 0

5: $\quad$ else return 1

Proof.   First note that when $n \geq 2f + 1$, procedure get-core takes $O(1)$ time.

By Lemma 14.10, the probability of terminating after one phase is at least ρ. Therefore, the probability of terminating after i phases is at least $(1 - \rho)^{i-1}\rho$. Therefore, the number of phases until termination is a geometric random variable whose expected value is ρ^{-1}.

Clearly, the time complexity of the common coin procedure dominates the time complexity of a phase. Thus each phase requires $O(T)$ expected time and therefore, the expected time complexity of the algorithm is $O(\rho^{-1}T)$. $\square$

14.3.2 A Common Coin with Constant Bias

As mentioned before, there is a simple f-resilient common coin algorithm with bias 2^{-n} and constant running time, for every $f < n$; each processor outputs a random bit with uniform distribution. Clearly, with probability 2^{-n} the value of the common coin for all processors is v, for any $v = 0, 1$. The expected time complexity of Algorithm 44 when using this coin is $O(2^n)$, by Theorem 14.11.

To get constant expected time complexity, we present an implementation for the procedure common-coin with constant bias. The different invocations of common-coin in the different phases of Algorithm 44 need to be distinguished from each other; this can be achieved by adding the phase number to the messages.

We present a common coin algorithm with bias $\frac{1}{4}$; the algorithm tolerates $\lceil \frac{n}{2} \rceil - 1$ crash failures. The key idea of the common coin algorithm is to base the value of the common coin on the local (independent) coin flips of a set of processors. Procedure get-core (from the previous section) is used to ensure that there is a large *core* set of processors whose local coin flips are used by all nonfaulty processors; this increases the probability that nonfaulty processors obtain the same return value for the common coin.

Processors begin the algorithm by randomly choosing 0 or 1 (with carefully selected asymmetric probabilities) and exchange their flips by using get-core. Processor p_i returns 0 for the common coin procedure if it received at least one 0 flip; otherwise, it returns 1. The pseudocode appears in Algorithm 45.

The correctness of the algorithm depends on all processors executing it; we can modify Algorithm 44 so that the procedure is executed in every phase, regardless of whether the processor needs the coin in that phase.

The common coin procedure assumes that the channels are secure and cannot be read by the adversary—only the recipient of a message can learn its contents. This assumption corresponds to a weak adversary, that is, one that takes as input the pattern of messages, but not their contents; because the message pattern is the same regardless of the random choices, the adversary can obtain no information at runtime about the random choices.

Lemma 14.12 *Algorithm 45 implements a* $(\lceil \frac{n}{2} \rceil - 1)$*-resilient coin with bias* $\frac{1}{4}$*.*

Proof. Fix any admissible adversary and initial configuration. All probabilities are calculated with respect to them.

First we show that the probability that all nonfaulty processors see the coin as 1 is at least $\frac{1}{4}$. This probability is at least the probability that every processor that executes Line 1 obtains 1. (Of course, there are other cases in which all nonfaulty processors terminate with 1, but it is sufficient to consider only this case.) The probability that an arbitrary processor obtains 1 in Line 1 is $1 - \frac{1}{n}$, and thus the probability that every processor that executes Line 1 obtains 1 is at least $(1 - \frac{1}{n})^n$, because the different processors' random choices are independent. For $n \geq 2$, the function $(1 - \frac{1}{n})^n$ is increasing up to its limit of e^{-1}. When $n = 2$, this function is $\frac{1}{4}$ and we are done.

To show the probability that all nonfaulty processors see the coin as 0 is at least $\frac{1}{4}$, consider the set C of core processors, whose existence is guaranteed by Lemma 14.5. Since every processor that returns from Algorithm 45 observes the random choices of all processors in C, all nonfaulty processors see the coin as 0 if some processor in C obtains 0 in Line 1.

The probability that some processor in C gets a 0 in Line 1 is $1 - (1 - \frac{1}{n})^{|C|}$, which is more than $1 - (1 - \frac{1}{n})^{n/2}$. To verify that this last expression is at least $\frac{1}{4}$, it suffices to verify that $(1 - \frac{1}{n})^n \leq (\frac{3}{4})^2$. Since $(1 - \frac{1}{n})^n$ is increasing up to its limit, we must verify that the limiting value e^{-1} is at most $(\frac{3}{4})^2$. This holds since $e^{-1} \approx 0.46$ and $(\frac{3}{4})^2 \approx 0.56$. $\qquad\square$

Note that the time complexity of the common coin algorithm is $O(1)$. Because Algorithm 45 provides a $(\lceil \frac{n}{2} \rceil - 1)$-resilient common coin with bias $\frac{1}{4}$, Theorem 14.11 implies:

Theorem 14.13 *If* $n \geq 2f + 1$*, then there is a randomized consensus algorithm with* $O(1)$ *expected time complexity that can tolerate* f *crash failures in an asynchronous system.*

14.3.3 Tolerating Byzantine Failures

In this section, we describe modifications to the previous algorithm to tolerate Byzantine failures.

The first modification is to the broadcast primitive employed. Instead of using the basic broadcast from Chapter 8, we will use failure model simulations from Chapter 12. The first step is to mask the potential two-faced behavior of the Byzantine processors with the asynchronous identical Byzantine failures simulation (Algorithm 39). On top of that, we will need a validation procedure to eliminate inappropriate messages and simulate asynchronous omission failures; the synchronous validate procedure (from Algorithm 37) can be modified to work in the asynchronous case.

The second modification is to use a common coin procedure that tolerates f Byzantine failures with bias ρ. The simple common coin algorithm, in which each processor flips a local coin, tolerates any number of Byzantine failures with an exponential bias. However, the exponentially small bias leads to exponentially large expected time complexity for the resulting algorithm. The running time is dramatically improved if a common coin with constant bias is used. Implementing a common coin with constant bias that tolerates Byzantine failures requires sophisticated techniques; for more details, see the chapter notes.

We leave it to the reader as an exercise to prove that the modified Algorithm 44 solves randomized consensus in the presence of f Byzantine failures. Moreover, if the expected time complexity of the common coin algorithm is T, then the expected time complexity of the randomized consensus algorithm is $\rho^{-1}T$. (See Exercise 14.13.)

The proof of the lower bound of Chapter 5 (Theorem 5.8) can be extended to prove that randomized consensus is possible only if $n \geq 3f + 1$. Thus the algorithm sketched in this section is optimal in the number of processors.

14.3.4   Shared Memory Systems

We now discuss how randomized consensus can be achieved in shared memory systems.

One possible way is to run the algorithms for message-passing systems by using some simple simulation, for example, the one described in Section 5.3.3, in a shared memory system. This approach suffers from two major shortcomings: First, the resulting algorithms are not wait-free, that is, they tolerate only $n/2$ failures at best; in message-passing systems we cannot hope to tolerate more failures, but this is not the case in shared memory systems. Second, because we only care about tolerating crash failures in shared memory systems, the algorithm can cope with stronger adversaries, such as those that have access to the local states and the contents of shared memory.

Interestingly, randomized consensus algorithms for shared memory systems have a general structure very similar to that of the message-passing algorithms.

Again, we have a deterministic algorithm that operates in (asynchronous) phases: A processor has a preference for decision at each phase; the processor announces its preference and it checks to see whether there is support for some decision value; if there is strong support for some value, the processor decides on it; if there is weak support for some value, the processor takes this value as preference to the next phase; if no single value has support, then the processor flips a coin (typically using some common coin procedure) to get a preference for the next phase.

Unlike the message-passing algorithms, because the algorithm has to be wait-free, we cannot count on the existence of a certain number of nonfaulty processors in each phase. Therefore, support level is not determined by the number of votes for a value, but rather according to the largest phase in which some processor prefers this value. We do not discuss further details of this scheme here, and refer the reader to the chapter notes.

A simple common coin with exponential bias can be implemented by independent coin flips, as described for message-passing systems. More sophisticated techniques are required to obtain constant bias; they are also discussed in the chapter notes.

Exercises

14.1 Prove that every processor terminates Algorithm 41 after sending n messages.

14.2 Prove that at most one processor terminates Algorithm 41 as a leader.

14.3 Modify Algorithm 41 so that each message contains a single pseudo-identifier: The termination condition for the algorithm (Lines 6 and 7) needs to be modified.

14.4 Prove that both the one-shot and the iterated synchronous leader election algorithms (Algorithm 41 and its extension) have the same performance in the asynchronous case as they do in the synchronous.

14.5 Show that for synchronous anonymous ring algorithms, there is only a single adversary.

14.6 Complete the details of the proof of Theorem 14.3.

Try to prove a stronger result showing that there is no randomized leader election algorithm that knows n within a factor larger than 2. Formally, prove that there is no randomized leader election algorithm that works both for rings of size n and for rings of size $2n$.

14.7 Calculate the average message complexity of the randomized consensus algorithm (Algorithm 44), given a common coin with bias $\rho > 0$.

14.8 Calculate the average message complexity of the common coin procedure of Algorithm 45.

14.9 Prove that $n \geq 2f + 1$ is a necessary condition for solving randomized consensus in an asynchronous systems, in the presence of f crash failures.

Hint: Modify the proof for Theorem 10.22.

14.10 Prove Lemma 14.4.

14.11 Suppose we have a more restricted model, in which processors can choose random values only with uniform probability distributions (on a bounded range). Show how to pick 0 with probability $1/n$ and 1 with probability $1 - 1/n$, as needed for Algorithm 45.

14.12 Modify the pseudocode of Algorithm 44 so that processors terminate one phase after deciding. Prove that the modified algorithm solves randomized consensus.

14.13 Extend Algorithm 44 to tolerate $f > n/3$ Byzantine failures, using asynchronous identical Byzantine failures and a modified version of validate from Chapter 12. Assume the existence of a common coin procedure that tolerates f Byzantine failures, with bias ρ.

14.14 Prove that randomized consensus with probability 1 is possible only if $n \geq 3f + 1$, when there are Byzantine failures.

Hint: Extend the proof of Theorem 5.8, noting that every finite execution has at least one extension that terminates.

Chapter Notes

The book on randomized algorithms by Motwani and Raghavan [194] includes a chapter on distributed algorithms. The survey by Gupta, Smolka, and Bhaskar [127] covers randomized algorithms for dining philosophers, leader election, message routing, and consensus.

Itai and Rodeh [141] were the first to study randomized algorithms for leader election; the proof showing nonexistence of a uniform leader election algorithm in an anonymous ring is taken from their paper. In fact, they show that a necessary and sufficient condition for the existence of a randomized leader election algorithm for anonymous rings is knowing the number of processors on the ring within a factor of two (Exercise 14.6). Higham's thesis [136] describes improved algorithms and lower bounds for leader election and computation of other functions on rings.

Randomized leader election algorithms for systems with general topology were presented by Schieber and Snir [234] and by Afek and Matias [6].

An algorithm for mutual exclusion with small shared variables was suggested by Rabin [223]; this algorithm has average waiting time depending on m, the number of processors actually contending for the critical section, and requires a $O(\log \log n)$-bit shared variable. The algorithm we presented has average waiting time depending on n, the number of processors, and uses a constant-size shared variable; this algorithm appears in [223] and is credited to Ben-Or. Saias [232] has shown that the adversary can increase the expected waiting time of a processor, showing that the original algorithm of Rabin did not have the claimed properties. Kushilevitz and Rabin [151] have shown how to overcome this problem; Kushilevitz, Mansour, Rabin, and Zuckerman [150] proved lower bounds on the size of shared variables required for providing low expected bounded waiting.

The first randomized algorithm for consensus in an asynchronous message-passing system was suggested by Ben-Or [48]; this algorithm tolerated Byzantine failures and required $n > 5f$; its expected running time was exponential. A long sequence of randomized algorithms for consensus followed, solving the problem under different assumptions about the adversary, the failure type, the ratio of faulty processors, and more. A survey by Chor and Dwork [80] describes this research prior to 1988. Aspnes [21] surveys later advances in this area.

In 1988, Feldman and Micali [104] presented the first algorithm that tolerates a linear fraction of Byzantine failures with constant expected time; they presented a synchronous algorithm requiring $n > 3f$ and an asynchronous algorithm requiring $n > 4f$. The best asynchronous algorithm known to date, due to Canetti and Rabin [65], tolerates Byzantine failures with constant expected time and only requires $n > 3f$.

Our presentation follows Canetti and Rabin's algorithm, simplified to handle only crash failures; the procedure for obtaining a core set of values was suggested by Eli Gafni. The deterministic voting scheme of Canetti and Rabin's algorithm is inspired by Bracha [60]. Bracha's algorithm uses a simulation of identical Byzantine failures together with a validation (as in Chapter 12); Bracha's paper includes the answer to Exercise 14.13. Canetti and Rabin, on the other hand, embed explicit validation in their algorithm.

There is no upper bound on the running time of the consensus algorithm presented here that holds for *all* executions. Goldreich and Petrank [123] showed how to obtain a synchronous consensus algorithm (for Byzantine failures) that has constant expected time complexity and is guaranteed to terminate within $f + 2$ rounds.

There are also many randomized consensus algorithms for shared memory systems. Although there are many similarities in the overall structure, the common coin is typically implemented using different techniques than those in message-passing systems. These algorithms are wait-free but do not have to tolerate Byzantine failures. Therefore, they can withstand a strong adversary, which can observe the local states and the shared memory. Against such an adversary, cryptographic techniques are not helpful.

The first randomized consensus algorithm for shared memory systems was given by Chor, Israeli, and Li [81]; this algorithm assumed an adversary that cannot read the local states of processors. Later, Abrahamson [1] presented the first algorithm that can withstand a strong adversary. This was followed by a number of algorithms; to date, the best algorithm that tolerates a strong adversary is due to Aspnes and Waarts [23]. Aspnes [20] proved a lower bound on the number of coin flips needed for solving consensus.

The algorithms presented here demonstrate a general methodology for using randomization safely. A deterministic mechanism guarantees the safety properties regardless of the adversary (mostly as a separate module), for example, having only a single leader or having agreement and validity; randomization enters the algorithm only to guarantee liveness properties, for example, termination or bounded waiting.

15

Wait-Free Simulations of Arbitrary Objects

The results of Chapter 5 indicate that read/write registers memory do not suffice for wait-free coordination among processors; for example, consensus cannot be solved by using only reads and writes. Indeed, most modern and proposed multiprocessors provide some set of "stronger" hardware primitives for coordination. But are these primitives sufficient? Can they be used to provide a wait-free (fault tolerant) simulation of any desired high-level object in software?

In Chapter 10, we saw how stronger shared objects can be simulated with simpler shared objects, in a manner that is wait-free. A closer look at the objects studied in that chapter reveals that the operations they support involve either reading or writing portions of the shared memory. They differ in their size (whether the values read are binary or can take arbitrary values), in their access pattern (whether a single processor or several processors can read or write a location), and in their read granularity (whether a single location or several locations are read in a single step). However, none of them allows a processor to read and write in an atomic step, as happens in a *read-modify-write* or *test&set* operation.

In this chapter, we show that this is inherent, that is, that some shared objects cannot be simulated with other shared objects, in a wait-free manner. We investigate the following question: Given two types of (linearizable) shared objects, X and Y, is there a wait-free simulation of object type Y using only objects of type X and read/write objects? It turns out that the answer depends on whether X and Y can be used to solve the consensus problem.

Slightly weaker than wait-free simulations are nonblocking simulations. The idea of a *nonblocking* simulation is that, starting at any point in an admissible execution in which some high-level operations are pending, there is a finite sequence of steps by a single processor that will complete one of the pending operations. It is not necessarily the processor taking the steps whose operation is completed—it is possible that this processor will make progress on behalf of another processor while being unable to finish its own operation. However, this definition is not quite correct. For an operation to complete, technically speaking, the invoking processor has to do at least one step, the response. That is, another processor cannot totally complete an operation for another. To avoid this problem, we specify that an operation is *pending* if its response is not enabled.

The nonblocking condition is a global progress property that applies to the whole system, not to individual processors. The distinction between wait-free and non-blocking algorithms is similar to the distinction between no-lockout and no-deadlock algorithms for mutual exclusion.

We start this chapter by considering a specific object, the FIFO queue, and then extend the results to arbitrary objects. For convenience, we often identify an object type with the operations that can be applied to its instances.

15.1 EXAMPLE: A FIFO QUEUE

The approach we take is to compare the objects by their ability to support a wait-free consensus algorithm among a certain number of processors. To gain intuition, let us consider, first, a specific object, namely a FIFO queue, and see which objects cannot simulate it and which objects cannot be simulated with it. This example illustrates many of the general ideas we discuss later; furthermore, the FIFO queue is an important data structure widely used in operating systems software.

By the methodology of Chapter 7, the specification of a FIFO queue Q is as follows. The operations are [enq(Q, x),ack(Q)] and [deq(Q),return(Q, x)], where x can be any value that can be stored in the queue (x can be $\perp$ for the return). The set of allowable operation sequences consists of all sequences of operations that are consistent with the usual semantics of a sequential FIFO queue, namely, values are dequeued in the order in which they were enqueued. The events on FIFO queues are enq, deq, ack, and return.

Recall, from Chapter 5, that there is no wait-free consensus algorithm for any number of processors greater than one if we only have read/write objects. We now show that there is a wait-free consensus algorithm for two processors p_0 and p_1, using a FIFO queue and read/write objects.

The algorithm uses two read/write objects and one shared FIFO queue Q that initially holds 0. Processor p_i writes its input to a shared read/write object *Prefer*[i] and then dequeues the queue. If the dequeued value is 0, then p_i accessed the queue before the other processor did and is the "winner," and it decides on its own input. Otherwise p_i "lost" to the other processor and it reads *Prefer*[$1 - i$] and decides on that value (see pseudocode in Algorithm 46). The correctness of the algorithm is left as an exercise.

Lemma 15.1 *Algorithm 46 solves consensus for two processors.*

Algorithm 46 Consensus algorithm for two processors, using a FIFO queue: code for processor p_i, $i = 0, 1$.

Initially $Q = \langle 0 \rangle$ and $Prefer[i] = \bot$, $i = 0, 1$

1:   $Prefer[i] := x$ // write your input
2:   $val := \mathsf{deq}(Q)$
3:   if $val = 0$ then $y := x$ // dequeued the first element, decide on your input
4:   else $y := Prefer[1 - i]$ // decide on other's input

If there was a wait-free simulation of FIFO queues with read/write objects, then there would be a wait-free consensus algorithm, for two processors, using only read/write objects. Because there is no such algorithm, an immediate implication is:

Theorem 15.2 *There is no wait-free simulation of a FIFO queue with read/write objects for any number of processors.*

This is a special case of a general theorem we present below (Theorem 15.5).

There are objects that admit wait-free consensus algorithms for any number of processors, for example, *compare&swap*. It is simplest to present the sequential specification of a compare&swap object by the following procedure:

compare&swap(X : memory address; *old* , *new* : value) returns value
     previous : $= X$
     if *previous* = *old* then $X := new$
     return *previous*

Algorithm 47 solves consensus for any number of processors, using a single compare&swap object. The object, called *First*, is initially $\bot$. Processor p_i performs compare&swap on *First*, trying to store its own input, x_i in it, if *First* is still initialized. If the operation is successful, that is, if it returns $\bot$, the processor decides on its own input; otherwise, the compare&swap operation returns the input value, v, of some processor, and processor p_i decides on v.

On the other hand, FIFO queue objects (and read/write objects) cannot support a wait-free consensus algorithm for three processors or more.

Theorem 15.3 *There is no n-processor wait-free consensus algorithm using only FIFO queues and read/write objects, if $n \geq 3$.*

Proof. We must show that there is no three-processor consensus algorithm using queues and read/write objects in an asynchronous system in which up to two processors can fail. The proof of this theorem has the same structure as the proof of Theorem 5.18.

Assume, in contradiction, that there is such an algorithm for three processors, p_0, p_1, and p_2. Because shared objects are linearizable, we shall simplify our notation by combining invocations and matching responses on a shared object into a single step by the processor.

Algorithm 47 Consensus algorithm for any number of processors, using compare&swap: code for processor p_i, $0 \leq i \leq n - 1$.

Initially *First* = $\perp$

1:   $v := \text{compare\&swap}(First, \perp, x)$
2:   if $v = \perp$ then   // this is the first compare&swap
3:       $y := x$ // decide on your own input
4:   else $y := v$ // decide on someone else's input

By Lemma 5.16, the algorithm has an initial bivalent configuration, B.

As in the proof of Theorem 5.18, we let p_0, p_1, and p_2 take steps until we reach a critical configuration, C, such that $p_0(C)$, $p_1(C)$, and $p_2(C)$ are all univalent. Note that they cannot all have the same value, or C would not be bivalent. Without loss of generality, assume that $p_0(C)$ is 0-valent and $p_1(C)$ is 1-valent (see Fig. 15.1).

What are p_0 and p_1 doing in their steps from C? If p_0 and p_1 access different variables or access the same read/write object, then we can employ arguments similar to those used in the proof of Theorem 5.18 to derive a contradiction. So, the interesting case is when p_0 and p_1 access the same FIFO queue object, Q. We consider three cases.

Case 1: p_0 and p_1 both dequeue from Q. In this case, $p_0(C) \overset{p_2}{\sim} p_1(C)$. Since $p_0(C)$ is 0-valent, Lemma 5.15 implies that $p_1(C)$ is also 0-valent, which is a contradiction.

Case 2: p_0 enqueues on Q, and p_1 dequeues from Q (or vice versa). If Q is not empty in C, then in $p_1(p_0(C))$ and $p_0(p_1(C))$ all objects and all processors are in the same state, which is a contradiction since $p_1(p_0(C))$ is 0-valent whereas $p_0(p_1(C))$ is 1-valent.

If Q is empty, then p_1's dequeue in C returns an empty indication, whereas p_1's dequeue in $p_0(C)$ does not return an empty indication; so the previous argument does not apply. However, $p_0(C) \overset{p_2}{\sim} p_0(p_1(C))$. Since $p_1(C)$ is 1-valent, $p_0(p_1(C))$ is also 1-valent, and by Lemma 5.15, $p_0(C)$ is 1-valent, which is a contradiction.

Case 3: p_0 and p_1 both enqueue on Q. Suppose p_0 enqueues a and p_1 enqueues b (see Fig. 15.2). Let $k - 1$ be the number of values in Q in C. Thus in $p_0(C)$ the kth value is a, and in $p_1(C)$ the kth value is b.

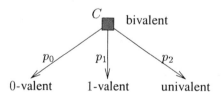

Fig. 15.1   The critical configuration, C.

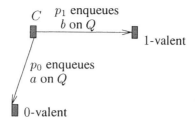

Fig. 15.2   Case 3 in the proof of Theorem 15.3.

We will show that we can run p_0 alone until it dequeues the a and then run p_1 alone until it dequeues the b. This means that even if a and b are enqueued in the opposite order, we can run p_0 alone until it dequeues the b and then run p_1 alone until it dequeues the a. Now p_2 cannot tell the difference between the two possible orders in which a and b are enqueued, which is a contradiction. The details follow.

Starting from $p_1(p_0(C))$, there is a finite p_0-only schedule, σ, that ends with p_0 deciding 0, since $p_0(C)$ is 0-valent and the algorithm is wait-free. We first argue that in σ, p_0 must dequeue the kth element. Suppose otherwise, that in σ, p_0 does fewer than k dequeues on Q, so that it never dequeues the a. Then, when we apply the schedule $p_0\sigma$ to $p_1(C)$, p_0 also decides 0, which contradicts the fact that $p_1(C)$ is 1-valent.

Thus p_0 must perform at least k dequeues on Q in σ. Let σ' be the longest prefix of σ that does not include p_0's kth dequeue on Q.

Starting from $\sigma'(p_1(p_0(C)))$, there is a finite p_1-only schedule τ that ends with p_1 deciding 0. We now argue that p_1 must dequeue from Q at some point in τ. Assume otherwise that p_1 never dequeues from Q in τ; namely, p_1 never dequeues b from the head of Q. Then when we apply the schedule τ to $\sigma'(p_0(p_1(C)))$, p_1 also decides 0, which contradicts the fact that $p_1(C)$ is 1-valent.

Thus it must be that p_1 dequeues from Q in τ. Let τ' be the longest prefix of τ that does not include p_1's dequeue on Q.

Consider two extensions from C (see Fig. 15.3):

First, consider the execution in which p_0 enqueues a on Q; p_1 enqueues b on Q; p_0 only takes steps in σ'; p_0 dequeues the a; p_1 only takes steps in τ'; p_1 dequeues the b. Let D_0 be the resulting configuration.

Second, consider the execution in which p_1 enqueues b on Q; p_0 enqueues a on Q; p_0 only takes steps in σ'; p_0 dequeues the b; p_1 only takes steps in τ'; p_1 dequeues the a. Let D_1 be the resulting configuration.

However, $D_0 \overset{p_2}{\sim} D_1$, and therefore, by Lemma 5.15, they must have the same valence. This is a contradiction since D_0 is reachable from $p_1(p_0(C))$, which is 0-valent, whereas D_1 is reachable from $p_0(p_1(C))$, which is 1-valent. $\square$

This implies:

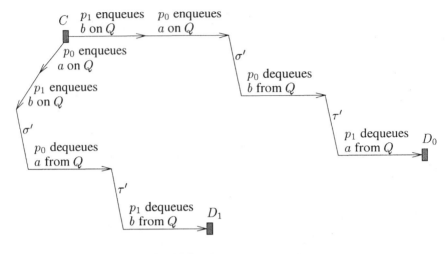

Fig. 15.3 Final stage in Case 3.

Theorem 15.4 *There is no wait-free simulation of a compare&swap object with FIFO queue objects and read/write objects, for three processors or more.*

15.2 THE WAIT-FREE HIERARCHY

The methods used for FIFO queues can be generalized into a criterion for the existence of wait-free simulations. The criterion is based on the ability of the objects to support a consensus algorithm for a certain number of processors.

Object type X *solves wait-free n-processor consensus* if there exists an asynchronous consensus algorithm for n processors, up to $n - 1$ of which might fail (by crashing), using only shared objects of type X and read/write objects.

The *consensus number* of object type X is n, denoted $CN(X) = n$, if n is the largest value for which X solves wait-free n-processor consensus. The consensus number is infinity if X solves wait-free n-processor consensus for every n. Note that the consensus number of an object type X is at least 1, because any object trivially solves wait-free one-processor consensus.

For example, the consensus number of read/write objects is 1. There is a trivial algorithm for one-processor consensus using read/write objects, and back in Chapter 5 we showed that there is no wait-free algorithm for two-processor consensus, using only read/write objects.

As shown in Section 15.1, the consensus number of FIFO queues is 2. Other examples of objects with consensus number 2 are test&set, swap, fetch&add, and stacks.

As implied by Algorithm 15.2, the consensus number of compare&swap is infinity. Other objects with infinite consensus number are memory-to-memory move, memory-to-memory swap, augmented queues, and fetch&cons (see Exercise 15.7). In fact, there is a hierarchy of object types, according to their consensus numbers; in particular, there are objects with consensus number m, for any m (see Exercise 15.8).

The consensus number of objects is interesting because of Theorem 15.5, which is the key result of this section.

Theorem 15.5 *If $CN(X) = m$ and $CN(Y) = n > m$, then there is no wait-free simulation of Y with X and read/write registers in a system with more than m processors.*

Proof. Suppose, in contradiction, that there is a wait-free simulation of Y with X and read/write registers in a system with $k > m$ processors. Denote $l = \min\{k, n\}$, and note that $l > m$. We argue that there exists a wait-free l-processor consensus algorithm using objects of type X and read/write objects.

Note that even if $l < k$, then there is also a wait-free simulation of Y with X in a system with l processors. Such a simulation can be achieved by employing $k - l$ "fictitious" processors, that never access the object Y.

Since $l \leq n$, there exists a wait-free l-processor consensus algorithm, A, which uses only objects of type Y and read/write objects. We can obtain another algorithm A' by replacing each type Y object with a wait-free simulation of it using objects of type X and read/write objects. Such a wait-free simulation of type Y objects exists, by assumption.

Then A' is a wait-free l-processor consensus algorithm using objects of type X and read/write objects. Therefore, X has consensus number at least $l > m$, which is a contradiction. $\square$

Corollary 15.6 *There is no wait-free simulation of any object with consensus number greater than 1 using read/write objects.*

Corollary 15.7 *There is no wait-free simulation of any object with consensus number greater than 2 using FIFO queues and read/write objects.*

15.3 UNIVERSALITY

In Section 15.2, we have used the consensus number of objects to prove that certain objects cannot be wait-free simulated by other objects, that is, to show impossibility results. It turns out the consensus number can also be used to derive positive results, that is, wait-free simulations of objects, as shown in this section.

An object is *universal* if it, together with read/write registers, wait-free simulates any other object. In this section we show that any object X whose consensus number is n is universal in a system of at most n processors. Somewhat counter-intuitively, this does not imply, say, that X is universal in any system with $m > n$ processors; this and other anomalies of the notion of universality are discussed in the chapter notes.

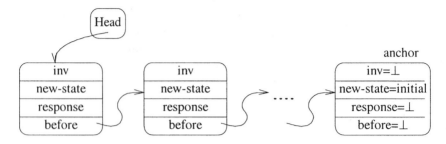

Fig. 15.4   Data structures for nonblocking simulation using compare&swap.

We prove this result by presenting a *universal* algorithm for wait-free simulating any object using only objects of type X and read/write registers. First, we present a universal algorithm for any object in a system of n processors using only n-processor *consensus objects* and read/write registers. Informally speaking, n-processor consensus objects are data structures that allow n processors to solve consensus; a more precise specification appears below. We then use X to simulate n-processor consensus objects.

15.3.1   A Nonblocking Simulation Using Compare&Swap

We start with a simple universal algorithm that is nonblocking but not wait-free. Furthermore, this algorithm uses a specific universal object, that is, compare&swap. This will introduce the basic ideas of the universal algorithm; later, we show how to use a generic consensus object and how to make the algorithm wait-free.

The idea is to represent an object as a shared linked list, which contains the ordered sequence of operations applied to the object. To apply an operation to the object, a processor has to thread it at the head of the linked list. A compare&swap object is used to manage the head of the list. Specifically, an operation is represented by a shared record of type *opr* with the following components:

inv:	The operation invocation, including its parameters
new-state:	The new state of the object, after applying the operation
response:	The response of the operation, including its return value
before:	A pointer to the record of the previous operation on the object

In addition, a compare&swap variable, called *Head*, points to the *opr* record of the last operation applied to the object. The initial value of the object is represented by a special anchor record, of type *opr*, with *new-state* set to the initial state of the object. Initially, *Head* points to the anchor record.

The *Head* pointer, the *opr* records, and their *before* pointers comprise the object's representation (see Fig. 15.4).

To perform an operation, a processor allocates an *opr* record, initializing it to the appropriate values, using the state information in the record at the *Head* of the list.

Algorithm 48 A nonblocking universal algorithm using compare&swap:
code for processor p_i, $0 \leq i \leq n - 1$.

Initially *Head* points to the anchor record

1: when *inv* occurs: // operation invocation, including parameters
2:      allocate a new *opr* record pointed to by *point* with *point.inv* := *inv*
3:      repeat
4:          *h* := *Head*
5:          *point.new-state*, *point.response* := apply(*inv*,*h*.*new-state*)
6:          *point.before* := *h*
7:      until compare&swap(*Head*, *h*, *point*) = *h*
8:      enable the output indicated by *point.response*   // operation response

---

Then it tries to thread this record onto the linked list by applying compare&swap to
Head.

In more detail, the compare&swap compares the current *Head* with the value of
Head obtained by the processor when it updated the new *opr* record. If the compare
finds that they are the same, implying that no new operation record has been threaded
in the meantime, then the swap causes *Head* to point to the processor's *opr* record.
Otherwise, the processor again reads *Head*, updates its new record, and tries the
compare&swap.

The pseudocode appears in Algorithm 48. It uses the function apply, which
calculates the result of applying an operation to the current state of the object. The
notation $X.v$, where X is a pointer to a record, refers to the v field of the record
pointed to by X.

Proving that Algorithm 48 simulates the object is straightforward. The desired
linearization is derived from the ordering of operations in the linked list.

The algorithm is nonblocking—if a processor does not succeed in threading its
operation on the linked list, it must be that some other processor's compare&swap
operation succeeded, that is, another processor has threaded its operation on the list.
Note that the algorithm is not wait-free because the same processor might succeed in
applying its operation again and again, locking all other processors out of access to
the shared object.

15.3.2 A Nonblocking Algorithm Using Consensus Objects

Algorithm 48 has three shortcomings: first, it uses compare&swap objects, rather
than arbitrary consensus objects; second, it is nonblocking, rather than wait-free;
and third, it uses an unbounded amount of memory. We now address each of these
problems, incrementally presenting the algorithm.

First, we show how to replace the compare&swap operations with an arbitrary consensus object. A *consensus object Obj* provides a single operation [decide(*Obj*, *in*),
return(*Obj*, *out*)], where *in* and *out* are taken from some domain of values. The set

of operation sequences consists of all sequences of operations in which all *out* values are equal to some *in* value. Consensus objects provide a data structure version of the consensus problem.

A first attempt might be to replace the *Head* pointer (which is a compare&swap object) with a consensus object. The consensus object will be used to decide which processor will thread its new operation on the list, that is, which operation will be applied next to the shared object being simulated. Note, however, that a consensus object can be used only once; after the first processor wins the consensus and threads its operation, the consensus object will always return the same value. Therefore, the consensus object cannot be used to thread additional records on the list.

The solution is to perform the competition (to decide which processor gets to thread its next operation) on a consensus object associated with the record at the head of the list. That is, we replace the *before* component of the record with a component called *after*, which is a consensus object pointing to the next operation applied to the object. To perform an operation, as in the previous algorithm, a processor creates an *opr* record and tries to thread it to the list. The attempt to thread is done by accessing the consensus object at the head of the list with the pointer to its *opr* record as preference. If it wins the consensus, then its operation has been threaded as the next operation on the simulated object, after the current head of the list. Note that the linked list is directed from the first to the latest entry now, instead of from the latest to the first.

There is one problem with the above idea, namely, how to locate the record at the head of the list. Note that we cannot hold a pointer in a simple read/write object (otherwise, we could wait-free simulate a queue), and a consensus object cannot change with time. This was not a problem in the previous algorithm, because we kept a pointer to the head of the list in a compare&swap object.

The way around this problem is to have each processor maintain a pointer to the last record it has seen at the head of the list. These pointers are kept in a shared array called *Head*. This information might be stale, that is, a processor might thread an operation to the list, save a pointer to the threaded operation in its entry in the *Head* array, and then be suspended for a long time. A processor following this pointer later might end up in the middle of the list because other processors may thread many operations in the meanwhile. So how can a processor know which of these records is the latest? It is not possible to check whether the consensus object *after* is already set, because the consensus object cannot be read without altering its value. Instead, we add sequence numbers to the records on the list. Sequence numbers are assigned so that later operations get higher sequence numbers. The record with the highest sequence number, to which an entry in the *Head* array is pointing, is the latest on the list.

The above ideas lead to the following algorithm, which is a nonblocking simulation of an arbitrary object (for n processors) using n-processor consensus objects. The algorithm augments the record type *opr* so it contains the following components (see Fig. 15.5):

seq: Sequence number (read/write)

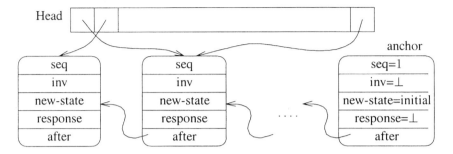

Fig. 15.5 Data structures for nonblocking simulation using consensus objects.

inv: Operation type and parameters (read/write)
new-state: The new state of the object (read/write)
response: The value to be returned by the operation (read/write)
after: Pointer to next record (consensus object)

In addition to the linked list of the operations applied to the object, the algorithm uses a shared array *Head*[0..*n* − 1]; the *i*th entry, *Head*[*i*], is a pointer to the last cell in the list that p_i has observed. Initially, all entries in *Head* point to the anchor record, which has sequence number 1.

The pseudocode appears in Algorithm 49.

Showing that Algorithm 49 simulates the object is rather straightforward. Given an admissible execution α of the algorithm, the desired linearization is derived from the sequence numbers of the records representing operations in the linked list. Clearly, this linearization preserves the semantics of the simulated object, and the relative order of non-overlapping operations.

We now study the progress properties of the algorithm.

For each configuration, C, in α, denote:

$$max\text{-}head(C) = \max\{Head[i].seq \mid 0 \le i \le n - 1\}$$

This is the maximal sequence number of an entry in the *Head* array in the configuration C. We abuse terminology and refer to *Head*[*i*].*seq* as the sequence number of the *i*th entry of the *Head* array.

Inspecting the pseudocode reveals that the sequence number of each entry of the *Head* array is monotonically nondecreasing during the execution. Furthermore, we have the following lemma, whose proof is left as an exercise to the reader (Exercise 15.12):

Lemma 15.8 *If a processor performs ℓ iterations of its repeat loop, then max-head increases at least by ℓ.*

Algorithm 49 A nonblocking universal algorithm using consensus objects: code for processor p_i, $0 \le i \le n - 1$.

Initially $Head[j]$ points to anchor, for all j, $0 \le j \le n - 1$

1:   when *inv* occurs: // operation invocation, including parameters
2:       allocate a new *opr* record pointed to by *point* with *point.inv* := *inv*
3:       for $j := 0$ to $n - 1$ do   // find record with highest sequence number
4:          if $Head[j].seq > Head[i].seq$ then $Head[i] := Head[j]$
5:       repeat
6:          *win* := decide($Head[i].after,point$)   // try to thread your record
7:          *win.seq* := $Head[i].seq + 1$
8:          *win.new-state*, *win.response* := apply($win.inv,Head[i].new\text{-}state$)
9:          $Head[i] := win$ // point to the record at the head of the list
10:     until *win* = *point*
11:     enable the output indicated by *point.response*   // operation response

---

Therefore, if processor p_i performs an unbounded number of steps, then *max-head* is not bounded. This implies that *max-head* is nondecreasing during the execution; furthermore, if α is infinite, then *max-head* is not bounded.

The above observation can be used to show that the algorithm is nonblocking. Assume that some processor, p_i, performs an unbounded number of steps, without threading its operation to the list. Then *max-head* increases without bound, and therefore, the sequence numbers are increasing. It follows that other processors succeed in threading their operations to the list.

The algorithm is still not wait-free because the same processor might succeed in applying its operation again and again, locking all other processors out of access to the shared object.

15.3.3   A Wait-Free Algorithm Using Consensus Objects

As mentioned, the algorithm of the previous section is nonblocking, and it is possible that a processor will never get to thread its *opr* record to the linked list. To make the algorithm wait-free, we use the method of *helping*. This method means performing the operations of other processors, not letting them be locked out of access to the shared object.

The key to this idea is to know which processors are trying to apply an operation to the object. This is done by keeping an additional shared array $Announce[0..n-1]$; the ith entry of this array, $Announce[i]$, is a pointer to the *opr* record that p_i is currently trying to thread onto the list (see Fig. 15.6). Initially, all entries in *Announce* point to the anchor record, because no processor is trying to thread an operation.

Given that it is known which processors are trying to apply an operation, the first question is how to choose the processor to help, in a way that guarantees that this processor will succeed in applying its operation.

Announce

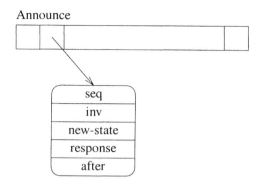

Fig. 15.6 Additional data structures for wait-free simulation using consensus objects.

The idea is to give priority, for each new sequence number, to some processor that has a pending operation. Priority is given in a round-robin manner, using the processors' ids; that is, if processor p_i has a pending operation, then it has priority in applying the kth operation, where $k = i \bmod n$. Thus if the sequence number at the head of the list is $k - 1$, where $k = i \bmod n$, then any competing processor checks whether p_i has a pending operation, and if so, it tries to thread p_i's operation to the list. Clearly, if all competing processors try to thread the same operation, they will succeed in doing so.

A final problem that arises is the issue of coordination between processors that concurrently try to thread the same record to the list. In the simple case in which operations are deterministic, the details of this coordination are relatively simple. In this case, it is safe for different processors to write the new state or the response, because they all write the same value (even if at different times). A processor detects that its operation has been applied to the object, that is, threaded onto the linked list, by seeing an assignment of a nonzero value to the sequence number of the record associated with its operation. Nondeterministic operations are considered in Section 15.3.5.

The pseudocode appears in Algorithm 50.

Fix some execution, α, of the algorithm. Proving that Algorithm 50 simulates the object is done as in the nonblocking algorithm.

Let us argue why the algorithm is wait-free. Assume that p_i tries to apply an operation to the object. Let C_1 be the first configuration after p_i announces its operation, in Line 2. As in the previous algorithm, for any configuration C of α, we denote by $max\text{-}head(C)$ the maximal sequence number of an entry in the *Head* array, in C. As in the previous algorithm, $max\text{-}head$ grows without bound, if some processor performs an unbounded number of steps in α.

Because $max\text{-}head$ grows without bound, let C_2 be the first configuration after C_1 in which $max\text{-}head(C_2) = k = (i + 2) \bmod n$. We argue that p_i's operation is threaded by C_2. Assume not. Then when any processor p_j checks the if condition in Line 7 after configuration C_1, it finds that $Announce[i].seq = 0$. Therefore, all

---

Algorithm 50 A wait-free universal algorithm using consensus objects:
code for processor p_i, $0 \leq i \leq n - 1$.

Initially $Head[j]$ and $Announce[j]$ point to the anchor record,
for all j, $0 \leq j \leq n - 1$

1:	when *inv* occurs:	// operation invocation, with parameters
2:	allocate a new *opr* record pointed to by $Announce[i]$	
	with $Announce[i].inv := inv$ and $Announce[i].seq := 0$	
3:	for $j := 0$ to $n - 1$ do	// find highest sequence number
4:	if $Head[j].seq > Head[i].seq$ then $Head[i] := Head[j]$	
5:	while $Announce[i].seq = 0$ do	
6:	$priority := Head[i].seq+1$ mod n	// id of processor with priority
7:	if $Announce[priority].seq = 0$	// check whether help is needed
8:	then $point := Announce[priority]$	// choose other record
9:	else $point := Announce[i]$	// choose your own record
10:	$win := \mathsf{decide}(Head[i].after, point)$	// try to thread chosen record
11:	$win.new\text{-}state, win.response := \mathsf{apply}(win.inv, Head[i].new\text{-}state)$	
12:	$win.seq := Head[i].seq + 1$	
13:	$Head[i] := win$	// point to the record at the head of the list
14:	enable the output indicated by $win.response$	// operation response

---

processors choose $Announce[i]$ for the $(k + 1)$st decision; by the agreement and
validity properties of the consensus object, they all decide on $Announce[i]$ and thread
p_i's operation.

The above argument can be made more precise to bound the step complexity of the
simulation. As in the algorithm of the previous section, after p_i performs n iterations
of its while loop the value of *max-head* increases at least by n. Because each iteration
of the while loop requires $O(1)$ steps by p_i, a configuration C_2 as above is reached
after p_i performs $O(n)$ steps. This implies:

Theorem 15.9 *There exists a wait-free simulation of any object for n processors,
using only n-processor consensus objects and read/write objects. Each processor
completes any operation within $O(n)$ of its own steps, regardless of the behavior of
other processors.*

The calculations in the above analysis charged one step for each invocation of the
decide operation on the consensus object. A more detailed analysis of the cost should
be based on the step complexity of the decide operation, in terms of operations on
more basic objects.

This shows that Algorithm 50 is a wait-free simulation of an arbitrary object for
n processors, using n-processor consensus objects. We can now state the general
universality result.

Theorem 15.10 *Any object X with consensus number n is universal in a system with at most n processors.*

Proof. Algorithm 50 uses an arbitrary n-processor consensus object to wait-free simulate any object Y in a wait-free manner. We use objects of type X to wait-free simulate the n-processor consensus object. □

15.3.4 Bounding the Memory Requirements

We have presented a wait-free simulation of an arbitrary n-processor object using n-processor consensus objects and read/write objects. In this section, we show how to bound the memory requirements of the construction. Note that there are two types of memory unboundedness in this algorithm: The number of records used to represent an object as well as the values of the sequence numbers grow linearly, without bound, with the number of operations applied to the simulated object. Here, we describe how to control the first type of unboundedness—the number of records; handling the other type of unboundedness—the values of sequence numbers, is not treated here.

The basic idea is to *recycle* the records used for the representation of the object. That is, each processor maintains a pool of records belonging to it; for each operation, the processor takes some free record from its pool and uses it in the previous algorithm; eventually, a record can be reclaimed and reused for another operation. A record can be reclaimed if no processor is going to access it. The main difficulty is knowing which of the records already threaded on the list will not be accessed anymore and can be recycled.

To understand how this is done, we first inspect how records are accessed in Algorithm 50. Note that each of the records already threaded on the list belongs to some processor whose operation it represents. Such a record has an assigned sequence number, which remains fixed for the rest of the execution. Consider some record threaded on the list, belonging to processor p_i, with sequence number k; we refer to it as record number k.

Let p_j be a processor that may access record number k. It follows that $Head[j]$ after Line 4 is less than or equal to k, and therefore, p_j's record is threaded with sequence number $k + n$ or less. Note that p_j's record could be threaded by other processors helping it, yet p_j will not detect it (being inside the while loop) and will try to access record k on the list although its record is already threaded. However, once p_j detects that its record has been threaded, it will never access record k on the list anymore.

The above argument implies that the processors that may access record number k on the list are the processors whose records are threaded as numbers $k + 1, \ldots, k + n$ on the list. These records do not necessarily belong to n different processors but may represent several operations by the same processor. Considered backwards, this means that if p_j's record is threaded as number k', p_j should release records number $k' - 1, \ldots, k' - n$.

We add to the *opr* record type an array, *released*$[1, .., n]$, of binary variables. Before a record is used, all entries of the *released* array are set to *false*. If a record

---

Algorithm 51 A wait-free universal algorithm using consensus objects with bounded memory: code for processor p_i, $0 \le i \le n - 1$.

Initially $Head[j]$ and $Announce[j]$ point to the anchor record, for all j, $0 \le j < n$

```
 1:   when inv occurs:                          // operation invocation, with parameters
 2:       let point point to a record in Pool such that
                point.released[1] = ... =point.released[n] = true
                and set point.inv to inv
 3:       for r := 1 to n do point.released[r] := false
 4:       Announce[i] := point
 5:       for j := 0 to n − 1 do               // find highest sequence number
 6:           if Head[j].seq > Head[i].seq then Head[i] := Head[j]

 7:       while Announce[i].seq = 0 do
 8:           priority := Head[i].seq + 1 mod n      // id of processor with priority
 9:           if Announce[priority].seq = 0           // check whether help is needed
10:               then point := Announce[priority] // choose other processor's record
11:               else point := Announce[i]              // choose your own record
12:           win := decide(Head[i].after,point)        // try to thread chosen record
13:           win.before := Head
14:           win.new-state, win.response := apply(win.inv, Head[i].new-state)
15:           win.seq := Head[i].seq + 1
16:           Head[i] := win                   // point to the record at the head of the list

17:       temp := Announce[i].before
18:       for r := 1 to n do                               // go to n records before
19:           if temp ≠ anchor then
20:               before-temp := temp.before
21:               temp.released[r] := true                    // release record
22:               temp := before-temp

23:       enable output indicated by Announce[i].response
```

---

has been threaded as number k on the list, then $released[r] = true$ means that the processor whose record was threaded as number $k + r$ on the list has completed its operation. When a processor's record is threaded as number k', it sets $released[r] = true$ in record $k' - r$, for $r = 1, \ldots, n$. When $released[r] = true$ for all $r = 1, \ldots, n$, then the record can be recycled.

To allow a processor to move backwards on the list of records, we restore the component *before* to the *opr* record type; when a record is threaded on the list, its *before* component points to the previous record threaded on the list. Now the list is doubly linked. The modified pseudocode appears as Algorithm 51.

We leave the correctness proof (linearizability and wait-freedom) to the reader as an exercise.

To calculate how many records a processor's pool should contain, we need to know how many unreleased records there may be, that is, records with *false* in some entry of their *released* array. Note that if *released*[r] = *false* for record number k on the list, then the record number $k + r$ on the list belongs to an incomplete operation. Because each processor has at most one operation pending at a time, there are at most n records belonging to incomplete operations. Each of these records is responsible for at most n unreleased records. Thus, there are at most n^2 unreleased records. It is possible that all n^2 records belong to the same processor; therefore, each processor needs a pool of $n^2 + 1$ records, yielding a total of $O(n^3)$ records.

15.3.5 Handling Nondeterminism

The universal algorithms described so far assumed that operations on the simulated object are *deterministic*. That is, given the current state of the object and the invocation (the operation to be applied and its parameters), the next state of the object, as well as the return value of the operation, are unique. Many objects have this property, for example, queues, stacks, and read/write objects; however, there are object types with nondeterministic operations, for example, an object representing an unordered set with a *choose* operation returning an arbitrary element of the set. In this section, we outline how to modify the universal algorithm to simulate objects with nondeterministic operations.

For simplicity, we refer to the version of the algorithm that uses unbounded memory (Algorithm 50). Line 11 of this algorithm is where the new state and the response are calculated, based on the current state and the invocation. Because we assumed operations were deterministic, it is guaranteed that any processor applying the invocation to the current state will obtain the same new state and response. Thus it suffices to use read/write objects for the *new-state* and *response* fields of the *opr* record; even if processors write these fields at different times, they will write the same value.

When operations are nondeterministic, it is possible that different processors applying the invocation to the current state will obtain a different new state or response value. If we leave the *new-state* and *response* fields of the *opr* record as read/write objects, it is possible to get inconsistencies as different processors overwrite new (and different) values for the *new-state* or the *response* fields.

The solution is to reach consensus on the new state and the response. We modify the *opr* record type so that the new state and response value are stored jointly in a single consensus object. We replace the simple writing of the *new-state* and *response* fields (in Line 11) with a **decide** operation of the consensus object, using as input the local computation of a new state and response (using **apply**). The rest of the algorithm remains the same.

We leave the details of this algorithm, as well as its proof, to the reader as an exercise.

15.3.6 Employing Randomized Consensus

We can relax the Liveness condition in the definition of a linearizable shared memory (Section 9.1) to be probabilistic, that is, require operations to terminate only with high probability; this way we can define *randomized wait-free* simulations of a shared objects. Because randomized wait-free consensus algorithms can be implemented from read/write objects (see Chapter 14), they can replace the consensus objects in Algorithm 50. Thus there are randomized wait-free simulations of any object from read/write objects, and there is no hierarchy of objects if termination has to be guaranteed only with high probability.

Exercises

15.1 Prove that Algorithm 46 is a wait-free consensus algorithm for two processors. What happens if three processors (or more) use this algorithm?

15.2 Prove that Algorithm 47 is a wait-free consensus algorithm for any number of processors.

15.3 Prove that $CN(\text{test\&set}) = 2$.

15.4 Prove that $CN(\text{stack}) = 2$.

15.5 Prove that $CN(\text{fetch\&inc}) = 2$.

15.6 The wait-free consensus algorithm for two processors using a FIFO queue relies on the fact that the queue was nonempty initially. Present a two-processor wait-free consensus algorithm that uses two queues that are initially empty and read/write objects.

15.7 Show that the consensus number of an augmented queue, which allows peek operations, that is, reading the head of the queue without removing it, is infinite.

15.8 Show that for every integer $m \geq 1$, there exists an object with consensus number m.

Hint: Consider a variation of an augmented queue that can hold up to m values; once a processor attempts to enqueue the $(m + 1)$st value, the queue "breaks" and returns a special $\perp$ response to every subsequent operation.

15.9 Show that consensus numbers also determine the existence of nonblocking simulations. That is, prove that if $CN(X) = m$ and $CN(Y) = n > m$, then there is no nonblocking simulation of Y by X in a system with more than m processors.

15.10 Prove the linearizability property of Algorithm 48.

15.11 Prove the linearizability property of Algorithm 49.

15.12 Prove Lemma 15.8.

15.13 Consider the following modification to Algorithm 50: First try to thread your own operation and only then try to help other processors. Show that the modified algorithm is not wait-free.

15.14 Consider the following modification to Algorithm 50: Add an iteration of the for loop (of Lines 3–4) inside the while loop (of Lines 5–13). What is the step complexity of the new algorithm? Are there situations in which this modification has improved step complexity?

15.15 Present a universal wait-free algorithm for simulating an n-processor object type with nondeterministic operations, using n-processor consensus objects; follow the outline in Section 15.3.5. Present the correctness proof for this algorithm.

15.16 Consider the same modification as in Exercise 15.14 to Algorithm 51: Add an iteration of the for loop (of Lines 5-6) inside the while loop (of Lines 7-16). What is the step complexity of the new algorithm? Are there situations in which this modification has improved step complexity?

15.17 Complete the correctness proof for Algorithm 51.

15.18 Show an execution of Algorithm 51, where n^2 records belonging to the same processor are not released.

15.19 A way to slightly reduce the memory requirements of Algorithm 51 is to have all processors use the same pool of records. Develop the details of this algorithm, which requires $O(n^2)$ records.

Chapter Notes

The results in this chapter indicate that there is a rich hierarchy of object types, and that some objects can be used to solve more problems than others. As mentioned in the introduction to this chapter, modern and proposed multiprocessors typically provide hardware primitives more powerful than just reading and writing. One would like to program at a higher level of abstraction than register operations, using shared objects of arbitrary types. As we have shown, if an object has a low consensus number, then it cannot be used, either alone or with additional read/write registers, to wait-free simulate an object with a high consensus number. Many common objects are universal and can be used to solve consensus among any number of processors, for example, compare&swap, or load-linked and store-conditional. Universal objects are desirable in hardware as they promise solutions for many other problems.

It is tempting to classify object types according to their consensus number. One way to do that, mentioned in passing before, is to organize object types into a *hierarchy*, where level n of the hierarchy contains exactly those objects whose consensus number is n. This classification into levels of a hierarchy is meaningful only if object types at a higher level are somehow "stronger" than object types at lower levels.

The term "robust" has been applied to the notion of a meaningful hierarchy. A reasonable definition of robustness is that objects at a lower level cannot be used to simulate objects at a higher level. In more detail, a hierarchy is defined to be *robust* if any collection of object types $\mathcal{T}$, all at level k (or lower) of the hierarchy, *cannot* wait-free simulate an object type T that is at level $k + 1$ (or higher) of the hierarchy. Jayanti [144] asked whether the wait-free hierarchy is robust and showed that if the consensus number is defined without allowing the use of read/write registers, or by allowing only a single object of the lower type, then the hierarchy is not robust. Our definition of the consensus number is consistent with this result, because it allows read/write registers and multiple objects of the lower type.

It turns out that the answer to the robustness question depends on additional aspects of the model. One aspect is whether operations of the object are deterministic or not; that is, whether the result of applying an operation to the object is unique, given the sequence of operations applied so far. Lo and Hadzilacos [172] showed that if objects are not deterministic, then the hierarchy is not robust. If the objects are deterministic, then the issue of robustness depends on some delicate assumptions concerning the relationships between the processors and the "ports" of the objects. Think of a port as a conduit through which operations can be applied to an object. An object may or may not be able to return different values, depending on which port is in use, and various rules concerning the binding of processors to ports are possible. The complete story has not yet been discovered; see a recent survey [105] for more information and references.

Another reasonable definition of robustness is that objects at a higher level can solve more problems than objects at a lower level. Specifically, consider two object types T and T', such that $CN(T) = m < CN(T') = n$. Under this interpretation, a robust hierarchy would mean that by using T' we can solve a strictly larger set of problems than by using T. However, such a hierarchy does not exist: It was shown by Rachman [224] that for any N, there exists an object type T, which can be accessed by $2N + 1$ processors, whose consensus number is 1; furthermore, T can be used to solve 2-set consensus (defined in Section 16.1) among $2N + 1$ processors. However, any number of N-consensus objects and read/write registers cannot be used to solve 2-set consensus among $2N + 1$ processors. Thus T, an object type at level 1, can be used to solve the 2-set consensus problem, but an object at level N (N-consensus) cannot be used to solve the same problem. This anomalous behavior is possible because the number of processors is larger than the number for which N-consensus is universal.

Most of this chapter is based on Herlihy's work on impossibility and universality of shared objects [134]. Universality results for a specific consensus object (*sticky bits*) were presented by Plotkin [216]. Universality results using *load-linked* and *store-conditional* were presented by Herlihy [131]. Other general simulations were given by Prakash, Lee, and Johnson [219], by Shavit and Touitou [241], and by Turek, Shasha, and Prakash [254].

There have also been suggestions to modify the operating system in order to support more efficient nonblocking simulations of objects; interesting research in this direction was presented by Alemany and Felten [8] and by Bershad [51].

16

Problems Solvable in Asynchronous Systems

The impossibility result proved in Chapter 5 shows that consensus cannot be solved deterministically in failure-prone asynchronous systems. As shown in Chapter 15, the impossibility of solving consensus implies that many other important problems cannot be solved deterministically in failure-prone asynchronous systems. However, there *are* some interesting problems that can be solved in such systems.

In this chapter we survey several such problems. The first problem is *set consensus*, a weakening of the original consensus problem in which a fixed number of different decisions are allowed. We present a lower bound that relates the number of different decisions to the number of processor failures. The second problem is an alternative weakening of consensus, called *approximate agreement*, in which the decisions must lie in a sufficiently small range of each other. The third problem is *renaming*, in which processors must choose new identifiers for themselves. We also discuss *k-exclusion*, a fault-tolerant variant of mutual exclusion in which multiple processes can be in the critical section at a time. Solutions to the renaming problem can be used to solve a variant of *k*-exclusion, in which processes must each occupy a specific "place" in the critical section.

Throughout this chapter we assume the asynchronous shared memory model with crash failures. The maximum number of crash failures allowed in an admissible execution is denoted f. The simulation presented in Chapter 10 (Section 10.4) allows us to translate these results to the message-passing model, with $f < n/2$ crash failures.

16.1 K-SET CONSENSUS

The consensus problem for crash failures (studied in Chapter 5) required that all nonfaulty processors eventually decide on a single value, where that value is one of the original input values. We can loosen this problem statement to require only that the number of different values decided upon by nonfaulty processors be at most some quantity, say k, while still requiring that every decision value be some processor's original input. Obviously, this problem is only challenging to solve if the number of values, k, is less than the number of processors, n; otherwise, the trivial algorithm, in which every processor decides on its input value, is a solution to this problem that tolerates any number of failures. The original consensus problem can be viewed as a special case of this problem, where $k = 1$.

We now give a more formal definition of the *k-set consensus* problem. Each processor p_i has special state components x_i, the *input*, and y_i, the *output*, also called the *decision*. Initially x_i holds a value from some set of possible inputs and y_i is undefined. Any assignment to y_i is irreversible. A solution to the consensus problem must guarantee the following, in every admissible execution:

Termination: For every nonfaulty processor p_i, y_i is eventually assigned a value.

k-Agreement: $|\{y_i : p_i \text{ is nonfaulty}, 0 \le i \le n - 1\}| \le k$. That is, the set of decisions made by nonfaulty processors contains at most k values.

Validity: If y_i is assigned, then $y_i \in \{x_0, \dots, x_{n-1}\}$, for every nonfaulty processor p_i. That is, the output of a nonfaulty processor is one of the inputs.

In this section, we show that the k-set consensus problem is solvable in an asynchronous system subject to crash failures as long as f, the number of failures to be tolerated, is at most $k - 1$. Afterwards, we show that this bound is tight. In the wait-free case, where the number of failures to be tolerated is $n - 1$, it follows that k-set consensus is possible only if $k = n$; in this case, the trivial algorithm, in which each processor decides on its own input, solves the problem.

We now describe a simple algorithm for k-set consensus. This algorithm, like most algorithms in this chapter, is presented for the shared memory model, and employs an atomic snapshot object, as defined in Chapter 10.

The snapshot object initially holds an empty indication in each segment. Each processor p_i writes its input x_i to its segment in the snapshot object; then, it repeatedly scans the snapshot object until it sees at least $n - f$ nonempty segments. Processor p_i decides on the minimum value contained in its last scan of the snapshot object. The pseudocode appears as Algorithm 52. The name of the atomic snapshot object is not explicitly included in the calls to the update and scan procedures.

Theorem 16.1 *Algorithm 52 solves k-set consensus in the presence of f crash failures, where $f \le k - 1$.*

Proof.   We show that the above algorithm solves k-set consensus. Fix an admissible execution of the algorithm.

Algorithm 52 k-set consensus algorithm for $f < k$ failures:
code for processor p_i, $0 \leq i \leq n - 1$.

1:   $\text{update}_i(x)$ // write input value to snapshot segment
2:   repeat
3:       $values := \text{scan}_i()$
4:   until $values$ contains at least $n - f$ nonempty segments
5:   $y := \min(values)$ // decide on smallest element of $values$

Consider any nonfaulty processor p_i. Termination follows since there are at most f crash failures. Because processors fail only by crashing, every value that is ever put into a processor's local variable $values$ is the input value of some processor. Therefore, p_i decides on the input value of some processor, and the validity condition is satisfied.

Let S be the set of all values v such that v is the minimum value contained in the final scan of the snapshot object by some nonfaulty processor. We now prove that the set S contains at most $f + 1$ distinct values. Suppose, in contradiction, that S contains at least $f + 2$ distinct values, and let v be the largest among them. It follows that there are $f + 1$ distinct input values that are strictly smaller than v, say $x_{i_0}, \ldots, x_{i_f}$ (the input values of $p_{i_0}, \ldots, p_{i_f}$). Let p_i be a nonfaulty processor such that v is the minimum value contained in its final scan. Thus p_i's final scan does not include the input values of $p_{i_0}, \ldots, p_{i_f}$, but then p_i's last scan missed at least $f + 1$ input values, which contradicts the code.

Since the set S is exactly the set of decision values of nonfaulty processors, we have just shown that the number of nonfaulty decisions is at most $f + 1$, which is at most k, which implies the k-agreement condition. $\square$

The obvious next question is, what happens when the number of failures exceeds k? Is k-set consensus still solvable? As we shall see next, the answer is negative.

Lower Bound

We now show that there is no algorithm for solving k-set consensus in the presence of $f \geq k$ failures. For $k = 1$, this amounts to the impossibility of solving the consensus problem, proved in Chapter 5. We first prove the lower bound for $k = 2$ and $n = 3$ and later discuss how to extend the result for other values of k and n.

For the purpose of the lower bound, we assume that all communication is via an atomic snapshot object[1] with a single segment for each processor and that an algorithm consists of an alternating sequence of updates to the processor's segment

---

[1] Almost the same proof works if processors communicate by ordinary read and write operations; we assume a snapshot object because it slightly simplifies matters, and to be consistent with the other algorithms in this chapter.

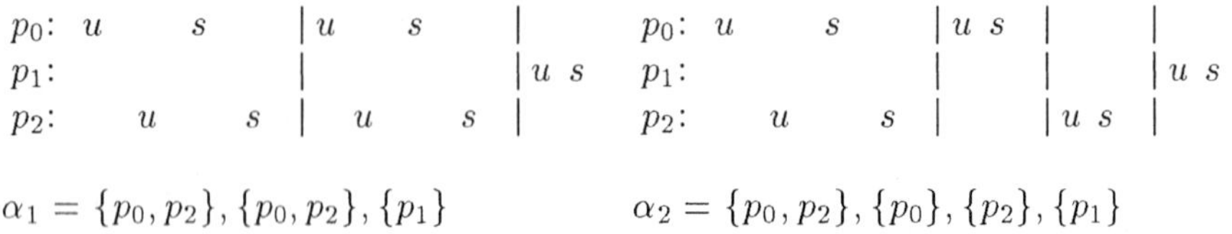

p_0: u s | u s | | p_0: u s | u s | |
p_1: | | u s p_1: | | | u s
p_2: u s | u s | p_2: u s | | u s |

$\alpha_1 = \{p_0, p_2\}, \{p_0, p_2\}, \{p_1\}$ $\alpha_2 = \{p_0, p_2\}, \{p_0\}, \{p_2\}, \{p_1\}$

Fig. 16.1   Two block executions α_1 and α_2; u denotes an update operation and s denotes a scan operation; perpendicular lines separate blocks.

and scans of the snapshot object. Moreover, a processor maintains a local step counter that is written in each update.

A *block B* is an arbitrary nonempty set of processor ids, that is, B is a subset of $\{0, \ldots, n-1\}$. A block B induces a schedule fragment in which, first, each processor in B updates its segment of the snapshot object, and then each processor in B scans the snapshot object. For concreteness, we will assume that the updates are done in increasing order of processor id, as are the scans; however, the internal order of the update operations and the internal order of the scan operations are immaterial, as long as all update operations precede all scan operations.

Fix some *k*-set consensus algorithm A. A *block execution* of A is an execution whose schedule is a sequence of schedule fragments, each of which is induced by a block, and whose initial configuration has each processor starting with its own id as input, that is, p_i starts with $i, 0 \leq i \leq n-1$. Thus a block execution, α, is completely characterized by the sequence of blocks $B_1, B_2, \ldots, B_l$ that induces its schedule. We abuse notation and write $\alpha = B_1, B_2, \ldots, B_l$. For notational convenience, we do not include steps of processors once they have decided.

The lower bound proof considers only admissible block executions of A in which there are no failures. Of course, A has to work correctly for all (admissible) executions, including those with failures, and all inputs; in fact, it is the requirement that A can tolerate failures that allows us to make crucial deductions about block executions with no failures.

Although they are very well-structured, block executions still contain uncertainty, because a processor does not know exactly which processors are in the last block. Specifically, if p_i is in B_k and observes an update by another processor p_j, p_i does not know whether p_j's update is in B_{k-1} or in B_k. Consider, for example, the block executions in Figure 16.1. First note that p_1 and p_2 do not distinguish between α_1 and α_2. However, because each processor increments a counter in each of its steps and includes it in its segment, p_0 distinguishes between α_1 and α_2 — in α_1, p_0 reads the second update of p_2, whereas in α_2, it reads the first update of p_2.

In Chapter 4 we defined the notion of similarity between configurations (Definition 4.1); here, we define an extended notion of similarity between block executions.

Let $\alpha = B_1, \ldots, B_l$; the *view of processor p_i after block B_k* is p_i's state and the state of all shared variables in the configuration after prefix of α that corresponds to $B_1, \ldots, B_k$. The *view of processor p_i in α*, denoted $\alpha|p_i$, is the sequence containing

p_i's view after each block in which p_i appears; $\alpha | p_i$ is empty if p_i does not appear in any block.

Two block executions, α and α', are *similar to some set of processors* P, denoted $\alpha \stackrel{P}{\sim} \alpha'$, if for any processor $p_i \in P$, $\alpha | p_i = \alpha' | p_i$. When $P = \{p_0, \ldots, p_{n-1}\} - \{p_j\}$, we use $\alpha \stackrel{\neg p_j}{\sim} \alpha'$ as a shorthand; for the nontrivial case $\alpha \neq \alpha'$, this means that p_j is the only processor distinguishing between α and α'.

We say that p_j is *unseen* in a block execution α if there exists $k \geq 1$, such that $p_j \notin B_r$ for every $r < k$ and $B_r = \{p_j\}$ for every $r \geq k$. Intuitively, this means that p_j's steps are taken after all other processors decide and none of them ever sees a step by p_j. Note that at most one processor is unseen in a block execution. For example, p_1 is unseen in executions α_1 and α_2 of Figure 16.1.

It is crucial to this proof to understand that it is *possible* to have an unseen processor p_i in an admissible execution of the algorithm A. The reason is that A is supposed to be able to tolerate the failure of (at least) one processor: If p_i takes no steps initially, the other processors must be prepared for the possibility that p_i has failed and thus they must decide without communicating with p_i. After the remaining processors have decided, it is possible for p_i to start taking steps.

Lemma 16.2 *If a processor p_j is unseen in a block execution α then there is no block execution $\alpha' \neq \alpha$ such that $\alpha \stackrel{\neg p_j}{\sim} \alpha'$.*

Proof. Let $\alpha = B_1, B_2, \ldots$. If p_j is unseen in α, then there exists some k such that $p_j \notin B_r$ for every $r < k$ and $B_r = \{p_j\}$ for every $r \geq k$. Assume, by way of contradiction, that there is a block execution $\alpha' = B_1', B_2', \ldots \neq \alpha$, such that $\alpha \stackrel{\neg p_j}{\sim} \alpha'$. Let l be the minimum index such that $B_l \neq B_l'$, that is, the first block in which α and α' differ.

If $l \geq k$ then $B_l = \{p_j\}$ in α, whereas in α', B_l' must include some other processor, p_i; however, p_i distinguishes between α and α', a contradiction. If $l < k$ then $p_j \notin B_l$. Since no processor in B_l distinguishes between α and α', then the same processors must be in B_l', again contradicting the assumption that $B_l \neq B_l'$. $\square$

If p_j is not unseen in α, then it is *seen*. Formally, a processor p_j is *seen in k*, if $p_j \in B_k$, and some processor $p_i \neq p_j$ is in B_r, for some $r \geq k$. If p_j is seen, then p_j is *last seen in k*, if k is the largest index in which p_j is seen. For example, p_0 and p_2 are seen in both α_1 and α_2 (Fig. 16.1); in α_1, p_0 is last seen in B_2.

Lemma 16.3 *If p_j is seen in a block execution α, then there is a unique block execution $\alpha' \neq \alpha$ such that $\alpha' \stackrel{\neg p_j}{\sim} \alpha$.*

Proof. Assume that in $\alpha = B_1, B_2, \ldots$, p_j is last seen in k. It is possible that p_j appears in blocks later than B_k, but in this case α can be written as $\alpha = B_1, \ldots, B_t, \{p_j\}, \ldots, \{p_j\}$. Define a block execution α' as follows:

1. If $B_k \neq \{p_j\}$, then take p_j into an earlier block by itself, that is,

$$\alpha' = B_1, \ldots, B_{k-1}, \{p_j\}, B_k - \{p_j\}, B_{k+1}, \ldots, B_t, \{p_j\}, \ldots, \{p_j\}$$

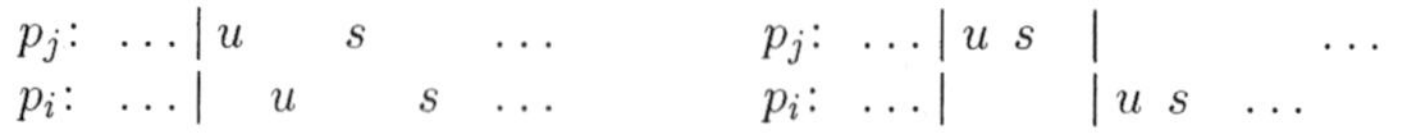

$$p_j: \ \ldots \ | \ u \qquad s \qquad \ldots \qquad\qquad p_j: \ \ldots \ | \ u \ s \ | \qquad\qquad \ldots$$
$$p_i: \ \ldots \ | \qquad u \qquad s \ \ldots \qquad\qquad p_i: \ \ldots \ | \qquad\quad | \ u \ s \ \ldots$$

$$\alpha = B_1, \ldots, B_{k-1}, B_k, B_{k+1}. \qquad \alpha' = B_1, \ldots, B_{k-1}, \{p_j\}, B_k - \{p_j\}, B_{k+1}.$$

Fig. 16.2   Illustration for first case in proof of Lemma 16.3, $B_k = \{p_i, p_j\}$.

where the number of final blocks consisting only of p_j is sufficient for p_j to decide (see Fig. 16.2).

2. If $B_k = \{p_j\}$, then merge p_j with the next block, that is,

$$\alpha' = B_1, \ldots, B_{k-1}, \{p_j\} \cup B_{k+1}, B_{k+2}, \ldots, B_t, \{p_j\}, \ldots, \{p_j\}$$

where the number of final blocks consisting only of p_j is sufficient for p_j to decide.

Clearly, $\alpha' \overset{\neg p_j}{\sim} \alpha$. Since p_j distinguishes between α and α' (Exercise 16.2), we have that $\alpha \neq \alpha'$. We now show that α' is unique.

If $B_k \neq \{p_j\}$ (Case (1)), then clearly, there is another processor $p_i \in B_k$. If $B_k = \{p_j\}$ (Case (2)), then there is another processor $p_i \in B_{k+1}$: B_{k+1} is not empty and does not include p_j. Moreover, if $p_j \in B_r$, for some $r > k$, then $B_{r'} = \{p_j\}$ for every $r' \geq r$ (otherwise, p_j would be last seen in $k - 1$ of α).

In both cases, for any block execution α'' that is neither α nor α', p_i distinguishes between α and α'', which proves the uniqueness of α'.   □

Now construct a graph $\mathcal{B}_n$. The nodes of $\mathcal{B}_n$ correspond to block executions with n processors; since the algorithm is wait-free, there is a finite number of block executions and, therefore, the graph has a finite number of nodes (Exercise 16.5). There is an edge between two nodes corresponding to block executions α and α' if and only if $\alpha \overset{\neg p_j}{\sim} \alpha'$, for some processor p_j; the edge is labeled with p_j. For example, the part of $\mathcal{B}_3$ for the two executions of Figure 16.1 has two nodes, one for α_1 and one for α_2, and an edge between them labeled with p_0 (Fig. 16.3).

By Lemma 16.2, a node with degree $n - 1$ corresponds to a block execution in which some processor p_i is unseen.

By Lemma 16.3, the degree of a node in $\mathcal{B}_n$ that corresponds to a block execution without an unseen processor must be n.

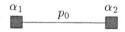

Fig. 16.3   Part of $\mathcal{B}_3$ for the executions of Figure 16.1.

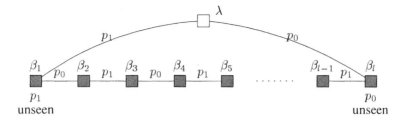

Fig. 16.4 The graph for block executions of two processors, $\hat{\mathcal{B}}_2$, with the imaginary node, λ.

We now color the edges of $\mathcal{B}_n$. If there is an edge between executions α and α' labeled with p_j then, by definition, $\alpha \overset{\neg p_j}{\sim} \alpha'$. Therefore, all processors other than p_j, namely, $p_0, \ldots, p_{j-1}, p_{j+1}, \ldots, p_{n-1}$, decide on the same values in α and in α'. The edge is colored with this set of decisions. Consider, for example, the executions of Figure 16.1; if p_1 decides on 1 and p_2 decides on 2 then the edge in Figure 16.3 is colored $\{1, 2\}$.

The discussion so far has applied to any number of processors; consider now the very simple case of a system with two processors. In this case, we can list all block executions; for example, if each processor (always) takes exactly two steps before deciding, then some of the block executions are:

$$\beta_1 = \{p_0\}, \{p_0\}, \{p_1\}, \{p_1\}$$
$$\overset{\neg p_0}{\sim} \quad \beta_2 = \{p_0\}, \{p_0, p_1\}, \{p_1\}$$
$$\overset{\neg p_1}{\sim} \quad \beta_3 = \{p_0\}, \{p_1\}, \{p_0\}, \{p_1\}$$
$$\overset{\neg p_0}{\sim} \quad \beta_4 = \{p_0\}, \{p_1\}, \{p_0, p_1\}$$
$$\overset{\neg p_1}{\sim} \quad \beta_5 = \{p_0\}, \{p_1\}, \{p_1\}, \{p_0\}$$
$$\vdots$$
$$\overset{\neg p_0}{\sim} \quad \beta_{l-1} = \{p_1\}, \{p_1, p_0\}, \{p_0\}$$
$$\overset{\neg p_1}{\sim} \quad \beta_l = \{p_1\}, \{p_1\}, \{p_0\}, \{p_0\}$$

Note that there are two nodes with degree 1—one for the single execution in which p_0 is unseen and one for the single execution in which p_1 is unseen. We add an imaginary node, λ, with edges to these nodes, labeled with the unseen processor. Let $\hat{\mathcal{B}}_2$ be $\mathcal{B}_2$ with the imaginary node. Figure 16.4 shows $\hat{\mathcal{B}}_2$.

In $\mathcal{B}_2$, the color of an edge is a single value—the decision of a processor not distinguishing between the two incident executions. The coloring of edges extends naturally to the edges adjacent to λ; an edge labeled with p_i is colored with the decision of p_{1-i}, the other processor. We concentrate on edges in $\hat{\mathcal{B}}_2$ colored with $\{0\}$ and define the *restricted degree* of a node v to be the number of edges colored with $\{0\}$ that are incident to v.

Consider a non-imaginary node v with one incident edge colored with 0 and another incident edge colored with 1 (that is, the restricted degree of v is exactly 1). Node v corresponds to an execution in which one processor decides 0 and the other processor decides 1. That is:

Lemma 16.4 *If the restricted degree of a (non-imaginary) node is 1, then the node corresponds to an execution in which $\{0, 1\}$ are decided.*

Clearly, the edge incident to the imaginary node, λ, labeled with p_1, is colored with $\{0\}$; the other incident edge, labeled with p_0, is colored with $\{1\}$. Thus the restricted degree of λ is exactly 1. The sum of the restricted degrees of all nodes must be even, because each edge is counted twice in the summation. Thus there is an odd number of non-imaginary nodes with odd restricted degree, that is, there is an odd number of non-imaginary nodes with restricted degree 1. That is:

Lemma 16.5 *There is an odd number of executions in which $\{0, 1\}$ are decided.*

Therefore, there is at least one execution in which $\{0, 1\}$ are decided. This provides an alternative proof for the impossibility of consensus; moreover, this can be used to prove the impossibility of wait-free three-processor algorithms for 2-set consensus, as shown next.

Let us now consider the case of three processors, p_0, p_1 and p_2. Recall that in block executions p_i starts with input i, namely, 0, 1, or 2, and by the problem definition, processors must decide on at most two different values and the decisions must be a subset of the inputs.

We consider the graph $\mathcal{B}_3$, defined as above, and add an imaginary node λ, with an edge to each node with degree 2, corresponding to a block execution with an unseen processor; the edge is labeled with the unseen processor. The extended graph is denoted $\hat{\mathcal{B}}_3$. After λ is added, the degree of each non-imaginary node is exactly 3; each of its adjacent edges is labeled with a different processor. In the same manner, the additional edges are colored with the set containing the decisions of all processors but the unseen processor.

For three processors, we concentrate on edges colored with the pair $\{0, 1\}$; this means that the pair of processors that do *not* distinguish between the two adjacent executions decide on 0 and on 1 (in both executions). Similarly to the two-processor case, the *restricted degree* of a node v is the number of edges colored with $\{0, 1\}$ that are incident to v. Exercise 16.6 asks you to show that a (non-imaginary) node cannot have restricted degree 3, that is, it cannot have three incident edges colored with $\{0, 1\}$.

Therefore, the restricted degree of a node is at most 2. As in the case of two processors, the restricted degree is interesting because we can prove:

Lemma 16.6 *If the restricted degree of a (non-imaginary) node is 1, then the node corresponds to an execution in which $\{0, 1, 2\}$ are decided.*

Proof. Let α be the block execution corresponding to a node v. Without loss of generality, assume that the single incident edge colored with $\{0, 1\}$ is labeled by processor p_0 and that p_1 decides 0 and p_2 decides 1 in α. We argue that p_0 decides 2 in α.

If p_0 decides 0 in α, then consider the edge incident to v labeled with p_1. This edge must exist since each node has n an adjacent edges, each labeled with a different processor. It must be colored with $\{0, 1\}$ (the decisions of p_0 and p_2). Similarly, if p_0 decides 1 in α, then consider the edge incident to v and labeled with p_2; it must be colored with $\{0, 1\}$ (the decisions of p_0 and p_1). In both cases, the restricted degree of v must be 2. $\square$

What is the restricted degree of the imaginary node? This is the number of block executions with an unseen processor in which $\{0, 1\}$ are decided by the seen processors. By the validity condition, these can only be executions in which p_2 is unseen. Thus these are block executions in which p_0 and p_1 run on their own, not seeing p_2 at all, and p_2 runs after they decide. It can be shown (Exercise 16.8) that these executions have a one-to-one correspondence with all two-processor block executions, as captured by $\mathcal{B}_2$. By Lemma 16.5, there is an odd number of two-processor block executions in which $\{0, 1\}$ are decided. Therefore, the restricted degree of λ is odd.

Because the sum of restricted degrees of nodes in the extended graph $\hat{\mathcal{B}}_3$ (including λ) is even, there must be an odd number of non-imaginary nodes with odd restricted degree. Because the restricted degree of a node is at most two, it follows that an odd number of nodes have restricted degree 1. Therefore, at least one node has restricted degree 1. By Lemma 16.6, this node corresponds to an execution in which $\{0, 1, 2\}$ are decided, which proves:

Theorem 16.7 *There is no wait-free algorithm for solving the 2-set consensus problem in an asynchronous shared memory system with three processors.*

For wait-free algorithms, the lower bound for any value of k is proved by considering $\mathcal{B}_k$, colored as before. Define the *restricted degree* of a node to be the number of edges colored with $\{0, \ldots, k - 2\}$ that are incident on the node. The above combinatorial argument can be extended, by induction, to show that an odd number of nodes has restricted degree 1 (Exercise 16.10). The lower bound then follows from the natural extension of Lemma 16.6 for $\mathcal{B}_k$ (Exercise 16.11).

The lower bound can be extended to any number of failures $f \geq k$, in the same manner that the impossibility of consensus is extended from wait-free algorithms to any number of failures (Chapter 5). The simulation of Section 5.3.2 needs to be extended to work for any number of simulating processors (not just two); more details appear in Exercise 16.12 and the chapter notes.

Finally, the simulation of atomic snapshot objects from read/write registers (Algorithm 30), together with the simulation of read/write registers in message-passing systems (described in Section 5.3.3), imply that the same lower bounds hold for asynchronous message-passing systems, as long as $f > n/2$. If $f \leq n/2$, this problem, as well as all the other problems in this chapter, cannot be solved in asynchronous message-passing systems; the proof is similar to proof of Theorem 10.22.

16.2   APPROXIMATE AGREEMENT

The approximate agreement problem is another weakening of the standard consensus problem, which, like k-set consensus, admits fault-tolerant solutions in asynchronous systems. Instead of allowing limited disagreement in terms of the number of different values decided, a *range* is specified in which decision values must fall.

Processor p_i's input value is denoted x_i and its output value is denoted y_i, $0 \le i \le n - 1$. Input and output values are real numbers. The following conditions should be satisfied in every admissible execution by a solution to the ϵ-*approximate agreement* problem, for some positive real number ϵ:

Termination: For every nonfaulty processor p_i, y_i is eventually assigned a value.

ϵ-*Agreement:* For all nonfaulty processors p_i and p_j, $|y_i - y_j| \le \epsilon$. That is, all nonfaulty decisions are within ϵ of each other.

Validity: For every nonfaulty processor p_i, there exist processors p_j and p_k such that $x_j \le y_i \le x_k$. That is, every nonfaulty decision is within the range of the input values.

Below, we present two wait-free algorithms for approximate agreement: a simple algorithm that depends on knowing the range of possible input values and an adaptive algorithm that does not require this knowledge.

16.2.1   Known Input Range

We now present an algorithm that solves the approximate agreement problem for up to $n - 1$ failures. The algorithm proceeds in a series of asynchronous rounds. In each round, processors exchange values and apply an averaging function (specifically, computing the midpoint) to the values exchanged in order to compute new values, which are used in the next round. Values are exchanged by having each processor first update its segment of an atomic snapshot object and then scan the snapshot object. The exchange of values is asymmetric in that a fast process might see many fewer values in the snapshot object than a slow one; however, it is guaranteed to see at least one (its own).

As will be shown, each round reduces the spread of the values held by processors by a factor of 2. The number of rounds required until the spread is within the specified ϵ is the log of the range of the inputs divided by ϵ. The intuition behind this calculation is that the number of factor-of-2 reductions required to shrink the spread from its original range to ϵ is the log (base 2) of the ratio of the old and new ranges. Later, we discuss how to modify the algorithm to work with an unknown input range.

For simplicity of presentation, the algorithm uses a separate snapshot object for each round r, ASO_r. Initially each segment in ASO_r holds an empty indication. The pseudocode appears as Algorithm 53. Given a nonempty set X, the function range(X) returns the interval $[\min(X), \max(X)]$, and the function spread(X) returns the length of this interval, that is, $\max(X) - \min(X)$; the function midpoint(X) returns the middle of range(X), that is, $\frac{1}{2}(\min(X) + \max(X))$.

Algorithm 53 Asynchronous round $r \geq 1$ of wait-free ϵ-approximate agreement algorithm for known input range: code for processor p_i, $0 \leq i \leq n - 1$.

Initially $v = x$ and *maxRound* $= \lceil \log_2 \frac{D}{\epsilon} \rceil + 1$,
where D is the maximal spread of inputs

```
1:   update_i(ASO_r,v)
2:   values[r] := scan_i(ASO_r)
3:   v := midpoint(values[r])
4:   if r = maxRound then y := v and terminate                    // decide
```

The algorithm uses a separate snapshot object for each round, but they can be replaced with a single snapshot object, in which each processor writes the concatenation of its values for all rounds so far (see Exercise 16.13).

The following lemmas are with respect to an arbitrary admissible execution of the algorithm.

For each $r \geq 1$ and each processor p_i, denote by V_i^r the value of p_i's local variable *values*[r] after Line 2 of asynchronous round r. For each $r \geq 1$, denote by U^r the set of all values ever written to ASO_r; this can be by either faulty or nonfaulty processors. Denote by U^0 the set of input values of all processes.

Let M be the value of *maxRound*. Note that U^r is not empty, for every r, $0 \leq r \leq M$. The key for the correctness of the algorithm is the next lemma.

Lemma 16.8 *For every asynchronous round* r, $0 \leq r < M$, *there exists a value* $u \in range(U^r)$, *such that* $\min(U^{r+1}) \geq (\min(U^r) + u)/2$ *and* $\max(U^{r+1}) \leq (\max(U^r) + u)/2$ *(see Fig. 16.5)*.

Proof. Let u be the first value written (in Line 1) with round number r, by some processor p_j. We argue that u satisfies the claim of the lemma.

By the properties of the atomic snapshot object, each processor that participates in round $r + 1$ reads u when calculating its value for round $r + 1$. This holds since if p_j overwrites u, it is with a round number larger than r, so scans that are linearized after p_j overwrites u will be used for a round strictly bigger than $r + 1$. Thus $u \in V_i^r$, for any processor p_i calculating a value v_i^{r+1} for round $r + 1$. The lemma follows by proving that $(\min(U^r) + u)/2 \leq v_i^{r+1} \leq (\max(U^r) + u)/2$, which we leave as an exercise to the reader (see Exercise 16.16). □

As Figure 16.5 makes obvious, the above lemma implies:

Fig. 16.5 Illustration for Lemma 16.8.

Lemma 16.9 *For every* r, $0 \leq r < M$, range$(U^{r+1}) \subseteq$ range(U^r).

Moreover, the spread of values is reduced by a factor of 2 at each asynchronous round.

Lemma 16.10 *For every* r, $0 \leq r < M$, spread$(U^{r+1}) \leq \frac{1}{2}$spread$(U^r)$.

Theorem 16.11 *Algorithm 53 solves wait-free ϵ-approximate agreement when the input range is known.*

Proof.   Fix an admissible execution of the algorithm.

Termination follows since each processor performs at most *maxRound* asynchronous rounds and each asynchronous round completes within a finite number of steps.

To prove validity, consider some nonfaulty processor p_i. By repeated application of Lemma 16.9, its decision y_i is in the range of all the input values.

We now consider ϵ-agreement. Consider any two nonfaulty processors p_i and p_j. By definition, $maxRound = \lceil \log_2(D/\epsilon) \rceil$; clearly, $maxRound \geq \log_2(\text{spread}(U^0)/\epsilon)$. By repeated application of Lemma 16.10,

$$\text{spread}(U^{maxRound}) \leq \text{spread}(U^0) \cdot 2^{-maxRound}$$

Substituting the above lower bound on *maxRound* shows that

$$\text{spread}(U^{maxRound}) \leq \epsilon$$

By the code, p_i's decision, y_i, and p_j's decision, y_j, are in $U^{maxRound}$. Hence, $|y_i - y_j| \leq \epsilon$. $\square$

We can state an explicit bound on the number of steps taken by a nonfaulty processor.

Theorem 16.12 *A nonfaulty processor performs* $O(\lceil \log_2(D/\epsilon) \rceil)$ *scan and update operations on a snapshot object before deciding, in any admissible execution of Algorithm 53.*

16.2.2   Unknown Input Range

Algorithm 53 depends on knowing D, an upper bound on the spread of input values. Such a bound is not always available, and even when it is available, the bound can be very large compared with the actual spread of input values in the execution. We now describe an algorithm that does not rely on knowing D.

A close look at the algorithm reveals that what we really need is a bound on the spread of inputs in the execution. A first idea would be to modify the current algorithm so it calculates the number of rounds dynamically at each round, based on the spread of the inputs of processors that have started the execution so far. However, consider the case where some processor, say p_0, takes a solo execution in which it

---

Algorithm 54 Wait-free ϵ-approximate agreement algorithm for unknown input range: code for processor p_i, $0 \leq i \leq n - 1$.

1: $\text{update}_i(\langle x, 1, x \rangle)$
2: **repeat**
3:      $\langle x_0, r_0, v_0 \rangle, \ldots, \langle x_{n-1}, r_{n-1}, v_{n-1} \rangle := \text{scan}_i()$
4:      $maxRound := \log_2(\text{spread}(x_0, \ldots, x_{n-1})/\epsilon)$ // assume that $\log_2 0 = -\infty$
5:      $r_{\max} := \max\{r_0, \ldots, r_{n-1}\}$
6:      $values := \{v_j \mid r_j = r_{\max}, 0 \leq j \leq n - 1\}$
7:      $\text{update}_i(\langle x, r_{\max} + 1, \text{midpoint}(values) \rangle)$
8: **until** $r_{\max} \geq maxRound$
9: $y := \text{midpoint}(values);$ // decide

---

writes its input, executes some number of rounds, K, and then decides, without p_1 taking any steps. It can be shown that, in this case, p_0 must decide on its input, x_0 (see Exercise 16.15). Suppose after p_0 decides, processor p_1 starts a solo execution with an input x_1, such that $|x_0 - x_1| > \epsilon \cdot 2^{K+2}$; p_0 writes its input, reads x_0, x_1 and calculates a number of rounds to execute, $K' > K + 2$. Note that by asynchronous round $K + 1$, p_1's preference is still more than ϵ away from x_0. Later, when executing asynchronous round $K + 2$, p_1 reads only its own preference for round $K + 1$, so p_1's preference remains the same until it decides. Thus p_1 decides on a value that is more than ϵ away from x_0, contradicting the ϵ-agreement property.

To avoid this problem, a processor does not go from one round to the next round, but rather skips to one more than the maximal round r that it observes in a scan, taking the midpoint of the values already written for this round r (and possibly ignoring its own input value).

The pseudocode appears as Algorithm 54.

The correctness proof assumes an arbitrary admissible execution of the algorithm.

We use the same notation of U^r and V_i^r as in the proof of the previous approximate agreement algorithm, but with slightly modified definitions because space is reused. For $r \geq 1$, U^r is the set of all values ever written (in Line 1 or Line 7) to the atomic snapshot object with round number r (middle element of the triple). U^0 is defined to be the set of input values of all processors. For $r \geq 1$, V_i^r is the value of p_i's variable *values* after executing Line 6 with $r_{\max} = r$. (If p_i never has its $r_{\max}$ variable equal to r, then V_i^r is undefined.)

Let M be the largest r such that U^r is not empty. Convince yourself that U^r is not empty, for every r, $1 \leq r \leq M$. The proof of Lemma 16.8 remains almost exactly the same (except that u can be written either in Line 1 *or* in Line 7 of the algorithm). Therefore, we can derive Lemma 16.9 and Lemma 16.10.

Theorem 16.13 *Algorithm 54 solves wait-free ϵ-approximate agreement when the input range is unknown.*

Proof. Fix an admissible execution of the algorithm.

To show that termination holds, we must show that no processor can keep increasing *maxRound* forever. *maxRound* only can increase if another processor starts executing the algorithm, thus increasing the spread of observable inputs. Since there is a finite number of processes, *maxRound* can only be increased finitely many times.

Validity follows in a manner similar to the proof for Theorem 16.11.

We consider ϵ-agreement. Let R be the smallest round in which some nonfaulty processor p_i decides. We claim that spread$(U^R) \leq \epsilon$. By Lemma 16.9, for any round R' such that $R < R' \leq M$, range$(U^{R'}) \subseteq$ range(U^R), which, together with the claim, implies ϵ-agreement.

We now verify the claim that spread$(U^R) \leq \epsilon$. Consider some value $v_j^r \in U^R$ written for round R by p_j. If p_j writes its input value (i.e., performs its first update) before p_i computes *maxRound* for the last time, then the claim follows as in the proof of Theorem 16.11. If, on the other hand, p_j writes its input value after p_i computes *maxRound* for the last time, then the maximal round number seen by p_j in its first scan is at least R. (In this case, p_j ignores its input.) Thus, the value written by p_j for any round greater than or equal to R is in the range of the values written so far for round R, which proves the claim. ☐

16.3 RENAMING

The coordination problems considered so far in this chapter—k-set consensus and approximate agreement—require processors to decide on values that are close together. We now present a problem in which processors should decide on *distinct* values, but in a small range.

The *renaming problem* considers a situation in which processors start with unique names from a large domain (the *original names*) and, for some reason, they need to shrink it. Thus each processor should pick a *new name* from some small name space $[1..M]$. Denote by y_i the new name chosen by processor p_i; the main requirements of the renaming problem are:

Termination: For every nonfaulty processor p_i, y_i is eventually assigned a value.

Uniqueness: For all distinct nonfaulty processors p_i and p_j, $y_i \neq y_j$.

The goal is to minimize M, the size of the new name space. A superficial solution is to let processors choose their index, that is, processor p_i takes i as its new name; the new name space is of size n. Yet this solution is not good if the indices are larger than the actual number of processors. To rule out this solution, we make the following additional requirement:

Anonymity: The code executed by processor p_i with original name x is exactly the same as the code executed by processor p_j with original name x.

The uniqueness condition implies that M must be at least n. Here we show renaming algorithms with $M = n + f$, where f is the number of crash failures to be tolerated.

Algorithm 55 Wait-free renaming algorithm: code for processor p_i, $0 \le i \le n-1$.

```
1:   s := 1
2:   while true do
3:       update_i(⟨x, s⟩)
4:       (⟨x_0, s_0⟩, ..., ⟨x_{n-1}, s_{n-1}⟩) := scan_i()
5:       if s = s_j for some j ≠ i, then
6:           let r be the rank of x in {x_j ≠ ⊥ | 0 ≤ j ≤ n − 1}
7:           let s be the rth integer not in {s_j ≠ ⊥ | 0 ≤ j ≠ i ≤ n − 1}
8:       else
9:           y := s                                    // decide on s as new name
10:          terminate
```

16.3.1 The Wait-Free Case

We start with the wait-free case, namely, $f = n - 1$. For this case, there is a renaming algorithm whose output domain contains $n + f = 2n - 1$ names, namely, $M = 2n - 1$. This algorithm is simpler than the algorithm for arbitrary f, because it uses a larger name space.

The idea of the algorithm is quite simple; processors communicate using some atomic snapshot object containing for each processor its original name and a new name it suggests for itself. Each processor, p_i, starts the algorithm by writing its original name to its segment in the snapshot object. Then p_i scans the snapshot object and picks some new name that has not been suggested yet by another processor (the exact rule will be defined later). Processor p_i suggests this name by writing it to its segment in the snapshot object and scans the snapshot object again. If no other processor suggests this name, p_i decides on it; otherwise, it picks another new name and suggests it again.

The pseudocode appears in Algorithm 55. In this algorithm, the rule for picking a new name is to choose the rth ranked integer from the free (not suggested) numbers in the range $[1..2n - 1]$, where r is the rank of the processor's original name among all the original names of participating processors. The algorithm uses a single atomic snapshot object, whose name is left implicit in the calls to the update and scan procedures. The ith segment of the snapshot object contains a pair of values: p_i's original name x_i and p_i's current suggestion s_i for its new name.

The following lemmas are with respect to an arbitrary admissible execution α of the algorithm. Obviously, anonymity is obeyed.

Lemma 16.14 (Uniqueness) *No two processors decide on the same name.*

Proof. Assume by way of contradiction that two processors, p_i and p_j, decide on the same name, say y. Let $(⟨x_0, s_0⟩, ..., ⟨x_{n-1}, s_{n-1}⟩)$ be the view returned the last time p_i executes Line 4 before deciding. By the code, $s_i = y$, since p_i writes its suggested name before its last scan. Similarly, let $(⟨x'_0, s'_0⟩, ..., ⟨x'_{n-1}, s'_{n-1}⟩)$ be the view returned the last time p_j executes Line 4 before deciding, and again, $s'_j = y$.

Without loss of generality, we may assume that p_i's scan precedes p_j's scan, by the linearizability property of the atomic snapshot object. Also, p_i does not change its suggestion after it decides, and thus $s'_i = y$. This violates the condition for deciding, and yields a contradiction. $\square$

Note that the lemma does not depend on the specific rule used for picking the suggested name, as it does not consider Lines 6–7, where the new name is picked. This rule is important only for bounding the size of the new names and for guaranteeing termination of nonfaulty processors, as done in the next two lemmas.

The rank of a processor is at most n, and at most $n - 1$ integers are already suggested by other processors, so the highest integer a processor may suggest is $2n - 1$. Because a processor decides only on a name it has previously suggested:

Lemma 16.15 *The new names are in the range* $[1..2n - 1]$.

The delicate part of the correctness proof is arguing termination; that is, proving that a processor cannot take an infinite number of steps without deciding, regardless of the behavior of other processors.

Lemma 16.16 (Termination) *Any processor either takes a finite number of steps or decides.*

Proof. Assume, by way of contradiction, that some processor takes an infinite number of steps in the execution α without deciding; we say that such a processor is *trying*. Consider a finite prefix of α such that all trying processors have already executed Line 3 at least once and all other processors have either decided or taken all their steps. Denote by α' the remaining suffix of α; note that only trying processors take steps in α'. Let p_i be the trying processor with smallest original name; we argue that p_i decides in α', which is a contradiction.

Let *NF* (for "not free") be the set of suggested names appearing in the atomic snapshot object at the beginning of α' in the segments of processors that are not trying; note that this set remains fixed in α'. Let F (for "free") be all the remaining names, that is, $F = [1..2n - 1] - NF$; assume that $F = \{z_1, z_2, \ldots\}$, where $z_1 < z_2 < \ldots$.

Consider a point in α' where all trying processors have written a suggestion (for a new name) based on a view returned by a scan that started in α'. Since no processor performs Line 3 for the first time in α', it follows that all views contain the same set of original names; therefore, each processor gets a distinct rank.

Let r be the rank of p_i's original name x_i in this view. By choice of p_i, r is the smallest rank among all the trying processors.

We first argue that no trying processor other than p_i ever suggests a name in $\{z_1, \ldots, z_r\}$ once every trying processor has done an update based on a scan that started in α'. Consider another trying processor p_j. When p_j performs a scan in α', it sees every name in *NF* in use and possibly some other names as well. Thus the free names from p_j's perspective form a set $F' \subseteq F$. Since p_j's original name has rank greater than r, p_j suggests a name greater than z_r.

Algorithm 56 A renaming algorithm resilient to f failures:
code for processor p_i, $0 \le i \le n - 1$.

```
 1:   s := ⊥
 2:   repeat
 3:       update_i(⟨x, s, false⟩)
 4:       (⟨x_0, s_0, d_0⟩, ..., ⟨x_{n-1}, s_{n-1}, d_{n-1}⟩) := scan_i()
 5:       if (s = ⊥) or (s = s_j for some j ≠ i) then
 6:           let r be the rank of x in {x_j ≠ ⊥ | d_j = false, 0 ≤ j ≤ n − 1}
 7:           if r ≤ f + 1 then
                  let s be the rth integer not in {s_j ≠ ⊥ | 0 ≤ j ≠ i ≤ n − 1}
 8:       else
 9:           update_i(⟨x, s, true⟩)                              // indicate decided
10:           y := s                                     // decide on s as new name
11:           terminate
12:   until false
```

We now argue that p_i will eventually suggest z_r in α'. If not, then p_i always sees z_r as someone else's suggestion. By definition, z_r is not a member of *NF*. Thus it is continually suggested by other trying processors. But by the previous claim, every other trying processor will eventually reach a point in time after which it only suggests higher names. Thus eventually p_i will stop seeing z_r as someone else's suggestion.

Thus eventually p_i will suggest z_r, see no conflicting suggestion of z_r, and decide z_r. □

16.3.2 The General Case

Let us now consider the general case of an arbitrary $f < n$; for this case, we present a renaming algorithm with $n + f$ new names. Although the wait-free algorithm will obviously work in this case as well, we pay a price in terms of an unnecessarily large name space when f is smaller than $n - 1$. Thus we are interested in more efficient algorithms for smaller numbers of failures.

The algorithm extends the idea of the previous algorithm by restricting the number of processors that are proposing names at the same time. A processor suggests a name only if its original name is among the $f + 1$ lowest names of processors that have not decided yet.

The only addition to the data in the snapshot object is a bit, where the processor announces that it has decided. The pseudocode is very similar and appears as Algorithm 56.

The uniqueness property follows by the same arguments as in Lemma 16.14.

Clearly, at most $n - 1$ integers are suggested or chosen by processors other than p_i itself, in any view returned in Line 4. A processor suggests a name only if its rank is at most $f + 1$; thus the name suggested by a processor is at most $(n-1) + (f+1) = n + f$.

Since a processor decides only on a name it has previously suggested, its new name must be in the range $[1..n + f]$.

The next lemma claims termination and is proved along the same lines as Lemma 16.16; the proof is left as an exercise for the reader (Exercise 16.21).

Lemma 16.17 *A processor either takes a finite number of steps or decides.*

16.3.3 Long-Lived Renaming

An interesting aspect of the renaming problem is in a *long-lived* setting, where processors request and release new names dynamically. For example, assume that we have a large potential set of processors $p_0, \ldots, p_{n-1}$, with original names $0, \ldots, n-1$; however, at each point in the execution at most k of them are interested in participating in the algorithm. There are reasons to reassign names to the participating processors, for example, to use small data structures, whose size depends on the number of participating processors, k, rather than on the total number of processors, n.

To specify the *long-lived renaming problem with k participants*, we need to use the tools from the layered model of Chapter 7; there are inputs and outputs to deal with and later in this chapter we describe an algorithm that layers two algorithms, one of which is an algorithm for long-lived renaming. The inputs for the specification are *request-name$_i$* and *release-name$_i$*, $0 \leq i \leq n - 1$; the outputs are *new-name$_i$(y)*, $0 \leq i \leq n - 1$, where y is a potential name. The allowable sequences of inputs and outputs are those satisfying the following properties:

Correct Interaction: The subsequence of inputs and outputs for each i is a prefix of *request-name$_i$*, *new-name$_i$*, *release-name$_i$*, repeated forever.

To define the next properties, we need a notion of a *participating* process: p_i is participating after a prefix of a sequence of inputs and outputs if the most recent input for i that has occurred is *request-name*. We also define a participating processor p_i to be *named y* if *new-name$_i$(y)* has occurred since the most recent *request-name$_i$*.

k-Participants: After every prefix of the sequence, the number of processors that are participating is at most k.

The uniqueness and termination properties need to be slightly reworded:

Uniqueness: If participating processor p_i is named y_i and participating processor p_j ($j \neq i$) is named y_j after any prefix of the sequence, then $y_i \neq y_j$.

Termination: The subsequence of inputs and outputs for each i does not end with *request-name*.

The anonymity requirement from before is modified to require that the range of the new names will only depend on k, the maximum number of concurrent participants, rather than on n, the total number of potential participants.

Algorithm 57 A long-lived renaming algorithm for k participating processors: code for processor p_i.

1: upon *request-name* event:
2:      $s := \bot$
3:      repeat
4:          $\text{update}_i(\langle x, s, \text{false}\rangle)$
5:          $(\langle x_0, s_0, d_0\rangle, \ldots, \langle x_{n-1}, s_{n-1}, d_{n-1}\rangle) := \text{scan}_i()$
6:          if $(s = \bot)$ or $(s = s_j$ for some $j \neq i)$ then
7:              let r be the rank of x in $\{x_j \neq \bot \mid d_j = \text{false}, 0 \leq j \leq n - 1\}$
8:              if $r \leq k$ then
                    let s be the rth integer not in $\{s_j \neq \bot \mid 0 \leq j \neq i \leq n - 1\}$
9:          else
10:             $\text{update}_i(\langle x, s, \text{true}\rangle)$ // indicate decided
11:             *new-name*(s) and exit
12:     until false

13: upon *release-name* event:
14:     $\text{update}_i(\langle \bot, \bot, \bot\rangle)$

Bounded Name Space: For each *new-name*$_i(y)$ output, y is in $\{1, \ldots, M(k)\}$, for some function M.

Simple modifications to Algorithm 56 give an algorithm that solves long-lived renaming for k participants with new name space $2k - 1$. See Algorithm 57.

The properties of the algorithm, uniqueness, $(2k - 1)$ name space, and termination are proved along the lines of the general renaming algorithm. Only the last property, termination, depends on assuming that at most k processors participate concurrently: If more than k processors participate, we are still guaranteed that new names taken concurrently by participating processors are unique and in the range $[1..2k - 1]$, but it is possible that some processor(s) will not terminate (see Exercise 16.24 to Exercise 16.26).

After translating the scan and update procedures into their constituent reads and writes, the number of steps performed by a processor between a *request-name* event and *new-name* event depends on n, the total number of processors; the chapter notes discuss algorithms whose step complexity depends on k, the number of participating processors.

16.4   *K*-EXCLUSION AND *K*-ASSIGNMENT

The section presents two problems that extend the mutual exclusion problem (studied in Chapter 4). In the first problem, *k-exclusion*, some number of processors (specified by the parameter k) are allowed to be inside the critical section concurrently. The

k-exclusion problem is a natural way to incorporate fault tolerance into the mutual exclusion problem, as will be discussed shortly.

The second problem, k-*assignment with m slots*, extends k-exclusion even further and requires each processor inside the critical section to have a unique number between 1 and m (a *slot*). The k-assignment problem is an abstraction of the situation when there is a pool of identical resources, each of which must be used by only one processor at a time; for instance, suppose a user needs to print a file but does not care which of the several available printers is used, as long as it gets exclusive access to the printer. The parameter k indicates the number of processors that can be using resources in the pool simultaneously, whereas m is the number of resources in the pool. In the absence of failures, k and m would be the same, but, as we shall see, the potential for failures indicates that m should be larger than k.

After defining the problems more precisely, we present an algorithm that solves k-exclusion in the presence of less than k failures. Then we show that k-assignment with m slots can be solved by combining a k-exclusion algorithm with a long-lived renaming algorithm for k participants whose new name space has size m.

The properties we require for k-exclusion are extensions of the properties required in the mutual exclusion problem.

k-*Exclusion:* No more than k processors are concurrently in the critical section.

k-*Lockout avoidance:* If at most $f < k$ processors are faulty, then any nonfaulty processor wishing to enter the critical section eventually does so.

Note that k-lockout avoidance (or even the weaker property of k-deadlock avoidance) cannot be attained if processors may get stuck inside the critical section. Thus, we assume that nonfaulty processors take only a finite number of steps in the critical section and eventually transfer to the exit and the remainder section. Faulty processors may fail inside the critical section, but because fewer than k processors can fail, this allows an additional nonfaulty processor to make progress and enter the critical section.

For the k-assignment problem with m slots we also require that processors in the critical section have a slot, denoted s_i for p_i, where s_i is an integer between 1 and m.

Uniqueness: If p_i and p_j are concurrently in the critical section then $s_i \neq s_j$.

As in the renaming problem, we would like to reduce the range of values held in s_i variables, that is, make m as small as possible.

16.4.1 An Algorithm for k-Exclusion

The algorithm is similar to the bakery algorithm for mutual exclusion (Algorithm 10) from Chapter 4 in that it uses tickets to order the requests by processes. (The chapter notes discuss how the tickets can be bounded.) When starting the entry section, a processor obtains a ticket, ordering itself among the processors competing for the critical section. Then it checks the tickets of the competing processors; if fewer than

---

Algorithm 58 A k-exclusion algorithm: code for processor p_i, $0 \le i \le n - 1$.

$\langle$Entry$\rangle$:
1: $ticket_0, \ldots, ticket_{n-1} := \mathsf{scan}_i()$
2: $\mathsf{update}_i(\max(ticket_j \ne \infty \mid j = 0, \ldots, n - 1) + 1)$
3: repeat
4:     $ticket_0, \ldots, ticket_{n-1} := \mathsf{scan}_i()$
5: until $|\{\langle ticket_j, j\rangle : \langle ticket_j, j\rangle < \langle ticket_i, i\rangle\}| < k$ // lexicographic order
$\langle$Critical Section$\rangle$
$\langle$Exit$\rangle$:
6: $\mathsf{update}_i(\infty)$
$\langle$Remainder$\rangle$

---

k of them have "older" tickets, it enters the critical section. In the exit section, a processor sets its ticket to ∞.

The algorithm uses a single atomic snapshot object, whose name is left implicit in the calls to the update and scan procedures. The ith segment of the snapshot object contains the current ticket of processor p_i. If p_i is not interested in the critical section, then its ticket is set to ∞, which is also the initial value. The pseudocode appears as Algorithm 58.

We now discuss why the algorithm provides k-exclusion and k-lockout avoidance. Fix an execution of the algorithm.

Lemma 16.18 *Algorithm 58 provides k-exclusion.*

Proof. Assume in contradiction there is a configuration in which more than k processors are in the critical section. Before entering the critical section, each of these processors executed a scan, stored a new ticket, and scanned again (at least once).

Let p_i be the processor who stored its ticket latest in the execution. The linearizability property of snapshots implies that the scan of p_i contains the tickets of all other processors. That is, p_i must see at least k smaller tickets, which contradicts the condition on Line 5.   □

The proof of k-lockout avoidance considers some processor p_i that gets stuck in the entry section. Eventually, all nonfaulty processors that enter the critical section before p_i exit; in addition, all nonfaulty processors that scanned before the update of p_i (in the linearizability order of the snapshot) enter the critical section as well and exit. In both cases, if these processors ever move to the entry section, they will get a ticket larger than p_i's ticket. Thus eventually the only processors with tickets smaller than p_i's are the faulty ones; because fewer than k processors are faulty, the condition in Line 5 will be satisfied and p_i will enter the critical section. This proves:

Lemma 16.19 *Algorithm 58 provides k-lockout avoidance.*

Together, the last two lemmas prove:

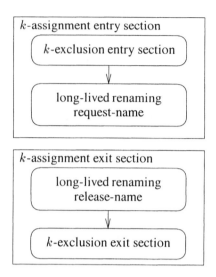

Fig. 16.6   A schematic view of the k-assignment algorithm.

Theorem 16.20 *Algorithm 58 solves the k-exclusion problem, if fewer than k processors are faulty.*

16.4.2   An Algorithm for k-Assignment

The reader might be tempted to suggest solving k-assignment with $2k - 1$ slots using the algorithm for long-lived renaming for k participants. The slot assignments are obvious because the renaming algorithm uses $2k - 1$ names, and indeed, as discussed at the end of Section 16.3.3, if too many processors wish to enter the critical section, some of them will be stuck. Thus the protocol provides k-exclusion as well. It is the lockout avoidance property that is not provided by long-lived renaming; when more than k processors are trying to obtain a new name, a processor in the entry section may be overtaken infinitely many times (see Exercise 16.27).

   The solution, however, is simple; we encompass a long-lived renaming algorithm for k participants (using $2k - 1$ names) with a k-exclusion algorithm (see Fig. 16.6). Formally proving the properties of the algorithm is left to the reader.

Exercises

16.1 Prove that in a solo execution of any k-set consensus algorithm, the processor must decide on its input value.

16.2 For both cases considered in the proof of Lemma 16.3, prove that p_j distinguishes between α and α'.

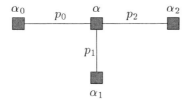

Fig. 16.7 Illustration for Exercise 16.6.

16.3 Consider the following block execution for four processors:

$$\alpha = \{p_0, p_2, p_3\}, \{p_2, p_3\}, \{p_0\}, \{p_1\}, \{p_1\}$$

1. Which processor is unseen in α?
2. Is p_0 seen in block 1 of α?
3. Is p_3 last seen in block 3 of α?
4. Construct the unique execution $\alpha' \stackrel{\neg p_i}{\sim} \alpha$, for every $i = 0, 1, 2, 3$.

16.4 Find a formula for the number of block executions with two processors, assuming that each processor always takes exactly s steps before deciding.

16.5 Prove that for a system with n processors there is a finite number of block executions.

16.6 Prove that the restricted degree of a non-imaginary node in $\hat{\mathcal{B}}_3$ cannot be 3.

Hint: Consider a non-imaginary node and its adjacent nodes, as described in Figure 16.7, and try to determine the decisions of all three processors in the four block executions corresponding to these nodes.

16.7 Extend the proof of Exercise 16.6 to show that in $\hat{\mathcal{B}}_k$ there is no non-imaginary node whose restricted degree is 3.

16.8 Let A be a k-set consensus algorithm for three processors. Show a one to one correspondence between the block executions of A in which p_2 is unseen and the block executions of a k-set consensus algorithm A' for two processors.

Hint: A' behaves like A behaves in block executions that do not contain any steps of p_2.

16.9 Explain how the definition of block executions should be modified so that the proof of Theorem 16.7 holds also when processors communicate by ordinary read and write operations, rather than update and scan operations.

16.10 Prove, by induction on $k \geq 2$, that an odd number of nodes in $\mathcal{B}_k$ have restricted degree 1.

Hint: Add an imaginary node connected to all nodes corresponding to block executions with an unseen processor; use the inductive hypothesis on k to prove that the restricted degree of the imaginary node is odd; complete the proof as was done for $k = 3$.

16.11 Extend Lemma 16.6 to any $k \geq 2$. That is, prove that if the restricted degree of a non-imaginary node in $\mathcal{B}_k$ is 1, then it corresponds to an execution in which $\{0, \ldots, k-1\}$ are decided.

16.12 Extend the simulation of Section 5.3.2 to prove: If there is a k-set consensus algorithm for a system of $n > k$ processors that tolerates the failure of k processors, then there is a wait-free k-set consensus algorithm for a system of k processors.

16.13 Modify the code of the approximate agreement algorithm to use only a single snapshot object, with possibly unbounded number of values in each segment.

16.14 Prove Theorem 16.12.

16.15 Prove that in a solo execution of any approximate agreement algorithm, the processor must decide on its input value.

16.16 Complete the proof of Lemma 16.8.

16.17 Use Lemma 16.8 to prove Lemma 16.9 and Lemma 16.10.

16.18 Prove that Algorithm 53 is correct even if processors use only an array of atomic single-writer multi-reader registers.

16.19 Modify the approximate agreement algorithm (Algorithm 54) and its correctness proof so that *maxRound* is calculated only in the first asynchronous round.

16.20 Present an execution of the renaming algorithm (Algorithm 55) in which some process takes an exponential number of steps before deciding.

16.21 Prove Lemma 16.17.

16.22 Describe an execution of Algorithm 56 that uses name $n + f$.

16.23 Prove that there is no wait-free renaming algorithm with new name space of size n.

Hint: Follow the ideas used to prove that there is no wait-free algorithm for solving consensus (Theorem 5.18).

16.24 Prove the uniqueness property of Algorithm 57, even when more than k processors participate concurrently.

16.25 Prove that $[1..2k + 1]$ is the new name space used by Algorithm 57, even when more than k processors participate concurrently.

16.26 Prove the termination property of Algorithm 57, when k processors or less participate concurrently.

16.27 Show an execution of Algorithm 57 with more than k participating processors (concurrently), in which some processor does not terminate.

16.28 Show an execution of Algorithm 57 with $2k$ participating processors (concurrently), in which all processors terminate.

16.29 Explain why Algorithm 58 needs a flag.

Hint: Assume that many processors (more than k) exit the critical section and are now in the remainder; now consider what happens when some processor wishes to enter the critical section.

16.30 Specify the k-exclusion and k-assignment problems using the model of Chapter 7. Then describe and prove correct the k-assignment algorithm mentioned in Section 16.4.2 using the layered model.

Chapter Notes

The study of solvable problems has been a prolific research area in the last five years, and our presentation has only touched it; here, we try to describe some of the key developments.

The k-set consensus problem was first presented by Chaudhuri [73], who also presented an f-resilient algorithm for k-set consensus, for any $f < k$. The lower bound showing that k-set consensus cannot be solved in the presence of $f \geq k$ failures was proved concurrently by Borowsky and Gafni [58], by Herlihy and Shavit [132], and by Saks and Zaharoglou [233].

Our proof of the lower bound for k-set consensus combines an operational argument about block executions and their similarity (and non-similarity) structure with a combinatorial argument about a coloring of a graph representing this structure. Block executions were defined by Saks and Zaharoglou [233] and by Borowsky and Gafni [58], who called them *immediate snapshot executions* because they correspond to executions in which restricted snapshot objects are employed. Lemma 16.2 and Lemma 16.3 were stated and proved by Attiya and Rajsbaum [32]. The graph representation of the similarity structure of block executions ($\mathcal{B}_n$) is new; it is inspired, in part, by the lower bound on the number of rounds for solving k-set consensus in the synchronous model, presented by Chaudhuri, Herlihy, Lynch, and Tuttle [75]. The combinatorial argument follows a graph-theoretic proof of Sperner's lemma given by Tompkins [253]; see also Bondy and Murty's standard text [57, pp. 21–23].

Approximate agreement was first presented by Dolev, Lynch, Pinter, Stark, and Weihl [96]; they considered message-passing models with crash and Byzantine failures. The algorithms we presented are based on an algorithm of Moran [190].

The renaming problem was first presented by Attiya, Bar-Noy, Dolev, Peleg, and Reischuk [26] for message-passing systems. The algorithms we presented here

(Algorithm 55 for the wait-free case and Algorithm 56 for the general case) are adaptations of the algorithm of Attiya et al. to shared memory systems.

Moir and Anderson [188] presented algorithms for long-lived renaming that are *fast* in the sense discussed for mutual exclusion, that is, in the absence of contention, a processor will pick a new name in a constant number of steps. Better algorithms for long-lived renaming were presented by Moir and Garay [189].

The k-exclusion problem was introduced by Fischer, Lynch, Burns, and Borodin [108]; we have presented an algorithm of Afek, Dolev, Gafni, Merritt, and Shavit [5], who also showed that the number of times a processor is overtaken is bounded in this algorithm. As for the algorithms of Chapter 10, a bounded timestamp system can be used instead of explicit tickets, to bound the memory requirements of this algorithm.

The k-assignment problem was introduced in message-passing systems under the name *slotted k-exclusion* by Attiya, Bar-Noy, Dolev, Peleg, and Reischuk [26]; the term k-*assignment* was coined by Burns and Peterson [64], who were the first to study this problem in shared memory systems. Burns and Peterson also showed that at least $2k + 1$ "slots" are required to solve this problem, by a proof that extends the methods of Fischer, Lynch, and Paterson [110].

All algorithms for variants of the renaming problem require the number of new names to be at least $n + f$, where f is the number of failures to be tolerated. An obvious question is whether the number of new names can be reduced. Attiya, Bar-Noy, Dolev, Peleg, and Reischuk [26] showed that at least $n + 1$ new names are needed (Exercise 16.23). Much later, Herlihy and Shavit proved that the number of new names must be at least $n + f$ [132].

Herlihy and Shavit derive the lower bounds for k-set consensus and renaming from a more general theorem characterizing the problems that can be solved by an f-resilient algorithm with only read and write operations [133]. This theorem uses techniques of algebraic topology. A simpler characterization theorem, relying only on graph-theoretic concepts, was proved by Biran, Moran, and Zaks [52] when only a single processor may fail. Their theorem is stated for message-passing systems, but simulations such as those presented in Chapter 5 and Chapter 10 can be used to translate it to shared memory systems.

17

Solving Consensus in Eventually Stable Systems

We have seen that fault-tolerant consensus is impossible to solve in an asynchronous system in which processors communicate via message passing or shared read-write registers. The key difficulty in trying to tolerate failures in an asynchronous system is distinguishing between a crashed processor and a slow processor. However, the assumption of complete asynchrony is often an overly pessimistic view of practical systems. If there are upper bounds on processor step time and message delays, synchrony can be used to detect failed processors, for instance, by having the processors exchange 'I'm alive' messages periodically.

A more abstract approach to detecting failures is to assume a service that does so but whose inner workings are not known to the users. This *failure detector* service could then be used in any kind of system, including an asynchronous one. The motivation for this approach is that there could be some other, and better, way to detect failures rather than imposing more stringent timing assumptions on the systems. This approach ignores the *operational features* of a failure detector and concentrates on the *properties* needed to solve consensus.

Strengthening the system assumptions, for instance, with failure detectors or stronger synchrony, is one strategy for circumventing the impossibility of consensus presented in Chapter 5. Recall from Chapter 5 that guaranteeing both safety (agreement and validity) and termination is impossible when the system is asynchronous.

A system may be poorly behaved for arbitrarily long periods, yet safety should nonetheless be preserved during these periods; that is, processors should never decide on conflicting or invalid values. We describe a simple mechanism to guarantee safety requirements, whereas termination is achieved only when the environment is well-behaved. Later, we describe how failure detectors encapsulate the treatment of the environment's behavior. A similar approach is taken in Chapter 14, where termination relied on lucky rolling of a dice.

The chapter starts with the mechanism for guaranteeing safety, which may terminate under fortunate circumstances. We present a formal model for failure detectors and define three types of failure detectors and show how they can be combined with the safety preserving algorithm to solve consensus, in both shared memory and message-passing systems. Possible implementations of failure detectors are discussed, as well as an application of these algorithms to state-machine replication.

17.1 PRESERVING SAFETY IN SHARED MEMORY SYSTEMS

This section presents a basic algorithm for guaranteeing safety; the algorithm is presented for asynchronous shared memory systems.

The algorithm consists of many invocations of a procedure called safe-phase. Each invocation has an associated *phase number* as a parameter. A processor may have several (non-overlapping) invocations of safe-phase; the numbers passed as parameters to the invocations of a particular processor are strictly increasing over the duration of the execution. Different processors may execute phases concurrently, but it is assumed that a *separate* set of phase numbers is used by each processor, for example, by appending the processor id as the "lower" bits of the phase number.

Calls to safe-phase also take a *value* parameter and return a value subject to the following conditions:

Validity: If an invocation of safe-phase returns $v \neq \perp$, then v is the *value* parameter in some invocation of safe-phase that begins before the return of v

Agreement: If an invocation returns $v \neq \perp$, then no invocation returns a value other than v or $\perp$.

Conditional termination: If there is an invocation of safe-phase with phase number r such that every other invocation that begins before this one ends has a smaller phase number, then the invocation returns a value $v \neq \perp$.

Each processor maintains its current *suggestion* regarding a return value in a shared register. Each phase consists of two stages: In the first stage, the processor chooses a value v, and in the second stage it tries to decide on v as its return value. Specifically, in the first stage, a processor writes its new phase number, and reads all the registers. If some other processor is observed to have reached a larger phase, the processor ends the phase without choosing. Otherwise, the processor chooses the observed value with the largest phase number and writes this value, tagged with its own current phase number, as its suggestion to its register. If no value has yet been suggested, then the processor suggests the value that was its input parameter. In the second stage, the processor reads all the registers; if all processors are still in a smaller phase, the processor decides on its chosen value.

In more detail, processor p_i has a single-writer multi-reader register R_i with the following fields:

Algorithm 59 safe-phase procedure for processor p_i.

---

procedure safe-phase(value x, integer r)
 // Stage 1: choose that value with largest phase tag
1:   $R_i.phase := r$ // other fields of R_i are written with their current values
2:   $maxPhase := 0$
3:   $chosenVal := x$
4:   for $j := 0$ to $n - 1$ do
5:      if $R_j.phase\text{-}tag > r$ then return $\perp$
6:      if $R_j.val \neq \perp$ then
7:         if $R_j.phase\text{-}tag > maxPhase$ then
8:            $maxPhase := R_j.phase\text{-}tag$
9:            $chosenVal := R_j.val$
10: $R_i := \langle r, chosenVal, r \rangle$
 // Stage 2: check that no other processor started a larger phase
11: for $j := 0$ to $n - 1$ do
12:     if $R_j.phase > r$ then return $\perp$
13: return $chosenVal$

---

phase The current phase number, initially 0.

val The value that p tried to commit in its last phase, initially $\perp$.

phase-tag The phase in which *val* was written.

Algorithm 59 presents the pseudocode.

Note that *chosenVal*, initially set to the argument x, is overwritten unless every other processor has a smaller phase and a $\perp$ value in its shared variable.

We first prove that the algorithm satisfies the validity property. The decision value is either processor p_i's input or a value read from some other processor's register. Simple induction shows this register contains only input values, which implies the validity of the algorithm.

Next, we prove the agreement property. Let p_i be the processor that decides with the smallest phase number, r_i, on some value v. This processor is well-defined because processors use distinct phase numbers.

We first argue that all processors that write a suggestion for a later phase (greater than r_i) suggest v. Otherwise, let p_j be the processor that first writes (in Line 10) a conflicting suggestion $v' \neq v$ for a phase $r_j > r_i$. (Again, this processor is well-defined because processors use distinct phase numbers and writes are atomic.) Note that p_i's second read from $R_j.phase$ (in Line 12) during phase r_i does not see r_j or a larger phase number, otherwise p_i would return $\perp$, and not v, from safe-phase. The invocations of safe-phase by p_i have increasing phase numbers and thus, p_j's first write to $R_j.phase$ (in Line 1) for phase r_j follows p_i's write of v to $R_i.val$ (in Line 10) for phase r_i. Hence p_j reads v from $R_i.val$ with phase number r_i during phase r_j. Because p_j is the earliest processor to write a conflicting value with phase number larger than r_i, p_j only sees the value v associated with phase numbers that are at least r_i during the for loop in Lines 11–12. Thus p_j suggests v, not v', for phase r_j.

Because processors decide only on values they suggest, no processor decides on a value different than v.

Finally, we verify conditional termination. Inspecting the code reveals that if a nonfaulty processor p_i executes an entire phase with the largest phase number, then p_i decides.

17.2 FAILURE DETECTORS

A way to capture stability properties of an asynchronous system is with the concept of a *failure detector*. When combined with the safety-preserving mechanism in Algorithm 59, failure detectors allow termination to be achieved. This section augments the formal model of computation given in Chapters 2 and 5 to model failure detectors.

Every processor p_i has a failure detector component called *suspect*$_i$ that contains a set of processor ids. The state transition function of a processor uses the current value of *suspect*$_i$ as one of its arguments (in addition to the current accessible state of p_i).

The state transition function does not change *suspect*$_i$. Instead, *suspect*$_i$ is updated by a *failure detector algorithm*, which we are not explicitly modeling. In each configuration of the system, the value of each *suspect*$_i$ component contains a set of processor ids. If p_j is in *suspect*$_i$, then we say that p_i *suspects* p_j (of being faulty). Below we put constraints on the values of the *suspect* variables in admissible executions to reflect the workings of a specific kind of failure detector.

What do we want a failure detector to do? First, it should tell us that a failed processor has failed. Such a condition is called "completeness." In particular, we shall insist that *eventually* every processor that crashes is permanently suspected by every nonfaulty processor. To rule out unhelpful failure detectors that would simply suspect everyone, we also would like a failure detector not to tell us that an operational processor has failed. Such a condition is called "accuracy." We first consider a fairly weak form of accuracy, in which eventually *some* nonfaulty processor is never suspected by any nonfaulty processor. Note that the failure detector is allowed to make some mistakes for a while before settling down to good behavior. Incorporating the above discussion into the formal model, we get the following definition.

Definition 17.1 *A failure detector is* eventually strong, *denoted* $\diamond S$, *if every admissible execution satisfies the following two properties:*

- *For every nonfaulty processor p_i and faulty processor p_j, there is a suffix of the execution in which j is in suspect$_i$ in every configuration of the suffix.*

- *There exists a nonfaulty processor p_i and a suffix of the execution such that for every nonfaulty processor p_j, i is not in suspect$_j$ in any configuration of the suffix.*

The accuracy property can be strengthened so that there is some nonfaulty processor that is *never* suspected.

Definition 17.2 *A failure detector is* strong, *denoted* S, *if every admissible execution satisfies the following two properties:*

- *For every nonfaulty processor p_i and faulty processor p_j, there is a suffix of the execution in which j is in $suspect_i$ in every configuration of the suffix.*

- *There exists a nonfaulty processor p_i such that for every nonfaulty processor p_j, i is not in $suspect_j$ in any configuration of the execution.*

A complementary approach equips every processor p_i with a component called $trust_i$ that contains a single processor id, instead of $suspect_i$. The indicated processor can be considered a leader. In a similar manner, the state transition function of a processor uses the current value of $trust_i$ as one of its arguments; $trust_i$ is updated by a *failure detection algorithm*, which we are not explicitly modeling; this algorithm can also be viewed as a leader election algorithm. If $trust_i$ is p_j, then we say that p_i *trusts* p_j (as being nonfaulty).

Analogously to the $\diamond S$ failure detector, we allow this failure detector, called Ω, to be initially unreliable; it can fail either by electing a faulty processor or by causing different processors to trust different leaders. More formally:

Definition 17.3 *A failure detector is a* leader elector, *denoted* Ω, *if every admissible execution satisfies the following property:*

- *Eventually $trust_i$ at every nonfaulty processor p_i holds the id of the same nonfaulty processor.*

17.3 SOLVING CONSENSUS USING FAILURE DETECTORS

17.3.1 Solving Consensus with $\diamond S$

A "rotating coordinator" paradigm is employed to solve consensus with $\diamond S$. The *coordinator* of phase r is the processor p_c, where $c = r \bmod n$, and it calls safe-phase with phase number r. A processor that is not the coordinator of phase r simply waits until either the coordinator completes phase r, or it suspects the coordinator. Then the processor increases its phase number and repeats.

The pseudocode appears in Algorithm 60.

We now show that, in any admissible execution of Algorithm 60, the hypothesis for conditional termination of safe-phase holds, that is, eventually there will be a processor that executes an entire invocation of safe-phase with the largest phase number. Consider a point in the execution when all the faulty processors have crashed and henceforth some nonfaulty processor p_c is never suspected. Let $r_{\max}$ be the maximum phase (according to $R_i.phase$) of any nonfaulty processor at that point. Let r be the smallest multiple of c that is larger than $r_{\max}$. Clearly, no nonfaulty

---

Algorithm 60 Consensus with $\diamond S$: code for processor p_i.

```
 1:   r := 0
 2:   while true
 3:       c := r mod n
 4:       if i = c then
 5:           ans := safe-phase(r,x)                       // x is p_i's input
 6:           if ans ≠ ⊥ then y := ans                     // and halt, y is p_i's output
 7:       else wait until c ∈ suspect or R_c.phase ≥ r     // not a coordinator
 8:       r := r + 1                                       // and repeat
```

---

processor gets stuck at any phase number unless it decides. Thus eventually p_c executes safe-phase with phase number r and is the coordinator of that phase.

Suppose, in contradiction, that there is another processor p_i that executes safe-phase with a phase number $r' \geq r$ concurrently with p_c's execution of safe-phase with phase number r. Because different processors use different phase numbers, $r' \neq r$, and thus $r' > r$. Because processors do not skip phases, p_i executed phase r at some earlier time. How did p_i finish phase r? Obviously p_c had not finished phase r yet, so p_i must have suspected p_c. But p_i executes phase r after the time when p_c is no longer suspected, because $r > r_{\max}$, which is a contradiction.

As stated, the conditional termination property ensures only that processor p_c terminates. It is possible to make all processors terminate in this case, by having a processor write its decision to a shared register once it has decided. A processor begins each iteration of the while loop by checking the decision registers of the other processors; if anyone else has decided, the processor decides the same value. This modification ensures that after p_c decides, eventually every nonfaulty processor decides as well.

Theorem 17.1 *Consensus can be solved in shared memory systems using $\diamond S$, for any number of crash failures.*

In contrast to the wait-freedom possible in shared memory, $n > 2f$ is necessary for solving consensus with $\diamond S$ when processors communicate by message passing. This result is shown using a familiar partitioning argument (cf. Theorem 10.22 in Chapter 10).

Theorem 17.2 *Consensus cannot be solved using the $\diamond S$ failure detector in an asynchronous system if $n \leq n/2$.*

Proof. Suppose in contradiction that there is an algorithm A that solves consensus using the $\diamond S$ failure detector in an asynchronous system with $n \leq 2f$. Partition the set of processors into two sets S_0 and S_1 with $|S_0| = \lceil n/2 \rceil$ and $|S_1| = \lfloor n/2 \rfloor$.

Consider an admissible execution α_0 of A in which all inputs are 0, all processors in S_0 are nonfaulty, and all processors in S_1 crash initially. Furthermore, suppose the failure detector behavior is such that every processor in S_0 permanently suspects every processor in S_1 and never suspects any processor in S_0. By the termination and validity conditions of A, some processor p_i in S_0 decides 0 at some time t_0.

Consider an analogous admissible execution α_1 of A in which all inputs are 1, all processors in S_1 are nonfaulty, and all processors in S_0 crash initially. Suppose the failure detector behavior is such that every processor in S_1 permanently suspects every processor in S_0 and never suspects any processor in S_1. Again, by the termination and validity conditions of A, some processor p_j in S_1 decides 1 at some time t_1.

Finally, consider an admissible execution α_2 of A that is a "merger" of α_0 and α_1. In more detail, all processors in S_0 have input 0, all processors in S_1 have input 1, and there are no faulty processors, but messages between S_0 and S_1 are delayed until time $t_2 = \max\{t_0, t_1\}$. Suppose the $\diamond S$ failure detector behaves as follows: Every processor in S_0 suspects every processor in S_1 until time t_2, and then it suspects no one. Every processor in S_1 suspects every processor in S_0 until time t_2, and then it suspects no one.

Executions α_0 and α_2 are indistinguishable to p_i until time t_2, so p_i decides 0 at time t_0 in α_2. But executions α_1 and α_2 are indistinguishable to p_j until time t_2, so p_j decides 1 at time t_1 in α_2. Thus α_2 violates the agreement condition for consensus. $\qquad\square$

The simulation of shared memory in a message-passing system (Section 10.4) can be applied to the algorithm of Theorem 17.1 to obtain Theorem 17.3.

Theorem 17.3 *Consensus can be solved in message-passing systems using $\diamond S$, assuming that $n > 2f$.*

17.3.2 Solving Consensus with S

In shared memory systems, the same algorithm used with $\diamond S$ (Algorithm 60) can be used to solve consensus with S. Because S guarantees that some nonfaulty processor p_j is never suspected by nonfaulty processors, the algorithm terminates when p_j takes on the role of coordinator. That is, the algorithm terminates within n phases.

When message-passing systems are considered, Theorem 17.2 cannot be extended to show that $n > 2f$ is required for solving consensus with S. In fact, consensus can be solved for any value of n and f when S can be employed.

One way to derive this algorithm (Exercise 17.3 explores another way) is to use S in order to simulate shared memory on top of message passing, without requiring that $n > 2f$.

Specifically, we modify the simulation of shared memory in a message-passing system (Section 10.4) so that processor p_i waits for responses from all processors not in *suspect$_i$*.

In more detail, when the writer wants to write a value to a register, it sends a message containing the new value and an incremented sequence number to all the processors. Each recipient updates a local variable with the value, if the sequence number is larger than what it currently has; in any event, the recipient sends back an acknowledgment. Once the writer receives acknowledgments from all processors it

---

Algorithm 61 Consensus with Ω: code for processor p_i.

1:    $r := 0$
2:    while true do
3:       if $i = trust$ then
4:          $ans := \mathsf{safe\text{-}phase}(r + i, x)$ // x is p_i's input
5:          if $ans \neq \perp$ then $y := ans$ // and halt, y is p_i's output
6:       $r := r + n$ // and repeat

---

does not suspect, it finishes the write. The properties of $\mathcal{S}$ guarantee that the writer eventually receives responses from all processors it does not suspect.

In a similar manner, in order to read the register, a reader sends a message to all the processors. Each recipient sends back a message with the value it currently has. Once the reader receives a responses from all processors it does not suspect, it returns the value with the largest sequence number among those received.

Failure detector $\mathcal{S}$ guarantees that there is some nonfaulty processor, say p_j, that is never suspected by any processor. Clearly, p_j is in the intersection of the set of processors sending an acknowledgment to the writer and the set of processors sending a response value to the reader. Exercise 17.4 asks you to show that the algorithm correctly simulates a shared register, following the proof of Theorem 10.21.

17.3.3 Solving Consensus with Ω

An alternative approach to solving consensus relies on the failure detector Ω. Algorithm 59 is executed together with failure detector Ω, which provides termination. Different processors use different phase numbers, in particular, processor p_i uses phase numbers $i, n + i, 2n + i, 3n + i, \ldots$. As long as processor p_i is a leader and has not yet decided, p_i calls safe-phase with increasing phase numbers.

The pseudocode appears in Algorithm 61.

To see why Algorithm 61 is correct, consider any admissible execution. Eventually, at some point in the execution, Ω ensures that every processor continuously trusts the same nonfaulty processor, call it p_c. All invocations of safe-phase that are in progress at that time are completed by some later time, after which no processor other than p_c invokes safe-phase any more. Processor p_c, however, continues to invoke safe-phase and thus eventually does so with a phase number that is larger than the phase number of any other invocation. This invocation satisfies the hypotheses for the conditional termination condition of safe-phase and thus it returns a non-$\perp$ value, causing p_c to decide. Termination of other processors can be handled in the same manner as for Algorithm 60.

For message-passing systems, it can be shown (Exercise 17.5) that $n > 2f$ is required for solving consensus, even when the system is augmented with the Ω failure detector. Under the assumption that $n > 2f$, Algorithm 61 can be executed in a message-passing system, using the simulation of Section 10.4.

17.4 IMPLEMENTING FAILURE DETECTORS

Because $\diamond \mathcal{S}$ can be used to solve consensus, it is not possible to implement $\diamond \mathcal{S}$ in an asynchronous system subject to crash failures. If it were, then consensus could be solved, contradicting the impossibility of doing so shown in Chapter 5. Obviously, the same observation holds for any failure detector that can be used to solve consensus, for example, $\mathcal{S}$ and Ω.

However, this observation is a theoretical one, which shows that for any proposed algorithm, there is a particularly adversarial execution in which it will fail. More practically speaking, there is a simple implementation of $\diamond \mathcal{S}$ based on timeouts. Each processor periodically sends an 'I'm alive' message to all the other processors. If a processor p_i does not hear from another processor p_j for some length of time (called the timeout interval for p_j), then p_i puts p_j in its suspect list. If p_i hears from p_j while p_i suspects p_j, then p_i removes p_j from its suspect list and increases the timeout interval for p_j.

Clearly this scheme satisfies the completeness property of $\diamond \mathcal{S}$: Because a processor that has failed never sends any more 'I'm alive' messages, this processor will eventually be put in every nonfaulty processor's suspect list and never removed. What about the accuracy property of $\diamond \mathcal{S}$? It is possible that a nonfaulty processor p_j will continually be added to and removed from the suspect list of another nonfaulty processor. This behavior, which violates the accuracy property, occurs if the messages from p_j to p_i always have delay longer than the current timeout interval for p_j being maintained by p_i. However, such a pattern of message delays is highly unlikely to occur.

A similar scheme implements $\mathcal{S}$ if some nonfaulty process *never* violates the timing assumptions.

Ω can be built on top of another failure detector, in particular, $\diamond \mathcal{S}$, or implemented directly using timing assumptions.

17.5 STATE MACHINE REPLICATION WITH FAILURE DETECTORS

Recall the state machine approach for implementing distributed systems, described in Section 8.4.2. In this approach, a system is described as a state machine, whose transitions are initiated by client requests and return responses. If the state machine is deterministic, then the key issue is *ordering* (or *sequencing*) the clients' requests.

A simple way to order the requests uses a single coordinator (server), who receives requests from clients, applies them to the state machine, computes responses, and sends them back to the clients. Obviously, in this scheme, the server is a single point of failure. Fault tolerance can be improved by replacing the single server with a collection of servers.

One approach to state machine replication has one of the servers act as the coordinator in normal execution mode; when the coordinator fails, one of the remaining servers is elected to replace it as the new coordinator. When the system is asynchronous, leader election must rely on timing assumptions or other mechanisms for detecting failures; the leader election mechanism may fail to converge, when the system does not obey the timing assumptions. This behavior can be encapsulated within failure detector Ω.

Ω may produce erroneous results for a while, causing several servers to consider themselves coordinators until Ω stabilizes and elects a single leader. If each (self-proclaimed) coordinator orders clients' request on its own, different processors' views of the state machine transitions will diverge and become inconsistent. Instead, agreement among coordinators must be used to order clients' requests. Servers that consider themselves coordinators invoke a copy of Algorithm 61 for each state machine transition; their input is the next client request they wish to commit. The coordinators invoke the algorithm for transition $\ell + 1$ only after transitions $1, \ldots, \ell$ are decided, and the state of the machine after the first ℓ transitions is fixed.

Note that even when the system is stable, with a unique nonfaulty coordinating server, the coordinator still calls Algorithm 61 for every transition of the state machine. The reason is that other processors may erroneously suspect the coordinator is faulty and try to replace it.

Exercises

17.1 Modify the proof of Theorem 17.2 to show that nonfaulty processors must continue to send messages in order to solve consensus with $\diamond S$.

17.2 Show optimizations to the message and time complexity of the simulation of shared memory by message passing in the context of Theorem 17.3.

17.3 Directly derive a consensus algorithm for message-passing systems, with any number of faulty processors, using S.

Hint: Follow Algorithm 15.

17.4 Expand the ideas presented in Section 17.3.2 to show a simulation of a shared register in a message-passing system, with any number of failures, assuming failure detector S.

Hint: Follow Theorem 10.21.

17.5 Modify the proof of Theorem 17.2, to show that consensus cannot be solved using the Ω failure detector in an asynchronous system if $n \leq 2f$.

17.6 Suppose that the completeness property of the $\diamond S$ failure detector is weakened to require that eventually every crashed processor is suspected by *some* nonfaulty processor (instead of every one). Either show how to convert this weaker failure detector into $\diamond S$ in an asynchronous system with $n > 2f$, or prove that it is impossible.

Can this weaker failure detector be used to solve consensus in an asynchronous system?

17.7 Suppose that the accuracy property of the $\diamond S$ failure detector is strengthened to require that eventually *no* nonfaulty processor is suspected by any nonfaulty processor. Either show that consensus cannot be solved in an asynchronous system with this stronger failure detector when $n \leq 2f$ or describe an algorithm using this failure detector that works when $n \leq 2f$.

17.8 $\diamond \mathcal{P}$ is a failure detector that guarantees that eventually each processor's suspected list contains exactly the faulty processors. Can you use $\diamond \mathcal{P}$ to simulate Ω?
Can you use Ω to simulate $\diamond \mathcal{P}$?
Either give algorithms or give impossibility proofs. Assume a message passing system with crash failures.

Chapter Notes

The original paper introducing failure detectors was by Chandra and Toueg [67], who proposed a variety of completeness and accuracy conditions. They also presented consensus algorithms for message-passing systems, using various failure detectors. Lo and Hadzilacos [171] studied failure detectors in shared-memory systems, and presented consensus algorithms using $\diamond S$ and S.

Our presentation is inspired by the work of Delporte-Gallet, Fauconnier, and Guerraoui [89], who studied shared memory simulations using failure detectors. (The solution to Exercise 17.4 can be found in this paper.) Algorithm 59 is based on algorithms presented by Lo, and Hadzilacos [171] and by Gafni and Lamport [116].

The failure detector in Exercise 17.6 is $\diamond W$; Chandra, Hadzilacos, and Toueg [66] showed that no weaker failure detector can solve consensus.

In the crash failure model, a failed processor is indistinguishable from a slow processor. In contrast, in the *failstop model*, described in Chapter 8, it is possible to tell whether a processor has failed. Sabel and Marzullo [230] use failure detector $\diamond W$ to simulate failstop processors in the presence of crash failures.

Failure detectors have been applied to several other problems, including various kinds of broadcasts [67], atomic commitment [126], leader election [231], and group membership [41, 79, 114, 169]. Additional work has addressed the relationships between different failure detector specifications [67, 83], and failure detectors in shared memory [171, 197].

Algorithm 61 is the shared memory version of the *Paxos* algorithm for message-passing systems, presented by Lamport [161], originally in 1989. Our description is inspired by the so-called *Disk Paxos* algorithm of Gafni and Lamport [116]. De Prisco, Lampson, and Lynch [220] describe an alternative way to derive Algorithm 61, by embedding the leader election into the algorithm. Their algorithm uses processor ids to break ties when there are several conflicting proposals for the same phase and terminates when certain timing assumptions hold.

In the state machine replication scheme described in Section 17.5, Algorithm 61 is invoked for each transition of the state machine, because it is not clear whether the system is stable or a new coordinator is being elected. Lamport [161] optimizes the normal case, where the system is stable and there is a single coordinator. The coordinator performs the first stage of safe-phase for several transitions at once. Thus, ideally, a leader will be able to commit several waiting transitions fairly quickly.

It is worth comparing the Paxos approach to state machine replication, discussed in this chapter, with state machine replication using totally order broadcast, described in Chapter 8. The latter approach is more flexible because applications can trade off weaker semantics of the broadcast service for better performance; this allows the development of applications in an incremental manner, first prototyping using strong semantics, then gradually weakening the semantics provided by the broadcast service in order to improve performance, while preserving correctness. On the other hand, the safety mechanism embedded in the Paxos approach, when translated to message passing, requires a processor to communicate only with a majority of the processors, whereas broadcast-based replication requires all group members to acknowledge each operation.

References

1. Karl Abrahamson. On achieving consensus using a shared memory. In *Proceedings of the 7th Annual ACM Symposium on Principles of Distributed Computing*, pages 291–302. ACM, 1988.

2. Sarita Adve and Mark Hill. Weak ordering—A new definition. In *Proceedings of the 17th Annual International Symposium on Computer Architecture*, pages 2–14, 1990.

3. Yehuda Afek, Hagit Attiya, Danny Dolev, Eli Gafni, Michael Merritt, and Nir Shavit. Atomic snapshots of shared memory. *Journal of the ACM*, 40(4):873–890, September 1993.

4. Yehuda Afek, Geoffrey Brown, and Michael Merritt. Lazy caching. *ACM Transactions on Programming Languages and Systems*, 15(1):182–205, January 1993.

5. Yehuda Afek, Danny Dolev, Eli Gafni, Michael Merritt, and Nir Shavit. A bounded first-in, first-enabled solution to the *l*-exclusion problem. *ACM Transactions on Programming Languages and Systems*, 16(3):939–953, May 1994.

6. Yehuda Afek and Yossi Matias. Elections in anonymous networks. *Information and Computation*, 113(2):312–330, September 1994.

7. Marcos Kawazoe Aguilera and Sam Toueg. A simple bivalency proof that *t*-resilient consensus requires $t + 1$ rounds. *Information Processing Letters*, 71(3-4):155–158, 1999.

8. J. Alemany and E. W. Felten. Performance issues in non-blocking synchronization on shared-memory multiprocessors. In *Proceedings of the 11th Annual ACM Symposium on Principles of Distributed Computing*, pages 125–134, 1992.

9. Y. Amir, D. Dolev, S. Kramer, and D. Malki. *Total Ordering of Messages in Broadcast Domains*. Technical Report CS92-9, Dept. of Computer Science, The Hebrew University of Jerusalem, 1992.

10. Y. Amir, L. E. Moser, P. M. Melliar-Smith, D.A. Agarwal, and P. Ciarfella. The totem single-ring ordering and membership protocol. *ACM Transactions on Computer Systems*, 13(4):311–342, 1995.

11. Yair Amir, Danny Dolev, Shlomo Kramer, and Dalia Malki. Transis: A communication sub-system for high availability. In *Proceedings of the 22nd Annual International Symposium on Fault-Tolerant Computing*, pages 76–84, 1992.

12. Cristiana Amza, Alan L. Cox, Sandhya Dwarkadas, Pete Keleher, Honghui Lu, Ramakrishnan Rajamony, Weimin Yu, and Willy Zwaenepoel. TreadMarks: Shared memory computing on networks of workstations. *IEEE Computer*, 29(2):18–28, February 1996.

13. James Anderson. Composite registers. *Distributed Computing*, 6(3):141–154, April 1993.

14. James Anderson. Multi-writer composite registers. *Distributed Computing*, 7(4):175–196, May 1994.

15. James H. Anderson, Yong-Jik Kim, and Ted Herman. Shared-memory mutual exclusion: major research trends since 1986. *Distributed Computing*, 16(2–3):75–110, 2003.

16. Thomas E. Anderson. The performance of spin lock alternatives for shared-memory multiprocessors. *IEEE Transactions on Parallel and Distributed Systems*, 1(1):6–16, January 1990.

17. Dana Angluin. Local and global properties in networks of processors. In *Proceedings of the 12th ACM Symposium on Theory of Computing*, pages 82–93, 1980.

18. ANSI/IEEE. *Local Area Networks: Token Ring Access Method and physical Layer Specifications, Std 802.5*. Technical report, 1989.

19. Eshrat Arjomandi, Michael J. Fischer, and Nancy A. Lynch. Efficiency of synchronous versus asynchronous distributed systems. *Journal of the ACM*, 30(3):449–456, July 1983.

20. James Aspnes. Lower bounds for distributed coin-flipping and randomized consensus. *Journal of the ACM*, 45(3):415–450, 1998.

21. James Aspnes. Randomized protocols for asynchronous consensus. *Distributed Computing*, 16(2–3):165–175, 2003.

22. James Aspnes and Maurice Herlihy. Wait-free data structures in the asynchronous PRAM model. In *Proceedings of the 2nd Annual ACM Symposium on Parallel Algorithms and Architectures*, pages 340–349, 1990.

23. James Aspnes and Orli Waarts. Randomized consensus in expected $O(N \log^2 N)$ operations per processor. *SIAM Journal on Computing*, 25(5):1024–1044, October 1996.

24. Hagit Attiya. Efficient and robust sharing of memory in message-passing systems. *Journal of Algorithms*, 34(1):109–127, 2000.

25. Hagit Attiya, Amotz Bar-Noy, and Danny Dolev. Sharing memory robustly in message-passing systems. *Journal of the ACM*, 42(1):121–132, January 1995.

26. Hagit Attiya, Amotz Bar-Noy, Danny Dolev, David Peleg, and Rudiger Reischuk. Renaming in an asynchronous environment. *Journal of the ACM*, 37(3):524–548, July 1990.

27. Hagit Attiya, Cynthia Dwork, Nancy Lynch, and Larry Stockmeyer. Bounds on the time to reach agreement in the presence of timing uncertainty. *Journal of the ACM*, 41(1):122–152, January 1994.

28. Hagit Attiya and Roy Friedman. A correctness condition for high-performance multiprocessors. *SIAM Journal on Computing*, 27(6):1637–1670, 1998.

29. Hagit Attiya, Amir Herzberg, and Sergio Rajsbaum. Clock synchronization under different delay assumptions. *SIAM Journal on Computing*, 25(2):369–389, April 1996.

30. Hagit Attiya and Marios Mavronicolas. Efficiency of semisynchronous versus asynchronous networks. *Mathematical Systems Theory*, 27(6):547–571, Nov./Dec. 1994.

31. Hagit Attiya and Ophir Rachman. Atomic snapshots in $O(n \log n)$ operations. *SIAM Journal on Computing*, 27(2):319–340, March 1998.

32. Hagit Attiya and Sergio Rajsbaum. The combinatorial structure of wait-free solvable tasks. *SIAM Journal on Computing*, 31(4):1286–1313, 2002.

33. Hagit Attiya, Marc Snir, and Manfred Warmuth. Computing on an anonymous ring. *Journal of the ACM*, 35(4):845–876, October 1988.

34. Hagit Attiya and Jennifer L. Welch. Sequential consistency versus linearizability. *ACM Transactions on Computer Systems*, 12(2):91–122, May 1994.

35. Hagit Attiya and Jennifer L. Welch. *Distributed Computing: Fundamentals, Simulations and Advanced Topics*. McGraw-Hill Publishing Company, May 1998.

36. Baruch Awerbuch. Complexity of network synchronization. *Journal of the ACM*, 32(4):804–823, October 1985.

37. Baruch Awerbuch. New distributed depth-first-search algorithm. *Information Processing Letters*, 20(3):147–150, April 1985.

38. Baruch Awerbuch. Reducing complexities of distributed maximum flow and breadth-first-search algorithms by means of network synchronization. *Networks*, 15(4):425–437, Winter 1985.

39. Baruch Awerbuch. Optimal distributed algorithms for minmum weight spanning tree, counting, leader election and related problems. In *Proceedings of the 19th ACM Symposium on Theory of Computing*, pages 230–240. ACM, 1987.

40. Baruch Awerbuch and David Peleg. Network synchronization with polylogarithmic overhead. In *Proceedings of the 31th IEEE Symposium on Foundations of Computer Science*, volume II, pages 514–522, 1990.

41. Ozalp Babaoglu, Renzo Davoli, and Alberto Montresor. Group communication in partitionable systems: Specification and algorithms. *IEEE Transactions on Software Engineering*, 27(4):308–336, 2001.

42. Ozalp Babaoglu and Keith Marzullo. Consistent global states of distributed systems: Fundamental concepts and mechanisms. In Sape Mullender, editor, *Distributed Systems*, chapter 4. Addison-Wesley Publishing Company, Wokingham, 2nd edition, 1993.

43. Henri E. Bal, M. Frans Kaashoek, and Andrew S. Tanenbaum. Orca: A language for parallel programming of distributed systems. *IEEE Transactions on Software Engineering*, 18(3):180–205, March 1992.

44. Amotz Bar-Noy, Danny Dolev, Cynthia Dwork, and H. Raymond Strong. Shifting gears: Changing algorithms on the fly to expedite Byzantine agreement. *Information and Computation*, 97(2):205–233, April 1992.

45. Valmir Barbosa. *An Introduction to Distributed Algorithms*. MIT Press, 1996.

46. Rida A. Bazzi and Gil Neiger. The complexity of almost-optimal coordination. *Algorithmica*, 17(3):308–321, March 1997.

47. Rida Adnan Bazzi. *Automatically Improving the Fault-Tolerance in Distributed Systems*. PhD thesis, College of Computing, Georgia Institute of Technology, 1994. Technical Report GIT-CC-94-62.

48. Michael Ben-Or. Another advantage of free choice: Completely asynchronous agreement protocols. In *Proceedings of the 2nd Annual ACM Symposium on Principles of Distributed Computing*, pages 27–30, 1983.

49. J. K. Bennett, J. B. Carter, and W. Zwaenepoel. Munin: Distributed shared memory based on type-specific memory coherence. In *Proceedings of the 2nd*

Annual ACM Symposium on Principles and Practice of Parallel Processing, pages 168–176, 1990.

50. Pioter Berman and Juan Garay. Cloture votes: $n/4$-resilient distributed consensus in $t + 1$ rounds. *Mathematical Systems Theory*, 26(1):3–19, 1993.

51. B. N. Bershad. Practical considerations for non-blocking concurrent objects. In *Proceedings of the 13th International Conference on Distributed Computing Systems*, pages 264–274, 1993.

52. Ofer Biran, Shlomo Moran, and Shmuel Zaks. A combinatorial characterization of the distributed 1-solvable tasks. *Journal of Algorithms*, 11(3):420–440, September 1990.

53. Ken Birman and Tommy Joseph. Reliable communication in the presence of failures. *ACM Transactions on Computer Systems*, 5(1):47–76, February 1987.

54. Ken Birman, Andre Schiper, and Pat Stephenson. Lightweight causal and atomic group multicast. *ACM Transactions on Computer Systems*, 9(3):272–314, August 1991.

55. Ken Birman and Robert van Renesse (eds.). *Reliable Distributed Programming with the Isis Toolkit*. IEEE Computer Society Press, 1993.

56. R. Bisiani and M. Ravishankar. PLUS: A distributed shared-memory system. In *Proceedings of the 17th Annual International Symposium on Computer Architecture*, pages 115–124, 1990.

57. J. A. Bondy and U. S. R. Murty. *Graph Theory with Applications*. MacMillan, London and Basingstoke, 1976.

58. Elizabeth Borowsky and Eli Gafni. Generalized FLP impossibility result for t-resilient asynchronous computations. In *Proceedings of the 25th ACM Symposium on Theory of Computing*, pages 91–100, New-York, 1993.

59. Elizabeth Borowsky, Eli Gafni, Nancy Lynch, and Sergio Rajsbaum. The BG distributed simulation algorithm. *Distributed Computing*, 14(3):127–146, 2001.

60. Gabriel Bracha. Asynchronous Byzantine agreement protocols. *Information and Computation*, 75(2):130–143, November 1987.

61. James E. Burns. *A Formal Model for Message Passing Systems*. Technical Report 91, Indiana University, September 1980.

62. James E. Burns, Paul Jackson, Nancy A. Lynch, Michael J. Fischer, and Gary L. Peterson. Data requirements for implementation of n-process mutual exclusion using a single shared variable. *Journal of the ACM*, 29(1):183–205, January 1982.

63. James E. Burns and Nancy A. Lynch. Bounds on shared memory for mutual exclusion. *Information and Computation*, 107(2):171–184, December 1993.

64. James E. Burns and Gary L. Peterson. The ambiguity of choosing. In *Proceedings of the 8th Annual ACM Symposium on Principles of Distributed Computing*, pages 145–158, 1989.

65. R. Canetti and T. Rabin. Fast asynchronous Byzantine agreement with optimal resilience. In *Proceedings of the 25th ACM Symposium on Theory of Computing*, pages 42–51, 1993.

66. Tushar Deepak Chandra, Vassos Hadzilacos, and Sam Toueg. The weakest failure detector for solving consensus. *Journal of the ACM*, 43(4):685–722, 1996.

67. Tushar Deepak Chandra and Sam Toueg. Unreliable failure detectors for reliable distributed systems. *Journal of the ACM*, 43(2):225–267, March 1996.

68. K. Mani Chandy. *Essence of Distributed Snapshots*. Technical Report CS-TR-89-05, California Institute of Technology, 1989.

69. K. Mani Chandy and Leslie Lamport. Distributed snapshots: Determining global states of distributed systems. *ACM Transactions on Computer Systems*, 3(1):63–75, February 1985.

70. Ernest Chang and Rosemary Roberts. An improved algorithm for decentralized extrema-finding in circular configurations of processes. *Communications of the ACM*, 22(5):281–283, May 1979.

71. Jo-Mei Chang and N. F. Maxemchuk. Reliable broadcast protocols. *ACM Transactions on Computer Systems*, 2(3):251–273, August 1984.

72. Bernadette Charron-Bost. Concerning the size of logical clocks in distributed systems. *Information Processing Letters*, 39:11–16, July 1991.

73. Soma Chaudhuri. More choices allow more faults: Set consensus problems in totally asynchronous systems. *Information and Computation*, 103(1):132–158, July 1993.

74. Soma Chaudhuri, Rainer Gawlick, and Nancy Lynch. Designing algorithms for distributed systems with partially synchronized clocks. In *Proceedings of the 12th Annual ACM Symposium on Principles of Distributed Computing*, pages 121–132, 1993.

75. Soma Chaudhuri, Maurice Herlihy, Nancy A. Lynch, and Mark R. Tuttle. Tight bounds for k-set agreement. *Journal of the ACM*, 47(5):912–943, 2000.

76. Soma Chaudhuri, Martha J. Kosa, and Jennifer L. Welch. One-write algorithms for multivalued regular and atomic registers. *Acta Informatica*, 37(3):161–192, 2000.

77. D. R. Cheriton and W. Zwaenepoel. Distributed process groups in the V kernel. *ACM Transactions on Computer Systems*, 2(3):77–107, May 1985.

78. To-Yat Cheung. Graph traversal techniques and the maximum flow problem in distributed computation. *IEEE Transactions on Software Engineering*, 9(4):504–512, July 1983.

79. Gregory Chockler, Idit Keidar, and Roman Vitenberg. Group communication specifications: A comprehensive study. *ACM Computing Surveys*, 33(4):427–469, December 2001.

80. B. Chor and C. Dwork. Randomization in Byzantine agreement. In *Advances in Computing Research 5: Randomness and Computation*, pages 443–497. JAI Press, 1989.

81. Benny Chor, Amos Israeli, and Ming Li. Wait-free consensus using asynchronous hardware. *SIAM Journal on Computing*, 23(4):701–712, August 1994.

82. Randy Chow and Theodore Johnson. *Distributed Operating Systems and Algorithms*. Addison-Wesley Publishing Company, 1997.

83. Francis Chu. Reducing Ω to $\diamond \mathcal{W}$. *Information Processing Letters*, 67:289–293, 1998.

84. Brian A. Coan. A compiler that increases the fault-tolerance of asynchronous protocols. *IEEE Transactions on Computers*, 37(12):1541–1553, December 1988.

85. G. Coulouris, J. Dollimore, and T. Kindberg. *Distributed Systems, Concepts and Designs*. Addison-Wesley Publishing Company, 2nd edition, 1994.

86. F. Cristian, R. Beijer, and S. Mishra. A performance comparison of asynchronous atomic broadcast protocols. *Distributed Systems Engineering Journal*, 1(4):177–201, 1994.

87. Flaviu Cristian. Probabilistic clock synchronization. *Distributed Computing*, 3(3):146–158, July 1989.

88. Flaviu Cristian, H. Aghili, Ray Strong, and Danny Dolev. Atomic broadcast: From simple message diffusion to Byzantine agreement. *Information and Computation*, 118(1):158–179, April 1995.

89. Carole Delporte-Gallet, Hugues Fauconnier, and Rachid Guerraoui. Failure detection lower bounds on registers and consensus. In *Proceedings of the 16th International Conference on Distributed Computing*, pages 237–251, 2002.

90. E. W. Dijkstra. Solution of a problem in concurrent programming control. *Communications of the ACM*, 8(9):569, 1965.

91. Danny Dolev. The Byzantine generals strike again. *Journal of Algorithms*, 3(1):14–30, March 1982.

92. Danny Dolev, Cynthia Dwork, and Larry Stockmeyer. On the minimal synchronism needed for distributed consensus. *Journal of the ACM*, 34(1):77–97, January 1987.

93. Danny Dolev, Joseph Y. Halpern, Barbara Simons, and H. Raymond Strong. Dynamic fault-tolerant clock synchronization. *Journal of the ACM*, 42(1):143–185, January 1995.

94. Danny Dolev, Joseph Y. Halpern, and H. Raymond Strong. On the possibility and impossibility of achieving clock synchronization. *Journal of Computer and System Sciences*, 32(2):230–250, April 1986.

95. Danny Dolev, Maria Klawe, and Michael Rodeh. An $O(n \log n)$ unidirectional distributed algorithm for extrema finding in a circle. *Journal of Algorithms*, 3(3):245–260, September 1982.

96. Danny Dolev, Nancy A. Lynch, Shlomit S. Pinter, Eugene W. Stark, and William E. Weihl. Reaching approximate agreement in the presence of faults. *Journal of the ACM*, 33(3):499–516, July 1986.

97. Danny Dolev, Dalia Malki, and H. Raymond Strong. *An asynchronous membership protocol that tolerates partitions*. Technical Report CS94-6, Institute of Computer Science, The Hebrew University, 1994.

98. Danny Dolev and Nir Shavit. Bounded concurrent time-stamping. *SIAM Journal on Computing*, 26(2):418–455, April 1997.

99. Danny Dolev and H. Raymond Strong. Authenticated algorithms for Byzantine agreement. *SIAM Journal on Computing*, 12(4):656–666, November 1983.

100. M. Dubois and C. Scheurich. Memory access dependencies in shared-memory multiprocessors. *IEEE Transactions on Software Engineering*, 16(6):660–673, June 1990.

101. Cynthia Dwork and Yoram Moses. Knowledge and common knowledge in a Byzantine environment: Crash failures. *Information and Computation*, 88(2):156–186, October 1990.

102. Cynthia Dwork and Orli Waarts. Simple and efficient bounded concurrent timestamping and the traceable use abstraction. *Journal of the ACM*, 46(5):633–666, September 1999.

103. E. Allen Emerson. Temporal and modal logic. In J. van Leeuwen, editor, *Handbook of Theoretical Computer Science*, volume B, chapter 16, pages 996–1072. Elsevier Science Publisher B. V., Amsterdam, 1990.

104. P. Feldman and S. Micali. Optimal algorithms for Byzantine agreement. In *Proceedings of the 20th ACM Symposium on Theory of Computing*, pages 162–172, 1988.

105. Faith E. Fich and Eric Ruppert. Hundreds of impossibility results for distributed computing. *Distributed Computing*, 16(2–3):121–163, 2003.

106. C. Fidge. Logical time in distributed computing systems. *IEEE Computer*, 24(8):28, August 1991.

107. Michael J. Fischer and Nancy A. Lynch. A lower bound for the time to assure interactive consistency. *Information Processing Letters*, 14(4):183–186, June 1982.

108. Michael J. Fischer, Nancy A. Lynch, James E. Burns, and Allan Borodin. Distributed FIFO allocation of identical resources using small shared space. *ACM Transactions on Programming Languages and Systems*, 11(1):90–114, January 1989.

109. Michael J. Fischer, Nancy A. Lynch, and Michael Merritt. Easy impossibility proofs for distributed consensus problems. *Distributed Computing*, 1(1):26–39, January 1986.

110. Michael J. Fischer, Nancy A. Lynch, and Michael S. Paterson. Impossibility of distributed consensus with one faulty processor. *Journal of the ACM*, 32(2):374–382, April 1985.

111. Greg N. Frederickson and Nancy Lynch. Electing a leader in a synchronous ring. *Journal of the ACM*, 34(1):98–115, January 1987.

112. Roy Friedman. *Consistency Conditions for Distributed Shared Memories*. PhD thesis, Department of Computer Science, The Technion, 1994.

113. Roy Friedman. Implementing hybrid consistency with high-level synchronization operations. *Distributed Computing*, 9(3):119–129, December 1995.

114. Roy Friedman and Robbert van Renesse. Strong and weak synchrony in horus. In *Proceedings of the 16th IEEE Symposium On Reliable Distributed Systems*, 1996.

115. Eli Gafni. Perspectives on distributed network protocols: A case for building blocks. In *Proceedings IEEE MILCOM '86*, 1986.

116. Eli Gafni and Leslie Lamport. Disk paxos. *Distributed Computing*, 16(1):1–20, 2003.

117. Robert Gallager. Finding a leader in a network with $o(e) + o(n \log n)$ messages. MIT Internal Memorandum, 1977.

118. Robert Gallager, Pierre Humblet, and Philip Spira. A distributed algorithm for minimum-weight spanning trees. *ACM Transactions on Programming Languages and Systems*, 5(1):66–77, January 1983.

119. Juan Garay and Yoram Moses. Fully polynomial Byzantine agreement for $n > 3t$ processors in $t + 1$ rounds. *SIAM Journal on Computing*, 27(1):247–290, February 1998.

120. Hector Garcia-Molina and Annemarie Spauster. Ordered and reliable multicast communication. *ACM Transactions on Programming Languages and Systems*, 9:242–271, August 1991.

121. Vijay K. Garg and Brian Waldecker. Detection of weak unstable predicates in distributed programs. *IEEE Transactions on Parallel and Distributed Systems*, 5(3):299–307, March 1994.

122. K. Gharachorloo, D. Lenoski, J. Laudon, P. Gibbons, A. Gupta, and J. Hennessy. Memory consistency and event ordering in scalable shared-memory multiprocessors. In *Proceedings of the 17th Annual International Symposium on Computer Architecture*, pages 15–26, 1990.

123. Oded Goldreich and Erez Petrank. The best of both worlds: Guaranteeing termination in fast randomized Byzantine agreement protocols. *Information Processing Letters*, 36(1):45–49, October 1990.

124. Ajei Gopal and Sam Toueg. Inconsistency and contamination. In *Proceedings of the 10th Annual ACM Symposium on Principles of Distributed Computing*, pages 257–272, 1991.

125. Gary Graunke and Shreekant Thakkar. Synchronization algorithms for shared-memory multiprocessors. *IEEE Computer*, 23(6):60–69, June 1990.

126. Rachid Guerraoui. Non-blocking atomic commit in asynchronous distributed systems with failure detectors. *Distributed Computing*, 15(1):17–25, 2002.

127. Rajiv Gupta, Scott A. Smolka, and Shaji Bhaskar. On randomization in sequential and distributed algorithms. *ACM Computing Surveys*, 26(1):7–86, March 1994.

128. Vassos Hadzilacos. *Issues of Fault Tolerance in Concurrent Computations*. PhD thesis, Aiken Computation Laboratory, Harvard University, June 1984.

129. Vassos Hadzilacos and Sam Toueg. *A modular approach to fault-tolerant broadcasts and related problems*. Technical Report TR 94-1425, Cornell University, Dept. of Computer Science, Cornell University, Ithaca, NY 14853, May 1994.

130. Joseph Y. Halpern, Nimrod Megiddo, and A. A. Munshi. Optimal precision in the presence of uncertainty. *Journal of Complexity*, 1(2):170–196, December 1985.

131. Maurice Herlihy. A methodology for implementing highly concurrent data objects. *ACM Transactions on Programming Languages and Systems*, 15(5):745–770, November 1993.

132. Maurice Herlihy and Nir Shavit. The asynchronous computability theorem for *t*-resilient tasks. In *Proceedings of the 25th ACM Symposium on Theory of Computing*, pages 111–120, 1993.

133. Maurice Herlihy and Nir Shavit. The topological structure of asynchronous computability. *Journal of the ACM*, 46(6):858–923, 1999.

134. Maurice P. Herlihy. Wait-free synchronization. *ACM Transactions on Programming Languages and Systems*, 13(1):124–149, January 1991.

135. Maurice P. Herlihy and Jeannette M. Wing. Linearizability: A correctness condition for concurrent objects. *ACM Transactions on Programming Languages and Systems*, 12(3):463–492, July 1990.

136. Lisa Higham. *Randomized Distributed Computing on Rings*. PhD thesis, Department of Computer Science, University of British Columbia, 1989. Technical Report 89-05.

137. Lisa Higham and Teresa Przytycka. A simple, efficient algorithm for maximum finding on rings. *Information Processing Letters*, 58(6):319–324, 1996.

138. Lisa Higham and Jolanta Warpechowska-Gruca. *Notes on Atomic Broadcast*. Technical Report 95/562/14, University of Calgary, Department of Computer Science, 1995.

139. D. S. Hirschberg and J. B. Sinclair. Decentralized extrema-finding in circular configurations of processors. *Communications of the ACM*, 23(11):627–628, November 1980.

140. Amos Israeli and Ming Li. Bounded time-stamps. *Distributed Computing*, 6(4):205–209, July 1993.

141. Alon Itai and Michael Rodeh. Symmetry breaking in distributed networks. *Information and Computation*, 88(1):60–87, September 1990.

142. Joseph JaJa. *An Introduction to Parallel Algorithms*. Addison-Wesley Publishing Company, Reading, Massachusetts, 1992.

143. B. Janssens and W. K. Fuchs. Relaxing consistency in recoverable distributed shared memory. In *Proceedings of the 23rd Annual International Symposium on Fault-Tolerant Computing*, pages 155–165, 1993.

144. Prasad Jayanti. Robust wait-free hierarchies. *Journal of the ACM*, 44(4):592–614, July 1997.

145. David B. Johnson and Willy Zwaenepoel. Recovery in distributed systems using optimistic message logging and checkpointing. *Journal of Algorithms*, 11(3):462–491, September 1990.

146. Frans Kaashoek, Andy Tanenbaum, S. Hummel, and Henri Bal. An efficient reliable broadcast protocol. *Operating Systems Review*, 23(4):5–19, October 1989.

147. Sundar Kanthadai and Jennifer L. Welch. Implementation of recoverable distributed shared memory by logging writes. In *Proceedings of the 16th International Conference on Distributed Computing Systems*, pages 116–124, 1996.

148. J-H. Kim and N. H. Vaidya. Recoverable distributed shared memory using the competitive update protocol. In *Proceedings of the 1995 Pacific Rim International Conference on Fault-Tolerant Systems*, pages 152–157, 1995.

149. Martha J. Kosa. Making operations of concurrent data types fast. In *Proceedings of the 13th Annual ACM Symposium on Principles of Distributed Computing*, pages 32–41, 1994.

150. Eyal Kushilevitz, Yishay Mansour, Michael O. Rabin, and David Zuckerman. Lower bounds for randomized mutual exclusion. *SIAM Journal on Computing*, 27(6):1550–1563, 1998.

151. Eyal Kushilevitz and Michael O. Rabin. Randomized mutual exclusion algorithms revisited. In *Proceedings of the 11th Annual ACM Symposium on Principles of Distributed Computing*, pages 275–284, 1992.

152. T. H. Lai and T. H. Yang. On distributed snapshots. In Zhonghua Yang and T. Anthony Marsland, editors, *Global States and Time in Distributed Systems*. IEEE Computer Society Press, 1994.

153. Leslie Lamport. A new solution of Dijkstra's concurrent programming problem. *Communications of the ACM*, 18(8):453–455, August 1974.

154. Leslie Lamport. The implementation of reliable distributed multiprocess systems. *Computer Networks*, 2:95–114, 1978.

155. Leslie Lamport. Time, clocks, and the ordering of events in a distributed system. *Communications of the ACM*, 21(7):558–564, July 1978.

156. Leslie Lamport. How to make a multiprocessor that correctly executes multiprocess programs. *IEEE Transactions on Computers*, C-28(9):690–691, September 1979.

157. Leslie Lamport. Using time instead of timeout for fault-tolerant distributed systems. *ACM Transactions on Programming Languages and Systems*, 6(2):254–280, April 1984.

158. Leslie Lamport. On interprocess communication, Part I: Basic formalism. *Distributed Computing*, 1(2):77–85, 1986.

159. Leslie Lamport. On interprocess communication, Part II: Algorithms. *Distributed Computing*, 1(2):86–101, 1986.

160. Leslie Lamport. A fast mutual exclusion algorithm. *ACM Transactions on Computer Systems*, 5(1):1–11, February 1987.

161. Leslie Lamport. The part-time parliament. *ACM Transactions on Computer Systems*, 16(2):133–169, 1998.

162. Leslie Lamport and P. M. Melliar-Smith. Synchronizing clocks in the presence of faults. *Journal of the ACM*, 32(1):52–78, January 1985.

163. Leslie Lamport, Robert Shostak, and Marshall Pease. The Byzantine generals problem. *ACM Transactions on Programming Languages and Systems*, 4(3):382–401, July 1982.

164. F. Thomson Leighton. *Introduction to Parallel Algorithms and Architectures: Arrays, Trees, Hypercubes*. Morgan Kaufmann, 1992.

165. Gérard LeLann. Distributed systems, towards a formal approach. In *IFIP Congress Proceedings*, pages 155–160, 1977.

166. Kai Li. *Shared Virtual Memory on Loosely-Coupled Processors*. PhD thesis, Yale University, New Haven, Connecticut, September 1986. Number: YALEU/DCS/RR-492.

167. Kai Li and Paul Hudak. Memory coherence in shared virtual memory systems. *ACM Transactions on Programming Languages and Systems*, 7(4):321–359, November 1989.

168. Ming Li, John Tromp, and Paul M. B. Vitányi. How to share concurrent wait-free variables. *Journal of the ACM*, 43(4):723–746, July 1996.

169. Kal Lin and Vassos Hadzilacos. Asynchronous group membership with oracles. In *Proceedings of the 13th International Conference on Distributed Computing*, pages 79–93, 1999.

170. Richard Lipton and John Sandberg. *PRAM: A Scalable Shared Memory*. Technical Report CS-TR-180-88, Computer Science Department, Princeton University, September 1988.

171. Wai-Kau Lo and Vassos Hadzilacos. Using failure detectors to solve consensus in asynchronous sharde-memory systems. In *Proceedings of the 8th International Workshop on Distributed Algorithms*, pages 280–295, 1994.

172. Wai-Kau Lo and Vassos Hadzilacos. All of us are smarter than any of us: Non-deterministic wait-free hierarchies are not robust. *SIAM Journal on Computing*, 30(3):689–728, 2000.

173. Michael C. Loui and Hosame H. Abu-Amara. Memory requirements for agreement among unreliable asynchronous processes. In *Advances in Computing Research, Vol. 4*, pages 163–183. JAI Press, Inc., 1987.

174. Jennifer Lundelius and Nancy Lynch. An upper and lower bound for clock synchronization. *Information and Control*, 62(2/3):190–204, Aug./Sept. 1984.

175. Nancy Lynch. *Distributed Algorithms*. Morgan Kaufmann, 1996.

176. Nancy Lynch and Michael Fischer. On describing the behavior and implementation of distributed systems. *Theoretical Computer Science*, 13(1):17–43, January 1981.

177. Nancy A. Lynch and Mark R. Tuttle. Hierarchical correctness proofs for distributed algorithms. In *Proceedings of the 6th Annual ACM Symposium on Principles of Distributed Computing*, pages 137–151. ACM, 1987. A full version is available as MIT Technical Report MIT/LCS/TR–387.

178. Stephen R. Mahaney and Fred B. Schneider. Inexact agreement: Accuracy, precision, and graceful degradation. In *Proceedings of the 4th Annual ACM Symposium on Principles of Distributed Computing*, pages 237–249, 1985.

179. Dahlia Malkhi and Michael K. Reiter. Byzantine quorum systems. *Distributed Computing*, 11(4):203–213, 1998.

180. Keith Marzullo and Susan S. Owicki. Maintaining the time in a distributed system. *Operating Systems Review*, 19(3):44–54, 1985.

181. Friedemann Mattern. Virtual time and global states of distributed systems. In M. Cosnard et. al, editor, *Parallel and Distributed Algorithms: Proceedings of the International Workshop on Parallel and Distributed Algorithms*, pages 215–226. Elsevier Science Publishers B. V., 1989.

182. Marios Mavronicolas and Dan Roth. Linearizable read/write objects. *Theoretical Computer Science*, 220(1):267–319, 1999.

183. P. M. Melliar-Smith, Louise E. Moser, and Vivek Agrawala. Broadcast protocols for distributed systems. *IEEE Transactions on Parallel and Distributed Systems*, 1(1):17–25, January 1990.

184. John M. Mellor-Crummey and Michael L. Scott. Algorithms for scalable synchronization on shared-memory multiprocessors. *ACM Transactions on Computer Systems*, 9(1):21–65, 1991.

185. Michael Merritt. Notes on the Dolev-Strong lower bound for Byzantine agreement. Unpublished manuscript, 1985.

186. David L. Mills. Internet time synchronization: The Network Time Protocol. *IEEE Transactions on Communications*, 39(10):1482–1493, October 1991.

187. David L. Mills. Improved algorithms for synchronizing computer network clocks. *IEEE/ACM Transactions on Networking*, 3(3):245–254, June 1995.

188. Mark Moir and James H. Anderson. Wait-free algorithms for fast, long-lived renaming. *Science of Computer Programming*, 25(1):1–39, October 1995.

189. Mark Moir and Juan A. Garay. Fast long-lived renaming improved and simplified. In *Proceedings of the 10th International Workshop on Distributed Algorithms*, volume 1151 of *Lecture Notes in Computer Science*, pages 287–303. Springer-Verlag, 1996.

190. Shlomo Moran. Using approximate agreement to obtain complete disagreement: The output structure of input free asynchronous computations. In *Proceedings of the 3rd Israel Symposium on Theory of Computing and Systems*, pages 251–257, 1995.

191. Carol Morgan. Global and logical time in distributed systems. *Information Processing Letters*, 20(4):189–194, May 1985.

192. L. E. Moser, Y. Amir, P. M. Melliar-Smith, and D. A. Agarwal. Extended virtual synchrony. In *Proceedings of the 14th International Conference on Distributed Computing Systems*, pages 56–65, 1994.

193. Yoram Moses and Mark R. Tuttle. Programming simultaneous actions using common knowledge. *Algorithmica*, 3(1):121–169, 1988.

194. Rajeev Motwani and Prabhakar Raghavan. *Randomized Algorithms*. Cambridge University Press, 1995.

195. Sape Mullender, editor. *Distributed Systems*. Addison-Wesley Publishing Company, 2nd edition, 1993.

196. Gil Neiger. Distributed consensus revisited. *Information Processing Letters*, 49(4):195–201, February 1994.

197. Gil Neiger. Failure detectors and the wait-free hierarchy. In *Proceedings of the 14th Annual ACM Symposium on Principles of Distributed Computing*, pages 100–109, 1995.

198. Gil Neiger and Sam Toueg. Automatically increasing the fault-tolerance of distributed algorithms. *Journal of Algorithms*, 11(3):374–419, September 1990.

199. Gil Neiger and Sam Toueg. Simulating synchronized clocks and common knowledge in distributed systems. *Journal of the ACM*, 40(2):334–367, April 1993.

200. Nuno Neves, Miguel Castro, and Paulo Guedes. A checkpoint protocol for an entry consistent shared memory system. In *Proceedings of the 13th Annual ACM Symposium on Principles of Distributed Computing*, pages 121–129, 1994.

201. Bill Nitzberg and Virginia Lo. Distributed shared memory: A survey of issues and algorithms. *IEEE Computer*, 24(8):52–60, August 1991.

202. Gary Nutt. *Centralized and Distributed Operating Systems*. Prentice-Hall, Inc., 1992.

203. Susan Owicki and David Gries. An axiomatic proof technique for parallel programs I. *Acta Informatica*, 6(4):319–340, 1976.

204. Susan Owicki and Leslie Lamport. Proving liveness properties of concurrent programs. *ACM Transactions on Programming Languages and Systems*, 4(3):455–495, July 1982.

205. J. Pachl, E. Korach, and D. Rotem. Lower bounds for distributed maximum-finding algorithms. *Journal of the ACM*, 31(4):905–918, October 1984.

206. Boaz Patt-Shamir and Sergio Rajsbaum. A theory of clock synchronization. In *Proceedings of the 26th ACM Symposium on Theory of Computing*, pages 810–819, 1994.

207. Marshall Pease, Robert Shostak, and Leslie Lamport. Reaching agreement in the presence of faults. *Journal of the ACM*, 27(2):228–234, April 1980.

208. David Peleg. *Distributed Computing: A Locality-Sensitive Approach*. SIAM Mongraphs on Discrete Mathematics and Applications. Philadelphia, PA, 2000.

209. David Peleg and Jeffrey D. Ullman. An optimal synchronizer for the hypercube. In *Proceedings of the 6th Annual ACM Symposium on Principles of Distributed Computing*, pages 77–85, 1987.

210. Kenneth J. Perry and Sam Toueg. Distributed agreement in the presence of processor and communication faults. *IEEE Transactions on Software Engineering*, 12(3):477–482, March 1986.

211. Gary L. Peterson. Myths about the mutual exclusion problem. *Information Processing Letters*, 12:115–116, June 1981.

212. Gary L. Peterson. An $O(n \log n)$ unidirectional algorithm for the circular extrema problem. *ACM Transactions on Programming Languages and Systems*, 4(4):758–762, October 1982.

213. Gary L. Peterson. Concurrent reading while writing. *ACM Transactions on Programming Languages and Systems*, 5(1):46–55, January 1983.

214. Gary L. Peterson and Michael J. Fischer. Economical solutions for the critical section problem in a distributed system. In *Proceedings of the 9th ACM Symposium on Theory of Computing*, pages 91–97, 1977.

215. Larry L. Peterson, Nick C. Buchholz, and Richard D. Schlichting. Preserving and using context information in interprocess communication. *ACM Transactions on Computer Systems*, 7(3):217–246, August 1989.

216. S. A. Plotkin. Sticky bits and universality of consensus. In *Proceedings of the 8th Annual ACM Symposium on Principles of Distributed Computing*, pages 159–175, 1989.

217. Athanassios S. Poulakidas and Ambuj K. Singh. Online replication of shared variables. In *Proceedings of the 17th International Conference on on Distributed Computing Systems*, pages 500–507, 1997.

218. David Powell, Peter Barrett, Gottfried Bonn, Marc Chérèque, Douglas Seaton, and Paulo Veríssimo. The Delta-4 distributed fault-tolerant architecture. In Thomas L. Casavant and Mukesh Singhal, editors, *Readings in Distributed Systems*. IEEE Computer Society Press, 1994.

219. S. Prakash, Y. Lee, and T. Johnson. A nonblocking algorithm for shared queues using compare-and-swap. *IEEE Transactions on Computers*, 43:548–559, May 1994.

220. Roberto De Prisco, Butler W. Lampson, and Nancy A. Lynch. Revisiting the PAXOS algorithm. *Theoretical Computer Science*, 243(1-2):35–91, 2002.

221. J. Protic, M. Tomasevic, and V. Milutinovic. A survey of distributed shared memory systems. In *Proceedings of the 28th Hawaii Conference on System Sciences*, volume I, pages 74–84, 1995.

222. Jelica Protic, Milo Tomasevic, and Veljko Milutinovic, editors. *Distributed Shared Memory: Concepts and Systems*. IEEE Computer Society Press, August 1997.

223. Michael O. Rabin. N-process mutual exclusion with bounded waiting by $4 \cdot \log n$-valued shared variable. *Journal of Computer and System Sciences*, 25(1):66–75, August 1982.

224. Ophir Rachman. Anomalies in the wait-free hierarchy. In *Proceedings of the 8th International Workshop on Distributed Algorithms*, volume 857 of *Lecture Notes in Computer Science*, pages 156–163. Springer-Verlag, 1994.

225. M. Raynal. *Algorithms for Mutual Exclusion*. MIT Press, 1986.

226. Michel Raynal. *Networks and Distributed Computation: Concepts, Tools, and Algorithms*. MIT Press, 1988.

227. Michel Raynal, Andre Schiper, and Sam Toueg. The causal ordering abstraction and a simple way to implement it. *Information Processing Letters*, 39(6):343–350, September 1991.

228. Michael K. Reiter. Distributing trust with the Rampart toolkit. *Communications of the ACM*, 39(4):71–74, April 1996.

229. G. G. Richard III and M. Singhal. Using logging and asynchronous checkpointing to implement recoverable distributed shared memory. In *Proceedings of the 12th IEEE Symposium on Reliable Distributed Systems*, pages 58–67, 1993.

230. Laura Sabel and Keith Marzullo. Simulating fail-stop in asynchronous distributed systems (brief announcement). In *Proceedings of the 13th Annual ACM Symposium on Principles of Distributed Computing*, pages 399–399, 1994.

231. Laura Sabel and Keith Marzullo. *Election vs. Consensus in Asynchronous Systems*. Technical Report TR95-411, UC San-Diego, 1995.

232. Isaac Saias. Proving probabilistic correctness statements: The case of Rabin's algorithm for mutual exclusion. In *Proceedings of the 11th Annual ACM Symposium on Principles of Distributed Computing*, pages 263–274, 1992.

233. Michael Saks and Fotios Zaharoglou. Wait-free k-set agreement is impossible: The topology of public knowledge. In *Proceedings of the 25th ACM Symposium on Theory of Computing*, pages 101–110, 1993.

234. Baruch Schieber and Marc Snir. Calling names on nameless networks. *Information and Computation*, 113(1):80–101, August 1994.

235. Andre Schiper, Jorge Eggli, and Alain Sandoz. A new algorithm to implement causal ordering. In *Proceedings of the 3rd International Workshop on Distributed Algorithms*, number 392 in Lecture Notes in Computer Science, pages 219–232. Springer-Verlag, 1989.

236. F. B. Schneider, D. Gries, and R. D. Schlichting. Fault-tolerant broadcasts. *Science of Computer Programming*, 4(1):1–15, April 1984.

237. Fred B. Schneider. Synchronization in distributed programs. *ACM Transactions on Programming Languages and Systems*, 4(2):125–148, April 1982.

238. Fred B. Schneider. Implementing fault-tolerant services using the state machine approach: A tutorial. *ACM Computing Surveys*, 22(4):299–319, December 1990.

239. Reinhard Schwarz and Friedemann Mattern. Detecting causal relationships in distributed computations: In search of the holy grail. *Distributed Computing*, 7(3):149–174, 1994.

240. Adrian Segall. Distributed network protocols. *IEEE Transactions on Information Theory*, IT-29(1):23–35, January 1983.

241. Nir Shavit and Dan Touitou. Software transactional memory. *Distributed Computing*, 10(2):99–116, February 1997.

242. Barbara Simons, Jennifer Welch, and Nancy Lynch. An overview of clock synchronization. In *Fault-Tolerant Distributed Computing*, number 448 in

Lecture Notes in Computer Science, pages 84–96. Springer-Verlag, 1984. Also IBM Technical Report RJ 6505, October 1988.

243. Ambuj K. Singh, James H. Anderson, and Mohamed G. Gouda. The elusive atomic register. *Journal of the ACM*, 41(2):311–339, March 1994.

244. A. Prasad Sistla and Jennifer L. Welch. Efficient distributed recovery using message logging. In *Proceedings of the 8th Annual ACM Symposium on Principles of Distributed Computing*, pages 223–238, 1989.

245. T. K. Srikanth and Sam Toueg. Optimal clock synchronization. *Journal of the ACM*, 34(3):626–645, July 1987.

246. T. K. Srikanth and Sam Toueg. Simulating authenticated broadcasts to derive simple fault-tolerant algorithms. *Distributed Computing*, 2(2):80–94, August 1987.

247. Robert E. Strom and Shaula A. Yemini. Optimistic recovery in distributed systems. *ACM Transactions on Computer Systems*, 3(3):204–226, August 1985.

248. Michael Stumm and Songnian Zhou. Fault-tolerant distributed shared memory algorithms. In *Proceedings of the 2nd IEEE Symposium on Parallel and Distributed Processing*, pages 719–724, 1990.

249. Andrew Tanenbaum. *Modern Operating Systems*. Prentice-Hall, Inc., 1992.

250. Andrew Tanenbaum. *Distributed Operating Systems*. Prentice-Hall, Inc., 1995.

251. Andrew Tanenbaum. *Computer Networks*. Prentice-Hall, Inc., 5th edition, 1996.

252. Gerard Tel. *Introduction to Distributed Algorithms*. Cambridge University Press, 1994.

253. C. B. Tompkins. Sperner's lemma and some extensions. In E. F. Beckenbach, editor, *Applied Combinatorial Mathematics*, chapter 15, pages 416–455. John Wiley and Sons, Inc., New York, 1964.

254. John Turek, Dennis Shasha, and Sundeep Prakash. Locking without blocking: Making lock based concurrent data structure algorithms nonblocking. In *Proceedings of the 11th Annual ACM Symposium on Principles of Database Systems*, pages 212–222, 1992.

255. Russel Turpin and Brian Coan. Extending binary Byzantine agreement to multivalued Byzantine agreement. *Information Processing Letters*, 18(2):73–76, February 1984.

256. Robbert van Renesse, Kenneth P. Birman, and Silvano Maffeis. Horus: A flexible group communication system. *Communications of the ACM*, 39(4):76–83, April 1996.

257. K. Vidyasankar. Converting Lamport's regular register to atomic register. *Information Processing Letters*, 28:287–290, August 1988.

258. Paul M. B. Vitányi and Baruch Awerbuch. Atomic shared register access by asynchronous hardware. In *Proceedings of the 27th IEEE Symposium on Foundations of Computer Science*, pages 233–243. IEEE, 1986.

259. Jennifer Lundelius Welch. Simulating synchronous processors. *Information and Computation*, 74(2):159–171, August 1987.

260. Jennifer Lundelius Welch and Nancy A. Lynch. A new fault-tolerant algorithm for clock synchronization. *Information and Computation*, 77(1):1–36, April 1988.

261. J. H. Wensley et al. SIFT: The design and analysis of a fault-tolerant computer for aircraft control. *Proceedings of the IEEE*, 66(10):1240–1255, October 1978.

262. K.-L. Wu and W. K. Fuchs. Recoverable distributed shared virtual memory. *IEEE Transactions on Computers*, 39(4):460–469, April 1990.

263. Zhonghua Yang and T. Anthony Marsland, editors. *Global States and Time in Distributed Systems*. IEEE Computer Society Press, 1994.

Index

WILEY SERIES ON PARALLEL AND DISTRIBUTED COMPUTING
Series Editor: Albert Y. Zomaya